MARKETING MANAGEMENT

MARKETING MANAGEMENT

INTEGRATING THEORY AND PRACTICE

TONY PROCTOR

INTERNATIONAL THOMSON BUSINESS PRESS
I(T)P An International Thomson Publishing Company

London • Bonn • Johannesburg • Madrid • Melbourne • Mexico City • New York • Paris
Singapore • Tokyo • Toronto • Albany, NY • Belmont, CA • Cincinnati, OH • Detroit, MI

Marketing Management: Integrating Theory and Practice
Copyright © 1996

First published 1996 by International Thomson Business Press

I(T)P A division of International Thomson Publishing Inc.
The ITP logo is a trademark under licence

British Library Cataloguing-in-Publication Data
A catalogue record for this book is available from the British Library

---

First printed 1996
Typeset in 10/12 Usherwood by Florencetype Ltd, Stoodleigh, Devon, England
Printed in Hong Kong

ISBN 0–412–62350–1

International Thomson Business Press
Berkshire House
168–173 High Holborn
London WC1V 7AA

SHORT CONTENTS

CONTENTS

CASE EXAMPLES AND PROBLEMS

PREFACE

A sustainable competitive advantage is the goal of all organizations whose aim is a lasting and strong business position. Marketing is one of the chief mechanisms for achieving this ambition. Attainment of a sustainable competitive advantage rests on the ability to meet the needs of customers in a manner that is superior to the competition. Only by so doing will the organization obtain the kind of return it requires.

Irrespective of the organizational setting, there will always be a place for marketing. In health services, for example, the viability of certain specialist services depends on the ability of their providers to make the services and themselves known to potential users. Marketing is about communicating the benefits of a product or service to those who need or want it. If there is a specialist service available at a given hospital, for example, then those who make referrals – GPs and consultants in local hospitals – need to know about this service and how it can benefit their patients. Not only will this ensure satisfied GPs, consultants and patients, but it will also help to ensure the continued provision of the specialist service. It is the job of marketing to help ensure that awareness, interest, desire and action are stimulated.

We live in a world of rapid change. Among the most noticeable changes are those introduced by technology. In order to survive, providers of products and services have to keep abreast of change since this is particularly crucial in facilitating the establishment of a competitive advantage. Today, many firms are technology driven and establish their position in the market on the basis of having a competitive advantage in technology. But technology is not the only factor at work; society itself is evolving, at different rates and in different ways throughout the world. It is the ultimate user who determines what needs to be produced, and it is changes in the ultimate user's wants and needs that require close monitoring.

In writing this book I had in mind primarily undergraduate students starting to study marketing for the first time. The book will of course be of interest to anyone who wants a comprehensive introductory text on the subject of marketing. The way in which it is written and presented attempts to forge a link between theory and practice. The theoretical arguments of the marketing literature are illustrated through the use of short case examples and case problems, which pose interesting problems and points for discussion.

The book introduces marketing, and in particular the marketing concept and the nature of marketing management. Marketing activities take place in a constantly changing world and are affected by what is taking place in the business environment. The first four chapters examine marketing and the kind of environment in which it operates. The next two chapters provide an insight into the kind of mechanisms firms can use to analyse the market and the changing nature of the environment in order to identify opportunities to exploit and make more effective decisions. Marketing information systems and market research are seen as tools which can help in this activity.

Having studied the nature of the marketing environment, and been introduced to tools which help to define a firm's interaction with the market, the book examines the marketing decision-making process in more detail. Chapter 7 looks at various ways of segmenting a market so as to identify the best openings. Chapter 8 looks at market targeting and positioning, following the identification of profitable market segments. These two chapters show how the firm determines and selects the most profitable opportunities to exploit.

Marketing decisions should not be taken on an *ad hoc* basis. They are taken as part of a carefully worked out plan. Moreover, such plans have a strategic underpinning to them. Chapter 9 introduces the planning process and how it is linked to strategy. It provides a platform for Chapters 10 to 17 which look at specific marketing decisions relating to the elements of the marketing mix.

Having made and implemented marketing decisions, control needs to be effected. Control monitors how well the enterprise is faring, and enables corrective action to be taken where deviations from plan occur. All planning, decision making and analysis depend upon human effort and careful organization. Chapter 18 also looks at marketing organization.

While the book endeavours to introduce an international marketing approach throughout, a separate treatment of the subject of international marketing is warranted; this is the subject of Chapter 19.

Most of the ideas for this book have come about as a result of teaching. Many of the case examples I use are based on what can readily be found in the marketing press. I am also indebted for the constructive comments of those kind reviewers who gave of their time to peruse the manuscript at various stages during its completion.

LECTURERS' RESOURCE MANUAL

This book comes complete with a comprehensive lecturers' resource manual which is free to lecturers and teachers recommending the text book as an essential purchase for their students.

For more information call Mark Wellings (Senior Commissioning Editor) on 0171 865 0066 or order direct from the address below:

Anita Barnecut
Inspection Copy Requests
Chapman & Hall Ltd
Cheriton House
North Way
Andover
Hants SP10 5BE

Tel: 01264 342932
Fax: 01264 342765
email: rchinspection@itps.co.uk

GLOSSARY

Advertising – the use of mass media to communicate a non-personal message about an organization and/or its products and services to a target audience.

Barriers to entry – obstacles which discourage firms from entering a market or industry – e.g. R. & D. costs, high advertising costs, etc.

Barriers to exit – obstacles which discourage firms from leaving the industry or market – e.g. sunk capital and investment in the market, non-transferable resources.

Brand – a name, term, sign, symbol or design used to identify a supplier's goods or service and to distinguish them from similar products offered by competition.

Brand extension – making use of an existing brand for new or modified products.

Brand image – the perceptions and beliefs held by consumers about a particular brand of good or service.

Brand loyalty – the extent to which purchasers continue to buy a specific brand of product in preference to competing brands.

Brand switching – the decision by consumers to substitute alternative brands for the one they currently use.

Break-even points – where total costs equal total revenue derived from selling a product or service.

Buyer behaviour – the purchasing decisions of buyers as influenced by their functional and psychological motivations and needs.

Chain store – a retail business with many branches.

Channel – a marketing channel is a channel of distribution comprising a group of interrelated intermediaries who make products available to consumers.

Competition-based pricing – price determination which is based mainly on what competitors charge.

Competitive advantage – the possession by a firm of various assets and attributes (low costs, innovative brands, etc.) which provide it with an advantage over rival firms.

Competitive strategy – strategic plans which try to make sure a firm is able to match competitors in supplying a particular product or service.

Competitors – rival organizations which market similar or substitute products or services to the same groups of customers or target markets.

Cost-based pricing – pricing based on production and marketing costs.

Demand-based pricing – pricing based on the strength of demand.

Differential advantage – something possessed by a product, service or organization that cannot be matched by competition and which is desired by customers.

Differentiated marketing strategy – a strategy which reflects the use of various marketing mix formats, each aimed at a particular market segment.

Direct marketing – the means by which products or services are introduced to the customer through some form of non-personal medium – eg. telephone.

Direct selling – a form of direct marketing involving fact-to-face contact between buyer and seller.

Distribution – the manner in which goods and services are made available to customers.

Economies of scale – decreases in the average unit costs of producing and marketing products as the magnitude of the operation increases.

Family branding – the situation whereby all the products produced by a company are sold under the same brand name.

Joint venture – a business jointly owned by a number of independent companies who function independently except with respect to the joint venture business.

Marketing audit – a systematic review and examination of the objectives, strategies, organization, and performance of how a company markets its goods or services.

Marketing communications – information exchanged to facilitate the buying and selling of goods.

Marketing environment – the external forces influencing how a company fares industry-wide in developing its product markets. It includes technological, economic, legal, ethical, political, societal, customer and competitor influences.

Marketing information system – the system of information flow that assists marketing planning and decision making.

Marketing intelligence – the information about developments in a firm's marketing environment that can assist marketing executives in formulating marketing plans.

Marketing mix – the elements of product, price, distribution and promotion which are at the organization's disposal in marketing its products and services to buyers.

Marketing myopia – the tendency for firms to take a narrow view of the markets they currently serve. It is based upon current product offerings and thus tends to ignore broader market opportunities.

Marketing planning – The process of assessing marketing opportunities and marketing resources, determining marketing objectives and developing a plan to implement marketing strategies.

Marketing research – a formalized procedure for collecting information to be used in marketing planning and decision making.

Marketing strategy – a means of attaining specified marketing objectives.

Market segmentation – the identification of target customer groups where the latter are aggregated into groups with similar requirements and buying characteristics.

Market share – the proportion of the sales of a product market accounted for by sales of one brand or one company.

New product – a product which is new to a firm.

Opinion leaders – individuals possessing knowledge, skill or a personality that endows them with the capacity to influence others.

Own-label brand – a product which is sold by a retailer under the retailer's own brand name.

Positioning – the comparative position an organization's product market offering holds in the mind of the customer *vis-à-vis* competing offerings.

Price – the money value that a buyer has to pay to the seller of an item in order to effect purchase.

Product – a functional and saleable commodity with tangible and intangible attributes, including social and psychological utilities or benefits.

Product differentiation – the manner in which suppliers try to distinguish their own products from those of competitors.

Product life cycle – the phases of introduction, growth, maturity and decline through which most products, services and markets pass.

Product mix – the range of products and/or services offered by an organization.

Product portfolio – the mix of products or services a firm offers to an organization. The intention is to balance short-term losses with longer-term profitability.

Promotional mix – advertising, sales promotion, personal selling and public relations.

Psychological pricing – the setting of prices, bearing in mind the effect a product's price has on consumers' perceptions of the product.

Reference group – a social group with which a person identifies herself or himself or desires to join.

Sales promotion – activities or materials used to promote sales using added value or some other incentive. It is used with sales staff, distributors or customers.

Selling – a process of persuasion whereby one party attempts to induce the other party to part with money in return for goods, services or ideas.

Services – intangible products.

Strategic business unit – a division of a multi-product firm with quite distinct business activities.

Targeting – the act of identifying the market segments on which to concentrate resources and marketing activity.

1 THE MARKETING CONCEPT AND THE NATURE OF MARKETING MANAGEMENT

This chapter explores the nature of marketing. Differing business orientations are examined in the context of marketing as a business philosophy, and the nature and management of the marketing mix is studied, attention being given to how firms can gain competitive advantage. The chapter concludes by exploring the scope of marketing.

OBJECTIVES

After studying this chapter you should be able to:

- understand what marketing is, and what it means for a firm to be pursuing a 'marketing oriented' philosophy in its approach to business

- understand the nature of the marketing mix variables – price, product, promotion and distribution – and how they interrelate with one another

- understand the nature and purpose of marketing management

- understand what is meant by a differential advantage and how firms try to exploit it in developing products and marketing strategies

- appreciate the scope of marketing.

INTRODUCTION

It is possible to view marketing both as a functional aspect of a business and as a business philosophy (see Figure 1.1). As a functional aspect of a business, it is concerned with making decisions which enable the business to serve its customers effectively with products and/or services. This involves designing products, setting prices, choosing promotional methods and arranging distribution. From the point of view of a business philosophy, it is concerned with satisfying customer wants and needs in the pursuit of its stated objectives.

In this first chapter both of these viewpoints will be explored. Businesses have always had to carry out the functional aspect of marketing, but over the course of time organizations have adopted a variety of business orientations or philosophies. These differing orientations or philosophies are individually considered, along with their implications for how organizations perceive the market place for their goods or services. The chapter also draws on the clear distinction between selling and marketing.

Finding a way of making a product or service different from that of your competitors is seen as a key aspect of marketing strategy in both consumer and industrial markets. It is usually referred to as 'creating a competitive differential'. The nature of the marketing mix – product, price, distribution and promotions – is developed in detail.

THE NATURE OF MARKETING: A FUNCTION OF BUSINESS AND A BUSINESS PHILOSOPHY

NATURE OF MARKETING

There has been a plethora of definitions of marketing over the years and these definitions have changed with time. The important feature of any modern-day definition of marketing is that it should make a clear reference to identifying and satisfying customer needs and to building support mechanisms to facilitate this.

One such definition is offered by the American Marketing Association (AMA):

> Marketing is the process of planning and executing the conception, pricing, promotion and distribution of ideas, goods, and services to create exchanges that satisfy individual and organizational objectives.
>
> (*Marketing News*, 1985)

Numerous definitions of marketing can be found (see, for example, McDonald and Leppard [1991, pp.4–5] and Baker [1991, ch.1]). In all cases, historical definitions of marketing were considered to be apt and pertinent at the time they were made; for various reasons, however, they were superseded by new definitions which were considered to be more fitting to their times.

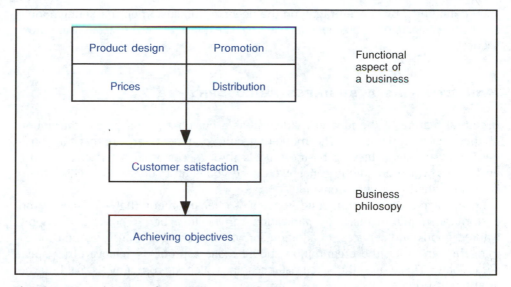

Figure 1.1   Marketing: a functional aspect of a business, and a business philosophy.

The official definition given by the Chartered Institute of Marketing is quite concise but also reflects the same basic ideas as those offered in the AMA definition:

> . . . the management process responsible for identifying, anticipating and satisfying consumer requirements efficiently and profitably.

Marketing facilitates the satisfying of exchange relationships; fundamental to this is the existence of a market. A market is a collection of people sharing a common want or need, and who are motivated to enter into exchange processes to satisfy the need or want. In practical terms markets embrace a number of product, spatial and physical dimensions, and may be defined in terms of the goods – or services which are viewed as substitute products by buyers. In spatial terms a market may be local, regional, national or international in scope. From a physical perspective, buyer and seller exchanges may be transacted in a well-defined market place, or in a less defined way.

Certain circumstances have to exist in order to bring about an exchange. First, people, individuals or organizations have to want to take part in an exchange; they must also possess something of value that others want. They must be prepared to give up something of value in order to obtain something of value. The objective of a marketing exchange is to obtain something that is wanted more than the thing that is given up to get it. In other words, a reward in excess of costs. Finally, those involved in the exchange have to be able to communicate with each other to make their something of value available (Kotler, 1988, p.6). When exchange occurs, products/services are traded for other products/services or for financial resources.

Definitions are often used to summarize in a rather succinct way what a subject is all about. This is true of marketing as in other fields. To get a real feel for what marketing is all about, we need to look in more detail at the ideas expressed in such definitions. By concentrating on the needs of the customer, marketing adopts a specific philosophical business stance. This is explored in more detail in the next section.

MARKETING AS A BUSINESS PHILOSOPHY

A central feature of the idea of marketing as a business philosophy is the notion of the marketing concept. The marketing concept reflects an approach to business that stresses achieving business goals through customer satisfaction. Those businesses which adopt the concept produce goods and services for which there is an identified customer demand.

Encapsulated in the marketing concept is the argument that by focusing on customers' requirements, an organization can be in a better position to supply wanted goods and services. In addition, provided it charges a fair price and other things are in order, the organization should make a profit or achieve other specified goals. These are the circumstances in which a company is said to be 'marketing oriented'.

To gain a better appreciation of the meaning of the marketing concept, it is necessary to have a clear understanding of what is meant by customer needs, wants and demands. People experience needs when they are deprived of some basic satisfaction. In order to satisfy these needs people develop 'wants'. For example, people may be lonely when they are deprived of the satisfaction of the company of others. They will want something or someone to alleviate their sense of loneliness. Demands are wants for specific products or services together with an ability and willingness to purchase them. A lonely person may have just sufficient money to go to a disco, deciding that this is the best way to spend his or her money to solve the loneliness problem.

An interesting question to ask is whether all firms actually adopt the marketing concept and display the marketing philosophy in their approach to business. The answer to such a question is that it is not the case. Firms may adopt a variety of business philosophies or orientations, which are reflected in different approaches to marketing. These different approaches and their implications for a business are explored in the next section.

BUSINESS ORIENTATIONS

Organizations adopt a variety of approaches to business. It is possible to classify these approaches as follows.

- production orientation
- product orientation
- sales orientation

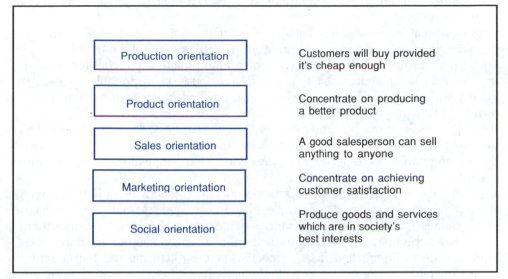

Figure 1.2 Business orientations.

● marketing orientation

● societal (marketing) orientation.

It can be argued that the various orientations have developed chronologically, but it is still possible to find firms practising one or other of each of these orientations today. The various orientations represent responses to the prevalent business conditions under which organizations operate, and thus may change as the firm encounters different conditions. It is not surprising, therefore, that the different orientations can be considered within a chronological framework, since over the years the nature and competitiveness of markets has changed considerably.

To a limited extent all of the approaches represent a degree of marketing orientation or an attempt to apply the marketing concept. With the exception of the marketing orientation itself and its modified form, the societal orientation, each approach has specific limitations which detract from their universal appeal as satisfactory business orientations.

THE PRODUCTION ORIENTATION

The 'production orientation' approach to business emphasizes finding a cheaper way to produce goods so that cost savings can be passed on to consumers, who will benefit as a result. Mass-produced goods offering no variation in terms of characteristics are typical of this kind of approach. There is an assumption that people want the basic product and are not too concerned about additional product features or options. Mass production and standardization of product features result in production economies of scale. The savings may then be passed on to consumers.

The classical example of production orientation, often quoted in the marketing literature, is to be found in the invention of movable type in the fifteenth century. Gutenberg's invention of movable type for printing made it possible for books to be produced much more cheaply than had previously been possible. The saving in cost was passed on to the user or consumer and many people were able to own books for the first time.

In more recent times, both the Model T Ford and the Volkswagen Beetle were examples of production orientation at work. In both cases, however, as competition emerged in their respective countries and in international markets, the firms changed their business orientations.

Technology is often associated with production orientation and the bringing about of benefits to society. For example, the harnessing of steam power to industry in the eighteenth and nineteenth centuries made it possible to mass produce many products for the first time, at an affordable price to the consumer. In more recent times the development and mass-production of the microchip has had a similar impact on some consumer products. In the early days of electronic digital watches, prices tended to be high. With the mass production of the microchip, however, electronic watches have become commonplace and can be bought at low prices – although some which are sold on the basis of their brand name nevertheless command high prices.

There is no doubt that production orientation can work in the consumer interest. However, it only goes a small part of the way towards a true marketing orientation. Production orientation still characterizes some firms, which assume that people will buy their products because they are cheaply priced. The case of the Blue Bell pub in the case example below is an instance of this approach. Where customers are more interested in obtaining the product than in its finer details, this belief may well be justified. In addition, production orientation may also work where a product's costs are unduly high and need to be brought down in order to expand the market. However, in adopting a production orientation, organizations may overlook certain opportunities, since they are not really sensitive to customer wants and needs.

PRODUCT ORIENTATION

More than a century ago the philosopher Ralph Waldo Emerson remarked: 'If a man writes a better book, preaches a better sermon, or makes a better mousetrap than his neighbour, though he builds his house in the woods, the world will make a beaten path to his door.'

A product orientation reflects a tendency on the part of a firm to think that if it produces a superior product or service to those of its competitors, then demand for its product will be assured. This kind of thinking often leads to an organization becoming intent on improving the nature of the product or service, rather than heeding what consumers want. An illustration of this is given in the Ozel case example on page 8.

THE BLUE BELL: BUSINESS ORIENTATION

The Blue Bell pub was located in a deprived area where incomes were low and unemployment high. It put on luncheons every day of the week for its customers. The menu offered each day was exactly the same, and there was no variation from week to week. The menu comprised tomato soup, egg and chips, and rice pudding. This made up a three-course meal, which at 49 pence the pub claimed was the cheapest three-course meal in town.

For a couple of years the management of the pub enjoyed a good steady income from both its bar trade and its lunch-time meals. Every day the pub was packed full of locals and the occasional passers-by. Some six months ago a Japanese-owned company opened a new assembly plant on a site close to the Blue Bell. The company recruited its assembly workers locally, and many people who formerly had been unemployed suddenly found themselves with jobs.

In the last six months business at the Blue Bell has slackened off altogether. Not only is there little demand for the 'cheapest three-course meal in town', but there has also been a substantial fall-off in all the bar trade, at lunch-times, evenings and weekends.

QUESTIONS

1. Can you account for what has happened?

2. What action do you think the Blue Bell management can take to restore its previous level of trade?

The growth of competition encourages firms to produce better and better products or services. Associated with this race to improve is the danger of over-engineering products or services. One can improve them to the point where they are more than what the customer really wants or is prepared to pay for. Improvements cost money, and firms need to recoup their additional investment costs. As long as sales increase as a result of improvement there is always the possibility that investment costs will be repaid, even if prices are held at the pre-improvement level. Where no increased sales are experienced as a result of improvement, however, then improvement costs can only be recovered either by raising prices or finding some way of reducing costs.

Over-engineering is a very real problem. Where customers expect a certain quality for a given price and can easily recognize the price–quality 'pitch', it is

CASE EXAMPLE

OZEL COMPANY: BUSINESS ORIENTATION

The Ozel Company manufactures industrial component products to a very high standard in the industry. The quality of Ozel's products is reflected in them being engineered to tighter specifications. Whereas competitors maintain product specifications to within a few hundredths of a centimetre, the Ozel Company works to tolerances which demand accuracy to within a few thousandths of a centimetre. This increased accuracy, however, is only achieved with the aid of costly plant and machinery which demands expensive maintenance. In addition, quality control standards have to be high and scrappage rates are known to be higher than those of competitors.

Working to such high engineering specifications means that the costs of production are substantially higher than those of competitors, and the price charged to customers is correspondingly higher. Many companies are prepared to pay the higher price because the precision engineered products give more durable service and customers experience fewer problems with the products in use than those produced by competing firms at lower prices.

Recently, however, the effects of recession have been felt by all Ozel's customers and cost-saving exercises have been implemented by all of them. Nearly all of Ozel's customers have indicated that unless Ozel can reduce its prices to the level of those of other potential suppliers, they will be forced to take their custom to Ozel's competitors.

The message clearly indicates that Ozel's customers gain insufficient benefit from their more precisely engineered products to warrant paying the premium price

QUESTION

1. What action would you recommend Ozel should take?

pointless for a firm to offer more quality for the same price unless it gains a sustainable competitive advantage from doing so. The danger lies in the fact that there is an almost inherent belief that if one creates a superior product, people will always want to buy that product in preference to any other that is available. To some extent this may be true, but this will only hold to the point where the product provides benefits which just meet with the customer's expectations at a given price level. Where it is difficult to judge the price–quality pitch, the boundaries for defining over-engineering may be less clear.

Product orientation is quite different to production orientation. The latter reflects the idea that if the price of a product or service can be reduced, then this will enable the product or service to be within the purchasing range of more customers and hence will lead to customer satisfaction en masse. Product orientation argues that creating a better product or service will lead to customer satisfaction. If the customer is primarily interested in either a cheaper or a better product, then one or other of these approaches may produce good results. However, neither of these approaches begins by trying to find out what the customer really wants.

SALES ORIENTATION

The level of competition in business has increased substantially during the 20th century. There have been peaks and troughs in terms of activity in the developed countries of the world, but overall living standards have risen, newly developed countries have come on the scene and more developing nations have begun to play a role in world trade. All this has led to an overall increase in the level of competition, both among firms and among nations.

This development, and particular early experience with the ups and downs of the economic cycle, have had an impact on the business philosophy pursued by many firms. Following the experience of the Depression of the 1920s and early 1930s, most firms in the Western world came to realize that they had to actively sell their products if they were to survive. While this notion itself was basically a good one, it still lacked that vital ingredient of first setting out to establish what the customer really wanted. The sales-oriented approach, as it has been called, makes the assumption that people will want to buy a product or service that a firm or other organization can supply. It does not consider whether it is first necessary to establish what the consumer really wants. The operationalization of this orientation then implies that it is only necessary to inform people about a product, persuade them that it is one which they require, and make it available for them to purchase.

Sales orientation is often encountered in firms with over-capacity. Over-capacity arises when firms have increased their production capacity to meet real or anticipated demand, only to find that the demand is either not sustained or never experienced. This approach involves firms selling what they can produce, rather than producing what they can sell. A sales-orientated firm does not question whether a market and sufficient demand for the product exists – it merely assumes that a good salesperson can sell anything.

Such an approach, of course, overlooks the crucial point that if one starts with consumer wants and needs and then produces a product to meet those needs, the task of selling is made easier. In addition it ignores the argument that by starting with consumers' wants and needs it is less likely that opportunities in the market place will be missed.

CASE EXAMPLE

BONNYRIGG CHOCOLATE COMPANY: BUSINESS ORIENTATION

The Bonnyrigg Chocolate Company manufactures a wide range of chocolate confectionery items. Recently, sales have begun to fall off in the face of a switch in consumer spending patterns. At a recent meeting of the board of directors the sales director indicated that he felt the firm might be able to increase sales by increasing advertising and promotional expenditure and more effective selling techniques. 'It is the quality of the message and the frequency with which it is imparted that will influence our sales,' He was quoted as saying.

QUESTION

1. Do you agree with the sales director? If not, why not? What would you do?

MARKETING ORIENTATION

A marketing orientation centres on the consumer and examines the ways in which the organization can try to satisfy consumer wants and needs, making a profit while doing so. This approach adopts the argument that by concentrating on the consumer, the enterprise is best able to identify profitable opportunities in the market place.

Four considerations define whether or not a firm is adopting a marketing orientation:

- the market
- the customer
- the marketing team
- making a profit or achieving some other company-defined objective.

A marketing orientation requires that target markets are tightly defined and that marketing programmes are designed specifically to match the needs of each target market. Experience indicates that such an approach is likely to lead to satisfied customers. Furthermore, a satisfied customer is likely to develop loyalty to the firm's products and remain a customer, recommend buying from the same source to friends and acquaintances, and be prepared to buy other products from the same source.

CASE EXAMPLE

GATEWAY: SATISFYING CUSTOMER WANTS AND NEEDS

Shopping can be an ordeal, particularly if you have a large family to feed and a very limited budget. In addition, if you are not very good at keeping a running tally of how much you spend then it can be both embarrassing and depressing to arrive at the till and not be able to pay for selected goods.

One foodmarket chain, Gateway, is the first company in the United Kingdom to introduce a shopping trolley with a calculator mounted on the handle. The company indicated it was constantly seeking to find innovative products and services that provide real and added value for their customers. It felt that the shopping trolley calculators were a simple but effective new service.

(Source: The Grocer, *8 January 1994, p.9)*

QUESTION

1. Do you think that the trolley calculators are likely to attract more customers into Gateway stores? Why or why not?

2. What alternative methods can stores such as Gateway use in order to provide real added value for their customers?

Another feature of a marketing orientation is that people in an organization's marketing department have to work together towards shared marketing goals, and have to share this viewpoint with other departments in an organization. The organizational ethos and structure has to facilitate the implementation of the marketing concept. All members of the organization who come into contact with customers or clients should see it as part of their role to adopt a marketing oriented approach to business.

Marketing exists to help an organization reach its stated goals. However, achieving customer satisfaction is not enough in itself. A producer which gives away free products to people more than likely will create considerable customer satisfaction. However, it will not generate any income. Any organization which concentrates entirely on the satisfaction of its customers will experience difficulties in attaining its own objectives.

SOCIETAL ORIENTATION

A more recent form of business orientation is a development from the marketing orientation. It is associated with consumerism – that is, the need to act in the best interests of the consumer. This orientation reflects a belief that long-term consumer satisfaction can best be achieved if firms and other organizations provide goods and services which are of good quality, which are safe to use and which do not damage or destroy the environment in which we live. The pursuit of these objectives can sometimes involve a conflict between what consumers apparently want and what it is in their best interests to be offered. For instance consumers may say that they want bright white paper or bright white fabric products because they look and 'feel' clean. Such materials, however, can contain harmful chemicals, the manufacture of which may under some circumstances endanger people's health.

As a consequence, in pursuing a societal marketing orientation, a firm may wish to produce and market only materials whose manufacture is safe. Unfortunately,

CASE EXAMPLE

EURO DATA PRODUCTS: AN EXAMPLE OF A SUCCESSFUL MARKETING ORIENTED COMPANY

Many small businesses start off by being based in someone's home. Joe Scanlon's first business was no exception when he started it in 1974, specializing in personalized business forms. This business is now run by his two sons and Joe has moved on to start another business.

Joe entered the magnetic media and computer ribbons market in 1988, forming a company called Euro Data Products. The company is now based in offices in Rose Lane, Liverpool, though initially Joe also operated this company from home. A branch of the company is run by Joe's brother, Ben, in Newport, Gwent. The company owns a 7000 sq. ft warehouse in Huyton, Merseyside and offers a wide range of consumables. The product range now includes business forms, impact printer ribbons, thermal labels, self-adhesive labels, printed books and pads, floppy discs, and a full range of laser printer consumables. Showing its awareness of environmental issues, it has started to market more environmentally friendly products and now supplies large quantities of recycled paper.

Joe has many years of experience in this type of business and all the staff of the company have a specialized knowledge of the trade. Three people are employed at the Rose Lane office and a further three people are employed at the warehouse. Keeping overheads down and prices low are seen as cornerstones of remaining competitive in the market place.

Besides supplying good quality products at competitive prices, the firm offers same-day service to local customers. Where delivery is national, a two to three days' delivery time is achieved. The firm has both large and small customers and is prepared to supply any size of order. It always takes the specific needs of the customer into account and tries to supply any product that it is asked for, as long as that product is currently available. The firm has achieved a £1.2m sales turnover, even in the face of a recession. Of course, the products it supplies are the mainstay of most businesses, but nevertheless the sales record represents a fine achievement.

The company's success is attributed to its loyal staff, who are committed to customer satisfaction. It aims to match its first class quality products with a first class service. Considerable customer loyalty exists and customers – who include Gateway Foodmarkets and Ford Motors – come back time and time again.

(*Source:* Business North West, *January 1994, pp. 43–5*)

QUESTION

1. To what would you attribute the success of this company?

such materials may not have the bright, white, 'clean' appearance that people say they want. This is because they do not contain the harmful chemicals, and may lead to a lack of consumer satisfaction with the new product. Consumers may even continue to buy the old product even though its manufacture is harmful. Indeed the consumer may have to be educated to see the benefits of the new product.

There are many other products, including food products, which contain artificial colouring to give the appearance of freshness and cleanliness or to appear more attractive in some other respects. As long as these additives are not harmful, then there is no reason for a firm producing those products to change its stance in the matter. One difficulty, however, concerns how the consumer will view such products. Consumers may not perceive why it is all right for the appearance of the product in one case to be bright and sparkling, and yet in another instance for it to be harmful.

The societal marketing concept:

- **Focuses on the customer** Starting with customer wants and needs it enables the organization to develop appropriate products and services for which there is a requirement.

- **Is concerned with the customer's long-term interests** The organization is concerned with both the customer's and society's long-term needs. This may necessitate educating buyers in the benefits of buying products or services which may not be immediately perceived as satisfying their immediate requirements.

Adopting a societal orientation means that firms do not seek profit as their primary purpose. While profits are recognized as a business requirement, the purpose of a business is to create and keep a customer (Levitt, 1983, p. 6).

As a result of not adopting a marketing or societal marketing orientation, in the past many firms have run into great difficulties, and some have even failed. This deficiency gave rise to the phenomenon known as 'marketing myopia'. Marketing myopia is discussed in more detail in the next section.

MARKETING MYOPIA

Theodore Levitt (1962, p.7) coined the phrase 'marketing myopia'. According to Levitt, this represents the failure of management to recognize the scope of its business. Managers of such firms tend to be product oriented rather than customer oriented. He argued that organizational goals need to be broadly defined and oriented toward customer needs. The aircraft manufacturer Boeing, for example, sees itself in the high technology transportation business, rather than in the aeroplane business (*Business Week*, 1985).

While marketing myopia is not a business orientation, it is a syndrome that often pervades organizations. The marketing environment (see Chapter 2) is constantly changing, and customers' wants and needs change as the environment changes. Firms which fail to respond to these changes risk becoming uncompetitive in the market place and eventually going out of business.

THE MARKETING MIX

So far we have concentrated on marketing as a business philosophy. Now we will turn our attention to marketing as a functional aspect of a business. This involves looking at the marketing mix elements and their management in a strategic sense, to obtain a competitive advantage for an organization in the market place. First, however, we need to dispel the myth that marketing and selling are the same thing, and to explain how selling relates to marketing.

MARKETING AND SELLING

There is confusion in some people's minds such that they think marketing and selling are the same thing. The distinction was made earlier between a marketing orientation to business and a sales orientation. Selling highlights the needs of the seller and concentrates on getting money for a product or service that an organization has created. Marketing, on the other hand, looks at the needs of the buyer, aiming to satisfy customer needs through the design characteristics of the product or service. Peter Drucker (1974, p.64) has argued that the aim of marketing is to know and understand the customer so well that the product or service will sell itself.

Selling is only one element of the firm's marketing mix. Marketing is concerned with the firm's strategy. The strategy could be to increase its sales and profits by selling more of what it currently produces to existing customers. Alternatively, the strategy may be to achieve growth by getting people who currently buy other firms' products or services to switch allegiance. Many different strategies can be used, and in order to implement strategy, use is made of tactics relating to pricing, distribution, the product and promotion. We refer to these tactical decision areas as the elements of the marketing mix. Selling, on the other hand, is an aspect of promotion.

ELEMENTS OF THE MARKETING MIX

The marketing mix consists of the range of measures that organizations can employ to market their products to buyers (Borden, 1991). Important facets of the marketing mix are:

- the product – quality, features, styling options, brand name, packaging, sizes, services, warranties and returns

- the price – list price, discounts, allowances, payment period, credit

- the method of promotion – advertising, personal selling, sales promotion, merchandising and public relations

- the method of distribution (place) – channels, coverage, locations, inventory and transport.

These are commonly referred to as the four Ps. There is an argument for including a fifth element, marketing intelligence, 'intelligence' covering 'marketing information' and 'marketing research'.

The relative importance of these elements will vary in accordance with the particular buyer characteristics of the market or the market segments which are served by a product. In the case of consumer goods advertising, sales promotion and packaging may be emphasized. In the marketing of industrial or business goods the emphasis may be upon technical features of the product, price and personal selling.

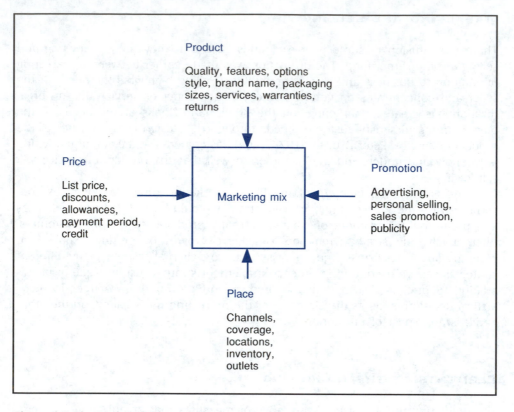

Figure 1.3 The '4 Ps' of the marketing mix

The elements of the marketing mix work together, rather than in isolation from one another. For instance, a high-quality consumer product would normally be marketed through up-market retail outlets, at a premium price and promoted through media that have an up-market or 'quality' image. Cartier watches have a high-quality image. They have a correspondingly high price tag, are advertised in quality glossy magazines and are sold through exclusive jewellery outlets.

Decisions have to be made with respect to the elements of the marketing mix, and the decisions made are reflected in marketing plans. Making such decisions and formulating such plans is part of the role of marketing management. In the next section we look in more detail at this role, in particular the task of implementing the marketing concept.

MARKETING MANAGEMENT

Marketing management implements the marketing concept. It finds out what customers want or need and relays this information back through the organization so that appropriately designed goods or services can be produced. Policies are set with regard to pricing, distribution and promotion and a strategy is devised in order that the organization's objectives can be attained through seeking out and exploiting opportunities in the market.

Management is about getting jobs done through people. This includes planning actions, organizing people to implement actions, co-ordinating efforts to achieve plans, controlling the plan so that it achieves objectives, and appraising performance.

Planning amounts to setting objectives and targets for future achievement. Such plans form the basis of future actions and let people in the organization know where the enterprise is going and what has to be accomplished within a given period of time. The marketing plan is linked with other plans in the firm. In the case of a manufacturing firm, for example, the other plans will relate to production, finance and personnel. All of these are part of what is called a 'corporate plan'. In large organizations, planning is a formalized process; it tends to be less formal in smaller firms. Small firms often maintain that they are too busy keeping up with current orders to have time to write down formal marketing plans.

The objective of organizing is to facilitate and produce efficient and effective working relationships between people, along with a sense of co-operation and purpose. This makes it easier to attain the goals and objectives set in the marketing plan. People in marketing management have to deal with other organizations. For example, in the course of advertising its products, a firm has to liaise with an advertising agency which will design and place advertisements on its behalf. In parallel, it has to get its sales people and its distributors to match their efforts so that they will support any advertising campaigns that are launched. Marketing management must also co-ordinate the activities of various departments within the organization, along with those of other organizations. Co-ordination is a very important dimension to marketing management activity.

Devising plans and making them available for implementation is not sufficient on its own. People are apt to set about doing things in their own particular way and at their own speed unless they are directed to do otherwise. Some things

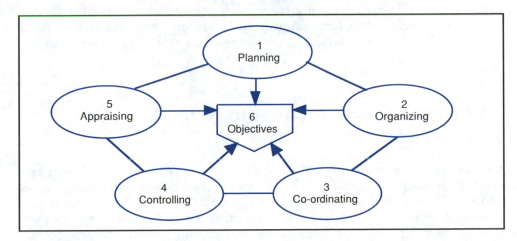

Figure 1.4 The management task

may not even get done at all. Organizations try to get around the problems that this can create by exercising control.

Control entails keeping people and other resources on track towards realization of the objectives which have been set. In many, cases organizations will be pursuing multiple objectives. For example, a firm could set itself a target of increasing its share of the market from 25% to 27% within six months of the initial planning date. In order to achieve this target it would be necessary to increase marketing expenditure. Targets for increased marketing expenditure would therefore have to be specified and set at the same time. Special sales promotion efforts might also have to be made to stimulate demand to the desired level. The cost and timing of these sales promotion exercises would have to be worked out and included as part of the plan.

Objectives set might include a certain increase in market share, maintaining profitability at the current level while so doing. However, if the firm subsequently incurred 50% more marketing expenditure than it had planned in achieving the market share objective, then it would be difficult to view control in this instance as having been been effective. Marketing plans involve the setting of multiple objectives, which must include provision for cost and resource utilization constraints.

Appraisal amounts to assessing what has been achieved and how well this has been done. This information can be used to help prevent the same kind of problems arising time and time again. For example, if the target was to sell 4000 carpets to department stores in Bristol over a 12-month period, but in actual fact only 2000 were sold, then appraisal amounts to accounting for this fact. It may be that stronger than expected marketing efforts by competitors have contributed to the shortfall in sales. In such a case, profitability on this form of distribution would also be lower than expected. Clearly, if a strategy could be evolved to gain an advantage over the competition, this would alleviate the problem. All this information would be pertinent to future marketing plans relating to carpet sales and profit targets through this kind of distribution outlet.

Plans and actions, while they are extremely important, are not sufficient in themselves. There has to be effective strategic thinking behind what goes into plans and decisions. The focus of such thinking should be on searching for a demonstrable differential advantage over competitors. The next section explores this in more detail.

SEARCHING FOR A DIFFERENTIAL ADVANTAGE

Competition occurs in nearly all aspects of business. Firms compete with one another for customers; those firms that are best able to satisfy consumer wants and needs are most likely to do well when the market is competitive. An organization can benefit by producing a strongly differentiated product or service from that of the competition. However, sometimes copying what the more successful firms are producing and marketing them can also be a very practical strategy.

Figure 1.5 Image, servicing, styling and support sell the product

For example, many IBM 'clone' microcomputer manufacturing firms have enjoyed success by adopting a 'me too' strategy.

PRODUCT DIFFERENTIATION

A product or service is made up of basic features and added values.

- **Basic features**: components, ingredients, performance.
- **Added values**: image, service, styling, support.

Product differentiation is achieved through making the added values more attractive to the customer, and occurs when users perceive that there are specific benefits attached to a particular company's product or service in comparison with the offerings of competitors. A product may be thought of as comprising of a set of basic features – components, ingredients, performance – and a set of added values – image, service, styling and support. Product differentiation can be attained through the added values (see, for example, Garvin, 1987, pp. 101–9). The more attractive the firm can make the added values then the more differentiated from competitive offerings it can make the product.

It is the benefits that the product or service provides to the user, rather than the product's features, which form the basis of differentiation. Differentiation results from offering customers benefits which are different to those obtainable from competing products or services. In this way differentiation is achieved through making the added values more attractive to the customer.

MARKETING STRATEGY AND A MARKETING PROGRAMME

To achieve its differential advantage, marketing management has to develop a marketing strategy and then design, construct and implement a marketing

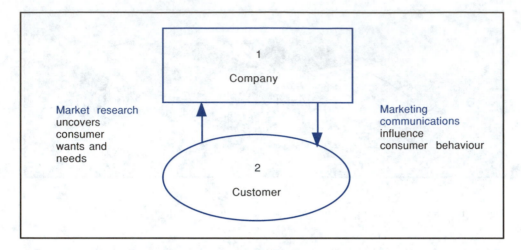

Figure 1.6 Marketing: a channel of information and influence

programme to enable it to achieve its objectives. Marketing strategy consists of identifying customers to target, along with the appropriate positioning of a product or service with respect to competitors' offerings in the market-place. The implementation of a marketing programme is facilitated through the marketing mix. Putting together a marketing strategy and an appropriate marketing mix requires a thorough understanding of customers, competitors and the marketing environment. Marketing research along with a systematic marketing information system provide useful ways of obtaining the desired information.

Following analysis of the market and the targeting of a specific group of customers, a marketing mix has to be developed which matches the wants of these targeted customers and which is superior, from the customers' perspective, to those of competitors. Firms which succeed in this respect develop a 'differential advantage' which reflects customers' reasons for preferring its products to those offered by competitors.

A key element in identifying and implementing resources which will produce a differential advantage is the two-way flow of marketing communication. This is explored below.

MARKETING: A CHANNEL AN INFLUENCE ON BEHAVIOUR

Marketing identifies customer needs and wants and facilitates the process of satisfying them. This may involve gathering information through specially commissioned market research studies. In addition, the organization will have many other ways of obtaining information on consumer needs and wants. It may have a formalized marketing information system, or it may simply make use of systematic feedback of information from all its staff who come in contact with customers and distributors.

Organizations need to inform prospective customers that they can satisfy customers' wants and needs. This they do with the aid of the promotional mix – a combination of advertising, personal selling, sales promotion and public relations. In addition because firms are in competition with one another they have to use marketing communications to inform the market that their product is superior to that of their competitors.

SCOPE OF MARKETING

There are some marked differences between how different kinds of organization use marketing. One important difference is in the marketing of industrial goods and consumer goods. The differences are explored below, along with a discussion of how marketing can be applied to all organizations.

INDUSTRIAL GOODS AND CONSUMER GOODS

Consumer goods are those goods which are bought by or on behalf of the ultimate user – washing machines and food are examples. Consumer goods marketing is a sophisticated business backed up by private marketing research companies and advertising agencies which undertake a considerable volume of work for consumer goods companies. Some companies spend millions of pounds each year on marketing activities.

Industrial goods are goods supplied to industry for use in the production of other goods. They may themselves be intermediate goods, not destined for use by the final consumer. Industrial goods include plant and equipment, raw materials and many different kinds of services.

Marketing is just as relevant to industrial goods as to consumer goods. The key differences in terms of marketing management emphasis when dealing with industrial buyers rather than consumers are:

- There are fewer industrial buyers than there are consumers, and the buying process can be more complex

- The nature of the marketing mix with respect to industrial markets can be substantially different to that directed at consumer markets.

One distinguishing feature which differentiates consumer markets from industrial markets is the number of customers. There are many more potential customers for consumer goods than for industrial goods. This influences the predominant methods of marketing communication that are used to reach the respective audiences – large numbers of consumers, often making rapid regular buying decisions in retail outlets, encourage consumer goods firms to use advertising of one form or another. It is often the cheapest and the most effective way of informing potential customers.

Advertising is also an important form of marketing communication for producers of industrial goods, and firms make use of advertising in trade journals to bring products to the attention of the industrial buyer. However, there is a much greater emphasis on personal selling in industrial marketing. Technical representatives or teams of marketing specialists with technical knowhow are often used to call on prospective buyers.

Marketing is broad in scope and includes such diverse areas as:

- consumer behaviour

- pricing

- purchasing

- sales management

- product management

- marketing communications

- comparative marketing

- social marketing

- the efficiency/productivity of marketing systems

- the role of marketing in economic development

- packaging

- channels of distribution

- marketing research

- societal issues in marketing

- retailing

- wholesaling

- the social responsibility of marketing

- international marketing

- commodity marketing

- physical distribution

The development of a marketing orientation is not just restricted to businesses. Marketing is relevant to any organization, whether it is a non-profit-making body, a public sector institution, a commercial organization, a commercial business or an industrial conglomerate (see Lovelock and Weinberg, 1984). Marketing attempts to understand customer wants and match them to the products or services that the organization is supplying.

CASE EXAMPLE

WINTER OLYMPICS: THE SCOPE OF MARKETING

'Successful marketing programmes provide opportunities for all parties involved to create value as well as to receive it,' – Richard W. Pound, member of the International Olympic Committee Executive Board.

It was anticipated that the 1994 winter Olympics in Lillehammer would generate higher than ever revenues from sponsorship and the sale of TV rights. In conjunction with the International Committee, the Lillehammer Olympic Organizing Committee created marketing programmes to try to maximize revenue for the Lillehammer Winter Olympics. At the same time, a priority was to make the event free from commercial clutter and organized for the primary benefit of athletes and spectators, both at the event and around the world.

Sport always attracts many viewers, both at the event itself and from a distance through the medium of TV. It was estimated that close on 1.5 million people would gather in Lillehammer to watch the 1994 Winter Olympics, and that they would be augmented by millions of TV viewers in different countries worldwide.

(Source: adapted from Marketing Week, *28 January, 1994, p.22).*

QUESTIONS

1. How might the marketing concept be applied in this case?

2. How might 'all parties involved create value as well as receive it'?

SUMMARY

Marketing is both a functional aspect of a business and a business philosophy. Firms have adopted various business orientations, with differing degrees of significance, for how to perceive the market place. Two important concepts have evolved: the 'marketing concept' and the 'societal concept'. Today, the latter is preferred – not only does it stress the need to satisfy customer wants and needs, but it also stresses the need to consider the long-term welfare of the parties involved. Selling is an important integral part of marketing – it is not an alternative to marketing, nor is it independent of marketing. It is part of the marketing mix.

Gaining a competitive advantage is a fundamental objective of marketing. It can be achieved by augmenting the benefits which are offered to customers in a way which is different to that of competitors. Organizations have a number of strategic tools at their disposal to win over customers to their products and service:

- product
- price
- promotion
- place (method of distribution).

Together they represent four elements of the marketing mix – the four Ps. Organizations must ensure that the marketing mix variables set for any product or service complement each other and add to the strategic impact of marketing activity. Decisions regarding individual elements of the marketing mix cannot be taken in isolation – they have to be considered in conjunction with the other elements of the marketing mix.

Marketing involves determining how the organization's objectives can be attained through seeking out and exploiting opportunities in the market. Marketing management is about getting this done through people. It includes:

- planning actions
- organizing people to implement actions
- coordinating efforts to achieve plans
- controlling the plan so that it achieves objectives, and
- appraising performance.

Marketing management develops a marketing strategy and then designs, constructs and implements a marketing programme to enable it to achieve its objectives. Marketing strategy consists of identifying customers to target along with the appropriate positioning of a product or service with respect to competitors' offerings in the market-place.

Marketing is equally relevant to both industrial goods and consumer goods. It is broad in scope and includes such diverse areas as: consumer behaviour; pricing; purchasing; sales management; product management; marketing communications; comparative marketing; social marketing; the efficiency/productivity of marketing system; the role of marketing in economic development; packaging; channels of distribution; marketing research; societal issues in marketing; retailing; wholesaling; the social responsibility of marketing; international marketing; commodity marketing; physical distribution.

DISCUSSION QUESTIONS

1. Indicate the key elements of a modern-day definition of marketing.

2. What is a market?

3. Explain what is meant by the phrase, 'marketing is both a business philosophy and a functional aspect of a business'.

4. Differentiate among the following:
   a. production orientation
   b. product orientation
   c. selling orientation
   d. marketing orientation
   e. societal (marketing) orientation.

5. Explain the notion of marketing myopia.

6. Differentiate between marketing and selling.

7. What do you understand by the term 'the marketing mix'.

8. What is involved in marketing management?

9. How might organizations achieve differential advantages?

10. What is marketing strategy and how does the idea of a marketing programme relate to this?

11. How is marketing a channel of information and an influence on behaviour?

12. Describe the various ways in which consumer goods marketing is:
    a. similar to industrial goods marketing
    b. different from industrial goods marketing.

REFERENCES

Baker, M. (1991) *Marketing: an Introductory Text*, 5th edn, Macmillan, Basingstoke.

Borden, N.H. (1991) Concept of the Marketing Mix, in *Marketing Classics*, 7th edn (eds B.M. Enis and K.K. Cox), Allyn & Bacon, Needham Heights, Mass.

Business Week, (1985) Boeing turns to guns for more of its bread and butter, 23 September, p.1.

Drucker, P. (1974) *Management Tasks, Responsibilities, Practices*, New York.

Garvin, D. (1987) Competing on the eight dimensions of quality, *Harvard Business Review*, November–December.

Kotler, P. (1988) *Marketing Management*: *Analysis, Planning and Control*, 6th edn, Prentice Hall, Engelwood Cliffs, N.J.

Levitt, T. (1962) *Innovations in Marketing*, McGrawHill, New York.

Levitt, T. (1983) *Marketing Imagination*, Free Press, New York.

Lovelock, C.H. and Weinberg, C.B. (1984) *Marketing for Public and Non-profit Managers*, John Wiley & Sons, New York.

McDonald, M. and Leppard, J. (1991) *The Marketing Audit*, Butterworth Heinemann, Oxford.
Marketing News (1985) AMA board approves new definition, 1 March, p.1.
Nicholas, R. (1994) Avon ads praise the real woman, *Marketing*, 27 January.

FURTHER READING

Groenross, C. (1989) Defining marketing: a market oriented approach. *European Journal of Marketing*, 23 (1).

Houston, F.S. (1986), The marketing concept: what it is not, *Journal of Marketing*, 81–7.

Litchenthal, D. and Wilson, D.T. (1992) Becoming marketing oriented, *Journal of Business Research*, May, 191–208.

McBurnie, T. and Clutterbuck, D. (1988), *The Marketing Edge*, Penguin Books, London.

McNair, M.P. (1968) Marketing and the social challenge of our times, in *A New Measure of Social Responsibility for Marketing*, (eds K. Cox and B.M. Enis), American Marketing Association, Chicago, Ill.

CASE PROBLEM 1.1

WELLIES: MEETING CUSTOMERS' REQUIREMENTS

In 1989 three metallurgists working in a German research laboratory discovered that when compounded with a number of other elements in certain proportions, aluminium foil could be produced which possessed entirely new properties. The foil could be produced in many different thicknesses, was flexible in whatever thicknesses were produced and was resistant to rust.

In the course of looking for commercial organizations who might be interested in making commercial use of the new compound, the firm came across Wellies, a British footwear manufacturer which, among other items, produced a line of rubber wellington boots. Wellies was an imaginative firm and saw immediate possibilities for marketing wellington boots made from the new aluminium compound.

During 1990–94 Wellies undertook technical development of the product. Development costs turned out to be quite high – nearly twice what they had originally envisaged.

The firm decided to market its new line of wellington boots under the name 'Wallies'. Changing the 'e' to an 'a' the chief executive said, would emphasize the fact that the boots were made out of aluminium. The firm decided to market the product through it existing outlets where its traditional wellington boots were made available to the members of the public.

Because of the unexpectedly high development costs and the fact that new processes had been installed to produce the new 'Wallies', the price

CASE PROBLEM 1.1 *CONTINUED*

to both retailers and other intermediaries was considerably higher than that of their more traditional wellington boots. However, the company felt that the customer was bound to perceive the superior quality of the boots, which would be reflected in the higher price which was charged.

The managing director felt that it would be unnecessary to advertise the new products, since the firm's existing distributors would be only too pleased to stock such an innovative new line. 'We have already spent millions of pounds developing this product – everyone will want to buy a pair so there is no point in spending more money', the managing director was quoted as saying.

The product was put onto the market in the summer of 1994. The company employed its own sales force, who called on a large number of wholesalers and retailers. The sales force encountered stiff resistance to the product from both wholesalers and retailers – less than 10% of the firm's distributors agreed to stock the product. Within a few weeks of the introduction of the product, all those distributors who had agreed to stock the product were asking the manufacturer to take back unsold stock (which amounted to 90% of what they had originally taken).

The company was dismayed at the apparent total failure of the new product, and the managing director decided to instigate an enquiry into the matter. A survey of wholesalers, retailers and consumers was undertaken with a view to finding out why the product had been rejected. The following comments were typical of the responses obtained.

Wholesalers and retailers:

'We couldn't take on a product like that. How could we be sure that there would be a demand for it?'

'Even if we did take on the product, we couldn't make a decent profit.'

' "Wallies" – you must be joking!'

'People would think we had mirrors in the window – not wellington boots.'

Consumers:

' "Wallies" – never seen or heard of them but they sound a bit daft!'

' "Metal Wellies"? – they can't be good for your feet.'

'I can't think of any occasion when I might want to use them.'

'I suppose if you were fashion conscious in the garden – it might give your neighbour a surprise. But think of the cost.'

'Are they for real?'

The managing director wondered what he should do with accumulated stocks of 'Wallies'.

QUESTIONS

1. What do you think went wrong?

2. What do you think the managing director of Wellies should do with respect to the current problem?

CASE PROBLEM 1.2

AVON: FINDING A COMPETITIVE DIFFERENTIAL

Do women buy cosmetics to cover up what nature has provided, or to enhance what nature has provided? Do women have different wants and needs as far as cosmetics are concerned? What kind of advertising appeals are likely to be most effective? Is there an element of fantasy in buying and using cosmetics? These are important questions that need to be answered.

In examining the glamour appeals in the advertising of cosmetics products to women, it will probably be noticed that they are usually portrayed by the faces of attractive celebrities or good looking young women. Despite the nature of the customary appeals used, the advertising agency handling Avon's account argue, however, that this is not what women want to see. On the contrary, Avon's group marketing communications manager believes that 'real beauty' comes from the inside and the company is intent on reflecting this in their advertising strategy.

In an attempt to modernize its image, Avon is developing two important themes in its advertising. Firstly, it wants to show that the products it has to offer are for 'real women', and secondly, it wants to show that it appreciates the nature of female friendship. After all, many of Avon's 160,000 representatives make most of their sales to friends.

Avon's new 1994 TV advertising campaign is the first since 1986. Its target audience is essentially women over 25 and under 50, positioned in the mid-market. Its main competitive products are Boots own brands and those produced by the Body Shop. The new advertising campaign planned by Avon follows a complete facelift to its entire product line during 1993.

CASE PROBLEM 1.2 *CONTINUED*

Avon's approach is novel and challenges the traditionally accepted notions of attractiveness in women. The managing partner of the agency handling the account was quoted as saying that the advertisements spurned the way in which imagery was associated with cosmetic products and in particular 'the preying on women's feeling of inadequacy'. He argued that cosmetics were not about covering up inadequacies, but rather about making the best of what women have.

In an attempt to bring female friendship and 'real women' into the advertising, one advertisement presents two friends talking about a new romance, along with the 'great for kissing' lipstick with moisturizer. In another advertisement an upset young mother, seeing her child off to school for the first time, is featured; a friend offers her a tear-proof mascara.

Friendship and 'realness' are also emphasized in press advertisements, where genuine friends are featured talking about each other. The actresses used in sequences have the appearance of 'real women'.

(Source: adapted from Nicholas, 1994, p.6)

QUESTIONS

1. How was Avon trying to achieve product differentiation?

2. Do you think that Avon's approach was justified? Why? Or why not?

2 THE MARKETING ENVIRONMENT

This chapter examines the environmental factors influencing demand and supply of products and services. Attention is also given to the legislation requiring organizations to market their goods in a responsible way. Changes in methods of distribution, and the shift towards a more responsible attitude to the environment, are also considered. Finally, the ethical issues involved in the marketing of goods and services are considered, along with different types of consumer protection agencies and watch-dog organizations.

OBJECTIVES

After studying this chapter you should be able to:

- understand how changes in environmental factors such as social and cultural values, political, fiscal and economic policies, and changes in technology have an impact on customers wants and needs for products and services and the kind of products and services that are produced

- understand the kinds of legislation that have been set up to try to ensure that organizations compete fairly in the market place and behave in a responsible way towards consumers

- understand how changes have taken place in the distribution of goods over the past 30 years or so, and what impact this has had on marketers of consumer products

- understand what the main 'Green' issues concerning the environment are, and the kind of steps that organizations can take to keep in line with 'Green' thinking

- understand the ethical issues involved in the marketing of goods and services

1   understand about the different types of consumer protection agencies and consumer watch-dog organizations that have been established to monitor business organizations and how they act in the interests of the consumer.

INTRODUCTION

Organizations function, in changing and at times inhospitable business environ-ments, rather like a ship at sea. It cannot be assumed that the environment will always accommodate the interests of the organization – sometimes the sea is rough and the ship has difficulty in making progress on its journey, sometimes it is calm and the weather clear, so that the ship can make steady progress. Sometimes the weather is malevolent: thick fogs and icebergs imperil the very

CASE EXAMPLE

THE BOILED FROG SYNDROME: RESPONSE TO ENVIRONMENTAL CHANGE

Charles Handy (1990, p.7) provides a graphic illustration of reaction to change with the 'boiled frog syndrome'. He tells how a group of French schoolchildren found that a frog would allow itself to be boiled to death when put in a pan of cold water, which was then slowly heated up.

However, if another frog was put into a pan of hot water it would immediately jump out. The generalizable conclusion he drew was that organisms react quickly to rapid environmental change, but may fail to respond to, or even recognize, slow changes. Large (1992) entended this allegory, suggesting that the 'boiled frog' company might also respond to sudden crisis and survive but that it might not perceive gradual changes in the economic, technological, social, political, cultural or competitive environments until it was too late to respond.

QUESTIONS

1. Why should firms not perceive gradual changes in the marketing environ-ment?

2. If firms do respond to sudden changes in the environment, what guarantee is there that they will always survive?

survival of the ship. The organizational environment presents this mixture of opportunities and threats.

To assure their continued well-being, organizations must respond and adapt to changing environmental conditions. This demands an understanding of those factors and forces which bring about the changes. In an ideal world, an organization will adapt to such changes as they occur, or even anticipate them in advance. An inability to do either of these can leave organizations in jeopardy.

The marketing or business environment is the setting within which a business operates, formulates policies and makes decisions. In examining the marketing environment it is usual to distinguish between the internal and external environments. The former usually comprises the various assets and resources possessed by an organization. That is, its workforce, plant and machinery, know-how, financial resources, etc. The latter refers to people, institutions and developments, etc. which exert an external influence on how the organization fares.

Organizations need to have a good understanding of the marketing environment in which they operate. They need to be able to anticipate the changes that are likely to take place in it for the foreseeable future. However, it is not simply a matter of adapting to change. Organizations can also exercise their own influence on the environment. They may do so, for example, by developing and commercializing new technological ideas. In turn, the new technologies then become part of the environment and have an impact upon what other organizations can do.

An organization can exert considerable control over its internal environment, but it cannot exert control in the same way or to the same extent over the external environment. It can only attempt to influence this, through various means. These may include activities such as lobbying among legislative groups. Organizations often do this when trying to influence the formulation of European Community directives on such things as product design, safety standards, etc.

In this chapter we will be looking at the external environment and how it impinges on the activities of organizations.

CHANGING PATTERNS AND STRATEGIES

Marketing policies, plans and decisions are put into practice in the context of an ever-changing external environment. The nature of the environment and the changes that take place within it offer opportunities, while also presenting threats and constraints, to an organization's activities.

The changing nature of markets requires entirely different marketing strategies to be adopted for the same products from time to time. There are fragmented markets and mass markets. Mass markets are markets in which there is a large volume demand for a standard product. Fragmented markets are based upon distinct market niches and segments.

There are many examples of changes in the marketing environment that impact heavily upon organizations and what they have to do in order to survive and prosper. For instance, from the point of view of technological change, the intro-

CASE EXAMPLE

HOLIDAYS ABROAD: THE IMPACT OF A CHANGING ENVIRONMENT ON CONSUMER WANTS

The change in the nature of the holiday market illustrates the impact that environmental forces can have on an industry. In the first half of the 20th century an improvement in living standards, accompanied by wider car ownership, produced a considerable increase in holiday traffic. Holiday resorts all over the UK began to develop and various infrastructures, entertainment businesses, hotel accommodation/guest houses and restaurants were established.

Over the last 30 years more people have started to take their holidays abroad. Places that people once only read about in books or saw on films are now familiar holiday destinations. Increasing affluence along with the development of air passenger transport have made this possible. Accompanying these developments there has been the introduction and growth of the travel agency business, an interest in learning languages and a growth in various aids to facilitate this, as well as the publication of a large number of books and guides on countries and foreign resorts.

QUESTIONS

1. What factors do you think led to more people taking their holidays abroad?

2. Can we attribute the growth of various ancillary industries such as language books, tapes and courses, or the development of travel agencies, only to the growth in people taking their holidays abroad? Discuss.

duction of the microchip has had a major impact on many types of consumer durables such as washers, cookers, etc. and on home entertainment, home-based office work and computer-based learning in education.

Over the last two decades there have been many changes in people's shopping habits as a greater emphasis has been put on convenience shopping. With increasing European integration, British firms and people are being influenced more and more by ideas expressed in other European countries and enacted through the European Parliament. Indeed, all the forces of the marketing environment have made an impact on what firms and people want and do throughout the world.

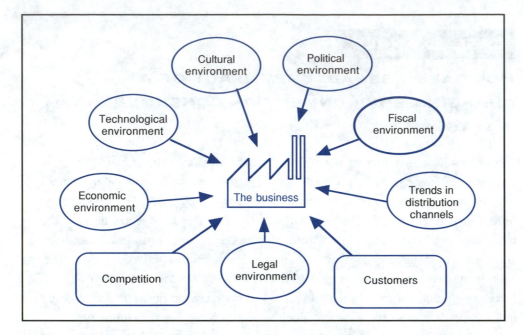

Figure 2.1 The business and its environments.

A number of different environmental variables affect consumers and firms. Social and cultural factors, political, fiscal and economic policies, as well as changes in technology, all have an impact on customers' wants and needs for products and services and the kind of products and services that are produced. Competitors as well as customers exert an influence; we will look at these two factors in detail in later chapters.

In the next section we will look specifically at social and cultural factors.

CHANGING SOCIAL AND CULTURAL ASPECTS OF CONSUMERS

In this section we will examine demography, the nature of cultural values, and changes in values and attitudes and how they impact upon the marketing activities of organizations.

DEMOGRAPHY

Demographic and cultural change can have society-wide influences that change and affect the marketing environment. In terms of demographic factors, the following are of interest to marketers:

- **population**: size, growth rate, distribution by gender and age, birth-rates, death rates, life expectancy

- **population density**: location, geographical/regional shifts
- **household/family**: size, make-up
- **income/wealth distribution**
- **socio-economic groups**: occupations, ethnic groups.

Such factors change slowly over time and exert powerful effects on the volume and nature of demand for most products and services. Some influences are obvious:

- the demand for children's products and services will be related to birth rate patterns
- the demand for products and services to meet the wants and needs of the elderly will be related to characteristics and trends of an ageing population.

In European countries in recent times there has been a declining birth rate. Along with this, an extension of life expectancy has resulted in a shift in the profile of the population to that of an ageing one. Many changes have also taken place in the make-up and size of family households. A situation of fewer marriages and fewer children, coupled with an increase in the labour force of married women has changed the basic nature of the family household. Career couples with no children are now quite common and are a target group of interest to many marketers because of their relatively high disposable income.

Another characteristic seems to have been a growth in non-family households. Some of these are made up of single, career people while others are made up of divorced or widowed adults. There has also been an increase in single-parent families. These changes in the structure and characteristics of households have had a major effect on the pattern of demand for a wide range of everyday goods and services.

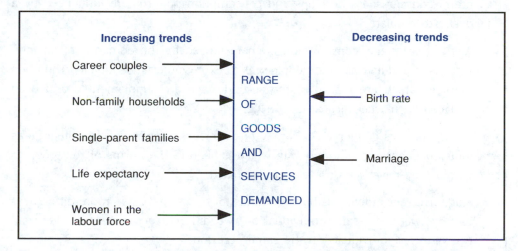

Figure 2.2 Trends in Europe and their impact on demand for goods and services.

CASE EXAMPLE

EASTERN PROMISE: ENVIRONMENTAL CHANGE AFFECTS ALL MARKETS WORLDWIDE

One tends to think of finding millionaires on the French Riviera or in the affluent regions of the USA. It may be surprising to know that there are over 500 000 dollar millionaires in the People's Republic of China, where there is also an emerging middle class (those with annual incomes in excess of $15 000 equivalent) which numbers more than 35 million people.

Another interesting point is that while European retail sales languish in the doldrums many Asian retail markets are experiencing annual sales growths of more than 10%. Of course the stage in development of the market may vary considerably from country to country, even within a particular region of the world. Malaysia in 1994 was a buoyant retail economy, but some of its neighbours such as Thailand, Cambodia, Vietnam and Laos did not share the same fortune.

It is possible to characterize the stage of economic development in a country and relate it to levels and types of marketing activity. The following typology is suggested by the Henley Centre.

- The first stage is where the formal cash economy is hardly developed and most consumption is of unbranded commodities.

- At the second stage incomes are in the range $2000 to $3000 per annum; brand consciousness develops and consumption patterns are influenced by a desire to emulate.

- At the third stage, consumption is characterized by the demands of an individualistic middle class and people seek to express their individuality. The mass markets which are typical of the second stage are supplemented and even replaced by market niches.

- Stage four sees gender, class, family or caste-based stereotypes disintegrate as individuals act and buy in a way which is alien to the norms of the group to whom they have been traditionally affiliated.

- Stage five sees individuals buying brands for occasions. Often more differences exist between the same individual on two different occasions than between two different individuals on the same occasion.

As far as income and wealth are concerned, the total gross domestic product of Europe is now greater than that of the USA, accounting for over one-third of world GDP and over 40% of world trade (Haliburton and Hunerburg, 1993). Within Europe there are quite wide disparities in terms of relative wealth. Switzerland, for example, has a per capita GDP approaching seven times that of Portugal. These differences seem to be widening, because of the unequal effects of the recent recession and the relatively higher population growth in the poorer countries.

There are also marked disparities of wealth distribution within individual countries in Europe – for example northern versus southern Italy, the south east of England versus the peripheral UK regions, and, to an extent, regional differences in Germany. It is not appropriate therefore to regard Europe as a single economic region for products which are directly influenced by the level of economic development.

THE NATURE OF CULTURAL VALUES

Often, different regions of a country exhibit different buying preference patterns that seem to reflect local cultural and traditional values. In addition, because many towns and cities throughout the world are now very cosmopolitan in nature, it is quite common to find large ethnic groups living in fairly large concentrations in urban areas. These groups have distinct cultural values which are reflected in their buying preference patterns. For example, in 1989 ethnic minorities made up less than 5% of the population of the UK. In the Greater London area, however, the figure was 17%, in the West Midlands 12% and in West Yorkshire it was 8%.

Culture is reflected in the prevalent core beliefs and values of people. These beliefs and values are evident in family and friendship relations, in social conven-

CASE EXAMPLE

TURKEY: CULTURAL INFLUENCE ON WAYS OF TRADING

At the gateway to Asia, yet still in Europe, lies the city of Istanbul. It is a historic yet commercial city in every possible way offering the visitor a wide range of spectacles from palaces, places of worship and views across the Bosphorous to one of its most famed commercial Turkish delights, the 'Grand Bazaar'

The Bazaar started off as a small warehouse at the time of Mehmet the Conqueror (the late 15th century) and expanded to cover a vast area as neighbouring shopkeepers started to put up roofs and porches so that commerce could be conducted comfortably in all kinds of weather. Important people built *hans*, or caravanserais, at the edge of the bazaar to enable caravans bringing wealth from all parts of the Ottoman empire to unload and trade right in the bazaar's precincts. Eventually, a system of locked gates and doors was provided so that the entire mini-city could be secured at the end of the business day.

Today there are some 4000 shops and several kilometres of streets in the bazaar. There are also mosques, banks, police stations and restaurants. The Grand Bazaar is as impressive a shopping precinct as one is likely to encounter in any part of the world; for the stranger it is relatively easy to become disoriented in the labyrinth of retail outlets that it comprises. An interesting characteristic of the bazaar is the way shops selling similar goods are clustered together in groups. For example, there is a goldsmith's quarter where a bewildering array of glitter meets the eye under the glare of well-lit shop-windows.

Perhaps the most striking thing about shopping in the Grand Bazaar, however, is the way in which business is conducted. There are no set prices – everything has to be haggled over. If you see a watch you want to buy, then you will be expected to haggle over the price. The shopkeeper usually asks a price much in excess of what he or she expects to obtain, and you are expected to make a counter offer (or to decline it, saying that it is far too expensive). If you walk away then you will almost certainly be pursued by the shopkeeper – a refusal to pay the initial price is almost certainly expected and the shopkeeper interprets your behaviour as being consistent with still wanting to haggle over the price. Only a polite but firm refusal is taken as 'no basis for a sale'.

The rate of inflation in Turkey in recent years has been extremely high and many shopkeepers in tourist places will be delighted to price their goods in

CASE EXAMPLE *CONTINUED*

Deutschmarks, American dollars, French francs or pounds sterling. They will often hold on to the foreign currency for many months before exchanging it for Turkish currency, hoping to add to their profit in doing so. Tourists can, in fact, often strike good bargains by making a deal in a stable foreign currency. This is certainly true in the Grand Bazaar, or at tourist places such as Side on the Mediterranean coast. Indeed, many shopkeepers have gone to the trouble to learn sufficient German, English or French to be able to negotiate a sale with visiting tourists.

One also has to be aware of the different style of approach in Turkish markets. Retailers there are much more proactive in their approach to selling than one expects in Europe or America. In Britain we might interpret this approach as 'touting' or 'soliciting' for business – something which is seen as undesirable in our own culture. In Turkish markets, however, it is seen as the normal and desirable way of doing business. There is no social security system in operation in Turkey and people without money can starve to death. In a such a country one has to fight to earn one's living.

There are markets or bazaars in most Turkish cities and towns. Even if one does not speak the language it a relatively simple matter to strike a bargain. One simply gets the retailer to write down the amount he or she wants. One then makes one's counter offer in a similar way, and so on.

QUESTION

1. Haggling over prices is common in many middle eastern countries, and elsewhere in the world. Can you explain why shopkeepers should prefer to haggle rather than ask a set price for their goods?

2. Why are Turkish shopkeepers and Turkish street traders more proactive in their selling approach than shopkeepers in Europe and the USA?

tions and rites, in social institutions and in social order itself. They take a long time to change since they are inextricably linked to such things as family upbringing, the education system, national history, religion and a variety of other institutional phenomena.

A variety of secondary beliefs and values, which are less durable and more situationally determined, are also to be found. For example, while a belief in law enforcement may be rooted in core values, attitudes towards private law enforcement and vigilantes reflect secondary values and beliefs. These beliefs are more likely to vary within society and to change over time. They may also be recognizable in subcultures within society. Subcultures evolve for a variety of reasons and commonly involve a grouping of people with common interests,

experiences and motivations. Subcultures may also be identified with age groupings, regional affiliations, religious or ethnic associations or even situational facets
of lifestyle (e.g. students).

From the point of view of international marketing, language is an aspect of
culture which is particularly relevant to marketing communications. Barring the
Swiss, the Dutch, and to a lesser extent, the Scandinavians and the Germans,
most Europeans experience major language hurdles. However, among the younger
generation of Europeans the situation is improving; 'International English' is also
growing in popularity. Another aspect of culture which has an influence on
consumers is religion. Religious beliefs, can have a major influence on consumer
attitudes and purchasing behaviour. This is often reflected in the kinds of food
that people consume, the drinks they purchase, even their style of dress. Business
practices themselves vary considerably between different areas and countries.

Marketers have to understand cultural values in all aspects of implementing the
marketing concept and managing the marketing mix.

CASE EXAMPLE

TOBACCO INDUSTRY: IMPACT OF PEOPLE'S CHANGING ATTITUDE TO SMOKING

The Tobacco Advisory Council maintains that the UK tobacco market is in a long-
term decline and that consumption has shown a downward trend since 1973. In
1991 a health survey found that 30% of British adults smoked with the proportions for men and women being equal. Figures show that the proportion of adults
smoking has declined considerably over the past ten years.

Regular exercise and healthy diets are prescribed as necessary conditions for
good health. This in turn has led to a dramatic change in lifestyles in recent
years. One consequence of this change in both attitudes and behaviour has been
the reduction in the proportion of smokers. Many people have stopped smoking
altogether, or have curtailed their smoking substantially.

From 1987 to 1992 there was a 55% increase (at current prices) in the UK
market value for cigarettes, to just over £10 bn. In 1993 the value was expected
to fall to £9.7 bn. While at constant prices the market growth has shown a 2%
rise, value increases are due almost entirely to rises in VAT and the imposition
of higher excise duty on tobacco. Duty represented 76% of the purchase price
in 1991, having risen by 44% over the period since 1987.

Taxation on tobacco has continued to increase significantly since 1990 and has
pushed price increases above the rate of inflation. The continued deep recession

led to a 6.7% drop in sales by volume in 1992, and it was estimated that in 1993 volume would have declined a further 4.5%. Cigarette production in the UK has been increasing, however, due to strong export demand and was up 12.7% in 1992.

Smokers and the tobacco industry have been the target of various pressure groups. These include ASH (Action on Smoking and Health) and PAT (Parents Against Tobacco). PAT was responsible for sponsoring a Parliamentary Bill to impose heavier fines on retailers selling cigarettes to children under the age of 16. ASH has helped to organize 'No Smoking Day', since its inception in 1984.

In an attempt to discourage smoking the Department of Health has sponsored anti-smoking advertisements. TV and radio advertising of cigarettes has been prohibited since 1973. There has been a voluntary agreement between the tobacco industry and successive governments since 1971, relating to tobacco advertising and promotion. However, the industry continues to use poster hoardings, campaigns, and sponsorship to promote its products.

(Source: The Grocer, *8 January 1994, pp. 31–3)*

QUESTIONS

1. 'No matter what action governments take to curb smoking, there will always be a large market for cigarettes.' Discuss.

2. What actions have tobacco manufacturers taken to offset the decline in cigarette smoking in the UK market?

CHANGES IN VALUES AND ATTITUDES

The 'permissive society' of the 1960s and its aftermath had a considerable influence on values and attitudes in the 1970s and 1980s. However, it would seem that in some respects these changes may now be undergoing a reversal. Today, people have in some ways returned to the social norms which prevailed before the 1960s. Even so, there are still many ways in which attitudes are considerably different to those of the pre-1960s.

Attitudes in the UK towards credit, for instance, have changed substantially over the last 20 years or so. Traditionally, credit purchasing was something which people tended to avoid. Indeed there was at one time a social stigma against purchasing on credit, except for major items such as homes and cars. This may have been a carry-over of Victorian values, or even a product of the hardships of debt which ensued during the interwar years of depression, in the 1920s and 1930s. Credit purchasing started to develop in the late 1950s as consumer confidence began to recover, following the hardships and rationing of the immediate post-war period. The Conservative government's message of the late 1950s and early 1960s – 'You have never had it so good' had a ring of truth about it. For many people, more affluent times have continued and today, credit is an intrinsic part in the marketing of many products.

Changes in society's attitudes towards health over a similar period of time have shaped the development of the multi-million pound industry centred on the supply of health products and services. People are now more weight-conscious, exercise-conscious, and diet-conscious. Moreover, smoking, which at one time was considered a social sophistication, is now widely considered to be anti-social.

There have been many changes in attitudes over the years which have had implications for marketing. One of the most far-reaching of these concerns the role of working women in Western society. In March 1992, roughly half of the working population of Britain was made up of women (*Employment Gazette*, June and September 1992).

At one time British women tended to stay at home and rarely held jobs with substantial incomes. This situation has changed considerably, and a high proportion of the workforce are women. This fact, with its implications for reduced leisure time and greater disposable incomes, may have contributed to the acceptance of convenience foods and the widespread adoption of home freezers and microwave ovens as well as to one-stop shopping.

THE INFLUENCE OF POLITICAL, FISCAL AND ECONOMIC POLICIES

Having examined one aspect of the environment – consumers and culture – and its impact on marketing activities, we now turn to examine those aspects which are usually under the control of the government: political, fiscal and economic policies.

POLITICAL AND FISCAL POLICIES

Governments are in a position to take actions which can substantially alter a company's marketing environment. In the UK, for instance, privatization of the public utilities has created new terms and conditions for the suppliers and subcontractors in these industries. The creation of an internal market within the health service has had a substantial impact on the way in which hospitals and other health service units go about their work. The transfer into private ownership of Jaguar and Rover in the car industry, and of British Airways, has created commercially competitive companies which have had a substantial impact on competitors in their respective industries. Deregulation in the EC has created both opportunities and threats across borders.

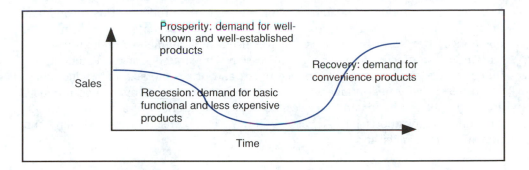

Figure 2.3 The effect of the economic cycle.

Legislation over such things as labelling, packaging, advertising and environmental issues all have to be taken into account when designing packaging and formulating advertising messages.

To discourage demand for certain imported goods, governments can impose tariffs on them. Firms wanting to import such goods then must find ways of getting round the problems that this creates. For example, a government may wish to encourage employment of local people in manufacturing industry. One way the government might seek to achieve this aim would be by imposing lower tariffs on sub-assemblies than on finished goods, so firms may prefer to import sub-assemblies instead of fully assembled goods. The reasons for imposing tariffs or taxes on imports are explored further in Chapter 19.

Political instability in a country can also have a marked effect on marketing methods used by exporters in accessing that country's markets. Under such circumstances it may be preferable, for example, to sell a licence to manufacture the product to a producer in the country concerned for a once-only royalty fee. Licences may be granted to produce or market goods and services. In the former case the license relates to know-how. Royalty payments can be one-off payments or they can be fixed as a percentage of subsequent sales.

THE ECONOMIC CYCLE

Traditionally the economy has been considered to follow a cyclical pattern consisting of four stages: boom, recession, slump (depression) and recovery. Various industries, markets and organizations can, of course, diverge from this trend, either demonstrating a decline in growth during a boom, or an expansion during a slump.

In each stage of the cycle there are different business patterns (see Figure 2.3). In times of prosperity, consumer spending is high. Organizations normally exploit this by expanding product lines, increasing promotional efforts, expanding distribution and raising prices, on the presumption that consumers are often willing to pay more for well-known and well-established products, and have the means to do so.

In times of recession, the purchasing power of consumers declines and may stagnate even when the economy enters into recovery. During a recession, consumers may shift their buying patterns to purchasing more basic, more functional, less expensive products, spending less on non-essential products. This means that decisions on the purchase of luxury items, such as cars or new homes, may be postponed. Not surprisingly, it is the producers and marketers of luxury goods who are most affected in a economic recession. The strategy for marketers during times of recession is usually to reduce prices and prune the size of product lines.

As the recovery gets under way, consumers start to buy convenience products and higher-priced goods and services. Assessing the strength of a recovery is difficult, and organizations have to assess how quickly consumers are making the transition from recession.

INFLATION

One of the most difficult phenomena to deal with during the economic cycle is inflation. Inflation is an increase in the general level of prices in an economy over time. It has two main causes:

- excess demand beyond the output capacity of the economy to supply goods and services
- increases in input costs – wages, raw materials and components.

Inflation produced by rising costs, results in reduced consumer buying power, creates problems for the marketer. Not only is uncertainty introduced into the market through the effect of inflation on costs and sales forecasts, but it is also difficult to determine the price to charge during the next budgeting period.

Inflation is not welcomed by the business community. It is administratively expensive to constantly change prices in line with inflation and it can affect a firm's competitive position in both domestic and foreign markets. High rates of domestic inflation, unless they are adjusted by corresponding changes in foreign exchange rates, effectively make imports cheaper and make exports more expensive.

THE INFLUENCE OF TECHNOLOGY

Next we will consider another of the environmental forces acting upon firms – technology.

In modern times the influence of technology in the marketing environment has come greatly to the fore. Technology has always been important but the rate of innovation has increased so rapidly in recent years that the impact of technology has become a principal driving force in business activity. In this section we examine the increasingly important role that technology has to play.

Technology is a driving force for change everywhere and has increased the potential losses or rewards associated with commercial success and failure. Technological progress depends on a process of successful innovation, which involves commercialization of ideas and an understanding of market needs. The

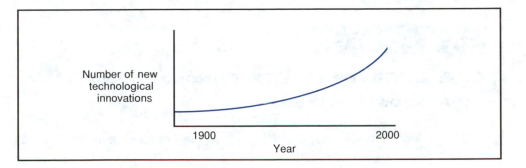

Figure 2.4   The rate of technological innovation during the 20th century.

role of marketing is to guide development efforts and facilitate commercialization. The Sony Walkman, for instance, is an example of a product that matched with customers' wants. In terms of technical sophistication it was basic and unexciting; the key element of its success was that it met a latent market need for a cheap, portable cassette player.

Technological advances and improvements are a feature of modern day business. The obsolescence of products within a relatively short period of their introduction is commonplace. Personal computers are a good example of where product obsolescence can be very rapid indeed. Moreover, it is increasingly the case that tomorrow's products are no longer news by the time they are put on the market. During the interval between the announcement of a new product and the time it can be made available to the consumer, competititors may already have announced improved or better versions of the same product.

Organizations that do not react to technological advances which are relevant to the kinds of products they produce run the risk of rapid product obsolescence and of going out of business.

Technology has a very strong influence on the type of products that marketers can offer. New technology can render existing products obsolete, forcing manu-facturers to incorporate the new technology into their products. Vinyl records gave some ground to the introduction of cassette tape recordings, then more ground was given to compact discs. Technology provides endless opportunities for brand new products – disposable 35mm cameras, cellular telephones, pocket computers and pocket-sized televisions are all examples of successful innovations that have created new markets.

Another important aspect of the environment which impacts on marketing activities is changes in distribution patterns. In the next section we will examine this important topic in some detail.

CHANGES IN DISTRIBUTION PATTERNS

The patterns of distribution have changed substantially over the past 30 to 40 years. The impact of changes in distribution patterns is perhaps greatest in the case of consumer goods marketers, particularly in retailing.

CASE EXAMPLE

C. & E. COVERDALE: TECHNOLOGY AND ITS IMPACT ON BUSINESS

Seamless Floors, a trading name of C. & E. Coverdale of Shaw, puts down around 250 000 square metres of flooring annually with the assistance of high-tech laser screed technology. Used in conjunction with a concrete mixer, the principles involved are similar to those used for laying floors manually. Concrete is placed slightly higher than is required and is then levelled with the laser screeder.

The laser screeder can reduce the cost of laying floors by about one-eighth, and the time taken to complete jobs can be reduced dramatically to around a quarter of the time taken by conventional methods. Up to 2000 square metres of flooring can be laid in a working day using this method, and for jobs of 1000 square metres and upwards it is the most cost-effective way of laying floors. In addition to cost-savings and improved efficiency in laying floors, the quality of the finished product is also improved. Using the new technology, floors are more denser and more durable. In addition they can also be made flatter and more consistent.

As a result of experience and the technology employed, the firm is able to offer a complete design and construct package which allows contractors to save as much as 80 per cent on contract time, compared with programmes using traditional methods. As a result of being able to complete floors faster, earlier access to following trades is allowed. Moreover, since this usually leads to a speedier completion of a project, lower overall costs associated with an entire project are commonly encountered.

(*Source:* Business North West, *January 1994, p.23.*)

QUESTIONS

1. What were the principal benefits that Coverdale acquired from making use of the new technology?

2. What benefits accrue to the customer as a result of the new technology? Are there any other beneficiaries?

CASE EXAMPLE

MONDEX: TECHNOLOGY-LED INNOVATION

A credit-card sized electrical purse contained in a wallet is about to replace money in our pockets, or so the creators of Nat West's Mondex want us to believe. Mondex works in the same kind of way as real money: there is no reference to a third party and no record is made of transactions – this differentiates it from a credit card.

The Mondex purse can even be filled with money over the telephone. It can be used to pay for goods, even newspapers and cigarettes, by sliding it through the vendor's own electronic wallet. Up to five different currencies can be held in a single purse and the device is sophisticated enough to allow customers to exchange money by sliding it through each other's electronic wallets and entering the amount to be debited/credited.

A pilot scheme is to be launched in Swindon. It is expected that 40 000 customers will initially receive a Mondex 'electronic purse' card and 'balance checker' – a smaller-sized electronic wallet through which the card is slid to give an instant balance of account. Two-thirds of retailers in the town are being fitted with the electronic wallets to accept Mondex transactions, and 11 000 payphones are being updated to take the card.

(Source: Bhoyrul, 1994, p.38)

QUESTION

1. What do you think are the main benefits to the consumer of the Mondex system? Can you see any problems with it?

In the UK, the growth in car ownership and the trend to a high percentage of husbands and wives both working has led to less time being available for shopping, but greater mobility for the shopper. All of these factors, in turn, have led to the need for one-stop shopping facilities and thence to the development of supermarkets to provide this facility. The British Market Research Bureau estimated that in 1991, 74% of regular grocery shopping was carried out once a week or less. Some 65.6% took place from Thursday to Saturday inclusive, and Sainsbury's, Tesco and Asda between them account for over 60% of regular major grocery shopping (*Regional Trends* vol. 27, 1992).

Many of the traditional retail outlets – fishmongers, butchers, pharmacists, etc. – have suffered severe competition as a result. Nevertheless, the corner shop is still a much-valued institution. According to one study, over 80% of consumers

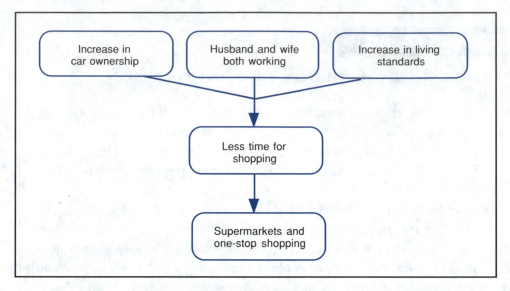

Figure 2.5 Factors giving rise to one-stop shopping.

feel this type of outlet offers a better level of personal service and greater convenience than supermarkets, both at home and abroad, especially for top-up and emergency purchases.

With the passage of time some of the chain stores such as Boots and Marks and Spencer have increased the range of products they offer to customers – for example, Marks and Spencer's move into food retailing. Large specialist retailing establishments (superstores) are now emerging to meet the needs of specific market segments – for example, Texas in the do-it-yourself homecare market. Halfords, traditionally retailers of cycle accessories and parts for the DIY motorist trade, now offer a car servicing/repair service to motorists at their new out-of-town stores.

HOW FIRMS ARE RESPONDING TO ENVIRONMENTAL CHANGE

Firms have adopted a number of ways of coming to grips with the ever-changing complexity of the environment. Foremost among these is the implementation of effective marketing information systems and the use of ongoing market research so that reaction time to change can be speeded up. These strategies will be considered in more detail in later chapters on marketing information systems and marketing research. Another approach involves what is called 'fast track' marketing. Increasing rates of technological change and the shortening of the life of products mean that companies have to act quickly when they are introducing new products to the market (the process of new product development is also discussed in a later chapter).

Late entrants to a market with a new product may find that the product does not offer attractive financial prospects, since a product's commercial life is likely to be much shorter than might have been typical, say, 20 years ago. This is obviously most applicable to those industrial markets where product development times can be counted in years – for instance, military and commercial aircraft. The response is to look for ways of reducing the amount of time needed for developing and testing a product. The implication of this is that organizations have to manage development 'in parallel', not sequentially. This means that instead of one stage following on from another, wherever possible development stages take place at the same time. Spending more money to speed up the process of innovation is another strategy, while spending more effort on planning things properly at the outset also appears to bear dividends.

One area of considerable public concern is preservation of the physical environment. Public awareness of the damage that processes and products can do to the environment has generated pressure on firms to act in a way that is seen as being more environmentally freindly. We explore ways in which firms are reacting to this challenge in the next section on 'Green marketing'.

Green marketing

Green principles relate to the preservation of the environment.There are a number of issues which have important implications for marketing. These issues are now being tackled and in many cases firms are taking advantage of the fact that they can promote certain products as being 'environmentally friendly'. The kinds of problems which exist and how firms are tackling these problems are discussed below.

It was found that damage was being caused by chlorofluorocarbons (CFCs) to the Earth's ozone layer. This led to the gradual removal of CFCs from all products, in particular from aerosol products.

The greenhouse effect (global warming), the result of certain gases being released into the atmosphere is another such issue. To counter this problem, less use of hydrocarbon-based energy has been advocated, with an emphasis being placed on energy conservation and products which promote energy conservation. Preservation of the tropical rainforests and the creation of new forests are other preventative measures to counter the greenhouse effect.

Acid rain is yet another product of civilization that damages the natural environment. It is produced by pollutants from power stations, factories and car exhausts. Proposed solutions to this problem are similar to those associated with the greenhouse effect.

Chemicals are a major force in environmental pollution. In an effort to make more productive use of land, intensive farming methods make use of artificial fertilizers and pesticides. Unfortunately these can have a detrimental effect on the environment. The use of phosphates and bleaches in household detergents and the dumping of waste into rivers and the sea can also damage the environment. Organizations are changing their working practices to prevent this, in response either to public opinion or to legislation.

The disposal of waste can also create environmental pollution. Packaging materials in which goods are transported are a major contributor to waste. Over-packaging is being discouraged and the use of reusable or recyclable materials encouraged.

Unspoilt countryside is rapidly disappearing in many parts of the world as urban expansion occurs, along with encroachment of commercial and industrial developments on the natural habitats of animals. More and better use of existing urban retailing and manufacturing sites is a partial answer to this problem.

As consumers become increasingly aware of the damage that can be caused to the environment by products, packaging, by-products and production processes, they may gradually come to demand more environmentally friendly products and, in particular, to reject throwaway products.

CASE EXAMPLE

JAQUES PRODUCTS LTD: GREEN ISSUES

Pollution has topped the agenda in many countries over the past 20 years and Britain is no exception. Environmental issues in turn have come to dominate the thinking of a good deal of British industry, all sectors of which have been compelled to examine their product and processes with a view to improving their environmental friendliness. Moreover, legislation has been introduced to force firms to conform to new requirements. In the case of the chemical industry, for instance, because of the non-biodegradable nature of polythene drums and containers, legislation is demanding that firms take responsibility for disposing of their product packaging.

Mandatory legal requirements have given rise to a virtually new drums and containers reconditioning industry. Moreover, the industry is populated with well-equipped entrepreneurial companies operating on a contract basis. One such company is Jaques Products Ltd of Stalybridge. The company has a large scale drum and container recycling operation which helps to satisfy legal requirements, as well as the objections of environmental pressure groups. An added benefit of the service is that it also offers significant cost savings to chemical companies which recycle their drums and containers.

Colin Jaques, the owner of the business, came up with the idea of laundering polythene drums 20 years ago in the days of the middle east crisis over oil. At that time, oil production was severely curtailed and the firm he worked for was unable to obtain sufficient petroleum-based polythene drums. Customers were therefore requested to return drums for laundering. Jaques' employers reprocessed many thousands of polythene drums during the next six years, and in so doing obtained significant savings for themselves and resolved disposal problems for customers.

Following redundancy in 1980, Colin Jaques surveyed northern chemical firms to assess the demand for a polythene drum laundering service. The survey showed that many polythene drums which could have been reused were at that time being destroyed.

In 1984 Jaques and his wife set up their own business to launder drums. Expansion was rapid and today Jaques Products provides a high-quality water-based chemical blending and polythene drum reconditioning service for the chemical and allied trades. The current size of the market for reconditioned drums is substantial, worth in the order of several million pounds.

(Source: Business North West, *January 1994, p.22)*

QUESTION

1. Reconditioning of products represents a good way of preserving 'Green' principles. Can you think of any other products which are reconditioned?

GREEN LABELS

The government's plans for an official eco-label on Green products were outlined in a Department of Environment White Paper in November 1991. The kind of products covered by the eco-labelling scheme would be those where there was a significant impact on the environment or where there was a high degree of consumer confusion about the environmental claims.

Green issues are increasingly seen as important by consumers, and this is reflected in the types of products consumers want to use. Organizations are having to change the nature of their products to meet these requirements. While many firms do appear either to possess a social conscience or to see the benefits of meeting the demands of Green consumers, this is not always the case. The legal infrastructure provides a remedy to this kind of abuse and many other kinds of business malpractice. In the next section we will examine this in more detail.

THE LEGAL ENVIRONMENT

While most firms willingly collaborate to act in the interests of society and behave in a reputable way, unfortunately there are some firms which do not. In this section we will look at how the legal dimension of the marketing environment seeks to preserve the best interests of customers and to ensure fair competition in the market place.

Sometimes, goods are sold that are not of merchantable quality and this is not apparent at the time of purchase. The law protects customers from unscrupulous manufacturers and dealers who produce shoddy, defective or dangerous goods. This also applies to the purchase of services.

Legislation also covers unfair trading practices, for example, when companies engage in trading practices that are not in the best interests of the customer. In the United Kingdom a variety of important Acts of Parliament have been passed which have either a direct or indirect effect on marketing. Similar kinds of laws exist in other countries, but this is not always the case.

Acts of Parliament pertinent to marketing which have been passed in the UK cover such things as requirements with respect to the labelling and advertising of foods; the provision of remedies where goods or services purchased do not match with the descriptions given for them; and making it an offence for anyone to demand payment for goods or services that have not been ordered.

There are also Laws concerning products offered at 'sale' prices, goods bought on credit, guarantees or conditions of sale, liability of traders for death or personal injury arising from negligence or from breach of duty, defects in products that give rise to damage, and the provision of a regulatory framework for the financial services industry. Legislation also covers anti-competitive practices in both public and private sectors.

ETHICS AND CODES OF PRACTICE

Laws are enacted to deal with behaviour which is generally considered to be wrong or unacceptable. Defining the boundary between what might be considered lawful and what is not lawful can sometimes be a difficult task. For instance, something might not technically be illegal, yet it might be widely considered to be undesirable and even immoral. In this section we pay attention to actions which, while not against the law, may be considered to be undesirable and not in the best interests of the consumer.

Ethics are studies concerning the principles of morality. In the setting of marketing, ethics relate to activities which while not actually illegal raise moral questions. It is important to differentiate between practices which are illegal and those which are unethical. It is necessary to make this distinction because of the way in which society reacts to violations of good behaviour. Where something is deemed to be illegal, the remedy is to seek redress through the law. Where something is considered to be unethical, however, one can only seek redress in less direct ways, such as through pressure groups or 'watch-dogs' (see below).

Marketing can involve many ethical issues. There is a view that marketing creates wants that did not previously exist, and perhaps which are not needed. Adherents to this philosophy argue that the creation of unnecessary wants is not in the best interests of society, since it can lead to all kinds of undesirable social consequences. In the case of products such as addictive or controlled drugs, legislation exists to outlaw trading except under medical supervision. However, there are certain other products – for instance, cigarettes, alcohol and pornography – that are more difficult to deal with, since the products themselves are not actually illegal.

Ethical issues arise also in connection with how organizations market their products. Advertising which makes misleading claims about products or services, or which operates at a subliminal level are examples. Price-fixing, while outlawed, may still operate covertly. Moreover, distributors may fail to comply with agreements they have made with producers.

Because ethical problems arise in business and because they cannot always be dealt with inside the legal framework, other ways have to be found for dealing with them. In the next section we look at the various ways in which these problems may be properly addressed.

PRESSURE GROUPS, WATCH-DOGS AND CONSUMERISM

Pressure groups have come into being to combat unethical or undesirable practices. The purpose of such groups is to bring to the attention of the public and government the need to outlaw or modify such practices.

'Watch-dog' organizations exist to deal with complaints about public sector and other organizations such as the various utilities. Complaints received from users of these services are publicized. There are also environmental watch-dog organizations, looking out for matters relating to the environment. They oppose plans to build factories or houses in the open countryside in some cases, and monitor environmental pollution caused by factories.

Consumerism is an organized movement, established to guard the economic interests of consumers by compelling companies to behave in a socially responsible manner. As a result of pressure from consumerism, many organizations now follow voluntary codes of practice relating to matters which may give rise to pollution. The government has established the Office of Fair Trading to encourage competition between organizations that is fair to them and to the consumer. There are various bodies which exist to protect the customer.

The Consumer Protection Advisory Committee was set up to deal with such things as:

● terms and conditions of sale

● prices

● advertising, labelling and promotion of goods and services

● selling methods.

CASE EXAMPLE

ADVERTISING STANDARDS AUTHORITY: UNSUITABLE ADVERTISING

What is acceptable advertising? When might something be judged obscene or distasteful? People seem to have differing opinions on the subject.

Complaints were received by the Advertising Standards Authority concerning leaflets for the September/October programme at the Norwich Arts Centre and Cinema City. The leaflets included advertisements headlined 'The sexiest jeans in Norwich', showing silhouettes of a couple seemingly engaged in sexual inter-course in various positions. The people making the complaints considered the advertisements to be obscene and distasteful.

The advertisers thought that the advertisements were in fact acceptable. Moreover, the advertisers had thought that the publishers would make any necessary enquiries prior to publication. Both publishers indicated that they had received complaints about the advertisements.

The complaints were upheld by the Advertising Standards Authority, which disapproved of the particular advertisements although it was noted that the advertisers and Cinema City regretted any offence caused and indicated that the advertisements would not be used again. The Advertising Standards Authority asked the advertisers not to use such an approach again, and asked the publishers to consider their readers' sensibilities in future.

(Source: Advertising Standards Authority, 1993, p.10)

QUESTION

1. What criteria do you think should be adopted when trying to assess whether an advertisement is obscene or distasteful?

The National Consumer Council deals with presenting the opinions of consumers to industry and government. County council trading standards and consumer protection departments deal with complaints from members of the public, and district council environmental health departments enforce laws relating, for instance, to food and drink which is unfit for sale, and any other matters relating to shop hygiene.

Another body, the Advertising Standards Authority, monitors advertisements. Complaints can be made by members of the public direct to this body. A monthly report is issued which lists complaints received and the action taken.

SUMMARY

Social and cultural values have an influence on customers wants and needs in the market place. This in turn affects the nature of goods and services which organizations offer in different regions or countries or to different cultural groups.

Political, fiscal and economic policies influence the demand for products both at home and abroad. Governments may try to curtail demand for certain goods for economic, fiscal or political reasons or to protect infant industries. This can present a marketing problem which exporters have to find ways of overcoming. The economic cycle also poses problems for marketers.

Technological advances can be used to advantage by many different kinds of firms. Such advances may have an impact upon manufacturing processes, as well as upon product or service design or performance.

Legislation is passed to protect consumers and prevent unfair competitive practices. These laws are regularly reviewed and amended.

Changes have taken place over the past 30 years which have had a marked impact on the marketing of consumer products. Conspicuous developments have been the use of the microchip, the growth of supermarkets aimed at providing convenience shopping, and the trend in specialist outlets.

Green issues are beginning to influence the way organizations think and do business. Environmental pollution has implications stretching far ahead into the future. As a consequence, organizations are starting to take steps required to keep in line with Green thinking.

Ethical issues involved in the marketing of goods and services are important. Some activities fall short of actually being illegal, but they may still be socially unacceptable.

Quite apart from enacted legislation, various bodies have been set up to monitor and report on organizations subject to agreed standards. Other bodies called watchdogs report on matters which, while not illegal, may be considered to be not in the best interests of the consumer or society. Such organizations form part of the ever-increasing 'consumerism' movement.

DISCUSSION QUESTIONS

1. What factors might give rise to inhospitable marketing environments?

2. Why should some firms react only slowly to changing environments?

3. Discuss the various ways in which an organization can try to change its external environment.

4. What is a 'mass market'? Why should there have been a shift away from these kinds of markets in the USA and Europe over the years?

5. Why do you think people's shopping habits have changed over the past 30 years? What impact do you think that this had on the kind of shopping facilities now available?

6. Discuss the various ways in which demographic characteristics and changes in these characteristics can influence consumer purchasing patterns.

7. Examine the various ways in which culture influences both consumer behaviour and the way in which businesses market their goods and services.

8. Cultural values can change over time. How might this be reflected in consumer attitudes?

9. Examine the effect that changes in consumers' attitudes may have on their purchasing behaviour.

10. How can governments influence the nature of the marketing environment?

11. What are the stages of the economic cycle, and what kind of impact does each stage have on marketing activities?

12. How might firms attempt to achieve growth in sales and profits during times of recession? Justify your answer.

13. Advances in technology can have very significant impacts on the marketing environment. How might firms capitalize on such advances?

14. In what ways might firms attempt to come to grips with the changing complexity of the business environment?

15. What factors give rise to the need for 'Green' marketing? Some firms may be reluctant to change their approach to marketing. Why should this be the case?

16. What are the various factors which give rise to the need for legislation with respect to marketing activities?

17. If the marketing of certain goods, or the way in which they are marketed, is not illegal then why should attention be paid to people who want such goods or practices banned or controlled?

REFERENCES

Advertising Standards Authority (1993) Monthly report no. 31, December.

Bhoyrul, A. (1994) Think big, talk big, and you'll make it big. *Business Age*, February.

Haliburton, C. and Hunerberg, R. (1993) Marketing in a European environment, in *European Marketing: Readings and Cases,* (eds C. Haliburton and R. Hunerberg), Addison Wesley, Wokingham.

Handy C. (1990) *The Age of Unreason*, Arrow Books, London

Large, M. (1992) Eco-mapping – how to avoid boiled frogs. *MEAD*, 23(4), 317–25.

Tyrrell, R. (1994) Eastern Promise is worth all the pain of red tape. *Marketing,* 3 February.

FURTHER READING

Alderman, G. (1984) *Pressure Groups and Government in Great Britain,* Longman, Harlow.

Donaldson, P. *Economics of the Real World*, 3rd edn, Penguin books, Harmondsworth.

Ela, J.D. and Manley, R.I. (1983) Technology changes market boundaries, *Industrial Marketing Management*, July, 153–6.

Fortune (1988), Why inflation is not inevitable, 12 September 155–64.

Jain, S.C. (1984) Environmental scanning: how the best companies do it. *Journal of Long Range Planning*, April, 117–28.

Levitt, T. (1977) Marketing when things change, *Harvard Business Review*, November–December, 107–13.

Still battling the ozone stigma (1992), *Marketing Week* (1992), 16 March, 18–19.

Morrison, A. (1991) The role of litigation in consumer protection, *The Journal of Consumer Affairs*, Winter, 209–20.

Palmer, A. and Worthington, I. (1992) *The Business and Marketing Environment*, McGraw-Hill, Maidenhead.

Vandermerwe, S. and L'Huillier, M. (1989) Euro-consumers in 1992, *Business Horizons*. Jan/Feb.

CASE PROBLEM 2.1

ESSPEE GROUP: TECHNOLOGY BEATS RECESSION

Recession is usually associated with firms experiencing declining sales and profits. However, one group seems to have found a way to counter this tendency by making use of state-of-the-art technology. Esspee produces and stocks all types of insulation materials, as well as round, square or rectangular-section tubing in epoxy, paper or fabric laminates. Unlike many companies that have been suffering from the recession, the St Helens-based family-owned group has more than doubled its sales turnover in the past four years.

The approach adopted by Greg Smith, son of the founder and now managing director, involves reinvesting profits into modern machinery, thereby enabling the company to remain competitive in a changing market place. Through the regular addition of new machinery, Esspee can offer a faster service to customers who are operating on a just-in-time basis.

There are two firms: Esspee (James Cooke) Saws and Esspee Precision Engineering. The saw company offers the latest saw-sharpening facilities at very competitive prices. It also markets diamond tooling which is based on a new technology, derived from America's space programme. By employing this tooling, machinists of all types of composite materials can speed up their production and at the same time prolong tool life considerably.

(Source: Business North West, *January 1994, pp. 33–5.)*

QUESTION

1. How can the acquisition of the latest technology help to make firms more profitable during periods of economic recession?

CASE PROBLEM 2.2

BONNE CHANCE RECRUITMENT AGENCY: MARKETING AND THE LAW

The Bonne Chance Recruitment Agency places advertisements on behalf of information technology companies for a variety of skilled posts in the field of information technology. Twelve months ago the agency decided that it needed to modify its advertising strategy in order to get better respondents to apply for posts it was promoting.

'Programmers, analysts, officers, etc. are rather drab and uninteresting job titles,' commented the senior partner at a regular strategy meeting. 'What we need to do is to come up with more exciting, stimulating and provocative titles for the jobs our clients want to be filled.'

The other executives attending the meaning concurred with this point of view, and after some deliberation it was decided that the use of the word 'architect' in the job title might well prove very attractive to aspiring professionals in the business.

'After all,' the senior partner remarked, 'there are naval architects, landscape architects and even golf-course architects. So why should we not advertise on behalf of our clients for "technical architects", "desktop architects"and "systems architects"?'

The partners decided to implement the strategy straight away. Following the decision to advertise jobs in this way the agency noted a marked increase in the quality of applicants. Client companies were pleased with the improvement in the quality of recruits and the agency's business doubled over six months from its level just over one year earlier. Only this week, however, the firm has received an official letter from the Architects' Registration Council indicating that the agency risks prosecution under the 1938 Architects (Registration) Act if it falsely uses the term 'architect' in job ads.

QUESTION

1. What action would you recommend that the agency should take? Why?

3 UNDERSTANDING THE CUSTOMER

This chapter considers those factors which influence consumer behaviour, as well as how marketers define market segments. There is also an examination of the way in which messages pass from marketers to consumers. The complex nature of buying decisions is studied, together with the implications for marketing practice.

OBJECTIVES

After studying this chapter you should be able to:

- understand what factors help to influence and determine consumer behaviour

- understand how marketers define market segments by such attributes as social class, age, reference groups, and life style

- describe the way in which messages pass from marketers to consumers involving selective attention, selective distortion, selective remembering and cognitive consonance and dissonance – and the implications of this for marketing practice

- describe complex buying decisions in terms of a given model and be able to identify the model's implications for marketing practice

- describe the differences and similarities between industrial and consumer buying.

INTRODUCTION

Knowledge of how customers make purchase decisions, or how they use a product or service, are critical elements of successful marketing strategy. Consumer buying behaviour refers to that of the ultimate consumers who purchase goods for personal or household consumption; organizational buying behaviour is that of individuals or groups who purchase goods on behalf of their organization, for use by that organization.

Many of the factors that influence consumer buying behaviour reflect the characteristics of the consumers, such as demography, spending power, attitudes and personality, social pressures, etc. Consumer behaviour is therefore a study not only of how customers behave, but of why they behave in a particular way. Similar comments can apply to the more complex organizational buyer behaviour.

We will look first at consumer behaviour, and then at organizational buyer behaviour.

CONSUMER BEHAVIOUR

In order to be able to function effectively in the market place, firms need to know:

- who constitutes the market
- what the market buys
- why the market buys
- who participates in the buying
- how the market buys
- when the market buys
- where the market buys (Kotler, 1988).

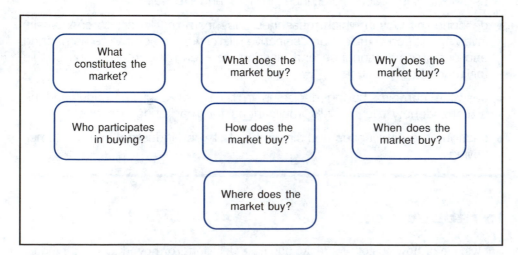

Figure 3.1 What the firm needs to know about the market.

To find the answers to questions such as these, it is usually necessary to undertake market research. It is also important to understand the major factors influencing consumer behaviour.

In studying consumer behaviour a distinction is made between complex decision-making situations, and those in which little consideration is given to the purchase being made. Where a product is relatively expensive and possibly technologically complex, prospective purchasers often go through a complex search and evaluation process prior to making a purchase. Where the product is relatively cheap and simple to understand, however, the process often involves little or no search, and evaluation is based upon prior experience of using the product. In both cases, however, attitudes and beliefs play an important part (see Assael, 1987, p.87, for a more elaborate classification of purchasing decisions).

Various models of consumer behaviour have been developed over the years, reflecting the different buying situations in which consumers find themselves. In the next section we will explore the principles behind these models.

MODELS OF CONSUMER BEHAVIOUR

Four main purchase situations are considered here:

- habitual purchase
- impulse buying
- limited decision making
- complex buying decisions.

We will examine each one in turn.

HABITUAL PURCHASES

Many food items are purchased at the supermarket out of habit – they tend to be low-priced, frequently purchased items. In such cases consumers do not undertake an extensive search for information, nor do they engage in extensive evaluation prior to making a purchase. Instead, they look for cues which give some idea about what the product is like. A cue such as the colour of the packaging, for example, may be perceived by consumers to infer a given level of quality.

Repeated use of a product raises the confidence people have in certain cues, and scanning becomes cursory in nature. Cues can stem from the product itself (intrinsic cues) – taste, texture, etc. – or follow from other attributes than the product itself (extrinsic cues) – brand name, packaging, advertising, etc. People develop confidence in the reliability of certain cues and learn to choose with the help of extrinsic cues.

Consumers can only process a restricted amount of information at any one time, and look for ways of compensating for this limitation by organizing their perceptions. For example, to facilitate their understanding of several competing brands, consumers mentally group them into a few categories, each of which has similar characteristics. When confronted by a new brand, consumers will consider its likeness to each of their mental categories and then judge its probable characteristics. In-store choice is predominantly based on the comparative assessment of rival brands.

Consumers purchase a particular brand because it is familiar and the familiarity is accentuated by different types of advertising. The main job of marketers of competing brands is to persuade the consumer to try a different brand. If consumers can be persuaded to try a different brand then there is the possibility that the behaviour of repeatedly buying the same brand will be transferred to the new brand.

Price and value for money are the principal factors which consumers consider in buying goods of this nature. Price and sales promotion are the key marketing variables used in such circumstances.

IMPULSE BUYING

Impulse buying comes from an urge to buy something immediately. For many people it may well be the main method of purchasing. However, it can involve emotional friction in the mind of the consumer. This is especially the case where the price of goods is substantial relative to the purchaser's resources.

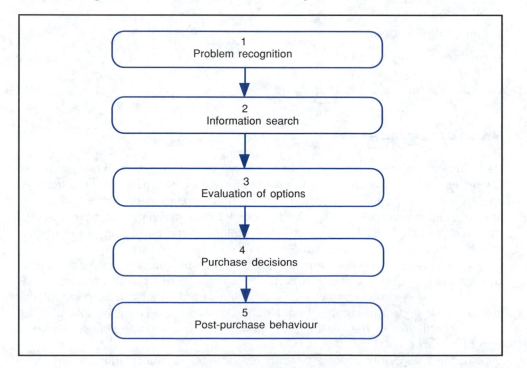

Figure 3.2 Five stages of the buying process.

LIMITED DECISION MAKING

Consumers engage in this form of pre-purchase activity when they buy products only occasionally and when information is required regarding an unfamiliar brand. People spend a moderate amount of time gathering information and deliberating upon it prior to making a purchase. For example, if a new improved version of a brand of shampoo is introduced, consumers will perhaps ask a friend who has used the product about its performance, or even watch a commercial, before they consider trying the product for themselves.

COMPLEX BUYING DECISIONS

Many people have studied consumer behaviour and a five-stage model of the buying process has been distilled from these researches (see, for example, Engel, Blackwell and Miniard, 1986). The implication is that consumers actually pass through all stages in buying a product or service. In actual fact, of course, as we have seen in the case of habitual purchases, this is not necessarily so. However, it is a useful framework from within which to view the purchase of many of the more expensive types of durable products and or services (Figure 3.2).

THE BUYING PROCESS

PROBLEM RECOGNITION

The notion here is that the prospective purchaser experiences a need to buy a certain product – for example, a new hi-fi system. The need or want can be triggered by a variety of stimuli, for instance the unsatisfactory performance of a current hi-fi system, or the fact that a neighbour has bought a new one. The marketer needs to identify the factors which give rise to the recognition of the problem and use these to advantage in marketing communications about the particular product, service or brand.

INFORMATION SEARCH

Once the problem has been recognized, prospective purchasers search for information about the product in question. A person who has recognized a felt need for a new hi-fi system may scan many hi-fi magazines for information on what is available and at what price. This scanning helps to identify locations where the products or service may be purchased, and the intending buyer may well visit these locations to obtain more information and possibly to listen to a number of different hi-fi systems.

The amount of research undertaken probably varies with the individual concerned, the amount of time available, and the availability of suitable products and services. From the marketer's point of view, key interest is shown in the sources of information that the prospective purchaser will consult and the kind of information which is likely to sway the consumer into buying one particular brand rather than another.

EVALUATION OF OPTIONS

It tends to be taken for granted that consumers make decisions on a conscious or rational basis, although we have to bear in mind that this may not necessarily always be the case. However, assuming a rational model of consumer choice, the process would seem to take account of the following:

- products are thought of as a bundle of attributes – e.g. bicycle: lightweight/ heavyweight, sports/touring, etc.

- relevant attributes vary from one product or service to another – e.g. size and speed are important with cameras, whereas the variety and packaging are emphasized in the case of chocolates

- some product attributes are more important to consumers than others – e.g. dependability and convenience may be more important than price when considering a business trip with an airline

- the degree of importance of different product attributes to different consumer groups can form the basis of market segmentation – e.g. fast courteous service at a restaurant

- consumers develop beliefs about products with respect to their various attributes – this forms a brand image – e.g. Volvo cars are safe

- consumers have utility functions with respect to each one of the attributes. Product/service satisfaction varies according to the fit between the product's performance on the attribute and the consumer's expectations – e.g. a small car's petrol consumption is considered satisfactory provided that it is more than 10km per litre

- attitudes towards brands are formed through the process of evaluation – e.g. Seiko watches are better value for money than competing brands because they offer the same product features and have equally elegant designs.

Firms need to understand what criteria consumers use to evaluate their products and services. If it is discovered that a product or service does not meet with consumers' expectations then the marketer can try one or more of a number of options:

- change the product so that it fits with consumer expectations

- change people's beliefs about the product or service

- change people's beliefs about competing brands and demonstrate that they are no better than the company's brand

- change people's perceptions of the importance of different brand attributes – if the product is considered weak on one attribute then the marketer could play down the importance of this attribute and stress the importance of others

- move the consumer perception of what comprises an ideal product more in the direction of the existing brand's profile of attributes.

PURCHASE DECISION

Intending purchasers are influenced by the attitudes of others. Other factors may also arise which prevent the purchase intention being put into practice. Unfortunately the marketer of the product can do little to counter these kinds of problems.

POST-PURCHASE BEHAVIOUR

Post-purchase cognitive dissonance is often experienced by consumers after making a relatively expensive purchase. There is a tendency to ask oneself whether one has done the right thing in making the purchase, or whether one would have been better off to have purchased a different brand, product or service altogether.

Consumers need to be reassured. If the marketer has exaggerated the benefits of the product then the consumer will more than likely experience dissatisfaction. This in turn can lead to poor word-of-mouth communication about the product to the consumer's circle of friends, relations and acquaintances.

Marketing people can do much to allay dissonance. Some of the methods include:

- directing specific advertising at people who have already bought the product, featuring contented, happy customers

- writing dissonance-reducing booklets to accompany the product or service

- arranging speedy redress of customer grievances.

Formal models of consumer behaviour help firms to establish a framework within which to both understand behaviour and formulate communication strategies to take advantage of their understanding. However one also needs to have an appreciation of the various factors that influence the consumer decision-making process. These are introduced in the following sections. First we will consider personal factors that can influence the buying decision process.

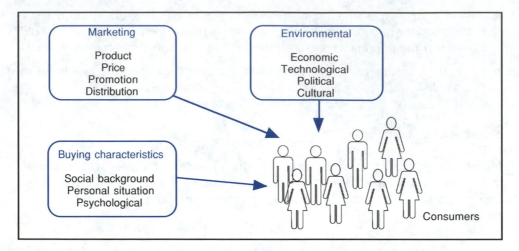

Figure 3.3 Factors influencing consumer behaviour.

FACTORS INFLUENCING THE BUYING PROCESS

The major factors influencing consumer behaviour are:

Marketing
- Product
- Price
- Promotion
- Place/distribution

Environmental
- Economic
- Technological
- Political
- Cultural

Buyer characteristics
- Demographic
- Situational
- Psychological
- Social

Elsewhere in the book we consider the impact of the marketing and environmental forces; here we will examine buyer characteristics.

DEMOGRAPHIC FACTORS

The market for a consumer good comprises all individuals or households purchasing goods or acquiring goods or services for personal consumption. Each market can be subdivided into 'sub-markets' or 'segments' each one of which could be regarded as a 'market' in its own right. There are many different ways in which sub-markets or segments can be defined (see below, and see also Chapter 7).

Markets can be defined in geographic terms, but there is usually so much variation in terms of purchase behaviour within markets defined in this way that further segmentation is nearly always required. The purchasing behaviour of individuals and groups within a market reflects different consumer characteristics, buying power, and wants and needs.

CASE EXAMPLE

THE SOCIAL DIVIDE: IMPLICATIONS FOR MARKETERS

In some countries, wealth is concentrated in the hands of only a few people, while in others it is more evenly distributed across the population. The distribution of wealth in a country is not constant over time – there is a tendency to think that as living standards rise, then everyone in a country becomes better off. However, this is not necessarily the case.

A 1994 report produced by Mintel showed that there was evidence of an increased polarization in the distribution of wealth in the UK. Some 40% of income in the UK is earned by only 20% of the population, and it seems that this disparity has widened since 1978, despite the fact that disposable income on the whole has increased by 255%.

The widening gulf between the 'haves' and the 'have nots' has implications for marketers. It means, for example, that while there is an increase in the demand for luxury goods and the like, there is also a growing demand for staple products and necessities, brought about by an increase in the proportion of households which only have sufficient income for these kinds of goods.

(Source: Cook, 1994, p.13)

QUESTION

1. Assuming that the gulf between rich and poor is going to continue to widen, produce a report indicating the precise areas of consumer purchasing activity which are most likely to be affected by the trend. Indicate also the implications that this is likely to have for marketers in the areas concerned.

There are over 300 million people in the European Community, and consumer characteristics, buying power and wants and needs vary considerably from one region to another. For example, some 30% of the population of Ireland is under 15 years of age, whereas in Germany and Italy the percentage is only around 15% (OECD, 1991). In Ireland the birth rate per 1000 of the population is around 17, while in Italy it is only 10 (Eurostat, 1990). Per capita GDP is $20 926 in Denmark and $8722 in Spain (OECD, 1990/91). Spending patterns vary substantially, also. The Germans spend three times as much as the Portuguese per person in terms of real purchasing power (Haliburton and Hunerburg, 1993). In Ireland approximately 40% of household expenditure goes on food, drink and tobacco while in the UK it is little more than 14%. The above figures represent extremes – the figures of constituent countries are spread out across the range.

Consumer expenditure by category predictably varies across countries according to purchasing power. In poorer countries, food and other 'basics' represent a higher percentage, compared to more luxury items such as leisure. Penetration of consumer durables also varies, even between some of the major countries (dishwashers 39% in West Germany to 12% in the UK; microwaves 57% in the UK to 13% in Spain). National buying habits still remain in many countries, although there may be signs of converging trends (Haliburton and Hunerberg, 1993).

In addition to consumer characteristics and buying power, climatic factors create differences among Europe's consumers. The climate of Northern Europe contrasts significantly with that of Mediterranean Europe, with implications for consumer buying behaviour with respect to a wide range of consumer durables ranging from clothes to washing machines and other domestic appliances.

All over the world consumers vary considerably from one region of a country to another in terms of age, income, educational level, mobility patterns and taste. Moreover, climatic conditions vary substantially in different countries. However, it is possible to distinguish groups of consumers who have much in common with respect to wants and needs. As is indicated above, these groups make up market segments, and firms develop products and services to serve the needs of these market segments.

SITUATIONAL FACTORS

Time available to make a purchase often plays an important role in determining what is purchased. For example, a last-minute purchase of a book to read when embarking on an air journey may involve very little consideration of what alternatives are available – one may simply take the first reasonably appealing front cover that one sees. Even substantial purchases like houses and cars can be subjected to the influence of time pressures.

Apart from time, there are several other situational factors that may influence purchases. For example, fear of unemployment may force would-be buyers of expensive domestic appliances to postpone their decisions. Inclement weather may create an unseasonal demand for waterproof clothing.

LEVEL OF INVOLVEMENT

Consumers will often undertake considerable research before purchasing high-priced goods that are visible to others. Such goods are known as 'high involvement' goods. Clothing, furniture, cars and houses are products which fall readily into this category.

The degree of involvement for certain products will vary between people. For example, some people undertake an extensive search when purchasing a birthday card. Another person buying a birthday card for the same person may undertake very little search. Nor is this necessarily just a function of the relationship that each person has with the recipient of the card. One person may simply put less value on the card than the other.

PSYCHOLOGICAL FACTORS

No two individuals are entirely alike in their behaviour, and individual psychological processes intervene. In this section we look at the various psychological processes involved.

PERCEPTION

People do not see the same event in exactly the same way. People differ in their perceptual process of:

- selective attention
- selective distortion
- selective retention.

Selective attention implies that people only pay attention to a small proportion of what is going on around them all the time. For example, when going about their daily work it is quite possible that they are exposed to hundreds of advertising messages but only actually 'perceive' a few of them. In all probability people would screen out all of them except for the odd one or two which were some way related to their current thoughts. Certainly, it is quite possible that they would be unable to recall any of them! The real test for the advertiser is to present messages in such a way that people will pay attention to them.

SELECTIVE DISTORTION

People assimilate incoming information so that it fits in with their preconceptions. It is possible, for example, that some people will ignore the typical type of drink-driving publicity showing horrific accidents, because they cannot relate to such a situation – they might assume that horrific accidents only happen to people who are habitually very drunk.

MOTIVATIONS

Marketers need to know what motivates people to buy a particular brand or service. Given this information, it may be possible to gain a competitive advantage in the design and/or marketing of a product. This can be done by persuading consumers that a product is better able to satisfy their wants and needs because of the benefits it offers.

There are various theories of motivation. Two of the most important, as far as marketing is concerned, were put forward separately by Freud and Maslow.

Freud suggested that people may be influenced at an unconscious level. Thus it may not be possible to get people to talk rationally about why they make certain purchases. A woman may say that she bought a particular dress because she liked the colour, or because it was of good 'quality'. It could also be, however, that the purchase was made in order to impress friends. All of these motivations could be behind the purchase, but the latter might never be disclosed in the course of asking the person to explain her motivation. Different methods of research have been developed to get at these hidden kinds of motivation.

Maslow suggested that human needs are ordered in a hierarchy of importance (Maslow, 1970). The most important needs are those to do with basic physiological needs, while the least important ones are to do with self-actualization. Maslow contended that people would not seek to satisfy the less important needs until the more important ones are satisfied. This theory helps us to clarify how various products may fit in with people's purchase plans. For example, a person may consider buying a home before purchasing a motor car. A householder who already has a car, a refrigerator, cooker, freezer, telephone, and washing machine may next be interested in purchasing a dishwasher.

LEARNING

Most human behaviour is acquired as the result of learning from experience. This also applies to the purchase of goods and services, and so learning is perhaps the most important factor underpinning consumer behaviour. Drives, stimuli, cues and responses and reinforcement are the key elements of learning. A drive is a force inside people that pushes them towards certain actions. Drives become motives when they are directed specifically towards a stimulus which will reduce the drive. Cues are minor stimuli which establish when, where and how a person will respond.

Firms build up demand for a product or service by linking it with strong drives, using cues to motivate people and providing positive reinforcement to people who respond. In effect this is really the whole basis of the marketing concept. Marketers seek to identify unsatisfied customer wants and needs (where there is a strong drive which is not fulfilled). The firm provides the product or service (stimulus) together with appropriate promotional messages (cues). The consumer responds by purchasing the product and the marketer follows this up with after-sales service or promotional messages, to reinforce the fact that the consumer has made a good choice.

CASE EXAMPLE

COCA-COLA: EXTENDING THE BRAND NAME

Some well-known companies have put their brand names on products which seem unrelated to their main business activity. Next and Bugatti, for example, have put their brand names on watches; the Bugatti label can even be found on gent's ties. Of course, these companies do not manufacture such products themselves – they have to rely on third parties for producing the goods.

Coca-Cola ventured into medium-priced men's and women's casual clothing in 1985. The clothes were distributed under license from Coca-Cola by Murjani International of New York and although the clothes were promoted as 'All-American', they were in fact manufactured in Asia.

The claim that the products were 'All-American', in view of the fact that they were produced in Asia, was the source of considerable controversy and disquiet. At the time, many thousands of textile workers in the USA had been laid off due to slow sales, attributable to competition from cheaper imported garments and textiles. To show their discontent, some American textile firms even removed Coca-Cola vending machines from their plants.

One textile worker is quoted as writing: 'I once had a dog who bit my hand when I fed him, and now it seems as if your company is doing the same thing to my company.'

(Source: Hendon, 1992, Classic Failures in Product Marketing, pp.30–1)

QUESTIONS

1. What explanation do you think consumer behaviour theory can offer for the reactions of people to what Coca Cola did?

2. What action do you think Coca Cola should have taken under the circumstances? Explain.

BELIEFS AND ATTITUDES

People have beliefs and attitudes which influence their purchasing behaviour. Brand images are related to the beliefs and attitudes of people and as a result of these images people make purchasing decisions. An attitude is a predisposition to act in a certain way towards an object under given circumstances. Attitudes are associated with the way in which people behave and act. Having a particular attitude towards something influences the way in which people behave.

Marketing communications try to inform customers that a product or service corresponds to their attitudes. Marketing communications are also concerned with correcting mistaken beliefs about a product or service.

PERSONALITY

A person's lifestyle goes beyond questions of social class. It is an expression of their personality. Some people may have a lifestyle which others might describe as avant-garde. Other people may be described as conservative, yet others as liberal-minded. Marketers have to look for relationships between their products and lifestyle groups which they can identify.

SOCIAL FACTORS INFLUENCING THE BUYING DECISION PROCESS

While personal and psychological differences exert an influence on the purchase behaviour of consumers, so too do a variety of social factors. Several people may have a part to play in making an individual purchase. We may not be conscious of this until we come to look at what is involved in the actual decision. For example, in talking with friends, something someone says may prompt us into deciding that it is time we did something about buying a new house. Someone else suggests that we should visit a new estate where some individualistic houses are being built. Finally we decide to buy a new house on the estate in question.

As can be observed, a number of people have been involved in this particular decision-making process. Each one, including ourselves, has played a role – a friend was the initiator, another friend the influencer, and we were the decider, buyer and actual user.

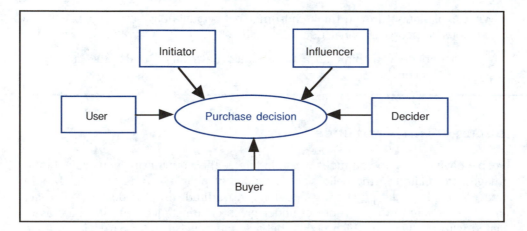

Figure 3.4 Roles in the purchase decision-making process.

A firm needs to be aware of the operation of different influences in this way – there are important implications for the various marketing communications that have to be made.

ROLES AND STATUS SYMBOLS

People join or become members of different groups. Within each group they take on a role which reflects their status with respect to that group. One of the most important measures of status is a person's job and how it is viewed by their various reference groups. People often buy products that relate to or reflect their role and status. Status symbols vary for different social groupings, and it is the job of the marketer to recognize what the status symbols are for different groups of people.

FAMILY INFLUENCE

Perhaps the strongest reference group which influences consumer behaviour is the family. It is not practical for marketers to attempt to identify the influence that families have on particular individuals' behaviour, but marketers are interested in the roles and relative degrees of influence of the various members of a family in the purchase of different products and services.

Traditionally, the wife or female partner in a family has tended to purchase the weekly shopping and buy small value items. Where there are children in a family, however, the children may exert considerable influence over what is actually purchased during a trip to the supermarket. In the case of expensive items there is generally joint decision making. The marketer's main task is to identify which members of the family have the greatest influence in choosing various products.

AGE AND LIFE CYCLE

People pass through various stages in their life cycle, and they have different life cycles according to whether or not they marry and have children. The table (over) illustrates the family life cycle concept. Different buying patterns are exhibited at every stage in the cycle.

There have been some critics of the usefulness of the family life cycle concept. Its major weaknesses include the exclusion of those couples who never have children, lack of account taken of one-parent families, undue emphasis on the age of children and the changing role of the father/husband but not of the mother/wife.

REFERENCE GROUPS

Reference groups are made up of people who directly or indirectly influence a person's attitudes or behaviours. Teenagers, for example may be influenced by

STAGES IN THE FAMILY LIFE CYCLE AND ASSOCIATED BEHAVIOURAL BUYING PATTERNS

Stage in the family life cycle	Buying interests
1. Single and young – away from home	Fashion clothes, sport and leisure products, cars, music centres and records, holidays
2. Young married couples – no children	Cars, consumer durables, holidays, furniture.
3. Married – small children	Washers, driers, baby items, economy food
4. Married – children under 13	Children's toys, education products, domestic appliances, many foods
5. Married – teenage children	Consumer durables, better furniture, hobby items.
6. Married – children left home – both/one still employed	Travel, recreation, self-education, investments, luxuries.
7. Older – retired	Cheaper holidays, value for money goods.
8. Solitary survivor	Economy living.

a pop-star cult. Marketers try to identify the reference groups of their target customers and make use of opinions reflected by such groups in their marketing communications.

SOCIAL CLASS

Social class reflects societal stratification. Members of a social class have similar values and attitudes, which are different to those of members of other social classes. Identification of the social class to which a person belongs can be rather an involved business, but in general it is based upon such matters as job, pay, wealth, education and value orientation.

Research appears to indicate that social classes have distinct product and brand preferences in areas such as clothing, leisure activities, home furnishings and motor cars. There are also signs that social classes have leanings with respect to media preferences – lower classes show a preference for television, while upper classes favour magazines and journals. Moreover, there is segmentation within a media division itself – for instance, with TV, we find upper classes favouring news and drama while lower classes prefer soap operas and quiz shows.

Although marketers may use social class as a means of market segmentation, many people in Britain do not like to be identified as belonging to a certain social

THE MARKET RESEARCH SERVICES CLASSIFICATION OF SOCIAL CLASS

Grade	% of population	Status	Head of household's occupation
A	3	Upper middle class	Higher managerial, administrative or professional
B	13	Middle class	Intermediate managerial administrative or professional
C1	23	Lower middle class	Supervisory or clerical junior managerial, administrative or professional
C2	32	Skilled working class	Skilled manual workers
D	19	Working class	Semi-skilled and unskilled manual workers
E	10	Those at lowest levels of subsistence	State pensioners or widows, casual or lowest grade workers

(Source: JICNARS National Readership Survey, 1981)

class. For example, many women's magazines are mainly read by 'working class' women. However, it is editorial policy to avoid any mention of social class, or any images which suggest that readers might be the wives of manual workers.

The ABCDE classification conceived by Market Research Services Ltd has in the past been the system most frequently used to classify people into social classes for marketing purposes. The method was invented years ago and is still often used. However, over the years there has been much social change which has produced greater social diversity. This method no longer explains consumer behaviour in many situations. Two newer systems are:

- **Sagacity**, employed by Research Service Ltd. This system also takes into consideration variations in aspiration levels and other behavioural patterns, in addition to income and stage of the life cycle. There are four main stages of the life cycle, which are subdivided by income and occupation groups.

- **Acorn**, produced by the C.A.C.I Marketing Analysis Group. The approach adopted reflects the fact that people living in particular residential districts tend to exhibit broadly similar patterns of behaviour.

CASE EXAMPLE

PROCTER & GAMBLE: MATCHING CULTURAL EXPECTATIONS IN JAPAN

Different cultures have different ideas about what is appropriate behaviour to be shown in advertisements and what constitutes poor taste. Nevertheless, even global companies can sometimes misjudge matters. For instance, a mistake was made by Procter and Gamble in Japan when promoting Camay soap.

The campaign advertisement used a popular European television advertisement showing a woman bathing. During the course of the televised sequence, the woman's husband enters the bathroom and touches her approvingly. Such behaviour was considered to be inappropriate and in poor taste for television by the Japanese.

P&G made another mistake in Japan with its promotion of Cheer laundry detergent, which asserted that the detergent was effective 'at all water temperatures'. Since the Japanese wash most clothes in cold water only, the promotion message was not appropriate.

(Source: Ricks, 1993, p.45)

QUESTION

1. Discuss the problem of promoting consumer products in a multicultural society. Do you think firms pay enough attention to this problem? Explain.

SOCIAL BACKGROUND

People's social background is reflected in their culture. Culture consists of values, perceptions, preferences and behaviours. Many Western societies value achievement, success and materialism. This is good for the sale of goods and services, which enables consumers to demonstrate their success and achievement through the kinds of products which they purchase. Other societies have somewhat different sets of values. While materialism is not absent in these other cultures, it has not been as prominent as it is in Europe and the USA. Moreover, many of the paraphernalia of Western societies are not generally revered in such countries. Nevertheless, we live in a changing world and there are signs of some Western artefacts being adopted in countries which have hitherto been slow to show an interest in Western ideas, values and goods.

Subcultures reflect nationality groups, religious groups, racial groups and geographic areas. One can observe the effects in the way consumers form preferences or tastes. Promises of material success may sell some products, but there is also a market for what is apparently anti-materialistic. One of the most rapidly developing business sectors at the present time is the occult 'mind, and spirit' sector, with its crystals, UFOs, alternative medicines and meditation. This is a profit-oriented business sector, despite its image of being anti-materialistic.

Many large cities are extremely cosmopolitan, with people from many nationalities and racial backgrounds making up their populations. People of similar ethnic background often tend to group together within particular areas of a city. Such communities have developed their own business activities, and in many instances this has led to the development of local retailing establishments which cater for the particular needs of the community. Such establishments recognize that the needs and wants of their local communities are in some ways different to those of the larger national community, and have been set up to serve those specific needs. Despite local provision by the smaller retailers, the specialist needs of ethnic minorities have usually been ignored as market opportunities by large established companies. There is a market niche which has been left to ethnic minority groups themselves to satisfy.

ORGANIZATIONAL BUYER BEHAVIOUR

So far we have looked at the behaviour of consumers. Equally important is the behaviour of people buying in organizations on behalf of the organizations. First we will look at some of the characteristics of industrial/business markets before going on to look specifically at the behaviour of organizational buyers.

Industrial buyers are those buying goods and services for some tangibly productive and commercially significant purpose. They buy on behalf of organizations operating in a wide variety of markets. The kinds of markets in which organizational buyers operate are as follows.

- **Producer markets** These consist of individual and business organizations that purchase products and services for the purpose of making a profit by using them to make other products. They include buyers of raw materials, components, semi-finished and finished goods.

- **Reseller markets** These are distribution intermediaries, such as wholesalers and retailers who buy finished goods for resale at a profit.

- **Government markets** These comprise national and local governments, seeking to provide the public with education, water, energy, national defence, road systems and health care.

- **Institutional markets** Organizations that seek to achieve charitable, educational, community or other non-business goals make up institutional markets. They include churches, some hospitals, libraries, museums, universities and charitable organizations.

Demand for industrial goods is derived from the demand for consumer goods. In this sense the demand is a derived demand. For example, in the car industry, there are firms which specialize in the production of electrical components for motor vehicles – for instance, Lucas. The demand for the electrical components depends upon the demand for the cars to which the components are fitted. If the motor industry is depressed, then the demand for electrical components will also be depressed. However, if the demand for a particular manufacturer's cars is depressed but the rest of the industry is buoyant, then only the demand for electrical components for that manufacturer's vehicles will be depressed.

The total demand for many industrial goods is relatively price inelastic – that is, it is not greatly affected by price changes. For instance, if the price of one or two minor components used in making a car is increased, this will not reduce the demand for those components since the added cost of incorporating them in the final consumer product – a motor vehicle – is negligible. Of course, where the added costs are substantial in relation to the final consumer product and the price rise is substantial, then demand may well be reduced.

DIMENSIONS OF ORGANIZATIONAL BUYING

First we will look at the nature of organizational buying decisions and consider how they are different or similar to the kinds of decisions consumers make.

CHARACTERISTICS OF ORGANIZATIONAL TRANSACTIONS

There are various differences between the customers in industrial or business markets and consumer markets. In particular, there are:

- fewer buyers
- larger buyers
- geographically concentrated customer groups.

Generally such purchases are made less frequently than consumer goods sales. The contract regarding the terms of sale of such items is often a long-term agreement, requiring renegotiation from time to time. In addition, purchasing decisions are often made by a committee, and often several people or departments in the organization will be involved in the negotiations.

ATTRIBUTES OF ORGANIZATIONAL BUYERS

Knowledge of marketing is just as important to the industrial buyer as it is to sales people. However, there are industrial buyers who simply place orders. They act on behalf of production management, and people in these jobs require little or no skill. More often, however, the role of the buyer is more important and the buyer needs to know all about the products and services. Buyers are also proactive, rather than reactive, and watch out for information which can enable them to make better purchase decisions.

PRIMARY CONCERNS OF ORGANIZATIONAL BUYERS

The primary concerns are:

- delivery
- service
- price.

Often, goods are bought on the basis of a set of expressed characteristics or specifications. The failure of a supplier to deliver products to a specification can often end in that supplier no longer being asked to supply goods to a firm.

Delivery is a key element in decision making. Failure of a supplier to make promised deliveries can hold up production and cause considerable lost sales to a company. Reliability in terms of keeping to promised delivery dates is an important concern of organizational buyers, since it can help to reduce the level of safety stocks kept and hence free up working capital.

Specific services required vary in terms of importance. Among the services usually required are market information, technical assistance, inventory maintenance, on-time delivery, repair service and credit facilities.

Price influences operating costs and costs of goods sold. These in turn affect the customer's selling price and profit margin. When purchasing major equipment, for example, an industrial buyer looks upon the price as the amount of investment necessary to obtain a certain level of return or savings. This leads to a comparison of the price of a machine with the value of the benefits that the machine will yield. Product quality and supplier service are considered in conjunction with the price when making a decision.

ORGANIZATIONAL BUYING DECISIONS

A firm that centralizes its buying decisions will adopt a different approach to purchasing than one in which purchasing decisions are made at individual user locations. Where purchasing is centralized, a separate organizational unit is given authority to purchase at regional, divisional, or headquarters level. Boeing, 3M and Xerox are examples of firms with centralized buying arrangements.

Factors that strongly contribute to the centralization of purchasing are (Corey, 1978, pp. 99–112):

- where two or more purchasing units within the organization have common requirements

CASE EXAMPLE

GENERAL MOTORS: CENTRALIZED BUYING

Prior to centralization of the buying function at General Motors, there were 106 buying locations spending more than $10 million annually on almost 24 million pairs of work gloves. Ninety sources supplied more than 200 styles. The cost savings generated from pooling the requirements for this item alone were substantial.

(Source: Hutt and Speh, 1992)

QUESTION

1. Since there appear to be so many benefits of buying centres, can you think of benefits which might accrue where buying is not centralized?

- where there are opportunities to strengthen bargaining position, obtain lower prices through the aggregation of a firm's total requirements, and achieve economies in inventory control
- where there is the opportunity to consolidate purchasing power and secure favourable terms and service when a few large sellers dominate the supply industry
- where engineering involvement is high and the engineering group is in close organizational and physical proximity.

STAGES OF THE ORGANIZATIONAL BUYING DECISION PROCESS

In the same way that there are models of the consumer decision-making process, there also models of the industrial buying decision process. Robinson (1967), identified eight buying phases in the industrial buying process:

- problem recognition
- general need description
- product specification
- supplier search
- proposal solicitation

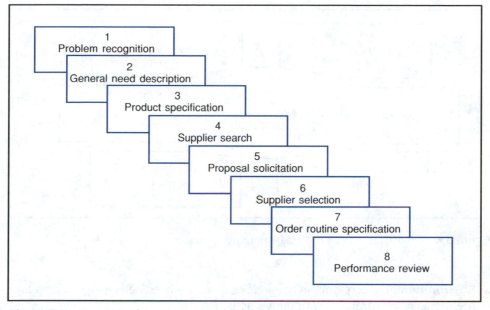

Figure 3.5 Stages in the organizational buying decision process.

- supplier selection

- order-routine specification

- performance review.

The model fits well where a product or service is being bought for the first time, but appears to be less applicable in other situations.

Organizational buyer behaviour is a complex process. While the job of buyer may exist in a firm, even so there may be many people concerned in the purchase decisions. Marketers have to identify the different roles played and then influence the various actors in the decision-making process.

INFLUENCES ON ORGANIZATIONAL BUYING DECISIONS

Industrial goods are bought by organizational buyers. More people influence business buying decisions than consumer buying decisions. Indeed, where the purchase of relatively expensive industrial goods is involved, there may be a buying committee, consisting of technical experts and senior management personnel. Even if this is not formally the case, the same people may still be involved or consulted in the course of making buying decisions (see Figure 3.6). Webster and Wind (1972, pp.78–80) provide a detailed account of the various influences on industrial buyers.

Industrial buyers respond to both rational economic and personal appeals when participating in buying decisions. The various influences on industrial buyers may be classified as follows:

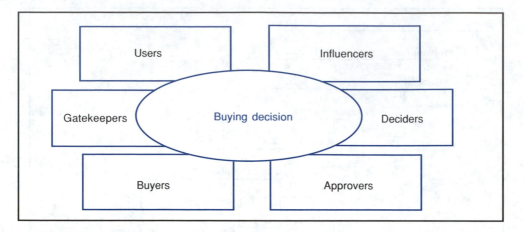

Figure 3.6 Influences on the organizational buyer decision.

- **Environmental** – economic recessions and resurgences, technological developments, legal constraints, competitive activities, etc.

- **Organizational** – objectives, procedures, structures and systems.

- **Interpersonal** – arising from status differences between people associated with the purchasing decision.

- **Individual** – associated with the age, income, education, job position, personality and attitude to risk of the buyer.

SIMILARITIES OF ORGANIZATIONAL BUYER BEHAVIOUR WITH CONSUMER BEHAVIOUR

Similarities with what we have outlined earlier in this chapter relating to consumer behaviour do in fact exist. As is the case of consumers making purchase decisions, there is a variety of people who exert an influence on the decision:

- **users** – who will use the product or service

- **influencers** – often technical personnel whose expertise is requested prior to making decisions

- **deciders** – those who actually have authority to take decisions

- **approvers** – those who hold the purse strings

- **buyers** – who select the supplier and arrange the terms of purchase

- **gatekeepers** – who can screen out information before it ever gets into the decision makers' in-trays.

Firms operating in industrial and business markets should be aware of the various influential roles in decision making. Moreover, they need to identify the key influential people and to persuade them that the product will meet a felt need.

SUMMARY

The consumer market is complex. It can be divided into segments in an almost infinite number of ways by classifying people according to social class, age, sex, ethnicity, marital status, lifestyle, reference groups and so on.

The motivations of consumers are complex too – there is a variety of theories to explain them. The marketer is interested in identifying those motives which prompt someone to buy one particular product rather than another.

The messages that marketers send to consumers are rarely received directly. People only attend selectively, interpreting messages in the light of their previous experience and existing ideas, and have very selective memories.

People make their purchasing decisions in a social context. Many purchasing decisions are made as part of everyday routines which are difficult to change. Other decisions are influenced by other people. Understanding the context in which consumer decisions are made is a key to successful marketing.

There are many similarities and there are also differences between consumer behaviour and organizational buyer behaviour. The decision making unit of a buying organization consists of people who play different roles in the process – those of user, influencer, buyer, decider, approver and gatekeeper. The industrial marketer has to identify these people and their roles when trying to market goods or services to an organization. The buying process comprises eight stages, which are similar to those encountered in consumer goods marketing.

DISCUSSION QUESTIONS

1. What do firms dealing with consumers want to know about them?

2. 'When deciding on the purchase of a new watch, I am the only person who has any influence on the decision regarding which make or brand I will buy.' How generalizable do you feel this statement is? Justify your answer.

3. Distinguish between 'habitual' and 'one-off' purchases.

4. Under what circumstances might consumers undertake 'limited decision making' when buying products or services?

5. Many consumer purchasing situations involve complex buying decisions. Describe some situations which illustrate this point and explain how the five-stage model of the buying process is relevant to these situations.

6. What is meant by impulse buying? Discuss how impulse buying situations might arise.

7. What do you consider to be the major factors that influence consumer behaviour?

8. How do situational factors influence consumer behaviour?

9. In what ways do people differ in how they perceive the same phenomenon?

10. What do you understand by the term 'cognitive dissonance'? What implications does the phenomenon have for marketers?

11. What influence have the viewpoints of Freud and Maslow had on ideas about consumer behaviour?

12. What role does 'learning' play in our understanding of consumer behaviour?

13. What are beliefs and attitudes? In what ways might they influence consumer behaviour?

14. 'The goods and services people buy represent an extension of their own personalities.' Discuss.

15. What are reference groups and how might they exert an influence on what, how, when and where people buy?

16. Discuss the nature of the family life cycle. How might it be relevant to an understanding of consumer behaviour?

17. What is social class? Some writers believe that this has an influence on consumer behaviour. Would you agree with this point of view? Justify your answer.

18. Distinguish between organizational buyers according to their principal attributes.

19. What do you consider to be the primary concerns of the organizational buyer?

20. What do you understand by the term 'buying centre'? Under what kinds of situations do you think firms should set up this form of buying?

21. What do you consider to be the main stages of the organizational buying decision-making process? Do you perceive any similarities with certain types of consumer decision processes? Explain.

22. 'In the same way that consumers are subjected to various influences on their buying behaviour, industrial buyers are also subjected to a variety of influences.' Expand on this statement.

REFERENCES

Assael, H. (1987) *Consumer Behaviour and Marketing*, Kent Publishing.

Cook, A. (1994) UK 1994: To have and to have not, *Marketing*, 3 February.

Corey, E.R. (1978) *The Organizational Context of Industrial Buying Behaviour*, Marketing Science Institute, Cambridge, Mass.

Engel, J.F., Blackwell, R.D. and Miniard, P.W. (1986) *Consumer Behaviour*, 5th edn, Holt Rinehart Winston, New York.

Eurostat (1990) *Basic Statistics of the Community*, 27th edn.

Haliburton, C. and Hunerberg, R. (1993) Marketing in a European environment, in *European Marketing: Readings and Cases* (eds C. Haliburton and R. Hunerberg), Addison Wesley, Wokingham.

Hendon, D.W. (1992) *Classic Failures in Product Marketing*, NTC Business Books, Lincoln, Ill.

Hutt, M.D. and Speh, T.W. (1992) *Business Marketing Management*, 4th edn, Dryden Press, New York.

Kotler, P. (1988) *Marketing Management: Analysis, Planning and Control*, Prentice-Hall, Englewood Cliffs, N.J.

Maslow, A.H. (1970) *Motivation and Personality*, Harper & Row, New York.

OECD (1990/91) *Economic Surveys*, UK, OECD, Paris.

OECD (1991) *Labour Force Statistics*, 1969–1989, OECD, Paris.

Ricks, D.A. (1993) *Blunders in International Business*, Blackwell, Oxford.

Robinson, P.J., Faris, C.W. and Wind, Y. (1967), *Industrial Buying and Creative Marketing*, Allyn and Bacon, Boston.

Webster, F.E. and Wind, Y. (1972) *Organizational Buying Behaviour*, Prentice Hall, Englewood Cliffs, N.J.

FURTHER READING

Chisnall, P.M. (1985) *Marketing: a Behavioural Analysis*, 3rd edn, McGraw-Hill, Maidenhead.

Enis, B. and Cox, K.K. (1991) *Marketing Classics*, 7th edn, Allyn and Bacon, Needham Heights, Mass., chapters 6–11.

Engel, J.F., Blackwell, R.D. and Miniard, P.W. (1986) *Consumer Behaviour*, 5th edn, Holt Rinehart Winston, New York.

Louder, D. and Dell Biota, A.J. (1988) *Consumer Behaviour: Concepts and Application*, 3rd edn, McGraw Hill, London.

Solomon, M.R., (1986) *Consumer Behaviour*, 5th edn, Holt Rinehart and Winston, New York.

CASE PROBLEM 3.1

COACH TOURS ENTERPRISES: DEVELOPING A MARKET STRATEGY

Coach Tours Enterprises was formed in 1983 as a holiday coach operating business in Newcastle under Lyme, Staffordshire. The firm grew surprisingly quickly and at first its target market was primarily the over-65s looking for holidays of up to ten days at different destinations throughout the United Kingdom. It soon became apparent that there were other target markets with different age profiles, interested in visiting a large variety of destinations. Western European destinations were particularly attractive, with 'grand tours' of European cities proving popular.

In 1990 the company formed a strategic alliance with an air tour operating company, Flightours, based at Walsall in the West Midlands. Flightours offered packaged holidays mainly to Mediterranean destinations – Spanish coastal resorts, Greek islands, the French Riviera, Malta, Cyprus, the Italian Riviera, the Aegean Coast of Turkey. Flights were from Birmingham and Manchester airports to holiday destinations and return.

There were many benefits to the alliance from the point of view of both firms. The firms shared marketing costs, took bookings for each other, and Coach Tours Enterprises organized a special fleet of coaches to ferry customers living in the West and North Midlands to Manchester and Birmingham airports.

The recession in Europe in the early 1990s did little to stimulate business. Indeed, sales of both companies, which had actually increased during the period immediately following the formation of the alliance actually showed signs of decline thereafter. The beginnings of recovery in the UK in 1994 filled both companies with more confidence and as a result they began to look for ways of expanding their existing businesses.

Both companies felt that they were not capitalizing on all the synergies of the alliance. People flying to holiday destinations abroad often wanted to travel about and see the sights. This was particularly true of island destinations such as Malta or the Aegean coastline of Turkey. While cars could be hired at most holiday destinations, and local coach operators plied their trade as well, not everyone who wanted to go sight-seeing wanted the hassle of self-drive and customers were critical of local coach-tour operators.

Several possibilities existed; forming more strategic alliances – networking, as it is called – represented one possibility. Where there were local coach tour operators, alliances might be struck with those operators possessing a good reputation with holiday-makers. Another possibility was to buy out a local operator at some destinations, provided the general business in the area was sufficiently attractive. A third alternative was to

CASE PROBLEM 3.1 *CONTINUED*

set up branch operating companies at very popular destinations. Again, this would need to be considered in the light of the overall local demand for coach tours and trips.

The chief executives of the two companies were mulling over the 'Persona behaviourgraphics' classification data and other demographic data which they found in the Lifestyle Pocket Book (published by the Advertising Association in conjunction with NTC Publications). Persona was developed by CCN Systems in conjunction with the National Shoppers Survey carried out by Computerized Marketing Technologies, and is based on people's leisure and shopping behaviour. The data are presented below. In all cases the percentage of UK households possessing the attribute is indicated:

1. Golf clubs and Volvo: husband career-oriented, materialistic; 3.7%.

2. The got set: higher income, well-educated, interested in arts; 1.8%.

3. Bon viveurs: winers, diners, articulate conversationalists; 4.3%.

4. Fast-trackers: young, middle income, interest in active sports, leisure: 3.6%.

5. The high-techs: motivated by technology, not necessarily high earners; 6.2%.

6. Faith, hope and charity: churchgoers and charity donors, generally with older/grown-up children, community-minded: 3.9%.

7. Safe, steady and sensible: mostly self-employed people with health and accident insurance, savings and pension plans; 3.9%.

8. Craftsmen and homemakers: little education but useful craft skills; 6.1%.

9. Trinkets and treasures: older, middle income group, intellectual rather than physical; 4.7%.

10. Cultural travellers: often elderly, love foreign holidays/theatre/concerts; 5.0%.

11. Carry on camping: outdoor types, like camping, walking, often in industrial and white collar work, particularly public sector; 3.8%.

12. Health and humanities: spiritual values, political/social change; 4.2%.

13. Wildlife trustees: older, better off with country pursuits, enjoy travelling; 5.5%.

14. Factories, fishing and football: active outdoor, mostly blue collar; 4.6%.

15. Lager, crisps and videos: sociable materialists, pleasure seekers, poorly paid with little education; 5.3%.

CASE PROBLEM 3.1 *CONTINUED*

16. Instant chic: lower-income young people, interested in modern styles, eager for new experiences; 4.9%.

17. Gardeners' question time: older suburban/rural owner-occupiers; 5.9%.

18. Pools, horses and pubs: poorer, less educated, few material comforts; 5.5%.

19. Survivors: very poor, little education or confidence; 9.1%.

20. Reading, religion and routine: low-income elderly, 'respectable' folk, give to charity and like to read, usually in small towns; 8.1%.

The two executives were wondering how this classification might apply to or be reflected in the behaviour of holiday makers. They knew that approximately 2 615 000 people live in the West Midlands – 4.7% of the population of Great Britain. The population of major towns between the River Mersey and the fringe of the North Midlands was estimated as follows:

Stoke-on-Trent	247 000
Macclesfield	152 000
Stockport	291 000
Stafford	119 000
Newcastle under Lyme	118 000
Chester	114 000

The following figures for the UK as a whole relate to family stage and household composition.

HOUSEHOLD COMPOSITION

Number in household	Total '000s	Aged 15+ '000s	Aged 18+ '000s	Full-time workers '000s
One	5630	6388	6550	8625
Two	7354	11 204	12 031	8260
Three	3693	2898	2534	4037
Four	3735	1351	865	977
Five +	1749	319	149	40
of which				
Six	314	52	23	
Seven +	139	14	9	

CASE PROBLEM 3.1 *CONTINUED*

HOUSEHOLD TYPE BY FAMILY STAGE

	Single parent '000s	Two adults + children <9, >4 or 1 child 10+ '000s	Other '000s
Adults only (16+)	47	238	339
Adults + child (5–15)	452	2047	1006
Adults + infant (5)	260	1355	114
Adults + child + infant	162	781	381
Adults + child (15)	452	1713	549
Adults + 2 children	299	2195	293
Adults + 3 children	81	275	446
Adults + 4 children	41		213

The two chief executives wondered whether the Persona classifications, or some other classification means, might be used to help them develop and justify an overall marketing strategy, and what use they could make of the demographic data. One of the two executives thought that there were ample data available, whereas the other thought that more information about consumers was required and that they ought to consider commissioning a market research study.

QUESTION

1. What advice would you offer in this case?

CASE PROBLEM 3.2

MITHRADITE BOX: INDUSTRIAL BUYER BEHAVIOUR

The Mithradite Box company has for many years made tough plastic containers for a wide variety of industrial and consumer goods applications. Recently, through informal sources, the company has learned that a major manufacturer of lead-acid accumulators, Lite-Power, is experiencing problems with one of its major suppliers of containers. The supplier in question has just won a contract with an even larger lead-acid accumulator company manufacturer and the terms of supply are extremely attractive. This has caused the supplier to want to renegotiate supply terms with Lite-Power.

Mithradite does not currently supply containers to lead-acid accumulator manufacturers but feels that it has the capabilities and resources to consider moving into that particular product market. Anxious not to overlook a possibly highly lucrative opportunity, Mithradite is keen to pursue the matter further.

Lite-Power is a public limited company. An outline organization chart is shown below.

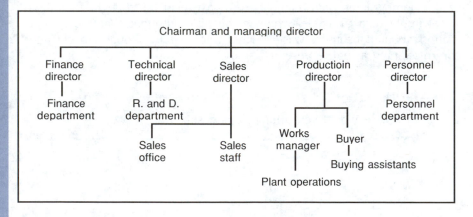

QUESTION

1. What steps might Mithradite take to pursue their interest?

4 COMPETITION

The nature of competition and the factors which influence it are explored in this chapter, along with how firms identify competitors and how they use product positioning to obtain a competitive advantage. Attention is paid to how firms define their marketing strategies and analyse the competitive positions of rivals. Consideration is given to the various sources of information available to firms that enable them to gauge competitors' strengths and weaknesses.

OBJECTIVES

After studying this chapter you should:

- understand the nature of competition, the factors which influence it and know how a firm identifies its competitors

- be able to describe the bases on which a competitive advantage may be attained and understand how competitive strategy relates to profitability

- know how leaders, challengers, followers and nichers define their marketing strategies

- know how firms analyse the competitive positions of rivals

- know the various sources of information available to firms that enable them to gauge competitors' strategies, strengths and weaknesses.

INTRODUCTION

Success in the market place depends not only on a firm's ability to identify customer wants and needs but also upon its ability to satisfy those wants and needs better than competitors are able to do. This implies that organizations need to look for ways of achieving a differential advantage in the eyes of the customer.

The differential advantage is often achieved through the product or service itself, but sometimes it may be achieved through other elements of the marketing mix.

Following a definition of what is meant by competition, attention in this chapter is given to Porter's five-forces model to portray the various factors which influence competition, and how this influence is effected. Actually identifying competition may not always be quite straightforward. It is important to be able to correctly identify different types of competitors, so that a suitable response to their marketing strategies and tactics can be put into practice as and when required.

The various bases of competitive advantage are discussed, and reference is made to Porter's strategic thrust typologies. This is then followed by a discussion of the various typologies of competitors that can be identified and the kind of strategy each one employs. Finally, the chapter ends by looking at how to assess competitors' strengths and weaknesses, and the sources of information that should be consulted when doing so.

NATURE OF COMPETITION AND IDENTIFICATION OF AN ORGANIZATION'S COMPETITORS

Competition is the process of active rivalry between the sellers of a particular product as they seek to win and retain buyer demand for their offerings (Pass *et al.*, 1991). The operational definition of competition, however, hinges upon the meaning of 'a particular product'.

Identification of an organization's competitors may not be as simple or as obvious as it might at first sight appear. The most obvious competitors are those which offer similar products or services to the same customers. The existence of substitute products and services highlights the nature of indirect competition, which must also be taken into account. Five levels of competition have been suggested: direct competition, close competition, products of a similar nature, substitute products and indirect competition.

- **Direct competition** Manchester City Football Club could be considered as a close competitor to Manchester United Football Club. Both offer similar products to the same general market, and geographically they are closely positioned. Moreover, at the time of writing, they both play in the Premier division of the English football league.

- **Close competition** In comparison with Manchester United and Manchester City, Blackburn Rovers and Bury football clubs both offer similar benefits to similar customers. Blackburn Rovers is geographically located at some distance from both Manchester clubs, but at the time of writing it plays in the same league. Bury, on the other hand, plays in a different league but is geographically placed in the same area of the country as the two Manchester clubs. Both Blackburn Rovers and Bury, and, for that matter many other football clubs, might be seen as close competition for the two Manchester teams.

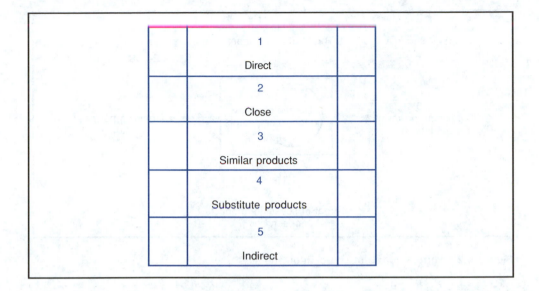

Figure 4.1 Levels of competition.

- **Products of a similar nature** Both Salford and Swinton have rugby league clubs. By and large, rugby matches are held there at a similar time of the week as football matches at either Manchester City or Manchester United. Salford and Swinton are also in close geographic proximity to Manchester. However, rugby league is a product of a similar nature to football, and there are also other rugby league clubs. All these sporting events are spectator sports, but there are also many other spectator sports which could be viewed as products of a similar nature to football. In fact we could classify most spectator sports as products of a similar nature. In all cases the spectator sports could be viewed as products of a similar nature to football matches at Manchester United or Manchester City.

- **Substitute products** What constitutes a substitute for watching a live spectatator sport? A televised one? A recorded one? A sport in which one participates rather than spectates? Here we are moving to considering alternative products or services, still in the arena of sport, which the consumer may prefer to a football match involving Manchester United or Manchester City.

- **Indirect competition** Under this heading there are very many possibilities. Lack of money, one week, for example, may cause a football spectator to indulge in another activity altogether – perhaps gardening.

From the above it can be seen that defining and identifying the competition can be quite a painstaking exercise. A firm should not only ask the question 'Who is the competition?', but should also ask 'Who is likely to be the competition in the near future?'

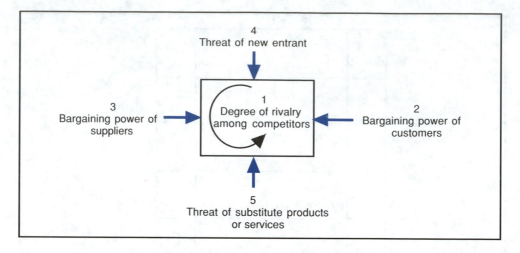

Figure 4.2 Porter's forces of competition model.

FACTORS INFLUENCING COMPETITION

Industries have distinctive idiosyncrasies of their own, and these idiosyncrasies alter over time. They are often referred to as the dynamics of the industry. No matter how hard a company tries, if it fails to fit in to the dynamics of the industry, ultimate success may not be achieved. Porter (1985) sees competition in an industry as being governed by five different sets of forces – see Figure 4.2.

Citing these five 'forces' is rather arbitrary – a sixth force, government regulation, is often the most significant influence in determining the profitability of an industry. In fact, when Porter studied the pharmaceuticals and airline industries, he discovered that government regulation and deregulation were important factors relating to profitability in both (Porter, 1988). We will now look at the five forces of the model in more detail.

1. Rivalry among competitors

Competition in an industry is more intense if there are many comparable rivals trying to satisfy the wants and needs of the same customers in the same market or market segment. Moreover, competiton increases where industry growth is slow, costs are high and there is a lack of product differentiation.

High exit barriers from a market or industry contribute to increased competition. Firms may find it difficult to get out of a business because of the relationship of the business with other businesses in which they are engaged. An organization may also have a considerable investment in assets which are used for the specific business and for which no valuable other use can be found. Less efficient firms or any firm wanting to exit a market or industry can be helped to do so by other firms either acquiring their physical plant or assets or offering to service and supply replacement parts to their customers (Harrigan, 1982, pp.45–8).

CASE EXAMPLE

BiC AND GILLETTE: COMPETITION

Disposable razors are the focus of cut-throat competitive rivalry between BiC and Gillette. While BiC operates at the budget end of the market, Gillette has a more up-market image. BiC, however, is to introduce a rival to Gillette's twin-blade range. A £2m. marketing campaign featuring TV and press advertisements is to support the launch of BiC Twin Select and Twin Pastel (for women).

The new BiC products are already on sale in the USA. Included in the new line is a sensitive variant which will be in direct competition with Gillette's planned extension to its Blue II Plus disposable brand, the first disposable razor to use technology developed for its showpiece product, the Sensor system razor, with a sales promotion budget of £1.3m. Most of this is to be spent on trial packs and merchandising. Gillette is working on the conjecture that consumers will switch first to the new disposables and then switch again to the premium razors.

BiC will probably boost margins through its move into the more lucrative twin-blade sector. This will impact on its volume to value ratio of share – 25.2% to 9% respectively (Nielsen). Standard BiCs are priced at 45p for five and the new variants are priced at £1.19 for five, well below Blue II Plus's price of £1.55.

(Source: Fox, 1994, p.2)

QUESTIONS

1. Evaluate the competitive strategies of Gillette and BiC.

2. How might other competitors in the market react to the competitive strategies of BiC and Gillette?

Increased competition also exists when there is considerable diversity of competition, or when there are high strategic stakes. In addition, the relative cost structures of the various firms in the market have a considerable bearing on the nature of competition. Moreover, a promising market attracts a high degree of competition as new entrants to a market try to establish themselves.

Rivalry or competition can take many forms. Bases of competition include price, quality, services, warranties, advertising and innovation. The relative dependence that competitors place on each of these can change over time, as competitors initiate fresh moves. Rivalry is thus dynamic, since current conditions are always being modified as companies launch new moves and countermoves.

CASE EXAMPLE

SONY AND PHILIPS: COMPETITION AND TECHNOLOGY

In 1993, Sony and Philips became embroiled in a bitter battle. The subject of the dispute was the £3.6 billion analogue tape cassette market. Philips announced its intention to recapture the market in December 1992. Its principal weapon was to be the Digital Compact Cassette (DCC), an improved quality tape with no hissing, and a price which compared favourably with the compact disc.

From Philips' point of view the DCC was a logical follow-on to the analogue tape, but Sony had different ideas and in retaliatory response launched its own alternative to analogue cassettes – the Mini-Disc. The Mini-Disc was a compact disc only 6.4 cm in diameter and designed for portable use. Philips spent £65m. developing DCCs; Sony incurred similar amounts in research. With both firms incurring high R. & D. costs, neither can really cut prices before recouping the investment.

As things stand, Philips has sold just 150 000 DCC players, against a forecast of almost one million units. Moreover, sales of the accompanying cassettes in high street stores have been very poor and a manufacturing plant in Illinois, built to produce 52 000 DCCs each week, stands idle, awaiting closure.

Sony has fared badly, too. Although it spent £30m. on advertising, it will not state how many MiniDisc players have been sold, but merely points to 'shipped' figures for last year of 300 000.

It is a sobering thought that there were more tape cassettes sold last year alone than the total number of CDs sold in the last ten years.

(Source: Bhoyrul, 1994, pp.28–9)

QUESTIONS

1. The case above indicates that in pursuing a competitive strategy all rivals may lose out sometimes. Is this not a logical argument for saying that there is little benefit to be derived by producers from competition?

2. Why do you think both companies 'failed' in this instance?

2. Bargaining power of customers

Customers can exert influence on producers. Where there is a small number of buyers, for example, or a predominant/single buyer, the producer's opportunities for action are limited. In the situation where one customer accounts for a significant proportion of a supplier's business, then that one customer can exert considerable influence and control over the price and quality of the products that it buys. Such firms can demand the highest specification in products, with tight delivery times (with just-in-time manufacturing, hence reducing their cost of raw material inventories), and customized products.

An example of customer power is to be found in the aerospace industry. When there is a downturn in the market for planes, supplying firms are affected by the power of their customers. Plane-makers, producing for the world's major airlines, are very dependent on the state of the world economy. When demand is low and margins are tight, they have to look for cost savings, irrespective of their production costs. Many companies have made large investments in plant, and cannot exit at will from the market. They know, however, that when the economic climate improves, demand will recover, forcing prices back to more profitable levels. The bargaining power of the customer is greater when demand is low and reduces when demand rises.

Many large companies operate as separate business centres, each with their own buyers. Where materials are used in many of their businesses, however, they take advantage of their buying power, negotiating as one company for such raw materials as petroleum products, transport and vehicles. This gives them a competitive advantage over smaller competitors with less leverage.

Buyers exert pressure in industries by hunting for lower prices, higher quality, additional service, and through demands for improved products and services. In general, the greater the bargaining power of buyers, the less advantage sellers will have. Not all buyers have equal bargaining power with sellers; some may be less sensitive than others to price, quality, or service. For example, in the clothing industry, major manufacturers face significant customer power when they sell to retail chains like Marks and Spencer and Burton. However, they can get much better prices selling to small, owner-managed boutiques.

3. Bargaining power of suppliers

Suppliers can exert pressure by controlling supplies. A powerful supplier is in a position to influence the profitability of a whole industry by raising prices or reducing the quality of the goods it supplies.

A firm that has few or only one potential supplier may have little control over the prices it pays for bought-in materials and components. It may also experience difficulty in controlling the quality of its raw materials and resources. If it is the only purchaser and constitutes an important part of the supplier's business, however, it is likely to have much greater control over both prices and quality.

Where a supplier has strength, through its relative size, it may decide to 'move downstream' and compete with some or all of its customers. It often happens that a company acquires its former customers in order to secure its own market from the competition. This demonstrates a company's recognition of the need to protect its route to market from its immediate competitors.

Another form of supplier power is 'lock-in'. This involves making it difficult or unattractive for a customer to change suppliers. It can be put into effect, for example, by offering specific services or product attributes that a competitor finds difficult to match.

Powerful suppliers can have the same adverse effects upon profitability as powerful buyers. Suppliers can exert bargaining power on participants in an industry by raising prices or reducing the quality of purchased goods and services, thereby squeezing profitability out of an industry which is unable to recover cost increases in its own prices. A supplier group is powerful if:

- it is dominated by a few companies and is more concentrated than the industry it sells to

- its product is unique, or at least differentiated

- it is not obliged to contend with other products for sale to the industry

- it poses a credible threat of integrating forward into the industry's business

- the industry is not an important customer of the supplier group.

(Source: Porter, 1980, pp.137–45.)

4. The threat of new entrants

The threat of new entrants can increase competitive activity in a market. Outsiders will be tempted to enter a market or an industry if they feel that the opportunity is sufficiently appealing in terms of profitability and sales. Markets which have grown to a substantial size become potentially attractive to large powerful firms, provided that the level of competitive activity enables them to achieve the kind of market share and profits and sales volume they expect.

This means that there is an incentive for firms already operating in a market to make the prospects appear less attractive to would-be entrants, by increasing the level of competitive activity. For example, lowering price levels would increase the competition between firms within the market and it might also deter other firms from entering because it would be more difficult for them to obtain high profitability levels. Much depends, however, on the cost structure of a would-be entrant. Firms adopting a low-cost strategy thrust with benefits of mass production and the latest technology and which could also achieve product differentiation might very well enter markets where price competition is reasonably tight since they could compete effectively.

Where a profitable market attracts new entrants, suppliers may expand downstream, or buyers may move upstream. This can cause increased competition and a likely reduction in margins. Methods of discouraging entry include raising the cost of entry into a market. This may be achieved by developing new products, through R. & D., which the competition find hard to match, or introducing new marketing initiatives, such as long term contracts with customers, or raising the cost of entry through economies of scale. Raising the cost of entry has long been common within many industries. In such cases larger, more expensive plants are continually built to gain competitive advantage.

New entrants to an industry tend to make it more competitive. The additional competitiveness may be due to a number of factors including the additional capacity which new entrants bring with them and their attempts to build market share.

The importance of the threat of entry depends on the barriers that are present, and on the reaction that the entrant can expect from existing competitors. If barriers to entry are high and a potential newcomer can expect sharp retaliation from the entrenched competitors, obviously there will be a reduced threat of entry. Porter (1980) lists seven major barriers to entry:

- economies of scale

- product differentiation

- capital requirements

- switching costs

- access to distribution channels

- cost disadvantages independent of scale, for example proprietary knowledge

- government policy.

Even if a potential entrant is willing to confront the entry barriers, it still faces the issue of how existing firms will react. It has to consider whether incumbent firms will react passively, or aggressively defend their market positions with price-cuts, increased advertising, product improvements, and whatever else will present difficulties for a new entrant. A potential entrant often thinks twice about entry when incumbents send strong signals that they will strongly defend their market positions against entry and with the financial resources to do so.

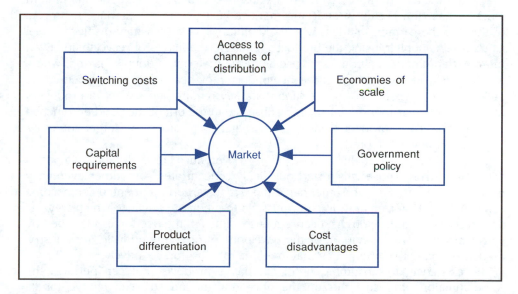

Figure 4.3   Barriers to entry.

5. The threat of substitute products or services

Suppliers in monopoly positions, or operating as members of a cartel, can exert influence on an industry in the short run. If there are alternative products or services available, however, then their power will be curtailed in the long run. In the 1970s, the oil-producers' cartel, OPEC, was able to impose large increases in the price of oil, because no other sources were available. The higher oil price made North Sea oil drilling an attractive economic proposition, and within a few years oil production in the North Sea was under way. At the same time there was a greater incentive for the oil-importing countries to economize on oil consumption and to look for alternative fuel sources.

It is not only competition from within the industry that must be considered, but also from other sources (both in services and goods). For instance, a manufacturer of profiled aluminium sheet for the building industry in the mid-1980s faced fierce competition from other aluminium suppliers. In addition, architects and builders had the choice of other building materials (asbestos, steel, etc.). Following the asbestos scare in the early eighties, approximately 30% of the building sheet market became available to substitute products, but aluminium was too expensive to take much of this cheaper end of the market. The steel suppliers, however, competed amongst themselves to exploit the new opportunities, installing new capacity to bring their prices down (Powell and Proctor, 1993).

Following this phase of expansion, the market stabilized. The steel producers had become accustomed to competition and product innovation in an expanding market, and looked for new opportunities. With a cheaper base product, they could now coat steel with long-lasting paint in more colours and offer new thermally-clad products that conserved heat, all still at lower prices than comparative aluminium products. Aluminium's market share dropped from 15% to 5% in a matter of 18 months.

Aluminium has traditionally been a substitute product itself. The aluminium industry has shown skill in attacking markets held by other materials. Examples of this are the canning market, where aluminium has successfully displaced steel as the main supplier, using the product's innate formability and recyclability. Even more extraordinary is aluminium's use as frame material in double glazing, where aluminium's qualities as an excellent conductor of heat have not prevented its utilization in a product where insulation is a key requirement. When a product is new to a particular market, it acts as a substitute to the established and entrenched competitor. As the product gains market share, it becomes the target for other competitors and their products.

Competition varies at different stages of the product life cycle and also varies across industries. Those which start out highly concentrated sometimes eventually become fragmented. On the other hand, those that start off fragmented can become concentrated. Unfortunately, it is not possible to predict in advance which way the pattern is likely to develop. As a consequence, although the five forces identified by Porter provide an explanation for the development of competition in an industry, market or market segment they may be difficult to use prescriptively.

The existence of substitutes, or of alternative products that can perform the same function, impose limits on the price that an industry can charge for its products. The presence of substitutes is not always obvious and may not easily

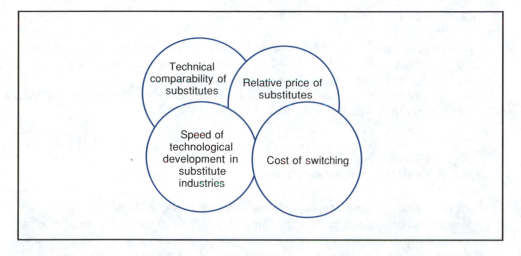

Figure 4.4 Factors governing the threat of substitute products.

be perceived by firms operating in an industry. Substitutes may even be preferred by customers, and may only be noticed when it is too late to arrest their dominance.

An example which illustrates the rise of a substitute product is the current proliferation of low-cost microcomputers coupled with low-cost, easy-to-use business packages in areas such as accounting, data base management and word processing. This 'product' has adversely affected the industry of specialist programmers and specialist computer bureaux. The threat of substitutes depends on technical comparability of substitutes, the relative price of substitutes, the speed of technological development in 'substitute' industries and the cost of switching (see Figure 4.4).

Substitute products that deserve the most attention strategically are those that are subject to trends improving their price–performance trade-off with the industry's product, or that are produced by industries earning high profits.

OVERALL EFFECT OF THE FIVE FORCES

The collective impact of the five competitive forces determines the ability of firms in an industry to earn, on average, rates of return on investment in excess of the cost of capital. The five forces determine an industry's profitability because they influence the prices, costs, and required investment of firms in an industry. Buyer power influences the prices that firms can charge, for example, as does the threat of substitution. The power of buyers can also influence the cost of investment, because powerful buyers demand costly service.

The strength of the five forces varies from industry to industry, and can change as an industry evolves. The result is that not all industries are alike from the standpoint of inherent profitability. In industries where the overall effect of the five forces is favourable, such as the soft drinks industry, many competitors earn attractive returns. However, in industries where there is fierce pressure from competitive forces, such as steel, few firms earn attractive returns.

In the next section we will will look at how firms can develop a sustainable competitive advantage for themselves in the market place in the face of all the forces of competition identified above.

COMPETITIVE ADVANTAGE

Traditionally, a competitor with a large or dominant market share is thought to have a competitive advantage. This, it is argued, arises from the well known effects of the experience curve and economies of scale in production, R. & D., administration, marketing, etc. However, the realization of a competitive advantage may depend on the definition of the market. A business can segment the market into smaller markets with particular needs (geographical, fast delivery, highest product specification or other factors). In choosing to focus on these needs, it can satisfy the requirements of this range of customers better than any of its competitors. The result is that it can then obtain a high market share within the smaller market.

A competitive advantage can be derived either from having a cost advantage or from having a 'value advantage', or even a combination of the two (see Figure 4.5). Having a cost advantage means that firms can produce and distribute their products at a lower cost than their competitors. A value advantage, on the other hand, means that the firm is able to offer a product which is perceived to provide differentiated benefits to customers – it has greater added value. These may be coupled with a focus strategy (narrow range of products and/or markets), pre-emptive moves (obtaining the best suppliers or channels of distribution by being first to market), or synergy moves (for example, acquiring a high-tech firm so that use can be made of its know-how in the original business).

A focus strategy entails concentrating on a relatively small buying group; focusing on a restricted portion of the product line; or operating in a limited geographical area. It can also involve targeting a market segment. The strategy can be used in conjunction with a low-cost or differentiation strategy. The advantage of a focus strategy is that it enables the concentration of effort to develop skills and apply resources over a restricted spectrum of activities. This can offset any disadvantages that may arise from an enterprise's lack of size.

A firm that is first to implement a strategy in a business area is following a pre-emptive strategy. Its success depends upon its ability to establish a competitive advantage by making it difficult for competitors to imitate or contest the initiative. Pioneering entry into a foreign market and gaining the best distributors ahead of competitors are examples. The pre-emptive move has many facets. From a production viewpoint it can entail securing preferential access to raw materials, or pre-empting in terms of acquiring scarce production equipment. It can also involve dominating supply logistics. In terms of the product it can amount to establishing a product position ahead of competitors; developing a dominant

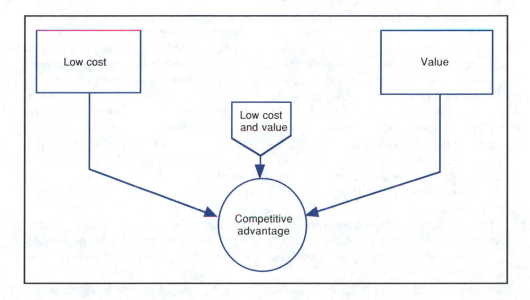

Figure 4.5 Sources of competitive advantage.

design; or securing superior product development personnel. From the perspective of production systems it may involve developing production processes; expanding capacity or achieving vertical integration. At the customer interface, it can amount to training customers in usage skills; encouraging customers to make long term commitments to the company's products; or acquiring specialized knowledge about a particular group of customers.

Finally, synergy is a characteristic of a situation where a business enjoys an advantage because it is linked to another business within the same enterprise. Both enterprises may benefit from shared resources, and in so doing reduce costs or investments. They may also be able jointly to offer a combination of complementary products. Synergy often results from some commonality in two operations, such as:

● distribution

● company or brand image and its impact on the market

● sales or advertising effort

● plant usage

● R. & D. effort

● operating costs.

In addition, it often produces increased revenues, decreased operating costs or reduced investment.

Economies of scale reflect the efficiencies that come with size. Fixed costs such as administration, facilities, equipment, staff and R. & D. can be spread over more units. Cost advantages arise where a producer derives economies of scale by having a large sales volume. Fixed costs can then be spread over a greater output. In addition there are the added benefits of what is called the 'experience curve'. The experience curve is similar to the learning curve with which we are familiar as people. As we perform a task or job again and again, we develop our skills. In time we become more efficient at doing the task or job. The experience curve extends this concept to show that efficiency increases and value added costs decline as the volume of production increases. Where a firm has the predominant market share, it should be able to reap the benefits of experience and hence enjoy cost advantages. These same benefits do not apply, however, where a firm has deliberately sought to increase its market share by buying it through price reductions, increased marketing effort and product development at the expense of long-run profitability.

The implication of cost advantages for marketing strategy is that they can be used to reduce prices or to earn higher margins at the same price. A preferable alternative, however, may be to reinvest in the product rather than run the risk of initiating price wars.

A value advantage or differentiation strategy, as it is sometimes called, is an attempt to distinguish a product or service in some way from its competitors through the benefit it offers to customers. In adopting this strategy an approach to the market based on careful segmentation is required. This approach recognizes that different groups of customers attach different degrees of importance to different benefits. (See Chapter 7 on segmentation.)

Given that firms will generally adopt a strategy based on a combination of value advantage and cost advantage, it is possible to make some general comments about how firms stand in this respect.

Firms which are able to derive little cost advantage and little value advantage are those which tend to operate in commodity market situations. In a mature market where it is difficult to increase market share, the only real prospect for development is in terms of moving towards a market niche strategy. Niche strategies are available to firms that are unable to gain any cost advantage but are able to find ways of achieving product differentiation. (These are discussed later in the chapter.)

Where a firm does not have a value advantage, it can only achieve a high cost advantage early in the life cycle of a product. With a cost advantage, the strategy followed by a firm can be to achieve price leadership. A firm which adopts this strategy can make it impossible for higher cost competitors to survive.

It is possible for a firm to successfully combine aspects of both cost leadership and differentiation. The most profitable firm in an industry could well be both a cost leader and a differentiator. Cases have been reported of firms which appear to successfully combine low-cost strategies with differentiation. Indeed, the strongest position is one where a firm enjoys the benefits of both a cost advantage and a value advantage. Streamlined, automated production facilities coupled with active and effective product differentiation strategies have enabled many Japanese consumer goods manufacturers to achieve very strong competitive positions which are very difficult to dislodge.

Honda motorcycles have maintained their initial success in America over the years by consistent actions to sustain a competitive advantage based on distribution and brand image in addition to low cost realized through high volume production (Wensley, 1987, p.39).

Finding ways of establishing a competitive advantage is a major task for marketing management. For many firms, the opportunities may be few. Companies can often find minor advantages to be exploited but these are soon copied by competitors – the advantage is only a temporary one. The implication of this is that firms need to be constantly finding new advantages.

Companies have to advertise their competitive advantage – they cannot assume that it will be automatically apparent to the market. A competitive advantage can arise from having a cost advantage, or a value advantage, or both. The strongest position is where both are enjoyed.

COMPETITIVE STRATEGY AND PROFITABILITY

A question of considerable general interest relates to how a business can maximize its profitability, or at least can become the most profitable performer in its industry. Maximum profitability can, in principle, only be achieved in one of two ways: either by minimizing costs, or by maximizing prices. Thus any useful business strategy must aim to follow one or other of these aims: to be the lowest-cost producer or the highest-price seller.

Porter argues that failure to make the choice between cost leadership and differentiation means that a company is 'stuck in the middle', with no competitive advantage, resulting in poor performance (Porter, 1988). The danger of this happening has long been emphasized by many other writers (e.g. Drucker's assertion that concentration is the key to real economic results (Drucker, 1964)). Moreover, the basic concept of strategic direction seems to suggest much the same thing. Many companies which have a clear direction and a distinct position are also demonstrably either cost leaders or differentiators, but not both. Names like Rolls-Royce, BiC, Cartier and KwikSave, for example, can be immediately classifed in one camp or the other. Some researchers have even suggested that the most effective strategies for some situations comprise systematic oscillation between cost leadership and differentiation (Gilbert and Strebel, 1988).

When 'focus' was introduced initially as a generic strategy it obscured the simple structure of the model, which argued that profits could be maximized either by achieving lowest costs or highest prices.

Competition reduces profits by the introduction of substitutes, new entrants, etc. as suggested by Porter. Moreover, perfect competition erodes profitability perfectly. Minimizing competition would minimize erosion of profits and this could be done by focusing on areas of the market where there are the fewest competitors. This in turn is a recommendation for the adoption of the 'focus strategy'. However, it is debatable as to whether 'focus' is really a strategy in its own right – at the end of the day, all strategies are focused to some extent. Even Ivory Soap, which has a very broad appeal, is carefully positioned as a multi-dimensional brand aimed at a fully researched customer profile (Clifford and Cavanagh, 1985).

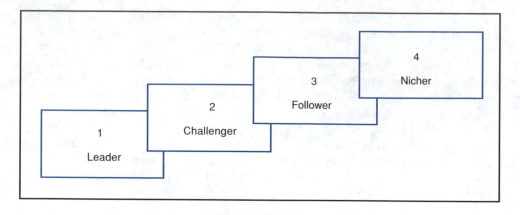

Figure 4.6 Typologies of market strategy.

STRATEGY TYPOLOGIES

While Porter's typologies represent one important way of looking at how firm's behave in the market place, there are other ways of looking at what firms do. Various suggestions have been put forward to account for the strategies adopted by firms. A commonly adopted framework is to consider firms according to the role they play in a market. The suggestion is that firms act as one of:

● market leader

● market challenger

● market follower

● market nicher.

These roles are considered below.

LEADER

The market leader is the enterprise that has the largest market share. Leadership is exercised with respect to price changes, new product introductions, distribution coverage and promotional intensity. Because of their large volume sales, market leaders enjoy the benefits of economies of scale and accumulated experience, which helps reduce costs and boulster profits. Not surprisingly, dominant firms want to stay in the leading position, and this requires them to:

● find ways of expanding total market demand

● protect market share

● even increase market share.

CASE EXAMPLE

KP: COMPETITIVE STRATEGY

KP announced its intention to double its advertising expenditure in 1994 to £12m. One eighth of this was to be spent in the first six months of 1994 on the new Publicis 'Crystal Maze' advertisement for Hula Hoops. In addition to Hula Hoops, the Skips and KP Nuts brands were to be the principal beneficiaries of the increased expenditure on advertising.

KP's biggest promotion was to take place in February 1994, when in conjunction with the Our Price music and video retailer, it was to offer money off CDs, videos, cassettes and computer games. The offer was to extend over the company's three largest brands – Hula Hoops, Skips and KP Nuts. It was intended that some 100 million special packs would go into the shops, giving away savings of £10m and a £1m TV campaign through Publicis was to support the promotion.

A company spokesman said that the promotion would link two market leaders, and had the essential elements of scale, simplicity and genuine added value. To maintain leadership of one of the most volatile and dynamic fast moving consumers goods markets, KP needed to outgun the competition in all areas of the marketing mix.

(Source: Marketing Week, *January 28, 1994, p.6).*

QUESTION

1. Do you think the strategy adopted by KP is a good one? Explain your point of view.

The market leader is conscious of economies of scale of operation, and is happiest when making inroads into large and substantial markets. Small specialist markets (niches) are not the prime interest of market leaders. For example, the Ford motor company produces a range of cars for high volume markets – for instance, the Fiesta for the small car market. Ferrari, on the other hand, specialize in producing high performance sports cars for a very small market segment that is prepared to pay a very high price for such cars.

CHALLENGER

Another group of competitors are referred to as 'market challengers'. These companies aspire to become market leaders, recognizing the benefits of holding that position. Challengers attack the leader and other competitors in order to try and gain market share, although it is uncommon for market challengers to attack the leader directly. They usually try to gain market share by attacking markets in which smaller and less efficient firms operate. Such markets, of course, do have to be of a significant size and not too small or specialized to be of concern to the larger firms.

There are a variety of strategies that challengers can adopt. One strategy is to produce an enormous variety of types, styles and sizes of products, including both cheaper and more expensive models. This was a strategy adopted by the Japanese Seiko company when it attacked the watch market. It accompanied this strategy with another which involved distributing its watches through every possible channel. The wide variety of models it had available (over 2000) meant that it could supply different types of channel with different models and thereby avoid the adverse effects of channel conflict.

FOLLOWER

A third role that firms can adopt is that of 'market follower'. Firms which undertake a good deal of innovation often have to recoup massive investment costs. Market followers are able to copy what the leading firms produce and can save themselves the burden of massive investment costs. This means that they can operate very profitably at the going price in a market. Such firms will obviously have to forgo the market share which comes from being first into the field.

Providing they can stay cost efficient and win a reasonable share of the market, they can survive. Less efficient ones, however, are open to attack from the market challengers.

NICHER

Most industries include smaller firms that specialize in producing products or in offering services to specific sectors of the market. In so doing they avoid the competitive thrusts of the larger firms, for whom specialization does not offer attractive economies of scale. That is, the segments are too small to generate the kind of return on investment that the larger firms require. This is called market niching.

Market niching is a strategy that is not only of interest to small firms but is also of interest to the small divisions of larger companies, seeking some degree of specialization. In cases where the latter occurs, the position of small firms is not quite so secure. From a firm's point of view an ideal market niche is:

● of sufficient size to be profitable to a firm serving it

● capable of growth

CASE EXAMPLE

CORLETT ELECTRICAL: MARKET NICHING IN THE INDUSTRIAL AND COMMERCIAL ELECTRICAL CONTRACTING INDUSTRY

Corlett Electrical Engineering Company regards service, quality and price to be its key success factors. Based in Wigan, the firm is an industrial and commercial electrical contractor. The firm's Managing Director, Ron Markey, started his career as an electrician in Rochdale, and worked his way up to foreman. Following the acquisition of Corlett by his employers in 1981, Ron was made manager of the Wigan operation and subsequently he acquired the Corlett business.

The company's industrial customer base has been successfully expanded over the past 13 years and today the company counts Barclays Bank, several well known industrial firms, local authorities, government departments, health authorities and British Waterways among its customers. The current size of the workforce is 32, including 18 fully qualified electricians and eight apprentices.

A variety of projects have been undertaken for different customers. These have included rewiring theatres at the Victoria Hospital, Blackpool; rewiring St John Rigby Sixth Form College; a complete electrical installation at St John Bosco School, Croxteth; all electrical work at the Special Care Baby Unit at Bolton General Hospital; a full electrical installation at a student recreation facility at Wigan College, Parson's Walk; installing new mains distribution at Ormskirk General Hospital; electrical work during the refurbishment of a Ward at Burnley General Hospital; and installing fire alarms at Pemberton Community High School.

(*Source*: Business North West, *January 1994, p.42.*

QUESTIONS

1. What basis or bases of market niching does Corlett use?

2. What factors, do you think, contribute to the firm's success?

- of negligible interest to major competitors
- a good fit with the firm's skills and resources.

Specialization is the cornerstone of market niching.

There is good evidence to show that a strong brand in a niche market earns a higher percentage return than a strong brand in a big market. In the case of large markets, competitive threats and retailer pressure can hold back profits even for the top brand (Drucker, 1964).

UNDERSTANDING THE MARKETING STRATEGIES OF COMPETITORS

A key task in establishing a sustainable competitive advantage in the market place is understanding the strategies adopted by competitors. If a firm is to analyse its competition properly it has to understand what strategy the competitors are following. Simply looking at which markets/segments in which competition is operating and examining market shares and financial performance of products/ services will provide the firm with a picture of what firms are doing. It will not, however, help to predict how things will develop in the future. To do this firms have to understand the strategies that competitors are pursuing.

NATURE OF COMPETITION ANALYSIS

Understanding competition is central to making marketing plans and strategy. A firm has to be constantly comparing its products, prices, channels of distribution and promotional methods with those of its competitors to ensure that it is not at a disadvantage. In doing so it can also identify areas where it can gain a competitive advantage.

WHO ARE THE COMPETITORS?

This may seem a simple question for most firms to answer. For example, at first sight Kellogg's main competitors might appear to be manufacturers of breakfast cereals. This is, of course, correct. However, product substitution has also to be considered. This involves looking more broadly at the types of business in which the firm operates. If this is done one can identify many producers of products that people consume at breakfast time. Many of these products could be used instead of Kellogg's cereals – i.e. they can be substituted.

Cross-elasticity of demand means that basically the same need can be satisfied by more than one product. Substitution occurs between products that have a high cross-elasticity of demand. For example, if the price of bitter beer rises in relation to the price of mild beer, then it is possible that some people may switch from drinking bitter to drinking mild.

ASSESSING COMPETITORS' STRENGTHS AND WEAKNESSES

Firms need to monitor their competition continually. The main need is for information regarding:

- sales
- market share
- profit margin
- return on investment
- cash flow
- new investment
- capacity utilization.

Knowledge of competitors' complete financial performance is useful. Such information enables firms to gain comprehensive impressions of their rivals that may be useful in predicting short term strategies to be adopted by competitors.

A knowledge of competitors' specific objectives would be very welcome, since these would give clues as to future strategies that competitors are likely to pursue. This kind of information may be difficult to obtain, but may be inferred from present or past activities.

SOURCES OF INFORMATION ABOUT COMPETITORS

Making good decisions can be improved by an adequate supply of relevant information. Knowing sources of information is an important first step. A starting point is to look at what competitors say about themselves and what others say about them. Sources of information fall into four categories:

- public
- trade and professional
- government
- investors.

PUBLIC SOURCES

Advertising, promotional materials and press releases are prime sources of information on what competitors have to say for themselves. Articles and newspaper reports provide a good source of information on what others have to say about them. In both of these cases, however, information may be biased or even distorted.

TRADE AND PROFESSIONAL SOURCES

Courses, seminars, technical papers and manuals prepared by competitors often provide detailed insights into their activities. Actually making sense of it all, however, can be very time consuming. It can take a considerable amount of time to distil and analyse it all. Distributors, the trade press and even customers are good sources of information when it comes to what other have to say about competitors.

GOVERNMENT

In the UK, firms have to lodge their annual reports at Companies House in London, Cardiff, Edinburgh or Belfast; the contents of these reports provide constructive insights into the operations of competitors. In the case of 'what others say about them', lawsuits, government ministries and national plans are other useful sources of information.

INVESTORS

Annual meetings, annual reports and prospectuses are primary sources of what competitors have to say about themselves. Credit reports and industry studies provide an outsider's viewpoint.

SUMMARY

Competition can arise from many sources and in many ways. Porter's five-forces model portrays the various factors which influence competition and how this influence is effected. Actually identifying competition is not always quite straightforward and it is important to be able to correctly identify different types of competition so that suitable reaction to competitors' marketing strategies and tactics can be put into practice as and when required.

The bases on which a competitive advantage may be forged fall into two categories: those based upon achieving a cost advantage, and those based upon obtaining a value advantage.

In the market place there are firms which can be thought of as market leaders, market challengers, market followers and market nichers. Each adopts a different marketing strategy to the other. Being able to classify firms in this way is helpful in predicting what moves competitors are likely to make in the near and more distant future.

Porter sees competition in an industry as being governed by different sets of forces: the threat of new entrants, bargaining power of suppliers, bargaining power of customers and the threat of substitute products or services.

Understanding competition is central to making marketing plans and strategy. A firm has to be constantly comparing its products, prices, channels of distribution and promotional methods with those of its competitors to ensure that it is not at a disadvantage. In doing this it can also identify areas where it can gain a competitive advantage.

A firm needs to have a continuous supply of information about competition. The main need is for information regarding sales, market share, profit margin, return on investment, cash flow, new investment, capacity utilization and financial performance. Naturally there would be benefits from knowing the specific objectives competitors are likely to pursue. These may be difficult to identify, but may be inferred from present or past activities.

One should look for what competitors say about themselves and what others say about them. Sources of information fall into four categories: public, trade and professional, government and investors. Knowledge of the various sources of information available to firms that enable them to gauge competitors' strategies, strengths and weaknesses is of key importance.

DISCUSSION QUESTIONS

1. How would you define 'competition'?

2. Give examples of:

   (a) direct competition
   (b) close competition
   (c) similar products
   (d) substitute products
   (e) indirect competition

   for the following products/services:

   (i) university education
   (ii) a local bus service into the town centre
   (iii) the Ford Mondeo motor car.

3. Elaborate on the five (six?) components of Porter's model of the factors influencing competition.

4. Outline the various bases of gaining a competitive advantage.

5. Porter argues that failure to make the choice between cost leadership and differentiation infers that a company is 'stuck in the middle', with no competitive advantage. How can this point of view be reconciled with the success of those firms which apply both of these strategic thrusts?

6. Differentiate among:

   (a) market leaders
   (b) market challengers
   (c) market followers
   (d) market nichers.

7. Discuss the various strategies which might be pursued by each one of the four categories identified in question 7.

8. Indicate the key information requirements about competitors that firms require.

9. How might a firm set about trying to collect information on a continuous basis about its competitors?

REFERENCES

Clifford, D.K. and Cavanagh, R.E. (1985) *The Winning Performance, How America's High Growth Midsize Companies Succeed*, Sidgwick and Jackson, London.

Drucker, P.F. (1964) *Managing for Results*, Harper & Row, New York.

Fox, H.L. (1994) BiC launch sets off razor wars, *Marketing*, February 3.

Gilbert, X. and Strebel, P. (1988) Developing competitive advantage, in *The Strategic Process* (eds J.B. Quinn, H. Mintzberg and R.M. James), Prentice Hall, Englewood Cliffs, N.J.

Harrigan, K.R. (1982) Strategic planning for end game, *Long Range Planning*, **15**(6), 45–8.

Pass, C., Lowes, B., Pendleton, A. and Chadwick, L., (1991) *Collins Dictionary of Business*, Harper Collins, London.

Porter, M.E. (1980) How competition forces shape strategy, *Harvard Business Review*, September–October, 137–45.

Porter, M.E (1985) Competitive Advantage, Free Press, New York.

Porter, M.E. (1988) video film and pamphlet: *Michael Porter on Competitive Strategy*, Harvard Business School Video Series, Cambridge, Mass.

Powell, D. and Proctor, R.A. (1993) Competition dynamics in aluminium, Working papers in Management, Keele University.

Wensley, R. (1987) Marketing strategy, *The Marketing Book* (ed. M.J. Baker), Butterworth-Heineman, Oxford.

FURTHER READING

Cravens, D.W. and Shannon, H.S. (1991) Market-driven strategies for competitive advantage. *Business Horizons*, Jan./Feb., 53–61.

Flax, S. (1984) How to snoop on your competitor, *Fortune*, 14 May, 29–33.

Haverty, J.L. and Myroslow, J.K. (1991) What happens when new competitors enter an industry, *Industrial Marketing Management*, **20**(2), 73–80.

Karakaya, F. and Stahl, M.J. (1989) Barriers to entry and market entry decisions in consumer and industrial goods, *Journal of Marketing*, April, 80–91.

Rothschild, W.E. (1984) *How to Gain and Maintain the Competitive Advantage*, Mcgraw Hill, New York.

CASE PROBLEM 4.1

ICPRO: PORTER'S FIVE-FORCES MODEL

In the last few years ICPRO sales revenue and volume had only shown moderate increases. Nevertheless, it was operating with an excellent return on capital employed and was showing healthy net and gross profit ratios. The market for food wrappings served by the firm was relatively static in terms of size, with the forecast for 1993 indicating only modest growth.

Increasing pressure on the main domestic market, produced by new foreign entrants to the industry, was exerting heavy downward pressure on prices and eroding profit margins. While the company was adopting a strategy of protecting its current product markets, where it held a very strong position, more profitable and cash generating business was sought to help offset diminishing returns in the prime product market. Ventures into certain European markets seemed to offer promising returns. But in addition to market expansion the firm was on the lookout for new products and ways of diversifying its current product market position.

Analysis identified entry onto the market of European competitors as a major threat. In terms of Porter's five-forces model this was seen as a possible 'new entrant'. This suggested that the cost structure of European competitors was an important factor to be taken into account when formulating strategy. The British and European markets are different – the European market is largely a commodity market – there is little brand loyalty or brand strength. The British and European markets are different. However, for certain sizes of the major brand, European manufacturers enjoyed a lower cost base than producers in the UK and could compete effectively in the market for these sizes.

Profit margins gained from the manufacture and sale of the major brand in the UK were considered to be higher than in Europe and could be considered attractive to overseas producers, currently operating in low margin commodity markets. This could also apply to American producers, although they would need a European base to make it an attractive proposition.

One idea ICPRO had was that of creating a unique selling proposition for the major brand, thereby creating a barrier to entry by forcing would-be entrants to spend heavily to overcome customer loyalty. Many suggestions and ideas were put forward, and some were agreed upon, shown below.

SELECTED SUGGESTIONS

The most effective way of deterring new entrants to the market is to raise entry barriers, making it difficult for a competitor to gain a position in the market, regardless of size and the amount it might spend on advertising. There were several ways to achieve this in the markets concerned:

- increasing advertising and promotional expenditure for the product, thereby increasing brand awareness and possible brand loyalty
- targeting specific households which are volume users of the major brand
- developing a unique selling proposition, such as use of a new material, that would set the product ahead of competitive products.

Implementation of one or all of these strategies would lead to an increase in brand awareness. The areas of the market that were not currently being reached by the product would be penetrated and new users would be brought to the brand. The barriers to entry would have been raised, and foreign competition deterred in the short term. Once these barriers have been raised they would have to be maintained and strengthened further to protect the market. Such a strategy would also stimulate the whole market and might cause it to grow in volume terms as new users were gained, or sales switched away from substitute products.

European manufacturers had strength in producing certain sizes of the major brand. It was very important that the company should promote other sizes and ensure that these were a feature of the UK market and that the consumer became accustomed to purchasing these versions. Advertising and promotional activity needed to be centred around this, thereby encouraging the consumer to remain loyal, not just to the brand but also to the variations of the product.

It was thought likely that these measures would only create a short term barrier, as foreign competition would invest in producing other versions more efficiently. Estimates showed, however, that it would be difficult for them to do so without significant investment. A more durable barrier would be to create a new brand. Such a brand might utilize a unique material that had special characteristics or some other benefit that would give the company a differential advantage.

The European companies had a cost advantage, so the firm had to reduce costs to match its potential competitors. This was important if competitors attempted to orchestrate a price war to gain market share. The firm had to be as competitive as possible, to be able to defend its position.

QUESTION

What strategy do you think ICPRO should follow to beat or match the competition? Justify your answer.

CASE PROBLEM 4.2

GOLDEN LADY: COMPETITIVE STRATEGY

Golden Lady claims it is European brand leader. According to its managing director Alan Cotton, the firm has 10% of sales in Poland and a strong presence in Russia. He feels that the market is oversupplied but that Golden Lady is gaining more ground, particularly in the UK.

Packing more products than competitors into limited store space is the name of the game for Golden Lady. It has done this by using small boxes in which to pack its hosiery lines. Despite the fact that the company only arrived in Britain three years ago, it lays claim to being in third position in the total market.

The company is now devising merchandising units to sell elsewhere in the stores, and Asda already has units which hold 2000 pairs. Alan Cotton, says that space is at a premium and the merchandising units give Golden Lady additional sites. He added that buyers were now considering their use, but with own-label taking around 42% of sales against 53% for brands, store owners would be careful not to detract from sales of their own labels, which sell at a few pence cheaper than the brands.

A range of 30 hosiery products is supplied by Golden Lady, but normally stores take around four products. Four new styles from Golden Lady have recently been launched:

- 60 denier knee highs in four shades, two pairs to a pack at £1.69

- Leda 15 denier tights in three sizes at £1.39

- a range of 15 denier stockings in packs of three retailing at £1.99

- a value for money two pair pack of knee high socks in 20 denier at 99p.

Alan Cotton indicated that for the current year the company had increased the range of knee highs which were enjoying rapid growth in fine and semi-sheer as women's fashion trends moved further towards wearing trousers. The company was hoping to increase sales through independents and symbol groups.

(*Source:* The Grocer, *8 January 1994, p. 27*)

QUESTIONS

1. Who are Golden Lady's main competitors?
2. Do you thing that the strategy being followed by Golden Lady is the correct one? Why or why not?

5 MARKETING INFORMATION SYSTEMS AND DECISION SUPPORT MECHANISMS

This chapter discusses main components of a marketing information system, along with decision support mechanisms. Both objective and subjective approaches to market measurement and forecasting are covered, along with the use of traditional management science/ operational research tools in marketing decisions. The use of various multivariate techniques and expert systems in marketing is also discussed.

OBJECTIVES

After studying this chapter you should be able to:

- describe the components of a marketing information system
- appreciate the nature of marketing decision support mechanisms
- understand the nature and purpose of both objective and subjective approaches to forecasting
- appreciate the use of traditional management science/operational research tools in marketing

- understand how various multivariate techniques may usefully be applied to marketing problems

- appreciate the use of expert systems in marketing.

INTRODUCTION

First we take a systematic look at the overall concept of a marketing information system and then we explore its various components in more detail. Attention is given first to methods of market measurement and forecasting, before moving on to examine the range of management science and operational research techniques which can be used to help in improving marketing decisions – decision support mechanisms.

We continue with decision support mechanisms by examining possible applications for two multivariate analytical techniques – cluster analysis and factor analysis. Consideration is also given to perceptual mapping techniques and the role they play in helping to analyse data.

Finally, we look at possible uses for expert systems as part of the decision support mechanism.

MARKETING INFORMATION SYSTEMS

Information systems are designed to make it easier to generate and provide information which can assist the smooth operation of the various functions which they support.

A marketing information system may comprise the following subsystems (Kotler, 1988, p.525).

- An internal reporting system containing data on sales, inventories, cash flows, accounts receivable, etc., all of which can be used to measure current activity and performance.

- A marketing intelligence system which collects everyday information regarding developments in the external environment, and in particular problems and opportunities.

- A marketing research system which gathers, evaluates and reports information on a specific environmental situation facing a company, providing sufficient information to minimize guesswork.

- An analytical marketing system which is able to undertake the complex analysis of business problems.

The last of these subsystems, the analytical marketing system, comprises a set of statistical tools and mathematical models. These are advanced statistical

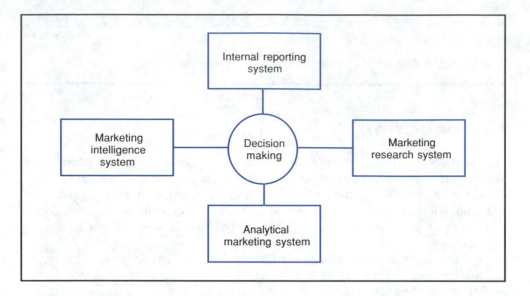

Figure 5.1 Components of a marketing information system.

procedures which assist executives to understand more about the relationships within sets of data, helping them to generate better marketing decisions. These tools and models are referred to as 'decision support mechanisms'.

One can define a marketing information system as one which scans and collects data from the environment, makes use of data from transactions and operations within the firm and then filters, organizes and selects data before presenting them as information to management.

DATA

Competitive information and information on customers wants and needs can be obtained from sales reports. Such reports can be entered into the information system in electronic form. This calls for the design of electronic forms which can easily be completed by sales staff. Sales reports tend to be filled in at home at weekends, or in hotel bedrooms during the working week. A portable laptop computer, directly connected via a modem link with the firm's mainframe computer, provides an attractive solution to the problem.

Data on the environment and competitive activity can often be bought from consultants and marketing research agencies. It is often already in an electronic form.

Data should as far as possible be kept in a disaggregated form in the database, so allowing anyone to manipulate and analyse the data to suit their own particular purposes. Summary statistical analyses of data may well be kept in a separate file within the database, if it is felt that it is information to which people may want to refer frequently. Having a computer-based information systems means that information in the form of reports can be made available quickly to management.

USERS AND USES OF A MARKETING INFORMATION SYSTEM

One of the main users of the marketing information system is sales management. It requires information to help it allocate the sales force effectively and assess the performance of sales staff equitably. Sales staff, too, should be able to access the system easily and get support and information about such things as:

● the quantity of the product on hand

● prices and price discounts

● status information on invoices, time of delivery and back orders

● delivery dates

● complete product specifications.

The information system facilitates analysis of the total sales revenue of a company over a period of time. The analysis examines total sales volume by product line, by salesperson, by territory and by customer groups. These sales are then compared with company goals and industry sales.

The information system can help to produce sales forecasts. Marketing budgets, sales strategies and sales quotas are influenced by these estimates. The sales

---

Sales force performance report:
calls made by sales staff
calls to sales ratios
contribution margin on products sold

Sales performance report:
analysis of total sales volume and sales profitability by –
    product line
    sales person
    territory
    customer groups
and comparison with company goals

Promotion report:
media guides for selecting among different media

Customer service report:
purchasing trends
lost customers
complaints

Figure 5.2 Some of the reports from a marketing information system.

forecasts also help in the planning and control of manufacturing, distribution management and advertising and promotion activities. In such sales forecasts, information on sales profitability is also made available. This shows the relative profitability of customers, territories, product lines, etc.

MARKETING RESEARCH AND THE MARKETING INFORMATION SYSTEM

Marketing research is seen as an element of the marketing information system, helping to define marketing problems. It also helps executives find new customers and adapt products to meet changing customer requirements. User-friendly software and large relational databases help advise users on which segments to target. Marketing research can tell customers how to price a product, which distribution channels to use and how to get more out of advertising and other promotional expenditure.

Outputs of the marketing information system can take the form of reports. There are obviously a large number of different reports that can be produced. Some of these are shown in Fig. 5.2.

DECISION SUPPORT MECHANISMS

Marketing decision support mechanisms comprise a collection of tools and techniques, with supporting software and hardware, by which an organization gathers and interprets relevant information from business and the environment and turns it into a basis for marketing action. The remainder of this chapter will examine the various decision support mechanisms that can be used. The main areas covered are:

- forecasting tools
- mathematical models
- statistical tools
- expert systems.

FORECASTING DEMAND

Marketing plans can only be prepared and delivered well if the size of current and future markets is carefully measured and estimated. Such information is a useful starting point from which to determine how resources should be allocated among markets and products or services.

DEFINING MARKET DEMAND

Demand can be measured at several different levels:

- **product levels** – product item sales, product form sales, product line sales, company sales, industry sales, national sales

- **space levels** – sales to individual customers, sales by territory, area or country and world sales

- **time levels** – short-range, medium range, long-range sales.

There are 'penetrated markets', 'potential markets', 'available markets', and 'served markets'. The current number of users of a product or service and the sales volume they generate constitutes the penetrated market. There may be figures readily available which indicate this or it may be necessary to establish it by sample survey.

These estimates do not take account of those people who have an interest in buying a particular product or service, but who currently do not do so. These people are important, since in looking at future demand they provide a measure of the potential market. Customers must be able to afford the product or service, so in assessing the potential market this must be established. This will redefine the market size.

The existence – or otherwise – of an opportunity to use a product or service also defines the size of the market. If it is not possible to use a product, then this will obviously restrict the market size. Taking this into account will define the available market. A company has only a limited amount of resources at its disposal, and so selects only certain market segments where it feels that it has the capacity to compete effectively and where the market size is sufficiently attractive. This becomes the 'served' or the 'target market'.

PREDICTING FUTURE DEMAND

A company's production schedules, planned manning levels and financial budgeting are all related to the sales forecast. Too optimistic a forecast can lead to excess stocks being accumulated, over-production and too high manning levels, and over-borrowing or inefficient deployment of financial resources. A pessimistic forecast can lead to large opportunity costs and the creation of frustration amongst potential buyers of the company's products because delivery is late or not forth-coming.

Firms adopt a variety of approaches to sales forecasting, but the basic approach is as follows:

1. Make an environmental forecast regarding inflation, employment, interest rates, consumer spending and saving, business investment, etc.

2. Make a forecast of sales and profits to be earned by the industry using the data in stage 1, together with other information which links industry figures to environmental trends.

3. Make a company sales forecast using the data in stage 2 and assuming a given market share.

Often, however, firms may not know the industry sales level. In such cases sales forecasts are made at the company level at stage 2, and, stage 3 is not used.

There are two basic approaches to forecasting sales for established products, both of which have a number of variants. On the one hand there are the methods which rely on asking questions of people and on the other hand there are those which involve the statistical or mathematical analysis of historical data.

ASKING PEOPLE QUESTIONS

Surveys of buyers' intentions

There are market research organizations which conduct periodic surveys of buying intentions. Using the results of regular sample surveys, predictions of the likely demand for various items are then prepared. Firms can of course carry out the surveys themselves, provided that they have the resources to do so. It is a method which can be applied effectively by producers of industrial plant, machinery and supplies.

Composite of sales force opinion

The sales force is in constant contact with the market and is in an excellent position to provide estimates on potential sales demand. When making use of estimates of the sales force, account has to be taken of any bias that may exist. For one reason or another, the sales force may be biased either in the direction of pessimism or in the direction of optimism. Another difficulty is that the sales force often may not really appreciate the larger economic factors which influence sales. Providing one can identify sources of bias and adjust for them in interpreting predictions, it is possible to make use of these estimates.

Expert opinion

Expert opinion is another method of forecasting. Experts may include dealers, distributors, suppliers, marketing consultants and even trade associations. A key factor which influences patterns of sales in a country is the state of its economy. Various economic experts can provide their opinions, and a government will produce its own forecast for the economy.

ANALYSING PAST DATA

Firms tend to base their forecasts on what they have achieved in the past. This approach to forecasting offers few opportunities for mistakes, except where there are large variations in sales from one year to the next. There are two basic methods of forecasting, each of which has a number of versions.

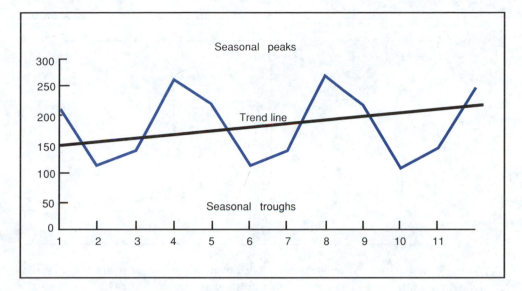

Figure 5.3   Elements of a time series analysis.

METHODS WHICH ADOPT A SOLELY TIME-DEPENDENT APPROACH

Classical time series analysis

The first set of methods is that based on time series analysis. In this case, it is assumed that sales simply vary as a function of time. The time effects are divided into:

- **cyclic** – fluctuations every few years (e.g. the trade cycle as various major economies in the world are hit by booms and slumps)

- **trend** – a general upward, downward or static (no trend) pattern (e.g. upward trend of sales of video recorders during the growth phase of the life cycle)

- **seasonal** – systematic variations at certain times of the year (e.g. additional sales of bathing costumes in the summer months)

- **erratic** – unpredictable or random variations (e.g. demand interrupted by an industry-wide strike).

Erratic variation is taken into account when making forecasts, but one does not attempt to predict it exactly. It is merely expressed as the error attached to the sales forecast. This method is most suitable for forecasting sales of products where the unexplained variation is small.

The trend component results from developments in a population, the formation of capital and developments in technology. It is evidenced by a general upward or downward shift in the pattern of sales. If there is no such pattern then there is assumed to be no trend.

Period	Year	Sales (tons)
1	1993	210
2		120
3		140
4		260
5	1994	220
6		125
7		145
8		270
9	1995	225
10		128
11		149
12		275

The cycle depicts the wavelike flow of sales over a number of years and is most useful when examining data for use in intermediate range forecasts (3–7 years). Traditionally, the cycle represents swings in economic activity.

The seasonal component refers to recurrent sales patterns that may exist within the period of a single year. This will reflect things such as weather factors, holidays, seasonal buying habits and so on.

Erratic variation comprises such things as strikes, fashions, and other unforeseen circumstances. These factors are unpredictable and need to be removed from past data in order to inspect the other three elements. Time series analysis consists of decomposing the original sales data into its trend, cyclical, seasonal and erratic components. The series is then recombined to produce a sales forecast.

For example, imagine the data in the above table represents quarterly data on shipments of a particular commodity:

There are several different approaches to forecasting time series data such as these; possibly the best is to use dummy variables and multiple regression analysis. Multiple regression is a statistical tool which can be applied to past data to discover the most important factors influencing sales and their relative influence. The dummy variables in this particular case represent the factors influencing sales. The approach consists of creating a variable for each of the four quarters, and the following equation is then estimated by multiple linear regression analysis:

$$\text{Sales} = B_0 + B_1 \text{ Time} + bP_2 \text{ Winter} + B_3 \text{ Spring} + B_4 \text{ Summer}$$

It should be noted that one of the dummy variables has to be left out so that the regression can be solved by computer – in this case, 'Autumn' is omitted. (See table on p. 127.)

The values obtained are:

$$B_0 = 256.6 \quad B_1 = 1.468 \quad B_2 = -45.6 \quad B_3 = -141.1 \quad B_4 = 122.2$$

Time	Sales	Winter	Spring	Summer	Autumn
1	210	1	0	0	0
2	120	0	1	0	0
3	140	0	0	1	0
4	260	0	0	0	1
5	220	1	0	0	0
6	125	0	1	0	0
7	145	0	0	1	0
8	270	0	0	0	1
9	225	1	0	0	0
10	128	0	1	0	0
11	149	0	0	1	0
12	275	0	0	0	1

We can forecast sales for subsequent periods by substituting values into the equation. For example:

$$\text{Period 13 forecast sales} = 256.6 + 1.468 \times 13 - 45.6 \times 1$$
$$= 230.1$$

Exponential smoothing

This is basically a technique which requires the minimum amount of data and is calculated by means of a simple equation. We will see how this is done below.

Many firms produce many hundreds or even thousands of products. Notable examples are the firms operating in the pharmaceutical industry. For such firms a simple forecasting technique is required which requires the minimum of data. In its simplest form exponential smoothing requires only three pieces of information:

- the period's actual sales Q_t

- the current period's smoothed sales q_t

- *a smoothing parameter, a,* a value between 0 and 1.

The sales forecast for the next period is given by the formula:

$$q_{t+1} = aQ_t + (1 - a)q_t$$

Such forecasts are handled by computer which, using an iterative procedure (trial and error) can regularly determine that value of a which gives the most satisfactory results in making forecasts. The value is the one which gives the best fit to past sales. Once the system has been set up, all that has to be done is to add new sales figures to the database as and when they occur. There are a number of more sophisticated variants on this approach – e.g. double exponential smoothing, exponential smoothing incorporating seasonal and trend components.

STATISTICAL DEMAND ANALYSIS

So far, the statistical or mathematical approaches we have considered treat the factors which seem to influence sales as regularly reccurring phenomena. The difficulty with this approach is that some patterns do not reappear at regular intervals. For example, while there are economic booms and slumps from time to time, their patterns are not so precise as to enable accurate forecasts to be made.

Statistical demand analysis attempts to identify the source of all influences on demand so that more accurate forecasts can be made. The basic statistical method to take account of such factors is multiple regression analysis. Experience seems to indicate that the factors most commonly considered are price, income, population, and marketing promotion.

The first stage in a regression analysis is to build a causal model in which one tries to explain sales in terms of a number of independent variables. For example, we might conjecture that industry sales of umbrellas are related to their relative price (P), personal disposable income (I), relative advertising expenditure and the absolute level of rainfall (R). We would express this relationship in the form of an equation:

$$S = a_0P + b_1I + b_2A + b_3R$$

What one has to do is to estimate the parameters for a_0, b_1 . . . b_3 and apply them to quantifications of P, I, A and R for the period of the forecast.

In principle, demand equations of this variety are acquired by fitting the best equations to historical or cross-sectional data. The coefficients of the equation are estimated according to what is called the 'least squares criterion'. According to this criterion, the best equation is that which minimizes a measure of the error between the actual and the predicted observations. The better the fit, the more useful will be the equation for forecasting purposes.

While this is a popular technique, one has to use it with care. There must always be an adequate number of observations – in making annual forecasts, 10–15 years' data are not unreasonable where there are four independent variables. Another problem is that what seem to be independent variables turn out to influence each other, and are not really independent at all. For example, relative price and relative advertising expenditure may well influence each other, since advertising costs can be reflected in the selling price. In addition there are other pitfalls to be watched for.

FORECASTING SALES OF NEW PRODUCTS

To forecast sales of new products one needs some initial sales figures with which to work. Given that early sales data are available, it is then generally possible by using one or other of a variety of mathematical models or 'curve fitting routines' to make some prediction for sales over a specified period of time. Alternatively, it may be possible to look at sales histories of similar new products and make

Year	Sales$_t$ '000	Y'_t '000	Y'^2_t
1	5	0	0
2	10	5	25
3	22	15	225
4	54.64	37	1369
5	104.71	91.64	8398
6	185.55	196.35	38 553
7	255	381.90	145 848
8	371.82	636.90	405 642
9		1008.72	

predictions by analogy. There are numerous examples of these models (Kotler and Lilien, 1983).

For example the epidemic model of initial sales developed by Bass (1969, pp. 215–27), facilitates sales prediction for new products:

$$p_t = p + q/m(Y_t)$$

where

p_t = probability of purchase, given no previous purchase was made
Y_t = total number who have tried
m = total number of potential buyers (saturation level)
q = parameter reflecting the rate of diffusion of the model
p = initial probability of first time purchase.

The model can be estimated by running a regression of current versus past sales (see data in table above):

$$\text{Sales}_t = c_0 + c_1 Y_t + c_2 Y_t^2$$

Analysis of the above sales gives the forecasting model:

$$\text{Sales}_t = 13.67 + 0.90 Y_t - 0.00054 Y_t^2$$

Forecasting sales of new products in retail outlets

Large retail chains often add new lines to their stock. Most of these retailers have benchmarks against which to judge whether a product is likely to be successful or not. A common practice is to offer the product for sale for a limited period in just one of its many shops. If the product fails to achieve a certain level of sales within the specified period, it is withdrawn from sale and not put on sale in other outlets.

APPLICATIONS FOR MATHEMATICAL MODELS IN THE MARKETING DECISION SUPPORT SYSTEM

Mathematical models are those referred to in the operations research literature. The main models are:

- linear programming
- transportation model
- assignment model
- network model
- decision trees
- inventory models
- queuing theory
- Markov analysis
- simulation
- game theory.

The various models or techniques have been applied in a wide variety of settings and can help to find solutions to problems in many different areas of marketing. Below, examples are shown (usually omitting calculations) of how these techniques may be applied to marketing problems. Interested readers can refer to books such as *MSIS* (Attaran, 1992), *Computer Models for Management Science* (Erikson and Hall, 1989), and the computer software which goes with such books to try out for themselves these kinds of problems.

LINEAR PROGRAMMING

Linear programming helps to determine how to minimize costs or maximize profits (or minimize/maximize some other factors), subject to a set of constraints.

For example an advertising manager has a budget of £5000 to spend and wants to maximize the 'reach' of magazine advertisements. The reach of one magazine (X_1) is 8000 potential customers, while that of another magazine (X_2) is 5000 potential customers. The number of potential customers with incomes of less than £10 000 per annum is 1000 and 400, respectively, per column inch of advertising in each magazine. The cost of an advertisement in magazine X_1 is £500 per column inch; it is £1000 per column inch in the case of X_2. The manager would like to reach at most 4000 potential customers whose incomes are less than £10 000 per annum. How many column inches should be bought in each of the magazines, so as to maximize profits?

This problem may be expressed as follows:

Objective: maximize $Z = 8000X_1 + 5000X_2$ (profit function)
subject to $X_1, X_2 \geq 0$ (negative amounts not allowed)
and $500 X_1 + 1000 X_2 \leq 5000$ (budget constraint)
$1000 X_1 + 400 X_2 \leq 4000$ (reach constraint)

Applying linear programming gives the answer: 2.5 column inches in magazine X_1 and 3.75 column inches in magazine X_2. The associated profit is £38 750.

TRANSPORTATION MODEL

The transportation model may be thought of as a special case of the linear programming model. A special algorithm is developed to solve such problems. Essentially, the idea is to allocate the flow of objects to sources and destinations in such a way as to minimize costs or maximize profits (or some other measure relating to minimization/maximization).

For example a company transports goods from three manufacturing plants to three warehouse sites. The supply capacities of the three plants, the demand requirements of the three sites and the transportation costs ($/ton) are as follows:

From plant	To warehouse site			Supply (tons)
	1	2	3	
1	$8	$5	$6	120
2	15	10	12	80
3	3	9	10	80
Demand (tons)	150	70	60	280

How should supply be equated with demand so as to minimize costs? The problem is expressed as:

Minimization problem

	Warehouse			
	1	2	3	Supply
Plant 1	8.00	5.00	6.00	120.00
Plant 2	15.00	10.00	12.00	80.00
Plant 3	3.00	9.0	10.00	80.00
Demand	150.00	70.00	60.00	280.00

The solution suggested gives:

| | Warehouse | | | |
	1	2	3	Supply
Plant 1	70.00	0.00	50.00	120.00
Plant 2	0.00	70.00	10.00	80.00
Plant 3	80.00	0.00	0.00	80.00
Demand	150.00	70.00	60.00	280.00

The solution value given is $1920 (cost minimized).

ASSIGNMENT MODEL

The assignment model helps to identify the minimum or maximum pay-off resulting from the matching of one set of items to a second set of items. The items may be people, projects, jobs, contracts, territories, etc. The potential applications for such a model in manpower planning are quite substantial. For example, one might be concerned with assigning people to jobs, assigning various contracts to people making bids, assigning sales people to territories, etc. An assignment problem may be thought of as one where only one from a set of items is assigned to only one from a set of other items.

This example involves getting a project completed in the shortest time. A marketing research department has received a request to carry out a study of the market for eight different products. Based on previous experience, the department knows that if it assigns the eight tasks individually to members of its department then it can expect to get the tasks performed in the following times (days).

| | Products | | | | | | | |
	1	2	3	4	5	6	7	8
John	5	3	4	3	6	3	C	7
Paul	5	2	3	2	5	4	6	7
Bill	3	C	5	4	4	5	7	5
Sam	4	6	6	3	3	2	8	6
Helen	6	7	7	C	6	3	7	7
Mary	4	4	3	6	4	6	6	8
Winifred	5	5	4	5	C	5	5	8
Alice	4	5	5	4	4	C	6	7
Arthur	3	4	C	3	5	3	7	6
Mark	6	3	4	4	6	2	7	6

Entries marked 'C' signify that the person would not have the skills or experience to carry out that particular study.

The overall aim is to get the task completed in the shortest possible time. Furthermore, the firm believes that it is desirable to have only one individual per project, since experience indicates that this is generally the quickest way to get things done. One way in which the firm has conducted the exercise in the past is to assign tasks according to the shortest available time indicated in each product study column. Thus the assignment made, based upon such a heuristic, might be:

Product study	Name	Time
1	Bill	3
2	Paul	2
3	Mary	3
4	John	3
5	Sam	3
6	Mark	2
7	Winifred	5
8	Arthur	6

This would give a completion time of 27 days. Using the assignment model and minimizing the amount of time, the solution indicates that the tasks can in fact be completed in 26 days with a different assignment of personnel:

Product study	Name	Time
1	Arthur	3
2	Paul	2
3	Mary	3
4	John	3
5	Sam	3
6	Mark	2
7	Winifred	5
8	Bill	6
		= 26 days

NETWORK MODELS

There are a variety of different network models, including critical path and PERT models (Figure 5.4). Here we will consider a simple type of network.

One particular market research study comprises ten activities, which have the following durations and precedences (see Table on page 134).

The task is to determine the minimum time that the project would take to complete. This is calculated to be:

A B E G I L   3 + 4 + 2 + 7 + 3 + 2 = 21 days

The minimum time of 21 days represents the critical path. To shorten the time to complete the project, an element on this route, or path, has to be shortened. It would be no use shortening C, D or K, for instance.

Activity	Duration (days)	Immediately preceding activities
A	3	
B	4	A
C	5	A
D	6	A
E	2	B
F	1	B
G	7	E
H	4	F
I	3	G, H
J	5	G, H, C, and D
K	6	D
L	2	I, J and K

NB: activities D, G and H must be completed prior to the commencement of J.

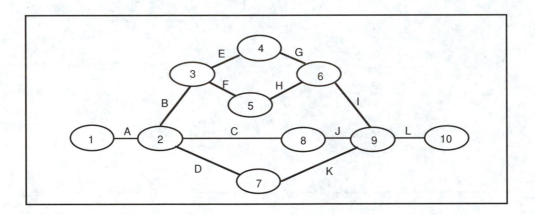

Figure 5.4   Network model.

DECISION TREES

Decision trees evaluate the expected pay-off of different alternatives. The PERT diagram shown in Figure 5.5 is a very simple one; much more complex ones can be built. The expected pay-off of the various alternatives are calculated and evaluated.

A marketing manager is deciding among a number of alternatives:

1. Undertake a promotional campaign that has a probability of 0.4 of making a £5m. profit if it is successful, and a probability of 0.6 of losing £1m. if it is unsuccessful.

2. Cut prices temporarily and stimulate market share. This would generate an additional £1.5m.

3. Do nothing for the present, so that there will be neither a gain nor a loss.

Which of these alternatives should be chosen?

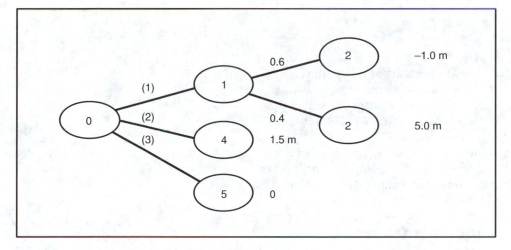

Figure 5.5 The decision tree for the problem.

The expected values of the three alternatives are:

1. $(0.6 \times -1.0) + (0.4 \times 5.0) = £1.4m$

2. £1.5m.

3. £0

Alternative 2 is therefore the best.

INVENTORY MODELS

Inventory models are concerned with deciding on the optimum level of stocks to maintain, the frequency with which to place orders and the quantities to purchase. The principal objective of developing inventory models is to minimize the total cost of the inventory system. The total inventory cost is the sum of total ordering costs and shortage costs. Ordering costs refer to the costs connected with placing orders and receiving inventory (salaries in purchasing and accounting departments, wages in the receiving area, etc.). Carrying costs are the costs associated with storage and are usually associated with warehouse rent and fuel costs, etc. Shortages are the costs associated with a lost sale and loss of customer goodwill.

Inventory models can be quite complex and take into account such things as quantity discounts, backorders and economic lot sizes. The model which is perhaps best known, and certainly the simplest, is the economic order quantity (EOQ) model, which aims to determine the optimum order quantity. It assumes deterministic demand, constant rate of demand, instantaneous replenishment of inventory, constant inventory costs and no shortages. The algorithm used is

$$Q^* = \sqrt{(2DC_0/C_h)}$$

where

Q^* = optimum order quantity
D = annual demand in units
C_h = holding cost per unit per year
C_0 = ordering cost per order.

However, the basic EOQ model may be unsuitable for many real world situations where the basic assumptions of the model do not apply. Further refinements to the model can enable these difficulties to be overcome.

QUEUING THEORY

Queues occur because facilities are unable to meet the demand for the service they have been set up to provide. The usual purpose of applying queuing theory models or techniques is to facilitate the identification of an adequate but not too liberal service facility. If the service provision is too generous then the service facility will often be idle and incur unnecessary costs – e.g. idle employees. On the other hand, where excessive waiting time exists because the facility is inadequate, customer dissatisfaction can occur and a loss of important goodwill ensue. The aim of these techniques is to establish the economic equilibrium between the cost of the service and the cost associated with possible loss of goodwill.

Solutions to queuing problems may be determined by algorithm. However, the situations in which they occur are complex and it is often preferable to use simulation methods (see below) to derive a solution.

MARKOV ANALYSIS

Markov analysis has been restricted in the main to brand switching behaviour and the impact it has had on market share.

For example consumer studies indicate the following probabilities that a person will buy a particular brand of soap, given that they purchased a specific brand on the previous occasion.

Transition matrix:

	Next purchase		
	Arnold's brand	Beryl's brand	Celia's brand
Last purchase			
Arnold's brand	0.6	0.3	0.1
Beryl's brand	0.2	0.7	0.1
Celia's brand	0.1	0.2	0.7

The current market shares of the brands are as follows:

Arnold's	30 %
Beryl's	40 %
Celia's	30 %

The task is to estimate the long run market share positions, given that the brand-switching probabilities remain constant.
   The solution is:

A	=	0.2917
B	=	0.4583
C	=	0.25

The main limitation of the model is the assumption of a stationary transition matrix.

SIMULATION

Simulations involve constructing simplified models of reality. The idea behind simulation is to find a satisfactory or close to best solution to a problem. Simulation does not employ an optimization algorithm, but simply portrays the performance of a particular system, given a set of input parameters. It is customary for simulation to be employed as a problem-solving technique when the problem under study is too complex to be treated by optimization techniques. In this latter respect a problem may be judged to be too complex when it either cannot be expressed mathematically, or the formulation is too involved for economic or practical purposes.
   Computer simulation can be of enormous benefit to a business. For instance, the Exxon Corporation developed a model of gasoline supply at a refinery which

was used to control the inventories of several blends of gasoline and to maximize storage tank utilization. Savings resulting from not building an additional storage tank amounted to $1.4 million (Golovin, 1979). In another instance a corporate simulation model was developed for Canterbury Timber Products Ltd to improve planning for domestic and export operations. The resultant ability to explore more alternatives with the model resulted in savings in direct and opportunity costs of at least $10 000 per annum (de Kluyver and McNully, 1980).

Simulation has been widely used by practitioners because of the degree of realism that can be included in simulation models, and the ease with which such models can be explained to non-technical decision makers (Hoover and Perry, 1989). In comparison with analytic techniques such as queuing theory, simulation models do not require the stringent assumptions that are necessary for tractable solutions. The logic and mathematical relationships are generally more easily understood.

Since simulation models the expected behaviour of a system, the model has to be built from the perspective of the executive who is studying the system. The executive can then experiment with different factors and with different scenarios to determine which give the most satisfactory results. The executive is experimenting with a model, rather than interfering with a system in order to understand the behaviour of that system.

The technique of simulation consists of taking random samples from the probability distribution that represents the real-world system under study. Many real world phenomena are 'normally' distributed, and so in many instances probability estimates using the normal curve can often be employed. In the case of queues, however, other kinds of distributions may be more appropriate – e.g. a uniform distribution or a random distribution – and one has first to establish how the events are distributed in reality. The inputs to the model consist of the observed values and the probabilities associated with each event.

Recent developments in software for desktop and laptop computers have made it possible for simulations to be developed with comparative ease. One such software package is MicroSaint, by Rapid Data Ltd of Worthing. Illustrations of its use can be found in Proctor (1994a, pp.50–5; 1994b, pp.18–23).

GAME THEORY

Game theory has been found to be useful when considering marketing strategy problems. It helps to determine the best strategy that competing firms can adopt. Games can be constructed for any number of 'players'; the simplest to undertand is the two-person game.

For example assume that two firms are competing for a market share of the sales for a particular product. Each firm is considering what promotional strategy to employ for the coming sales period. Assume also that the following pay-off matrix describes the increase in market share for firm A, and the decrease in market share for firm B. Questions to answer are:

- What would be the optimal strategy for each firm?
- Which firm would be the winner in terms of market share?
- Would the solution strategies necessarily maximize profit for either of the firms?
- If not, what might the two firms do to maximize joint profits?

	Strategies	Firm B		
		None	Moderate Promotion	Extensive
Firm A	None	5.00	0.00	−10.00
	Moderate	10.00	6.00	2.00
	Extensive	20.00	15.00	10.00

Solution:

Pay-off table:

Firm A

Strategies	None	Moderate	Extensive	Min row value
None	5.00	0.00	−10.00	−10.00
Moderate	10.00	6.00	2.00	2.00
Extensive	20.00	15.00	10.00	10.00*
Max column value	20.00	15.00	10.00*	

The row and column asterisked shows this game has a saddle-point (provides a solution) at value 10.0. This indicates the following optimal strategies for each firm to adopt, assuming no collusion and adoption of the minimax criterion.

A's strategy   = extensive

B's strategy   = extensive

The solution to the problem shows that both firms should undertake extensive promotion and that firm A will be the winner. However, the solution strategy will not maximize profits for either firm. To maximize profits, the frms need to collude.

STATISTICAL TOOLS AND DECISION SUPPORT

FACTOR ANALYSIS

Factor analysis is a generic name given to a class of multivariate statistical methods whose primary purpose is data reduction and summarization. Broadly speaking, it addresses the problem of analysing the interrelationships among a large number of variables and then explaining these variables in terms of their common underlying dimensions (factors). For example, a hypothetical survey questionnaire may consist of 100 questions, but since not all the questions are identical, they do not all measure the basic underlying dimensions to the same extent. By using factor analysis, the analyst can identify the separate dimensions being measured by the survey and determine a factor loading for each variable on each factor.

Factor analysis may be used to discover a set of dimensions that underlie or underpin a set of variables. Applications for factor analysis include:

- uncovering the factors which influence advertising readership

- ascertaining what personal characteristics are associated with preferring one brand of product to another

- uncovering the important dimensions of product/service quality

- uncovering factors which need to be taken into account in making decisions about such things as product design and promotion, etc.

When evaluating consumer views on a new toothpaste, for example, the impression of 'physical appearance of the toothpaste' might be measured by asking people to rate different toothpastes on attributes such as taste and colour. 'Medicinal properties' might be reflected in such attributes as 'prevents tooth decay' and 'prevents bad breath'. Attributes measure a slightly different aspect of the toothpaste's profile on a five point scale, where 5 denotes the definite presence of the perceived characteristic and 1 denotes little trace of it. The responses of six people might be as follows.

Respondent	Taste	Colour	Prevents tooth decay	Prevents bad breath
Tony	5	4	2	1
Roy	4	3	2	1
Bill	4	3	3	2
Janet	5	5	2	2
Jane	4	3	2	1
Anne	5	5	3	2

A factor is a weighted summary score of a set of related variables. For example, we could average 'taste' and 'colour' to produce a score for each person for 'physical appearance of the toothpaste' and then average 'prevents tooth decay' and 'prevents bad breath' to produce a score for 'medicinal properties':

Respondent	Physical appearance	Medicinal properties
Tony	4.5	1.5
Roy	3.5	1.5
Bill	3.5	2.5
Janet	5	2
Jane	3.5	1.5
Anne	5	2.5

The original four variables have now been supplanted by two factors, and the simple rule of averaging the relevant variables, or weighting each relevant pair of variables by 0.5 and the other pair by 0, has been used to produce the two factors. Namely:

• physical appearance = 0.5 taste + 0.5 colour + 0 prevents tooth decay + 0 prevents bad breath

• medicinal properties = 0 taste + 0 colour + 0.5 prevents tooth decay + 0.5 prevents bad breath.

This is essentially what is done when conducting a factor analysis, only we do not use such a simple rule as 'equal weighting' of the relevant variables. The weights to give to each of the variables in order to produce a weighted summary score have to be derived statistically.

In the above example using factor analysis we can produce two factors, which we can label as above, and where the factors are actually:

• physical appearance = 0.4 taste + 0.3 colour + 0.02 prevents tooth decay + 0.05 prevents bad breath

• medicinal properties = 0.01 taste + 0.04 colour + 0.45 prevents tooth decay + 0.37 prevents bad breath.

It should be noted that in the first equation the coefficients for taste and colour (0.4 and 0.3) are large, indicating these variables contribute significantly to the variation on the first factor (physical appearance). In addition, because taste has the larger coefficient, we could interpret this to mean that redesign expenditure which enhances consumer perceptions of physical appearance is likely to be more effective in terms of taste – assuming equivalent expenditure.

'Factor scores' can also be calculated for each subject. For example, in the case of Tony:

• physical appearance = $0.4 \times 5 + 0.3 \times 4 + 0.02 \times 2 + 0.05 \times 1 = 3.29$

• medicinal properties = $0.01 \times 5 + 0.04 \times 4 + 0.45 \times 2 + 0.37 \times 1 = 1.48$.

Scores for all six individuals can be plotted on a grid, as shown below.

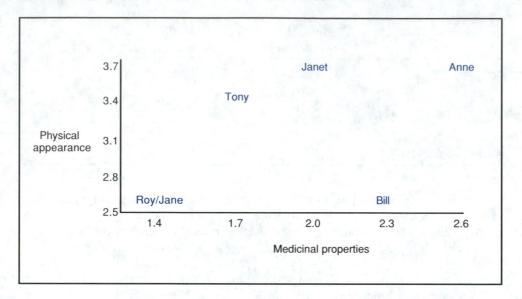

Figure 5.6

From the graph, we can see that Roy and Jane are not overly concerned about physical appearance or medicinal properties, whereas Anne is very concerned about both of these factors. Bill, on the other hand is concerned about medicinal properties, but not too concerned about physical appearance. On a sample size of 6, as is the case here, this information is not particularly valuable. However, on large sample data, the preferences of large clusters of individuals can be assessed.

The nature of the factors (that is, the names which we can attach to them) can be determined by examining the 'factor loadings'. Factor loadings are determined by calculating the correlation between each of the factors and each of the original rating variables. Each correlation coefficient represents the loading of the associated variable on the particular factor. In this case:

Variable	Physical appearance	Medicinal properties
Taste	0.85	0.10
Colour	0.76	0.06
Prevents tooth decay	0.06	0.89
Prevents bad breath	0.04	0.79

Variables which have a high loading on the factor serve to define it.

CLUSTER ANALYSIS

Cluster analysis is the name for a group of multivariate techniques whose primary purpose is to identify similar entities from the characteristics they possess. They identify and classify objects or variables, so that each object is very similar to the others in the cluster with respect to some predetermined selection criterion. Cluster analysis examines similarities between observations of subjects based on profiles of their scores on a number of measured characteristics. Applications include:

- determining the number and composition of market segments

- facilitating the selection of test markets

- identifying groups of people with common purchasing interests in segmentation studies – this helps to identify target markets and provides information for establishing product positioning and developing promotional themes.

For example, a panel of journalists has rated seven newspapers on various aspects. The ratings were made on a ten-point scale and an average rating obtained in each case.

Newspaper average ratings by journalists on selected aspects of seven newspapers:

	Guardian	Independent	Telegraph	Times	Financial Times	Mail	Express
Front page	8	7	6	6	6	7	8
Home news	8	6	7	6	4	5	6
Foreign news	7	8	8	7	8	5	5
Lead pages	6	6	6	5	6	6	5
Features	8	8	8	6	8	7	7
Books, art	8	8	8	6	8	3	3
Business	6	7	8	8	10	6	6
Sport	9	8	8	8	3	8	7
Photographs	9	8	5	7	3	7	6
Design	8	9	6	6	5	6	7

Using cluster analysis, the objective is to ascertain which newspapers appear to form clusters in terms of their similarities. There are various ways of conducting a cluster analysis, and readers interested in understanding more about this subject should consult a text such as Multivariate Statistical Methods, (Manly, 1993). In this case, the analysis was carried out using the squared Euclidean distance between all pairs of items in the table above, using the minimum variance method, and inputting the data in random order. The following results were obtained.

Node	Group 1	Number of objects Group 2	Sum of squares	In fused group
1	Express	Mail	3.000	2
2	Guardian	Independent	5.000	2
3	Telegraph	Times	7.500	2
4	Node 3	Node 2	19.750	4
5	Node 1	Node 4	42.917	6
6	Node 5	Financial Times	58.119	7

Dendrogram:

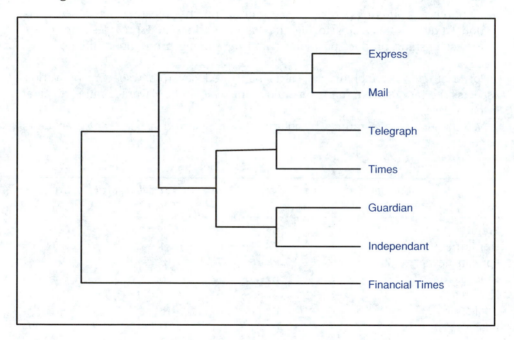

Figure 5.7

From the dendrogram, above, we can see that the *Express* and the *Mail* were perceived to be similar. The *Telegraph* and the *Times* clustered together, as also did the *Guardian* and the *Independent*. At a higher level of clustering, the *Express* and the *Mail* were clustered independently of the *Telegraph*, *Times*, *Guardian* and *Independent* while the *Financial Times* appeared on its own.

CONJOINT ANALYSIS

Conjoint analysis is a method of portraying consumers' decisions realistically as a trade-off among multi-attribute products or services. Conjoint analysis helps us to understand how people develop preferences for products or services and is based on the simple notion that consumers evaluate the utility or value of something by combining the separate amounts of utility provided by each attribute.

It is closely related to traditional experimentation. In situations where people are involved, we often need to conduct experiments with factors that we can control. For example, should a chocolate bar be slightly or very sweet to the taste? Should it be promoted as a weight-watcher's product or not? What price should be asked for the product?

In conjoint analysis the use of experimental design in the analysis of consumer decisions has two objectives. In the first instance, experiments may try to assess how the sweetness of the chocolate bar contributes to the willingness of the consumer to buy the bar. It may also seek to assess how much change in the willingness to buy can be accounted for by differences between the levels of sweetness. In the second instance the experiments may seek to establish a valid model of consumer judgements that is useful in predicting the consumer acceptance of any combination of attributes, even those not originally evaluated by the consumer.

MULTIDIMENSIONAL SCALING AND PERCEPTUAL MAPPING

It is easier to understand relationships between facts, events or objects if we can visualize these relationships spatially. There are a number of techniques which go under the heading of multidimensional scaling and perceptual mapping techniques which enable us to do exactly that. They allow us to see visually how products and services are perceived in relationship to one another by users. There are a variety of perceptual mapping programs and techniques designed to work with different kinds of data.

MDPREF

This is a mapping device which involves products being rated against a list of attributes. The average scores obtained for products against each attribute are then used as a basis for producing a map. For example:

A   Fruity flavour . . . . Non-fruity flavour
B   Low carbonation . . . . High carbonation
.
.
.
H   Not a Pick-me-up . . . . A Pick me up

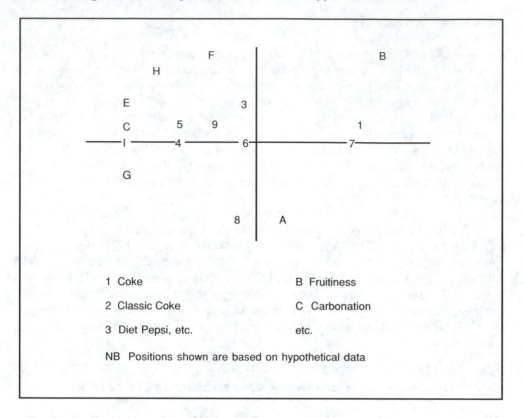

Figure 5.8 Brand maps produced by using MDPREF.

Products and ratings

	Coke	Coke Classic	7Up
A	5.79	6.49	2.86
B	3.42	3.90	3.90
.			
.			
H	3.07	2.72	4.16

MDPREF produces a map of the brands and the attributes (see above). NB Values shown are based on hypothetical data.

KYST

KYST works with data which have been rank ordered. For example, a list of 45 pairs of soft drinks is ranked in terms of similarity, from the most similar to the least similar. The number 1 is assigned to the pair that is the most similar, 2 to the next most similar pair, and so forth, until the highest value is assigned to the least similar pair.

	Rank
Coke – Coke Classic	_____
Coke – Diet Pepsi	_____
.	
.	
.	
Coke Classic – Diet Pepsi	_____
.	
.	
.	
Tab – 7Up	_____

The order of similarities between pairs of drinks is then ranked (see page 148).

Where more than one person makes a rating, which is usually the case, the diagonal matrix is redrawn to show average rankings. The lowest average ranking is then redesignated '1', and so on.

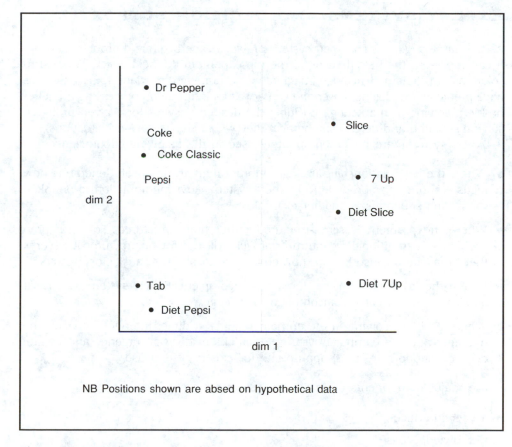

Figure 5.9 Brand map produced by using KYST.

	P	C	CC	etc.
Pepsi				
Coke	1			
Coke Classic	3	2		
Diet Pepsi	7	9	8	
Diet Slice	27	28	32	
Diet 7Up	41	42	43	
.				
.				
.				
Tab	12	11	10	

Dimension 1 = Cola flavour   Dimension 2 = Dietness

KYST can also be used in conjunction with with another mapping device, PREFMAP, to show how products are perceived with respect to 'ideal points'.

EXPERT SYSTEMS AND DECISION SUPPORT

As the name suggests, an expert system provides expertise to aid problem solving. It can represent the best thinking of the top experts in the field which can lead to solutions to problems which are imaginative, accurate and efficient. Expert systems have predictive modelling power and can act as an information processing model of problem solving in marketing, providing the desired answers for a given problem-solving situation and demonstrating how they would change for new situations.

Expert systems are most appropriately used in the following circumstances.

● Where the key relationships are logical rather than arithmetical. Generating new ideas is more appropriate for an expert system. Advising on action to be taken in specific situations is another example.

● Where the problem is semi-structured rather than structured. For structured problems, a traditional algorithm approach will do; for unstructured problems there may be an insufficient knowledge base to provide satisfactory results.

● Where the knowledge in the domain is incomplete. Expert systems are most applicable in domains of incomplete knowledge.

● Where problem solving in the domain requires a direct interface between the manager and the computer system. Situations of decision urgency and on-line decision support are most appropriate for expert system use.

The major components of an expert system are:

● a user interface
● a knowledge base
● an inference engine.

The knowledge base includes the definitions of the objects and variables in the system, including data, assumptions, production rules (if–then statements), heuristics and models. The inference engine manipulates the elements in the knowledge base and combines it with information from the user to solve a particular problem.

Expert systems can be used for a variety of purposes. These include:

- **interpretation** – inferring situation descriptions from sensor data. This is useful in observational market research studies

- **prediction** – inferring likely consequences of given situations. This is useful in forecasting

- **planning** – designing actions. Campaign planning or even marketing planning areas of application

- **diagnosis and monitoring** – inferring system malfunctions from observables. This is useful in the context of marketing control, monitoring performance against targets or budgets set

- **debugging** – prescribing remedies for malfunctions, recommending contingency action when plans are not achieved

- **design** – configuring objects under constraints. Product design is an area where expert systems can be applied

- **repair** – putting contingency plans into action.

Given the wide array of applications for expert systems in marketing, it is not appropriate to discuss or illustrate expert systems in the generic sense. However, there are different commercial packages available which suit specific purposes. A good example is that provided by project management systems software which incorporates an applications generator capable of facilitating the production of a marketing plan – e.g. Time Line, by Symantec Corporation of California.

SUMMARY

Marketing information systems exist to help marketing managers get to grips with the volumes of data with which they are constantly bombarded. The marketing information system provides management with a variety of reports to aid its decision making.

Marketing planning requires the size of current and potential markets to be carefully measured and estimated. There are several approaches to forecasting. Some methods rely on asking questions of people, while others involve the statistical analysis of historical data.

An indication and examples of how management science/operational research techniques and tools can be applied to marketing problems is given. Methods considered included linear programming, transportation models, assignment models, network models, decision trees, inventory models, queuing theory, Markov analysis, simulation and game theory.

Consideration is also given to factor analysis, cluster analysis and conjoint analysis, and how they may be used on marketing problems. Perceptual mapping techniques as means of portraying customers' views and attitudes towards products and services are also considered.

A growing area of interest and importance in the area of decision support systems is expert systems. There are numerous opportunities for the implementation of expert systems in marketing.

DISCUSSION QUESTIONS

1. How would you define a 'marketing information system'?

2. How does a marketing information system differ from marketing research?

3. What are marketing decision support mechanisms and how do they relate to the marketing information system?

4. Indicate the various ways in which sales management can make use of a marketing information system.

5. Why is it important to be able to measure the size of current and future markets?

6. What are the various levels at which market demand may be measured?

7. When forecasting future demand for products or services what should be the nature of the basic approach?

8. Under what circumstances might it be appropriate to undertake a survey of buyers' intentions in order to establish the nature of demand for a product?

9. When might expert opinion be an appropriate forecasting method?

10. Time series analysis is a method of statistical forecasting. What are the four components of a time series?

11. Multiple regression analysis is one of several ways of forecasting with the aid of time series analysis. Explain the principles involved in applying multiple regression analysis to time series forecasting.

12. Under what circumstances might exponential smoothing be a useful way of forecasting demand?

13. Statistical demand analysis employs multiple regression analysis to explain variations in demand for a product or service. How might it be used to forecast future demand?

14. Explain the principles involved in using epidemic models for forecasting the demand for new products.

15. How might one forecast the sales of a new product through multiple retail outlets?

16. Indicate the kinds of marketing problems to which the following might usefully be applied:
    (a) linear programming
    (b) transportation models
    (c) assignment models
    (d) network models
    (e) decision trees
    (f) inventory models
    (g) queuing theory
    (h) Markov analysis
    (i) simulation
    (j) game theory.

17. How can factor analysis enable marketing management to identify ways of improving a firm's competitive edge in the market?

18. Cluster analysis has several applications in marketing. Discuss some of these applications.

19. What is the purpose of conjoint analysis?

20. What do you think is the prime purpose of multidimensional scaling as applied to marketing problems?

21. There is a variety of multidimensional scaling techniques. How do they differ from one another?

22. Suggest potential applications for expert systems in marketing management.

REFERENCES

Bass, F. (1969) A new product growth model for consumer durables, *Management Science*, **15** (January), 215–27.

de Kluyver, C.A. and McNully, G.M. (1980) Corporate planning using simulation, *Interface*, **10**(3).

Golovin, L. (1979) Product blending: a simulation case study in double time, *Interface*, **9**(5).

Hoover, S.V. and Perry, R.F. (1989) *Simulation: A Problem Solving Approach*, Addison-Wesley, New York.

Kotler, P. (1988) *Marketing Management: Planning, Analysis and Control*, 6th edn, Prentice-Hall.

Kotler, P. and Lilien, G. (1983) *Marketing Decision Making: a Model Building Approach*, Harper & Row, New York.

Proctor, R.A. (1994a) Queues and the power of simulation in helping with business decisions and problems. *Management Decision*, 32(1), 50–5.

Proctor R.A. (1994b) Simulation in management services. *Management Services*, **38**(1), 18–23.

FURTHER READING

Attaran, M. (1992) *MSIS: Management Science Information Systems*, John Wiley, New York (includes a disk on which there are various management science tools, including a simulation program).

Burch, J. and Grudnitski, G. (1989) *Information Systems: Theory And Practice*, Wiley, New York.

Clarke, D.G. (1993) *Marketing Analysis and Decision Making*, The Scientific Press.

Emory, C.W. and Cooper, D.R. (1991) *Business Research Methods*, Irwin, Chicago, Ill.

Erikson, W.J. and Hall, O.P. (1989) *Computer Models for Management Science*, Addison Wesley, New York.

Green, P.E., Carmone, F.J. and Smith, S.M. (1989) *Multidimensional Scaling*, Allyn and Bacon, Needham Heights, Mass.

Hair, J.F, Anderson, R.E., Tatham, R.L. and Black, C.W. (1992) *Multivariate Data Analysis*, Macmillan, New York.

Little, J.D. (1979) Decision support systems for marketing managers, *Journal of Marketing*, **43**(3), 9–27.

Manly, B.F.J. (1993) *Multivariate Statistical Methods*, Chapman & Hall, London.

Markland, R.E. (1983) *Topics in Management Science*, Wiley, New York.

Watson, H.J. and Blackstone, J.H. (1989) *Computer Simulation*, Wiley, New York.

CASE PROBLEM 5.1

WILLIAM BRIGHT: MARKETING INFORMATION SYSTEMS

William Bright and Sons (Battery Manufacturers) are considering ways in which they can improve the quality of their marketing information system. The company is particularly interested in developing a decision support system and is wondering what use it might make of sophisticated fore-casting models, management science models, multivariate analytical methods such as factor and cluster analysis, and multidimensional scaling techniques.

The company manufactures and markets a wide range of electrical storage batteries for motorcars, trucks, lorries, vans and fork lift trucks. While the firm is profitable and does not face any particular serious short-term marketing crises, there are a number of questions to which it is trying to find answers. These include:

1. How can it improve the accuracy of its sales forecasts? Currently it uses salesmen's estimates; these often turn out to be widely inaccu-rate and in addition the company feels that its sales people tend to underestimate what the company can really sell.

2. How can the firm determine how its products are perceived by customers in relationship to competitors' products?

3. How can the marketing manager uncover the important dimensions of product/service quality in the firm's product-market offering?

4. How can the firm identify profitable market segments which it does not currently serve?

QUESTION

1. What advice would you offer the firm?

CASE PROBLEM 5.2

UMBRIA COMPANY: SALES FORECASTING

The Umbria Company markets a range of rainwear products, including gents' umbrellas. Industry sales for gents' umbrellas over the past years, along with disposable income, industry advertising expenditure and annual rainfall, are shown below.

Year	Industry sales (£'000)	Disposable income (£ '000 000)	Advert (£'000)	Rain (inches)
1979	361.00	10 291.00	1.04	30.60
1980	400.00	10 463.00	1.05	32.40
1981	431.00	10 674.00	1.03	34.10
1982	350.00	10 972.00	1.00	29.60
1983	614.00	11 573.00	1.21	39.70
1984	453.00	12 417.00	0.97	32.00
1985	597.00	13 001.00	1.20	37.80
1986	312.00	13 561.00	0.87	29.10
1987	307.00	13 972.00	0.79	26.80
1988	797.00	14 635.00	1.32	38.20
1989	890.00	15 239.00	1.37	40.20
1990	927.00	16 008.00	1.43	39.60
1991	720.00	16 541.00	1.01	31.70
1992	645.00	17 417.00	0.82	32.10
1993	841.00	17 908.00	1.00	31.70
1994	925.00	18 246.00	1.16	32.30

QUESTION

1. Assuming disposable income were to rise by 2% in 1995, what would be your best estimate of industry sales?

Hint: use the regression feature in Lotus 123, Aseasyas, or some other spreadsheet to help with the calculations.

6 MARKETING RESEARCH

This chapter examines the kinds of questions marketing research seeks to answer, indicating the sources of information which marketing researchers can consult. The research methods marketing researchers can employ are examined, and particular attention is given to how a survey might be conducted. Consideration is given to how a sampling plan is drawn up, how a simple questionnaire for use in a survey is put together, and the main ways of analysing data.

OBJECTIVES

After studying this chapter you should be able to:

- know to what kinds of questions marketing research seeks answers
- describe the sources of information which marketing researchers can consult
- understand what kind of research methods marketing researchers can employ
- describe the research process
- be able to describe how a sampling plan is drawn up and be conversant with different methods of probability and non-probability sampling methods
- be able to put together a simple questionnaire for use in a survey and understand how to conduct a survey
- explain the main ways of analysing data collected from sample data.

INTRODUCTION

Firms undertake marketing research to try to identify why people buy or do not buy products and services. It also provides information for making marketing mix decisions (pricing, product, distribution and promotion).

Research can be undertaken both in-house and by specialist marketing research companies. Where the latter are involved, research can be tailor-made to a client's requirements or bought 'off the peg', if a suitable omnibus research report is available. There is a variety of other sources which provide useful research data to companies. These include trade associations and government departments.

The research process involves:

- problem definition

- consulting company records and published data sources

- deciding whether field-work is required and, if so, what is the best research method

- specifying the location and size/type of sample

- collecting the data

- analysing the data

- evaluating the results

- setting down recommendations for action.

Various research methods are used in marketing research, including surveys, experiments and observational methods. Since virtually all research involves working with sample data, a key aspect of research concerns how the sample is drawn from the population. Quota sampling and simple random sampling methods are widely used in practice.

The bulk of marketing research that is carried out relies very much on survey methods. Questionnaire design and analysis along with sampling are key aspects of survey methods; they are given attention in this chapter.

There are costs and risks involved in undertaking research. These implications have to be fully appreciated before entering into research.

NATURE OF MARKETING RESEARCH

Information plays an important role in helping firms to make decisions. In the previous chapter we showed how marketing information systems and decision support mechanisms help in the process. In this chapter we will look at the role of marketing research.

A firm undertakes marketing research to uncover facts about both buyers and non-buyers of its products. This involves ascertaining the nature of wants and needs and assessing the current and potential demand for products and services. Information can help to reduce the element of uncertainty and guesswork in making marketing decisions. For instance, information on income levels and customer perceptions of a fair price can be used to advantage in setting prices.

Peter Chisnall (1991) has identified the main divisions of marketing research as follows.

- **Product research** – concerned with the design, development and testing of new products; the improvement of existing products and the prediction of trends in consumer preferences related to styling, product performance, quality of materials and so on.

- **Customer research** – covering such matters as buyer behaviour in relationship to social, economic and cultural factors.

- **Sales research** – examining the selling activities of a company, usually by sales outlets, territories, agencies and so on.

- **Promotion research** – concerned with testing and evaluating the effectiveness of the various methods used in promoting a company's products or services. This includes such things as exhibitions, public relation campaigns, merchandising, consumer and trade advertising, etc.

Many firms undertake their own marketing research, but there are also specialist consulting firms that undertake to collect and provide information, for a fee. This is particularly useful for small firms that do not have their own market researchers. There are also specialist market research firms that concentrate on specific aspects of marketing, such as branding or packaging. Even where firms do have market research departments, they can still benefit from the specialized service offered by such companies. In addition there are market research companies that collect trade or consumer data to sell to client companies on a fee-subscription basis.

INFORMATION SOURCES

There are many sources of information, but they tend to fall under two headings: information that the firm already has itself in company records, and information that it can obtain from outside sources.

COMPANY RECORDS

Firms have enormous amounts of useful marketing information filed away in their internal company records. These include customer sales records, salespersons' reports, and correspondence with individual customers. In addition there are the company's own sales statistics and competitive information gleaned from a variety of sources.

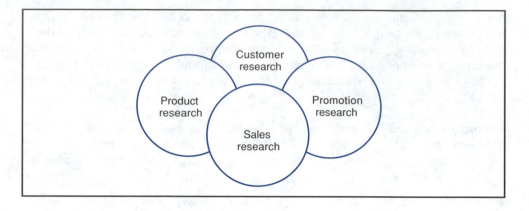

Figure 6.1 Types of marketing research.

OUTSIDE SOURCES OF INFORMATION

There are many different outside sources of information. Sources include trade associations, which produce reports, surveys and other statistics for member companies. Independently published reports and surveys on specific markets are also produced, by organizations such as Mintel and the Economist Intelligence Unit. Other sources of useful information include government statistics (census data, family expenditure surveys, national income statistics, etc.) and company reports and accounts produced by competitors. The latter can provide detailed information about competitors' future strategies and plans, and can be obtained from Companies House in London, Cardiff, Edinburgh or Belfast.

MARKETING RESEARCH SERVICES

There are firms, both large and small, of management consultants which offer their services to firms. They help with strategy formulation and also give advice on marketing problems. Such firms will readily undertake market surveys to measure consumer attitudes or to identify consumer wants and needs. In addition, because of the wealth of knowledge that they have accumulated, they are able to offer expert advice on marketing strategy.

There are also many marketing research companies located in different parts of the UK. One of the staple offerings of such firms is to undertake market surveys and appraise marketing opportunities. These companies undertake research on behalf of clients and also carry out omnibus surveys. The latter extend to cover a wide range of products and services and probe into people's attitudes and opinions about particular and other related matters. Information obtained in these surveys is sold to client companies on request. Omnibus surveys contain both relevant and irrelevant information as far as client companies are concerned. This means that although they are comparatively cheap to obtain their value is somewhat limited. Specific surveys relating to a company's products and those of

CASE EXAMPLE

NFO: MAIL PANELS

Mail panels are becoming more popular. NFO, the leading mail panel company in the USA, carries out over 2000 projects a year for more than 400 clients, using a panel of some 425 000 households. NFO argues that two major factors are contributing to their growing success:

- companies are starting to focus on smaller market segments, to provide selected products for targeted customers
- consumers are becoming less willing to participate in unsolicited surveys.

The latter trend has been attributed to the growth of dual wage-earner households, a growing preference for leisure time activities, and the ability to screen telephone calls using answering machines.

Taking into consideration growing dangers associated with door-to-door interviewing, these trends seem equally relevant in the UK. Moreover, given the efficiency of using pre-recruited panels, this US development may well be copied in Europe.

(Source: Factor, 1993, p.1)

QUESTIONS

1. What arguments can be put forward for suggesting that 'mail panels' are 'likely to be mirrored in Europe'?

2. Do you think that the days of traditional door-to-door and street corner surveys are numbered? Explain.

its competitors may also be commissioned; here the results are made known only to the clients sponsoring the research. Such surveys are more expensive than omnibus surveys.

Some marketing research firms specialize in collecting data on people's purchasing habits, usually in the form of consumer panel data. Retail audit data, based on continuous sampling of retail stocks, can be bought from market research firms.

Firms collecting data by 'panel' methods retain a group of people for a period of time, and all panel members are asked to keep a diary record of their purchases during this time. This method is preferable to other approaches to gathering longitudinal data, as people experience difficulty in remembering what they have purchased, and when. Panels, of course, do have to be representative of the population they represent and one difficulty in using consumer panels concerns assembling a representative panel and keeping it going. People drop out or even die, and finding a replacement who matches with the lapsed panel member can be difficult.

Audits of Great Britain Ltd have a panel of households which record purchases of packaged grocery, household goods, fresh food and other similar items. The panel is representative of the whole of Great Britain. Data are collected via personal data terminals which read bar codes. The terminals are linked via a modem to the telephone socket and data are polled overnight. In addition to personal data of the panel member, data are obtained on all purchases regarding:

- brand name
- size
- flavour/variety
- actual price paid
- weight of purchase
- quantity bought
- name and address of shop and type of shop.

Other British consumer panels include Nielsen (grocery consumer panel) and Taylor Nelson (family food panel) (Chisnall, 1992). There are also telephone panels who provide public opinion on topics ranging from housing, to violence and vandalism (Chisnall, 1992). There is also a trend towards mail panels.

THE PROCESS OF RESEARCH

Research has to be undertaken in a systematic manner, to ensure that problems are dealt with properly and that nothing is overlooked. The systematic way in which research is undertaken is referred to as the research process, to which there are a number of stages:

- problem definition
- consulting company records and published data sources
- deciding whether fieldwork is required, and if so, what is the best research method
- specifying the location and size/type of sample
- collecting the data
- analysing the data
- evaluating the results
- setting down recommendations for action.

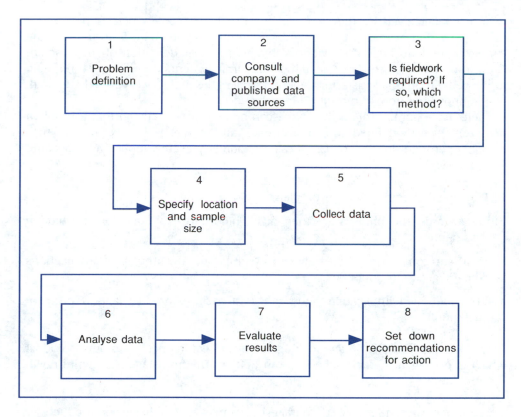

Figure 6.2 Stages in the marketing research process.

PROBLEM DEFINITION

The first stage in the research process is problem definition. This is an initial state-ment of the research objectives. Objectives are usually to provide information on people's:

- opinions
- attitudes
- beliefs
- intentions
- knowledge
- behaviour
- social background.

It is very easy to take the problem given as the one to find answers to. Quite often, however, the problem given masks an even more important problem, or is incorrectly perceived by the owner of the problem. People's perceptions reflect their own vision of reality, but sometimes these perceptions are distorted (see the earlier chapter on buyer behaviour). Obtaining a clear definition of the problem is an important first step in research. An incorrectly defined problem cannot lead to the generation of a satisfactory solution. Unless the problem is correctly defined, one cannot hope to ask the right kind of questions.

There are a number of methods one can apply to try to ensure that a problem has been correctly defined (see, for example, Van Gundy, 1993). An example which is highly pertinent in this context is called 'boundary examination'. The procedure is as follows.

1. An initial statement of the problem is written down.

2. Key words and phrases are then highlighted and examined for any hidden assumptions.

3. Without considering the validity of assumptions, the important implications they suggest are identified.

4. The identified implications are used as a basis to produce a new problem definition.

For example, imagine we are looking at ways of getting people to buy a product which is packaged in cans rather than in bottles. The first stage is to write down the problem:

In what ways might we encourage consumers to purchase our product packaged in cans?

At the next two stages (2–3), boundaries can be examined by considering whether the locus of responsibility might be shifted from the company to the consumer or others; whether consumers might be rewarded rather than just encouraged to purchase the product in cans – or perhaps punished in some way for not buying it in cans. One might also consider whether the focus might better be applied to using rather than buying the product in cans, since the purchasing decision is based more upon use than upon the act of purchasing.

Finally (stage 4) the problem might be redefined as:

How might customers be rewarded for using our product packaged in cans?

CONSULTING COMPANY RECORDS AND PUBLISHED DATA SOURCES

Once an acceptable definition to the problem has been obtained, the next step is to consult published data sources such as company records and previous reports provided by outside bodies and/or information in relevant periodicals. Some of these sources of data may provide answers to all or some of the aspects of the problem which have been identified. In addition, this kind of information can be obtained fairly cheaply.

Usually, one cannot expect to obtain answers to all aspects of a problem in this way, and it is often necessary to undertake field research to find out the specific information one requires. Field research involves finding things out by asking questions, doing experiments, making observations, etc., all of which generates 'primary data'.

Having decided to undertake field research, the next step is to decide whether to commission consultants to undertake the research work, or to undertake the work oneself. Much will depend on the size of the firm and its resources. Small firms usually do not have the resources to conduct their own marketing research.

The research method has also to be decided. From the point of view of the do-it-yourself approach to market research, this will probably mean that a survey of one kind or another will be undertaken. However, as we shall discuss below, there are other ways of obtaining data and it is here again that marketing research companies can be of considerable help.

FIELD RESEARCH

The main methods of conducting marketing field research comprise experimentation, observational methods and surveys.

EXPERIMENTATION

In conducting experiments we can create situations where we can assess the impact of one set of variables on another. We could wait for such events to occur naturally, but in reality this would be impractical. Not only would it take too long for all the naturally occurring conditions to happen but there would be many extraneous events impacting on what we want to examine. The latter would make it difficult to reach any meaningful conclusions.

Experiments are often used in supermarkets and large stores to assess the impact on purchase behaviour of varying amounts of space and shelf positioning given to different brands of goods. Both 'field' and 'laboratory' experiments are used to evaluate the effect of changes in a product or service, its price, type of packaging, distribution method or method of promotion. Field experiments study the effect of changes in these variables on customer reactions. Field experiments are usually carried out with fast moving consumer goods, and take place in selected stores or supermarkets.

One has to ensure that the stores or supermarkets used are representative of the universe of shops or stores with respect to what is being assessed. Certain towns and cities are known to contain populations which reflect national purchasing patterns and districts within these towns and cities have stores which also reflect these patterns. These retail outlets present good sites for field exper-iments. Distorted results, however, can occur if competitors start to undertake heavy promotions in the area. Sometimes competitors may deliberately intensify marketing activities in an area where they know controlled experiments are taking place.

A common field experiment carried out in stores is to assess the effect of varying the shelf space or shelf positioning given to goods. Some parts of a store attract more traffic or attention than others, and goods displayed at eye-level are more likely to be seen than if they are displayed below knee-level.

The difficulties associated with field experiments lead researchers to consider laboratory experiments as an alternative approach. Indeed, there are some kinds of marketing situations where laboratory experimentation represents the only really practical way of studying marketing phenomena. A laboratory experiment is a controlled method of assessing the effect of changes in the marketing mix vari-ables on customers' reactions. It takes place in a laboratory setting – that is, in a hall or room especially acquired by researchers for this purpose. Taste testing of products represents an example of such experiments. This is where subjects are asked to evaluate competitive brands and say which they prefer. Such tests are usually done 'blind' – that is, without the customer knowing the names of the various brands being assessed. Critics of laboratory testing argue that the situation in which participants find themselves is a contrived one, so they will not behave as they normally would.

OBSERVATION

Observation is a powerful research tool and can be effectively employed in many different marketing situations. For example, it may be used when trying to eval-uate the proposed siting of a new shop on a particular street. Simple head-counts of passers-by at different times over a prolonged period will give some idea of the amount of 'traffic' that passes by.

Observation, as a technique, can be applied in either a laboratory or a field research setting. Sometimes it may be difficult to distinguish between an experi-ment and observational research. A good example is where laboratory research is undertaken into advertising. There is a variety of mechanical contrivances that can be fitted to people to measure their reactions to different stimuli (usually advertisements). These include eye cameras, which measure changes in pupil size reflecting reactions to and interest in advertisements.

Traffic counters and television and radio audiometers are other examples of devices used in observation methods. Other methods include store/retail audits, pantry audits and information on brand or stock levels at retail outlets. Observing children's reactions to clothes or toys in shops can provide useful information that would not be available through formal interviews.

Some reported examples include the use of observational techniques by Honda, to research into how people load the boots of their cars. This resulted in a re-design of the Honda Civic hatchback (Skapinker, 1989). Another example is that of the manufacturers of Philips shavers identifying customer needs partly through observing, through a two-way mirror, a recruited sample's typical shaving techniques (Chisnall, 1992).

SURVEYS

A survey facilitates the collection of information from a large number of people. It involves posing a number of questions to people in order to ascertain facts, beliefs, opinions and attitudes from the participants with respect to some predefined object. Surveys can be carried out in person, over the telephone, or by post. The choice of method should pay attention to the type of information required, the amount of information required, and the cost, ease and accuracy of collecting answers to questions.

Technological advance has produced other methods of collecting survey data by electronic means. Respondents are invited to key answers into computer terminals which may be strategically placed in shopping malls.

Surveys can be conducted in person, over the telephone or by post. Each method has its advantages and disadvantages, which we will now examine.

PERSONAL INTERVIEWS

A major advantage of personal interviews is that they provide the opportunity to clarify potential ambiguities and misunderstandings in the questions that are posed. This is a strong point in favour of conducting personal interviews, since ambiguity can be a major problem in questionnaire design. Personal interviews also facilitate the presentation of visual material, which may be essential to the purpose of the research. While response rates to personal interviews tend to be good, and there are clear advantages in using personal interviews, it can be an expensive data collection method. In addition, interviewers can easily introduce personal bias into the recording of answers given by respondents.

All interviewers need to be trained. Personal bias can arise in recording what people say in interviews. This may be reflected in how both the interviewer and the interviewee behave. Interviewers will record their own interpretations of what other respondents say to them and, of course, depending on how a question is phrased a respondent may give a quite different response. Eliminating bias in soliciting and recording answers to questions in personal interviews is very important. Training in the use of a particular questionnaire can be used to standardize the approach adopted and to minimize this kind of error.

From the point of view of cost per respondent, interviews in respondents' homes are particularly expensive, whereas focus group discussions or interviewing in shopping centres tends to be less expensive. Interviewers can, however, aid with explanations, rephrase questions, use visual materials, etc. Nevertheless, the potential for interviewer bias is high and personal interaction between interviewer and interviewees can affect outcomes. On the other hand, the response to complex questions is good. Interviewers can explain and adjust questions to the needs of the situation.

TELEPHONE INTERVIEWS

Some 90% of homes in the UK now have a telephone (*Marketing Pocket Book*, 1993). Telephone interviews would seem therefore to represent a quick and convenient manner of collecting data, enabling a large number of interviews to be conducted in a short period of time, without the interviewer having to travel. The cost per interview is low and the sample can be spread out country-wide. There are, however, a number of drawbacks to using telephone interviews. For instance, only a short questionnaire can be used, in comparison to the personal interview method. The response rates associated with telephone interviews tend also to be lower. The range and type of questions that one can ask are limited. Attitude measurement and rating is not amenable to this form of interview, either.

The cost per respondent tends to be moderate. It includes both interviewers' time and telephone bills, but obviously there are significant savings on travel time and costs. There is only a moderate amount of flexibility to rephrase questions and tailor them to respondents, although there is some scope to explain and present complex issues. The potential for interviewer bias is only moderate, as there is only a limited opportunity for interaction to bias outcomes.

POSTAL SURVEYS

One of the cheapest ways of collecting survey data is by post. A covering letter and a stamped addressed envelope should accompany the questionnaire to encourage completion. It is usual to send a follow-up letter and a duplicate questionnaire, after a period of time has elapsed without a response. The main problem with postal questionnaires is the non-response rate, which typically is much higher than with any other method of inquiry. There are also problems associated with misunderstanding questions that cannot be corrected.

The cost per respondent tends to be low, consisting primarily of printing and postage costs. Flexibility is low and standard questions are required. Bias can arise from the phrasing of questions, and complex questions can be difficult to include.

SAMPLING

Virtually all marketing research makes use of sample data. This is the case irrespective of the method of research. What follows applies in principle to experimental, observational and survey methods. For reasons of convenience we will illustrate sampling in the context of survey research, bearing in mind the foregoing comments about its applicability to other research methods.

SAMPLING PLAN

Surveys aim to find things out about a population. Populations may comprise people or firms. The 'population' for a survey refers to all the persons or companies to which one would like to direct questions. The ideal would be to contact all members of a population and ask them to answer all the questions we wanted to put. If this were practical, it would produce very accurate results. However, only seldom is it possible to contact or gain a response from all the members of a population. The exception is in the case of industrial market research where the population is very small and it may be possible to contact all the firms that make up a particular population.

Large populations are the norm in marketing research and it would be impractical or too expensive to contact all members of such a population. In these cases we have to take a sample from the population – but we must ensure that the sample we choose represents the population as a whole.

There are three decisions to be taken in drawing up a sampling plan.

- **Who is to be surveyed?**   This defines the target population. Once this has been done, the next step is to develop a sampling frame – that is, a way of giving everyone in the target population a known chance of inclusion in the sample.

- **How many people/companies should be surveyed?**   Large samples give better results than smaller ones. However, even samples of less than 1 % of a population can provide good reliable information, if the sampling procedure is sound.

- **How should the samples of respondents be chosen?**

PROBABILITY SAMPLE

Probability samples permit the calculation of confidence limits for sampling error. Thus in taking probability samples one can attach probabilities to any point estimates that one is making. Cost and time often make it impractical to collect data through probability samples.

There are different kinds of probability sample:

- simple random sample

- stratified random sample

- cluster sample.

Simple random sample

In this case all members of the population have a known and equal chance of being included in the sample. For example, the names of every firm in a given population could be written onto slips of paper and the slips deposited in a box. The box could then be shaken so that all the slips of paper were thoroughly mixed up. A blindfolded person drawing successive slips of paper from the box would be taking a random sample of the population.

Simple random sampling works well when one is dealing with relatively small populations. For large scale consumer populations, however, the method is not appropriate since it is difficult to compile a list of all the people in a given population.

Stratified random sample

This approach is more suitable for sampling large consumer populations. It entails dividing the population into mutually exclusive groups and drawing random samples from each group. For example the population might be divided into five groups, A, B, C1, C2, D and E, reflecting the social backgrounds of the people involved. Random samples are then drawn from each group. Again, however, there remains the problem of obtaining suitable lists of people who make up the population and the various groups within it. Stratified sampling may be used in industrial marketing research where it is possible to identify a population of firms. A stratified sample is usually adopted to make sure that minority groups are adequately represented.

Cluster sample

Cluster sampling offers a more practical approach to sampling large consumer populations. Here the population is divided into mutually exclusive groups and the researcher draws a sample of the groups to interview. This time we are not interested in a person's social class but in where he or she lives, or some other characteristic. Assuming that residence is the key factor and that the objective is to interview household heads, then the first step is to divide up the locality under study into individual areas of housing. A random or stratified sample of the areas identified is then taken and interviews are held with every head of household within each area sampled.

This is a 'single stage' cluster sample, since only a sample of the blocks or areas of housing is taken. A 'two stage' cluster sample might involve undertaking the same number of interviews, making sure that a large number of blocks are covered but that only a sample of households in each block is interviewed. For example, if an area comprises three high-rise tower blocks of flats, one might randomly select one of the three blocks and interview all heads of households within that block.

NON-PROBABILITY SAMPLE

Researchers often use non-probability samples, particularly quota samples. Strictly speaking, sampling errors cannot be measured in such cases.

There is a variety of different non-probability sampling methods:

- convenience sample

- judgement sample

- quota sample.

Convenience sample

Here, the researcher takes the most accessible population members from which to obtain information. This happens, for example, when a firm producing a prototype domestic appliance gets some of its employees to test out the product in their own homes. Such a sample provides useful information to the researcher as long as the sample seems to be reasonably representative of the population being studied. However, asking a convenience sample of students about their reading habits might not be appropriate where one is interested in the reading habits of the population as a whole – i.e. all ages, occupations, etc.

Judgement sample

This type of sampling relies on sound judgement or expertise. It depends on selecting elements that are believed to be typical or representative of the population in such a way that errors of judgement in the selection will cancel each other out.

Judgement samples are also sometimes used in market research. They tend to be used more often in industrial market research than in consumer market research. In industrial market research a firm may get 50% of its business from ten large purchasers and the remaining 50% from 300 smaller firms. A judgement sample might therefore comprise five of the large purchasers (50%) and 150 of the remainder (50%). Judgement would be exercised to ensure that the firms chosen in the sample represented the subgrouping.

Quota sample

The first step of quota sampling is to estimate the sizes of the various subclasses or strata in the population. This is usually done through reference to some outside source, for example population census data. The relevant strata to the study have to be specified. For instance, a person's age may be something which a researcher may think is relevant to a particular study. As a consequence, age will have to be taken into account when drawing up the sample – if it is found that in the population, 25% of people are aged between 25 and 30, then the aim should be to make sure that 25% of the people in the sample are in this age band, and similarly that the other age bands reflect the composition of the population under study. Other factors than age might also be considered.

The procedures involved in quota sampling make choice of respondents the responsibility of interviewers. Unfortunately, this can lead to substantial bias which cannot be objectively measured (Yamane, 1967). Wide use has been made of quota sampling in marketing research, since it is relatively cost effective compared with other methods. However, with the development of random sampling techniques, researchers have become more critical of the drawbacks of the method (Chisnall, 1992). Properly applied, the method can be successful because it is possible to introduce representativeness by stratifying the quota sample by objective and known population characteristics such as age, sex, family status, socio-economic group, etc. Quota samples may be accurately constructed using classifications, such as Acorn, which are based on objective distributions of statistical variation in demographic, housing and occupational factors.

SAMPLE SIZE

The size of a sample affects the quality of the research data, and it is not simply a question of applying some arbitrary percentage to a specific population. The sample size that needs to be taken should reflect the basic characteristics of the population, the type of information required and, of course, the costs entailed. The larger the sample size, the greater its precision or reliability, but practical constraints of time, staff and other costs intervene.

When computing the size of a sample, the incidence of non-response should be borne in mind. If, for example, a final sample of 3500 is planned and the non-response rate is estimated at 30%, then it would be advisable to select an original sample of 5000. Such a correction will help to produce the number of responses required, but it will not correct the bias which arises from non-response – i.e. the fact that those who do not respond may have significantly different opinions, etc. from those who do respond.

The error of a sample varies inversely with the square root of the sample size. Thus a sample of 9000 is three times as accurate as a sample of 1000. Hence to treble the accuracy of a sample, its size must be increased ninefold. After a certain sample size has been reached, additional large increases in size do not significantly improve the statistical precision of a given sample. Costs,on the other hand, increase with larger samples.

In the case of random sampling one can fairly easily calculate the size of a sample required in order to achieve data of a stated degree of precision. This involves calculating a confidence coefficient which indicates the specific degree of certainty with which a particular sample estimate can be accepted as a true estimator of the population parameters or values. With simple random samples the formula for calculating sample sizes is as follows:

$$n = ((Z \times \text{s.d.})/E)^2$$

where n =   sample size
   Z =   Z statistic corresponding to the desired confidence level
   s.d. =   the estimated value of the standard deviation of the population parameter, estimated from a pilot survey
   E =   the maximum acceptable magnitude of error

For example, a researcher wants to draw a random sample such that there is a 95% chance that a sample mean of the people's estimates of how much they are likely to buy of a new product would be within 1.0 points of the true mean. A pilot study estimates the s.d. to be of the order of 20.0.

Since the 95% chance equates to a 95% confidence level this can be found in statistical Z tables to equate a value of $1.96 \times Z$.

Thus the required sample size is estimated to be:

$$\sqrt{n} = (1.96 \times 20)/1$$

$$n = 1537$$

DATA COLLECTION

Data collection methods vary according to the method of research adopted. Experiments and observations may have mechanical, computer assisted, or pencil and paper research instruments with which to collect data. The appropriate instruments vary considerably according to the subject of research and the nature of the research. It is easier to generalize about research instruments used in survey research, however, and for this reason we will examine data collection methods primarily pertaining to survey research.

Survey research data are usually collected by means of a questionnaire or interview schedule. Questionnaires are used where the researcher can list and identify specific questions to be posed to the respondents and where also it may be possible to anticipate some of the responses. They are used widely in structured interviews where the researcher knows precisely what information is required. Questionnaire construction and testing is discussed in some depth in the next sections.

Interview schedules are employed when the research is essentially exploratory in nature, or when it is only possible to semi-structure the interview. The interview schedule consists of a list of topics or general headings that the interviewer wants to raise with the interviewee.

QUESTIONNAIRES

Questionnaires must be carefully developed, tested and debugged before administering them. There are many potential errors that can be made when compiling a questionnaire, for example:

- including irrelevant questions – e.g., asking for a person's name and address in a survey where there is no need for such information

- including unanswerable questions – e.g., asking people what they think about products with which they have no familiarity – this may cause the respondent to terminate the completion of the questionnaire

- omitting important questions – e.g., in a survey of purchase intentions with respect to a given product or service, omitting to ask whether the respondents would be likely to buy or otherwise acquire that product or service

- including ambiguous questions – e.g., asking people whether they watch television regularly, without defining 'regularly'.

- including leading or biased questions – asking questions in such a way that there is an implied answer which the respondents are expected to give.

Questions can be open-ended, where the respondent must answer in his or her own way, or closed-ended where all possible answers are pre-specified. Open-ended questions can reveal more information and are often worthwhile during exploratory work when one wants to discover what people think. On the other hand, closed-ended questions are easier to tabulate and interpret.

Figure 6.3 Potential sources of misunderstanding in question phrasing.

The sequencing of questions is important. The earlier questions should attempt to create interest in the respondent. The questions should also follow a logical order, and questions relating to age, salary, etc. should be left to the last.

There is a variety of formats of questions that can be asked.

Closed ended

All possible answers are given with the question.

- **Dichotomous** A question suggesting two answers: usually yes and no.

  Did you buy your hi-fi on credit terms?   Yes ☐   No ☐

- **Multiple choice** Suggests three or more answers.

  Which of the following cities have you visited?

  London ☐   Paris ☐   New York ☐   Lisbon ☐   Munich ☐

  Ankara ☐   Bejing ☐   Dublin ☐

- **Likert scale** These measure attitudes and comprise statements with which the respondent has to agree or disagree

  'Persil washes whiter than white'

Strongly disagree	Disagree	Don't know	Agree	Strongly agree
1 ☐	2 ☐	3 ☐	4 ☐	5 ☐

● **Semantic differential** This, too, assesses people's attitudes and comprises a scale running between two bipolar adjectives. People indicate a point between the two extremes that reflects their own feelings towards a given product, service, etc.

British Airways Flights

Fast	❑	❑	❑	❑	❑	❑	❑	Slow
Comfortable	❑	❑	❑	❑	❑	❑	❑	Cramped
Economical	❑	❑	❑	❑	❑	❑	❑	Expensive

● **Rating scale**

In terms of value for money the Ford Mondeo is:

Excellent	Very good	Good	Fair	Poor
1 ❑	2 ❑	3 ❑	4 ❑	5 ❑

● **Stapel scale**

+5	+5
+4	+4
+3	+3
+2	+2
+1	+1
Helpful	Reliable
−1	−1
−2	−2
−3	−3
−4	−4
−5	−5

Here, respondents are asked to select a plus number for words that they think describe the service (or product) accurately. The more accurate they think the description is, the larger should be the plus number selected. Conversely, they must select a minus number for words which they feel do not describe the service (or product). The less accurate they believe the description to be, the larger should be the minus number selected.

Open-ended

These kind of questions do not suggest an answer. People are allowed to write whatever they wish.

- **Unstructured**

  'What do you think about Fry's Turkish Delight?'

- **Word association**   People are required to respond with the first word that comes to mind when presented with a selection of words:

  prison   ....

  train   ....

  shirt   ....

  tent   ....

  homely   ....

- **Sentence completion** People are required to suggest how a sentence might be completed. It is a mechanism that can be applied when trying to anticipate the reaction to words used in an advertising message or for a brand or company name.

  People who drink Coca Cola are ....

- **Story completion**   People are required to complete an unfinished story.

  Jackie missed the bus and knew she would be late for work. She went into the sweet shop on the high street. NOW COMPLETE THE STORY.

- **Picture completion**   An ambiguous picture is presented to someone in which one character is making a statement, shown in a 'balloon'. Respondents are asked to suggest what the other character may have to say by way of response.

Projective techniques such as sentence, story and picture completion are taken from the domain of Abnormal Psychology. They were devised in the belief that people have various psychological blockages which prevent them from verbalizing their true feelings. The assumption is that normal people, too, experience blockages and that the method is valuable in these circumstances, too.

Example of a postal questionnaire enclosed with the *Journal of Imaginative Marketing*

Reader Survey 1994

We at the *Journal of Imaginative Marketing* would like your help to improve your journal. The questions below will help you to tell us what you think of the magazine and how you would like to see it developed. Please return the completed questionnaire to JIM, Freepost 12324, Manchester M92 2ZZ by 14 July. You do not require a stamp. Thank you.

In answering the questions below, please put a tick in the appropriate box.

1. How often do you read JIM? (Please tick box)

    Every month   Yes ❑ –1
    Once every two months   Yes ❑ –2
    Once every three months   Yes ❑ –3
    Less than once every three months   Yes ❑ –4

2. Do you have any difficulties obtaining a copy of JIM?

    Yes ❑ –1   No ❑ –2

3. How many other people read your copy of JIM?

    None ❑ –1   1 ❑ –2   2 ❑ –3   3–5 ❑ –4   6–8 ❑ –5

    9–11 ❑ –6   12–15 ❑ –7   15+ ❑ –8

4. Some JIM items appear every month – please indicate how often you read them:

		Always	Often	Sometimes	Never
a.	Advertisements	❑ –1	❑ –2	❑ –3	❑ –4
b.	Editorial	❑ –1	❑ –2	❑ –3	❑ –4
c.	Notes on authors	❑ –1	❑ –2	❑ –3	❑ –4
d.	Book reviews	❑ –1	❑ –2	❑ –3	❑ –4

5. How interested were you in articles we published under the following categories in the past year?

		Very	Quite	Mildly	Not
a.	Branding	❑ –1	❑ –2	❑ –3	❑ –4
b.	New products	❑ –1	❑ –2	❑ –3	❑ –4
c.	Advertising	❑ –1	❑ –2	❑ –3	❑ –4
d.	Selling	❑ –1	❑ –2	❑ –3	❑ –4

6. How interested would you be in our publishing articles under the following categories?

		Very	Quite	Mildly	Not
a.	Exporting	❑ –1	❑ –2	❑ –3	❑ –4
b.	Pricing	❑ –1	❑ –2	❑ –3	❑ –4
c.	Selling	❑ –1	❑ –2	❑ –3	❑ –4
d.	Advertising	❑ –1	❑ –2	❑ –3	❑ –4

7. Which article that we published in the last 12 months did you like most?

Could you please supply some details about yourself?

8. Age

Under 25 ❑ –1   25 under 35 ❑ –2   36 under 45 ❑ –3

46 under 55 ❑ –4 56 under 65 ❑ –5   65 and over ❑ –6

9. Gender

Female ❑ –1   Male ❑ –2

10. Are you in full time education?

Yes ❑ –1   No ❑ –2   **If yes, go to question 15**

11. Are you in full time employment?

Yes ❑ –1   No ❑ –2   **If no, go to question 15.**

12. Which category does your job title fall into and in which type of industry?

JOB DESCRIPTION

Head of Department/Professor   ❑ – 1

Other academic   ❑ – 2

Chief executive   ❑ – 3

Director   ❑ – 4

Manager   ❑ – 5

Representative   ❑ – 6

Administrative   ❑ – 7

Clerical   ❑ – 8

Other   ❑ – 9

INDUSTRY

Insurance/banking/finance   ❑ –10

Government/national/local   ❑ –11

Manufacturing   ❑ –12

Distribution   ❑ –13

Media   ❑ –14

Education   ❑ –15

Consultancy   ❑ –16

Other   ❑ –17

13. Size of organization in terms of employees:

Up to 50 ❑ –1   51–100 ❑ –2   101–200 ❑ –3

201–500 ❑ –4   501–1000 ❑ –5   Over 1000 ❑ –6

14. Please indicate your income bracket:

Up to £10 000 ❑ –1   £10 001 – £15 000 ❑ –2

£15 001 – £20 000 ❑ –3   Over £20 000 ❑ –4

15. Which other marketing journals do you regularly read?

....

....

The numbers shown after the boxes in the above example are used to help with subsequent analysis of the questionnaire. The number beside the box which has been ticked will be the code which represents the answer given to that question.

Any questionnaire must be properly introduced to the respondent whatever method of data collection is employed. Interviewers must introduce themselves to the respondent indicating the purpose of the study and must establish their credentials. This is also true of postal questionnaires, but in the latter case either the introductory part of the questionnaire must do this or else an accompanying letter must explain the purpose and benefits of the study.

ANALYSING INFORMATION

The best method of analysing data varies according to the kind of study that has been undertaken and the kind of data that have been obtained. In this section we will illustrate the application of data analysis to data which have been collected by survey research. The same methods will sometimes be applicable to both observational and experimental research, and there may also be other forms of data analysis which can be used on survey data which are not covered here. Readers interested in a comprehensive review of data analysis methods in marketing research should consult a specialized text (see, for example, Green, Tull and Albaum, 1988, pp. 164–5).

Data analysis can be complicated and it is often too easy to draw erroneous conclusions. Data tabulation and cross-tabulation are the simplest ways to analyse findings from closed-ended questions. In addition, frequencies and percentages, averages and measures of dispersion can be worked out for major variables. Often this is sufficient to produce meaningful results. Of course, provided data are amenable to more sophisticated statistical analysis, and such analysis is warranted, then more sophisticated analysis can be conducted. However, it is the interpretation of data and the turning of data into information that often causes the greatest difficulty.

SIMPLE TABULATION OF DATA

A sample survey of 1000 men about their drinking habits revealed the following statistics:

Number of pints of beer consumed per day.	% of men
less than 1	77 – light drinkers
1–4	13 – moderate drinkers
5 or over	10 – heavy drinkers

From this we can see that there are significantly more men who drink less than one pint of beer per day than there are who drink a pint of beer or more a day. However, suppose we wanted to extend our observations to the entire population of British males. In this case we would want to attach confidence limits to our estimation of the proportion of men in the population who fell into each one of the three categories. We can do this by first establishing the standard error of the proportion. In the case of the light drinkers, for example, this would be:

$$SE_p = \sqrt{(pq/n)}$$

where p = proportion exhibiting the characteristic
q = proportion not exhibiting the characteristic
n = sample size

$$= \sqrt{(0.77 \times 0.23/1000)}$$

$$= 0.0133$$

The confidence interval is defined as:

$$p + Z \times SE_p,$$

where Z is the value on the normal distribution for the desired confidence interval. Since $Z_{99} = 2.58$ at the 99% confidence level, the sample value would lie in the area $0.77 \pm 2.58 \times 0.0133$, or between approximately 73.57% and 80.43%.

Again, suppose that it is ascertained from the sample survey of 1000 men that on average they consume one pint of beer per week (arithmetic mean). Suppose it is also estimated that the standard deviation of this sample is 0.5 pints. Assuming that drinking habits in the population of men are normally distributed, we can estimate the confidence interval for the population to be as follows:

$$x \pm Z \times S/\sqrt{n}$$

where
- x = sample mean
- Z = Z value on the normal distribution for desired confidence interval
- S = standard deviation of the sample

Hence, the 99% confidence interval estimate for the population is:

$$1 \pm 2.58 \times 0.5/\sqrt{(1000)}$$

$$= 1 \pm 0.04$$

That is between 0.96 and 1.04 pints of beer.

CROSS-TABULATION OF DATA

A more interesting example is as follows. Suppose we draw up a table (cross-tabulate) which shows the relationship between the age of the respondent and whether or not he or she owns a portable telephone.

	Age	
	< 35 years	≥35years
portable telephone owner	74	38
not an owner	226	262
	300	300

Suppose the above table represents the results of a survey of 600 people enquiring whether or not they own a portable telephone. Inspection of the data seems to indicate that younger people are more likely to own a portable telephone. However, when we introduce the gender of the respondent into the analysis, a different picture emerges:

	Age			
	Men		Women	
	< 35 years	≥35 years	< 35 years	≥35years
portable telephone owner	67	29	7	9
not an owner	83	121	143	141
	150	150	150	150

Inspection of the data suggests that it is men rather than women who are likely to own the phones. Amongst men the younger ones are more likely to own the phones, but amongst women age does not appear to be a factor.

Careful analysis of the data is thus required in order to draw the correct conclusions.

STATISTICS AND CROSS-TABULATION

The interesting question to answer is whether differences which we observe in cross-tabulating data are statistically significant. In other words, what is the probability that observed differences could have occurred by chance. Suppose analysis of survey data shows the following.

Question: Do you visit the cinema more than once a month?

	Occupation of respondent		
	Blue collar	White collar	Managerial
Yes	35	44	46
No	8	20	20
Total	43	64	66

We are interested to know whether the answers provided by the respondents from different occupational backgrounds could have occurred by chance. In this particular instance we can use the Chi-square test to see if this is the case (one should, however, consult standard statistical texts to appreciate the suitability of this test and understand its theoretical underpinning).

The Chi-square statistic is calculated by the formula:

Chi square $= \Sigma (O - E)^2 / E$

where O = the observed value and
E = the theoretically expected value assuming no difference between the occupational backgrounds of respondents in this instance.

| | Occupation of respondent | | | |
	Blue collar	White collar	Managerial	Total
Yes (O = observed)	35	44	46	125
(E = expected)	(43×125)/173 = 31.1	(64×125)/173 = 46.2	(66×125)/173 = 47.7	
No (O = observed)	8	20	20	48
(E = expected)	(43×48)/173 = 11.9	(64×48)/173 = 17.8	(66×48)/173 = 18.3	
Total	43	64	66	173

$$\text{Chi-square} = \Sigma(O - E)^2/E$$

$$= (35 - 31.1)^2/31.1 + (44 - 46.2)^2/46.2 + (4 - 47.7)^2/47.7 +$$

$$(8 - 11.9)^2/11.9 + (20 - 17.8)^2/17.8 + (20 - 18.3)^2/18.3$$

$$= 2.36 \text{ with degrees of freedom } (r-1)(k-1) = 2$$

where r = number of rows, k = number of columns.

χ^2 at 2 degrees of freedom at the 5% level = 5.99. Because 2.36 < 5.99, the difference noted in the sample is due to sampling error and is not statistically significant.

RISK AND COST OF RESEARCH

Since the marketing environment is changing rapidly, competition is usually exceptionally keen and failure to act at a precise moment in time can lead to a loss of strategic impetus and position. If a competitor gets in first with a new idea, it may be too late to respond.

Undertaking research can give advanced warning to a firm's competitors of its intended marketing strategy. Under these circumstances, undertaking research may be inadvisable.

Research can be both time consuming and expensive. Occasionally, it may even be undesirable. Having said that, it must be pointed out that the general rule to follow would be to undertake research unless there are good reasons not to do so.

The cost of collecting information must be weighed against the benefits to be derived from using the information. A knowledge of costs and benefits can help marketing researchers determine which projects should be carried out, which research designs to use and how big a sample size can be taken.

SUMMARY

Firms undertake research to find out why some people buy their products and others do not. Research is also undertaken to help provide information for making marketing mix decisions (pricing, product, distribution and promotion).

Research is undertaken both in-house (by a firm's own employees) and by specialist marketing research companies. In the latter case, research can be tailor-made to a client's requirements or bought 'off the peg', if a suitable omnibus research report is available. A variety of other sources can provide research data that are useful to companies. These sources include trade associations and government departments.

A wide variety of research methods are used, including surveys, experiments and observational methods. A key component of the research is how the sample has been drawn from the population.

Quota sampling and simple random sampling methods are widely used in practice.

The bulk of marketing research carried out is actually market research, which relies very much on survey methods. Questionnaire design and analysis along with sampling are key aspects of survey methods.

There are costs and risks involved in undertaking research. The implications of these have to be fully appreciated before entering into research.

DISCUSSION QUESTIONS

1. Why do firms undertake marketing research?

2. What are the main divisions of marketing research?

3. Indicate the main sources of marketing information.

4. Explain how a mail consumer panel operates. What advantage does it have over traditional kinds of consumer panels?

5. Indicate the main stages of the research process.

6. What kinds of information do the research objectives usually try to elicit?

7. What do you understand by the 'boundary examination' technique?

8. Indicate the main field research methods.

9. What is the purpose of experiments, and how might they assist marketing executives in solving problems?

10. Indicate potential applications for observation studies.

11. What are the main methods of undertaking surveys?

12. Explain what is meant by a sampling plan.

13. Distinguish between probability and non-probability sampling.

14. What principles are involved in taking a simple random sample?

15. What is a cluster sample? Under what circumstances might cluster sampling be appropriate?

16. Explain what is meant by a convenience sample, and indicate situations where the taking of such a sample might be appropriate.

17. How might a judgement sample differ from a convenience sample?

18. What is a quota sample? Indicate ways in which a quota sample may be obtained.

19. Indicate the general rules that should be applied when determining sample size.

20. A researcher wants to draw a random sample such that there is a 99% chance that a sample mean of people's estimates of how much they are likely to buy of a new product would be within 3.0 points of the true mean. A pilot study estimates the s.d. to be of the order of 25.0. What sample size should be taken, assuming no constraints as to time and costs?

21. Indicate the main sources of error that can arise when constructing a questionnaire.

22. Explain each one of the following:
    a. dichotomous questions
    b. multiple choice questions
    c. Likert scale
    d. semantic differential
    e. rating scale
    f. Stapel scale
    g. open-ended questions
    h. word association
    i. sentence completion
    j. story completion
    k. picture completion.

23. Differentiate between one-way and two-way cross-tabulation of data.

24. Analysis of survey data shows the following.

   Question: Do you buy your weekly groceries from Fresco's? Yes/No.

	Occupation of respondent		
	Shop floor	Office staff	Managerial
Yes	118	29	26
No	13	26	15
Total	131	55	41

Are the answers provided by the respondents from different occupational backgrounds statistically different from one another?

25. What are the essential differences between quantitative and qualitative data?

26. Discuss the various kinds of risks that are involved in undertaking research.

REFERENCES

Chisnall, P.M. (1991) *The Essence of Marketing Research*, Prentice Hall, Englewood Cliffs, N.J.

Chisnall, P.M. (1992) *Marketing Research*, 4th edn, McGraw-Hill, Maidenhead.

Factor, S. (1993) MR's Nora Batty finds the spotlight, *Research Plus*, September, 1.

Green, P.E., Tull, D.S. and Albaum, G. (1988) *Research for Marketing Decisions*, 5th edn, Prentice Hall, Englewood Cliffs, N.J.

Marketing Pocket Book (1993) The Advertising Association in conjunction with NTC Publications, London.

Mintel (1994) *Youth Lifestyles, 1993. Changing Attitudes*, Mintel.

Skapinker, M (1989) Why people watching is essential for product development, *Financial Times*, 2 February.

Van Gundy, A.B. *Techniques of Structured Problem Solving*, Van Nostrand Reinhold, New York.

Yamane, T. (1967) *Elementary Sampling Theory*, Prentice Hall, Englewood Cliffs, N.J.

FURTHER READING

Baker, M.J. (1991) *Research for Marketing*, Macmillan, Basingstoke.

Crouch, S. (1985) *Marketing Research for Managers*, Pan Books, London.

Curry, D.J. (1993) *The New Marketing Research Systems*, Wiley, Chichester.

Moutino, L. and Evans, M. (1992) *Applied Marketing Research*, Addison Wesley, Wokingham.

Webb, J.R. (1992) *Understanding and Designing Marketing Research*, Academic Press, London.

CASE PROBLEM 6.1

NEW SHOE COMPANY: DEFINING THE PROBLEM

The New Shoe Company, based in the English Midlands, is experiencing a fall in profits. The company measures profits in terms of the annual pre-tax return on capital employed earned by the company.

The sales director says that falling profitability is a reflection of the current slump in the market. Total demand in the market place is much less than it was 12 months ago and the company has struggled to maintain its market share at the previous level as competition has intensified. Competition from European manufacturers has been sharpened by changes in the EC trading regulations and Spanish manufacturers, in particular, have taken advantage of their lower cost structure to make inroads into the British market. At the same time the New Shoe Company has failed to take full advantage of opportunities in Europe. It has not fully developed its market niching strategy, where it can gain a competitive advantage. The sales director blames the firm's lack of competitiveness on the poor performance of the R. & D. team and the inability of the manufacturing departments to control costs.

The technical director claims that the firm's products are competitive with any that are produced world-wide. Indeed, in her view, the firm's products are by far the best available at the price offered. She points to the lack of marketing effort expended by the firm in the past year, pointing to the necessity to keep the firm's name before the public at all times, especially when competition is increasing in strength. At the same time, she recognizes that marketing effort requires financing and that this was not adequately provided during the period in question.

The production director points out that the company has been able to lower its manufacturing costs substantially through the introduction of new technology into the manufacturing process. However, he points out the accounting practices adopted by the firm distort the true picture. Profitability has in his view improved, though this is not truly reflected in the company's management accounts.

The finance director feels that the drop in profitability is attributable to recent acquisitions that the firm has made. Ventures into retailing have not been as profitable as had first been supposed. This might to some extent have been a reflection of bad timing on the part of the company, given the current recession.

The managing director points out that clearly there is a problem and that perhaps one should pay particular attention to what competitors are doing and how the firm is responding from a marketing viewpoint.

CASE PROBLEM 6.1 *CONTINUED*

QUESTIONS

1. Given the limited information in the case above, what do you think could be the real problem or problems in this example?

2. Depending upon the real nature of the problem identified, how might marketing research help in this instance?

CASE PROBLEM 6.2

YOUTH STYLES: INTERPRETING MARKET RESEARCH

A report produced by Mintel in 1994 indicated that young women are much more likely to wear stockings and suspender belts than older women. Figures show that 10% of **all** British women bought a suspender belt in 1993. Amongst the 20–24 year olds the figure was one third. More than a third of older women choose neutral coloured tights and stockings, but 91% of young women prefer black and more exotic colours. However, despite a preference for these kinds of goods young women are more modest in wanting private cubicles in shop changing rooms.

As far as holidays are concerned, young women are more enthusiastic about a holiday abroad than men of the same age. Some 40% of 15–24 year old women in the survey indicated that they 'love travelling abroad', compared with a third of young men.

Cinema attendance has increased dramatically among all age groups since 1984. The biggest increase has been among 15–24 year olds, where the proportion rose from 59% in 1984 to 89% in 1990. Newspaper readership also appears to be changing among younger people. Among 15–24 year olds, 28% said they bought the *Guardian* or one of the other national broadsheet newspapers in the last 12 months, compared with 19% for all adults.

Use of tobacco and drugs continues to be well established among young people. Some 43% of 20–24 year olds indicated that they smoke, compared with a third of all adults. As far as drugs are concerned, almost 30 per cent of 15–24 year olds say they use drugs – although most use only soft drugs. This was almost twice the level of usage reported in 1989.

(Source: Mintel, 1994)

CASE PROBLEM 6.2 *CONTINUED*

QUESTIONS

1. If you were in the cosmetics, lingerie, jeans or cigarette business, what use could you make of this kind of information?

2. What use might the information be to other kinds of business?

3. What other kinds of information might such a survey provide?

4. What other kinds of reports might Mintel produce?

7 MARKET SEGMENTATION

This chapter explores the concept of market segmentation and explains how organizations develop marketing strategies to exploit profitable product market opportunities. Market segmentation is a marketing tool which can be applied to all businesses and can take a variety of forms. This chapter explores the concept of market segmentation and explains how organizations develop marketing strategies to exploit profitable product market opportunities. The chapter provides a broad overview of both methods and applications of market segmentation noting that some forms are more applicable in given circumstances than others.

OBJECTIVES

After studying the chapter you should be able to:

- understand the importance and meaning of market segmentation
- understand how firms identify market segments
- identify the various bases for segmenting consumer markets
- describe the various underlying principles used for segmenting industrial markets
- outline how firms select segments
- describe how segment synergies can be achieved through selecting specific combinations of market segments.

INTRODUCTION

Products can be designed and marketed so as to have a more or less general appeal to most sections of a market. However, customers have varying wants and needs, and firms are likely to achieve a greater competitive advantage by producing a number of different offerings to meet the needs of specific segments. Attention is given to procedures for identifying market segments, choosing the best market segments in which to operate, and deciding the best strategy when entering market segments.

Segment selection is part of a systematic plan in which combinations of market segments, where obvious synergies exist, might be preferred to a choice of detached or isolated segments.

IMPORTANCE AND MEANING OF MARKET SEGMENTATION

Sometimes, markets are defined on the basis of products or industries – for example, the second-hand car market. However, there is a danger in adopting product-based market definitions, in that businesses may be defined too narrowly which might lead to missed opportunities and business failures. In order to avoid these problems, markets might be better defined in terms of 'generic need' (Levitt, 1960, pp. 45–56). This approach argues that the market is better considered in terms of what the customer buys, rather than what the organization or industry makes. In these terms a cosmetics company, for instance, might define its market (generic need) as the 'beauty market'. This is obviously a more customer-oriented and hence marketing-oriented method of defining markets.

Unfortunately, while the concept of generic needs helps to prevent a myopic view of markets, customers and competition, it is really too broad to be of operational use in helping to define market boundaries and in helping to develop strategic marketing plans. A way of overcoming these difficulties is to define a market in terms of customer function, technology and customer group (Abell, 1980). Thus one might define a particular microcomputer market as laptop colour computers (technology) supplied to academic users (customer group) for the purpose of carrying out academic research and related activities (customer function).

Segmentation is a marketing management technique which can help firms find ways of establishing a competitive advantage. A market segment is a section of a market which possesses one or more unique features that both give it an identity and set it apart from other segments. Market segmentation amounts to partitioning a market into a number of distinct sections, using criteria which reflect different and distinctive purchasing motives and behaviour of customers. Segmentation makes it easier for firms to produce goods or services that fit closely with what people want.

Theatres, for example, use several different methods of market segmentation.

CASE EXAMPLE

THE TEENAGE MARKET: DISCERNIBLE MARKET SEGMENTS

Teenagers form part of the population as a whole and one can only say that there is a teenage market in that they behave differently to other age groups. Comprising a distinct social group, as well as an age group, with their own pattern of buying behaviour and brand preference, they exercise strong influence on family buying decisions. Firms, in dealing with the special requirements of this segment, have created such things as compound beauty preparations specifically for adolescent complexions and also advertise directly, using copy and commercials phrased in teenagers' own language.

(Source: Proctor, 1992)

QUESTIONS

1. How might the language of teenagers differ from that of older people?

2. What kind of products lend themselves to special versions for teenagers?

3. The teenage market itself may be subdivided according to age. How might the demands of 19 year olds, for example, differ from those of 13 year olds?

One method reflects the day of the week and time of the day when customers prefer to go to the theatre. Friday and Saturday evening performances are very much in demand and are attended by people who would find it difficult to go at other times. Because demand is high, theatres can charge higher prices at weekends. Mid-week matinees, on the other hand, attract fewer people; as a consequence, prices are lower in order to stimulate demand. Mid-week performances may attract students, pensioners, the unemployed, etc. who might find it too expensive at weekends and who have more latitude over the time they can pick to go to the theatre. This pricing differential reflects an important point about market segmentation which we will develop in later chapters – different market segments will probably require different marketing mixes – different combinations of price, product, promotion and distribution strategies (Doyle, 1991).

Segmentation can be put into effect in a variety of ways. Markets comprise buyers of products and services, who differ from one another in various respects. The differences point to varying buyer wants and needs, the different resources at buyers' disposal, their place of residence, buying attitudes and buying practices. Any combination of these differences can be used as a basis for market

CASE EXAMPLE

WHITBREAD: REGIONAL SEGMENTS

There are strong regional preferences for beer in the UK, despite the existence of big brand names. One brewery, Whitbread, brews four local beers in the North West of England. In each case the beers reflect a leaning toward the local preference for light mild.

Whitbread also offers a 'Best Scotch' beer in the North of England, where there is a huge demand for such a full-flavoured beer. The company also produces a light bitter for the North East market and a smooth traditional ale, Durham Ale, for the Durham area in particular. The firm also has other regional beers to cater for the tastes of people in other areas of the country.

(Source: Whitbread News, *February 1985)*

QUESTION

1. To what extent do you think there are regional variations in tastes for fast moving consumer goods?

segmentation. The important thing that has to be remembered, however, is that a market segment exists only when people have common characteristics as buyers. Examples of market segments are illustrated in the following case examples.

There are classes of buyers, or market segments, where the difference is only slight in terms of product requirements. In such circumstances, the appropriate approach may be to identify broad classes of similar requirements and the common characteristics of people who share these requirements. Products can then be offered which meet the common wants of the identified segments and marketing communications relating to the products can be directed through suitable media to appeal to people possessing the identified characteristics. Airtours, for example, offers packaged holidays (flight, intermediate travel hotel accommodation and excursions) which appeal to groups of people who have slightly different ideas on how they will spend their holiday. There is sufficient commonality of interest in what Airtours has to offer, however, to attract these different groups to make use of the same packaged holiday.

Segmentation is a powerful component of marketing strategy. Failure to segment the market at all, when competitors are doing so, can lead to almost catastrophic consequences (see the following case example).

CASE EXAMPLE

FORD MODEL T: UNDIFFERENTIATED MARKETING

In the western world today we tend to take the motor car for granted, but it should be remembered that it was only a little more than a century ago, in 1886, that Gottlieb Daimler put together his first four-wheeled car. The vehicle was powered by a single-cylinder, 1.5-h.p. engine which enabled it to travel at up to 18 m.p.h. Daimler developed the motor car concept during the next three years and exhibited a four-seater, four-gear, model with a water-cooled engine at the 1889 Paris Exhibition. The licence to manufacture Daimler cars was acquired by a French firm of coachbuilders; today the Daimler name is owned by the Jaguar company (which is itself owned by Ford).

Detroit, which eventually became the motor car metropolis of the USA, had its first motor car in 1896. A young electrician called Henry Ford drove it and it had a two-cylinder, 4-h.p. engine. It was Henry Ford's belief that America, with its rapidly growing, opulent society and enormous physical distances, could make use of large quantities of motor cars. Despite his own optimism, however, there was considerable opposition to the idea, especially from horse-dealers, breeders, blacksmiths, and fodder merchants. These people had much to lose in a country where (in the 1890s) 18 million horses and mules were undertaking most of the transport work which could not be conducted via the railways.

Henry Ford was not really an inventor, he was more of an improver and organizer. He had watched the development of the motor car in Europe, but had come to the conclusion that most cars were built for sportsmen and enthusiasts. He did not think that these cars were for the ordinary person, who needed a car for the strenuous tasks of everyday life. However, Henry Ford did recognize that America required a foolproof, efficient, hardy vehicle, cheap to buy and economical to run. It was this insight which led him to build the 'Model T' – nicknamed the 'Tin Lizzie'.

A factory was built to facilitate production of the Tin Lizzie. Designed for the assembly line, or conveyor-belt method of mass production, the factory was one-fifth of a mile long. This was at a time when most European cars were still being made by craftsmen. Seen alongside modern cars, the Tin Lizzie of 1908, with its high body, small engine bonnet and open and doorless cabin looks comical. Nevertheless, it turned out to be very successful, 15 million Tin Lizzies being sold between 1908 and 1927.

CASE EXAMPLE *CONTINUED*

Henry Ford enjoyed considerable success in introducing the Model T to the market. There is no doubt about the success of the car and the strategy Henry Ford used in producing and marketing it. Indeed, for the time, the strategy was quite appropriate. The car was mass-produced in a standardized form, with no variations in terms of colour or other features, which allowed Ford to keep down the price of the car to the public and make it available to people who otherwise would not have been able to afford it. A similar strategy was later employed by Volkswagen in the mid-1930s when it introduced the renowned 'Beetle' car, which was to remain in production for over 40 years.

In pursuing the same strategy in the late 1920s, however, Henry Ford nearly encountered disaster. By then, competition had evolved as other manufacturers entered the market. Important competitors appreciated that there were customers with various and different needs in the market place (representing different market segments). Ford's competitors followed a strategy of differentiating their products from one another's by incorporating a variety of options – such as making cars available in different colours. Henry Ford did not react quickly to this new challenge and nearly went out of business as a consequence.

(Source: Hartley, 1992 and Larson, 1961)

QUESTIONS

1. Why was it correct for Henry Ford to pursue an undifferentiated strategy initially for the Tin Lizzie?

2. Why was Volkswagen able to pursue a similar strategy in Germany for the 'Beetle' during the 1930s?

3. The Tin Lizzie lasted only 20 years in production but the 'Beetle' lasted more than twice as long in production. Can you suggest an explanation for this?

SEGMENTATION, TARGETING AND PRODUCT POSITIONING

Having introduced the nature of market segmentation, it is now appropriate to examine how it relates to targeting and product positioning. Marketing executives employ the following steps:

- segment the market
- target the users
- position the products.

In order to segment a market, characteristics have to be identified which distinguish among customers according to their buying preferences. Profiles of market segments which reflect different combinations of these characteristics have then to be constructed.

To target the users, the financial appeal of all segments should be assessed and segments which have the greatest appeal should be selected for targeting. The selection criteria should take account of the relative financial attractiveness of the segments, and the organization's capability to exploit them.

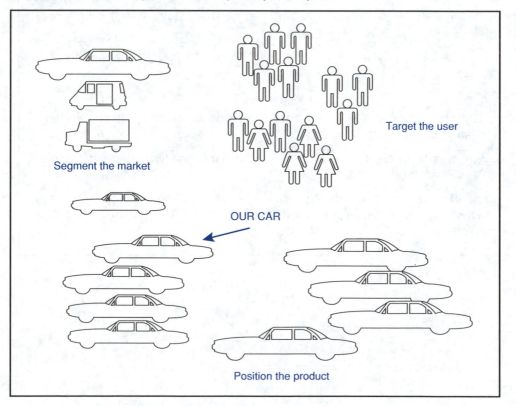

Figure 7.1 Segmentation, targeting and positioning.

In positioning a product, one should aim to match it with that segment of the market where it is most likely to succeed. This involves identifying possible positions for products within each target segment and then producing, adapting and marketing them towards the target market. The product or service should be positioned in such a manner that it stands apart from competing products. The positioning of a product or service indicates what the product represents, and how customers should evaluate it.

Positioning is accomplished through the use of the marketing mix variables, in particular product design and marketing communications. Positioning to achieve product differentiation applies equally to consumer and to industrial goods. Sometimes product positioning can be effected on the basis of tangible differences, such as product features. In many instances, however, customer perceptions about products can be utilized in order to differentiate and position products. Both positioning and targeting are discussed in greater detail in the next chapter.

In attempting to meet the specific needs of an identified market segment a firm can put itself in a better position to obtain a demonstrable competitive advantage for its product. Market segments must, of course, be:

- clearly identifiable, so that marketing communications can be easily directed at the segment

- large enough to generate the volume of sales and profits that the firm requires.

Having introduced the nature of market segmentation and looked at how this relates to targeting and positioning, we will now look at operational aspects of market segmentation. Various bases can be used to segment markets, and because the natures of consumer and industrial markets differ somewhat, we will see that bases for market segmentation also differ, according to whether we are considering consumer or industrial market applications. First we will examine the situation with respect to consumer markets.

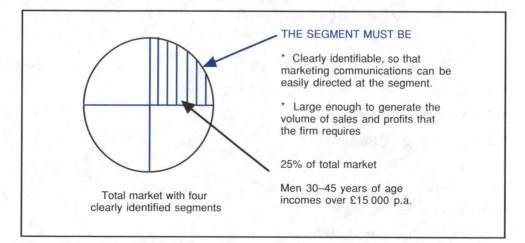

Figure 7.2   Requirements of a market segment.

BASES FOR SEGMENTING CONSUMER MARKETS

There are several approaches to segmenting markets for consumer goods. The methods reflect such things as geographic, demographic, psychographic and behavioural characteristics of consumers.

Geographic

- **Area of a country** – e.g. South-west England, Bavaria, Ardennes, Brittany.
- **Population size of the area** – e.g. under 5000, 5000–10 000, etc.
- **Predominant make-up of the area** – e.g. urban, rural.
- **Climate** – e.g. hot and dry, hot and wet, mild, cold.

Demographic

- **Age** – under 15, 15–24, etc.
- **Gender** – male, female
- **Family size** – 1, 2–3, 3–4, etc.
- **Income** – under £6000; £6000–10 000, etc.
- **Occupation** – skilled workers; executives; retired people; etc.
- **Education** – highest grade school; 6th form college; FE college; college of HE; university
- **Religion** – Muslim; Hindu; Christian; etc.
- **Race** – Afro-Caribbean; Asian; European; etc.
- **Nationality** – Irish; German; Spanish; Swiss; etc.

Psychographic

- **Social class** – A, B, C1, C2, D, E.
- **Lifestyle** – outdoors, party-goer.
- **Personality** – ambitious, retiring.

Behavioural

- **Occasions** – regular, special
- **Benefits** – quality, service, economy
- **User status** – non-user, ex-user, potential user, first timer, regular

- **Usage rate** – light, medium, heavy
- **Loyalty status** – none, medium, strong
- **Readiness stage** – unaware, aware, informed
- **Attitude toward product** – hostile, negative, indifferent, positive, enthusiastic.

GEOGRAPHIC AND DEMOGRAPHIC APPROACHES

Segmentation by gender has been found to be effective in the marketing of clothes, cosmetics, magazines, cars, and even cigarettes. In the USA, for example, Virginia Slim cigarettes have been marketed principally to women. Income segmentation can be applied to such product categories as clothes, cosmetics and cars.

Nationality segmentation can be used in export marketing, or if products are marketed in a multi-racial society. For example, the Hispanic market in the United States is large and diversified. By the late 1980s, there were over 18 million Hispanics, with a purchasing power of over $70 billion. Although over 40% were born in the United States, most have retained their subcultural identity and remain Spanish-speaking (Corchado, 1989).

Different nationalities have different habits, religions, traditions and cultures and these are reflected in their purchasing habits. Many companies also use geographic segmentation since market segments can easily be identified, measured and accessed on this basis.

More than one basis can be used for segmenting a market. The car market, for instance may be segmented by income and by the benefits sought by users which different models offer – economy, performance, etc.

Demographic segmentation entails using such factors as age, sex, income, occupation, family size, stage in the family life cycle, education, religion, race or nationality to distinguish between different customer groups. Care has to be taken in using these variables – some studies have shown that factors such as age, sex, income, occupation and race are in fact poor predictors of behaviour and therefore less than optimum bases for segmentation (see Haley, 1991).

The family life cycle has been put forward as a useful demographic tool that can be used when segmenting the market (Murphy and Staples, 1992). The stages are shown in Fig. 7.3.

The family life cycle is intended to show the various stages through which households progress. The implication for providers of goods and services is that linked to the different stages in the life cycle there are different purchasing needs. There have been some critics of the usefulness of the family life cycle concept. Major weaknesses are the exclusion of those couples who never have children, lack of account taken of one-parent families, undue emphasis on the age of children and the changing role of the father/husband but not of the mother/wife (Trost, 1974, pp. 37–47).

Demographic variables cannot be used effectively by themselves, but must be linked with each other to form an overall picture of the market segment. Age and income are two factors that are widely used, and they allow clearly identifiable groups to be pinpointed; for example, young, high-income earners.

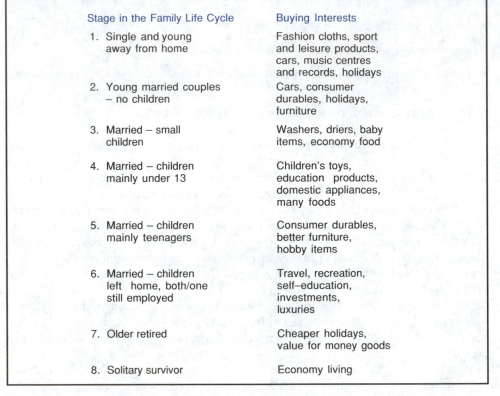

Stage in the Family Life Cycle	Buying Interests
1. Single and young away from home	Fashion cloths, sport and leisure products, cars, music centres and records, holidays
2. Young married couples – no children	Cars, consumer durables, holidays, furniture
3. Married – small children	Washers, driers, baby items, economy food
4. Married – children mainly under 13	Children's toys, education products, domestic appliances, many foods
5. Married – children mainly teenagers	Consumer durables, better furniture, hobby items
6. Married – children left home, both/one still employed	Travel, recreation, self–education, investments, luxuries
7. Older retired	Cheaper holidays, value for money goods
8. Solitary survivor	Economy living

Figure 7.3 Stages in the Family Life Cycle and associated buying preferences.

Geographic or geo-demographic segmentation is based on where people live. The premise is that people who live in similar types of residential districts have similar characteristics and hence similar behaviour patterns. Such a method of segmentation may be appealing to firms since they can normally target groups of people having somewhat similar needs. Firms using this method of segmentation can use one of the many systems that are commercially available. The following are major suppliers.

● CACI: Acorn, Monica, the Household classification

● CCN: Mosaic

● CDMS: Super Profiles

● Infolink: Define

● Pinpoint Analysis: PiN, FiNPin.

The use of Acorn (an acronym for 'A classification of residential neighbourhoods') is illustrated below. It is a way by which units of 150 addresses throughout Great Britain are divided into 38 different types of residential neighbourhoods. Addresses are classified on the basis of demographic, housing and socio-economic characteristics. It enables firms to use individual customer lists and market research survey data to identify the types of neighbourhood with the heaviest consumption of a particular product or service. This facilitates accurate targeting of retail and product distribution, product promotion and advertising on specific geographical demographic customer segments.

Using the postcode of their address, any customer can be categorized according to the Acorn classification. A firm which has a large customer database can take a sample of its customers and discover which Acorn categories are most valuable in terms of sales. From its records it can then determine what people in different categories buy and how much they spend per head, etc. On the basis of this information, messages and direct mailshots can be selectively targeted to those categories which are the firm's best customers.

Selected Acorn types and groups

- **Group C (older housing of intermediate status)**
    - C8: mixed owner-occupied and council estates
    - C9: small town centres and flats above shops
    - C10: villages with non-farm employment
    - C11: older private housing, skilled workers.

- **Group J (affluent suburban housing)**
    - J33: inter-war semis, white-collar workers
    - J34: spacious inter-war semis, big gardens
    - J35: villages with wealthy older communities
    - J36: detached houses, exclusive suburbs.

(Source: CACI Market Analysis, 1989)

PSYCHOGRAPHIC APPROACHES

Psychographic segmentation entails dividing buyers into different groups based on their social class, lifestyle and/or personality characteristics. Lifestyle and personality segmentation are growing in popularity. The method involves attempting to endow a product with characteristics that correspond to the target group of consumers' self-perceptions. It is maintained that these factors reflect people's values and opinions and thus enable researchers to ascertain why customers prefer certain products and services to others.

Fear is a psychographic variable which can be used to good effect in marketing communications. It is particularly good in establishing new market segments and works best with people who are low in anxiety and high in self-esteem, who are not interested in the topic of fear itself and believe that they are not very vulnerable. A 'social fear' appeal is better than a 'physical fear' appeal – advertisements for deodorants and mouthwash use the theme (Burnett and Oliver, 1979).

There is an argument that social class groupings are no longer useful for segmentation purposes because society is experiencing a changing social structure. The suggestion is that people are no longer primarily concerned with accumulating material possessions and moving up a social hierarchy, but are more concerned with their quality of life. Nevertheless, the social grading system of combined demographic and geographic characteristics is still used by some leading marketing research companies in the UK when undertaking usage and attitude surveys for fast moving consumer goods on behalf of firms. This reflects the continuous use of such characteristics as market segmentation variables.

Based upon a knowledge of customer lifestyle and personality characteristics, firms are in a position to appreciate people's wants and needs and this in turn helps them to develop products which are suited to the needs of their customers. Moreover, if a firm can ascertain people's aspirations, then it is in a better position to provide the services that people will need in order to realize their ambitions. Psychographic variables can be used in conjunction with other demographic and geographic variables.

Many psychographic segmentation systems are commercially available. The main ones are:

● SRI International (VALS (values and lifestyles))

● Taylor Nelson (MONITOR)

● NDL International (Lifestyle Selector).

BEHAVIOURISTIC APPROACHES

Behaviouristic segmentation entails dividing customers into groups according to their knowledge, attitude, and use or response to a product or service. Behavioural patterns can be differentiated by occasions, benefits, user status and usage rate. Occasions are situations where one can distinguish between buyers according to when they purchased or used a product or service. User status reflects non-users, ex-users, potential users, first-time users and regular users of a product or service. Usage rate reflects light, medium, or heavy use of products or services.

Behavioural segmentation methods can be applied to products which are purchased to celebrate an occasion. Examples include holidays, weddings, birthdays or seasonal events such as Christmas or Easter. The kissagram 'service' and associated complementary services are examples.

Benefit segmentation is popular with certain producers of consumer products. Producers of wrist-watches offer underwater diving watches, sports watches with stop-watch facilities, fashion watches with ornate dials to be worn for party-going, etc., all of which reflect the marketer's use of segmentation by benefits.

There are groups of individuals who can be classified according to the benefits they seek from the products they buy (see Figure 7.4) (Haley, 1991). Some of these segments appear among the customers of almost all products and services.

Rate of usage of the product or service represents another means of market segmentation. Heavy users of certain products – e.g. beer – often have many other similar habits in common. This may includes the type of media they choose to read or view. Armed with such information, firms can devise specific marketing strategies. The physical size of products is also influenced by rate of usage. Looking

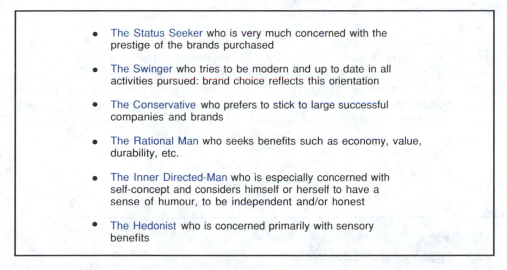

- The Status Seeker who is very much concerned with the prestige of the brands purchased

- The Swinger who tries to be modern and up to date in all activities pursued: brand choice reflects this orientation

- The Conservative who prefers to stick to large successful companies and brands

- The Rational Man who seeks benefits such as economy, value, durability, etc.

- The Inner Directed-Man who is especially concerned with self-concept and considers himself or herself to have a sense of humour, to be independent and/or honest

- The Hedonist who is concerned primarily with sensory benefits

Figure 7.4 Segmentation by benefits.

around the supermarket at the various goods on sale, one sees that there are large pack sizes aimed at families, and smaller packs aimed at single people and couples. Producers of detergents and many food items make use of this form of market segmentation.

Understanding the requirements of different market segments and matching these with appropriate product offerings is a key element of successful marketing.

Market segmentation is a method by which the total market is broken down into sub-markets or segments sharing some measurable commonality such as demographics, lifestyle, benefits, etc. It entails dividing a market into distinct groups of buyers who might require separate products and/or marketing mixes. Market segmentation amounts to breaking up a market into well-defined smaller groupings of consumers with common needs and wants, enabling these needs and wants to be met with specific products and services.

Market segmentation permits firms to identify target markets. In doing so it is also possible to identify the kind of appeals that should be directed towards the target market. To be effective, the right services and accompanying promotional messages have to be aimed at the right market segments.

Having looked at segmentation in consumer markets, we will now go on to look at segmentation in industrial markets.

SEGMENTATION IN INDUSTRIAL MARKETS

As in the case of consumer goods there are different approaches to segmentation. These may be based upon demography, the standard industrial classification index, geographic location, purpose for which the product is to be used and a number of other factors.

DEMOGRAPHY

Industrial markets can be segmented on demographic grounds but in this case demography refers to such factors as the industries that can use the product or service – e.g. automotive industry, furniture industry, or the size of company likely to make use of the product. (NB size may be judged by number of employees or sales turnover, or some combination of both of these factors. Size is a relative factor and should be determined within the specific context in which it is being applied.)

CASE EXAMPLE

MARY QUANT: SEGMENTATION

Women's skirts and dresses have changed over the ages but a change occurred in the 1960s which revolutionized designs as well as women's wants and needs with respect to appearance. Mary Quant did this when she introduced the mini-skirt. Wearers of the new mini-skirts rejected the constriction of the traditional girdle. A segmentation study was undertaken both in Germany and in the UK to find out which women still required girdles and what was required in their place by those who did not want girdles. Perhaps not surprisingly, the results of the studies showed different wants and needs according to age group and body type. These differences in buyers' wants and needs reflected the existence of different market segments.

Perhaps one of the most interesting findings was that segmentation also existed by personality type. The study focused on seven personality styles, ranging from the uninhibited and extroverted woman who wished to experiment with her image, through the middle range of those who wished to present themselves as fashion-conscious but restrained, to the very introverted woman who wanted to be inconspicuous and above all 'safe'. At one extreme the girdle was visualized to be chafing, old-hat and restrictive; at the other extreme it was seen as a means of being safely held together, conferring respectability on the wearer by way of giving a neat conforming image.

These personality groups were present in each of the age and income sub-groups, and in the cultural traditions of various geographical groupings. This made it possible to identify 'free-spirited swingers' who were also grannies, and 'hide-

CASE EXAMPLE *CONTINUED*

bound' 17 year olds who were terrified of appearing 'morally loose' if they did not restrain their body with strong foundation garments.

In more recent times, the mini-skirt has come in and out of fashion, as skirt lengths have oscillated above and below the knee. What was fashionable 30 or even 50 years ago may well be fashionable tomorrow, or today. Personality appears not to recognize the boundaries of time.

(Source: adapted from Walker, 1986)

QUESTIONS

1. Market segments need to be clearly identifiable, so that marketing communications can be easily directed at the segments, and also large enough to generate the volume of sales and profits that the firm requires. Using segmentation by personality type, how could a producer of women's clothes make use of the kind of information found in the two studies mentioned in the case study?

2. While people may wish to satisfy the needs of their personalities, they are constrained by the size of their purses. How might producers of ladies fashionwear seek to overcome this problem?

3. What practical uses would you envisage women's garment producers making of the kind of information derived from the two studies mentioned in the case study?

STANDARD INDUSTRIAL CLASSIFICATION

A very popular method employed by industrial goods producers involves using the Standard Industrial Classification index (SIC). This classifies all places of business into one of ten divisions covering the entire range of economic activity:

1. Agriculture, forestry and fisheries

2. Mining

3. Construction

4. Manufacturing

5. Transportation, communication, electric, gas and sanitary services

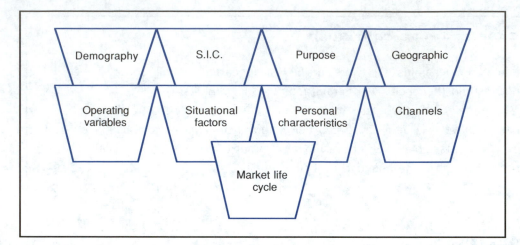

Figure 7.5 Some methods of segmenting industrial markets.

6.   Wholesale and retail trade

7.   Finance, insurance and real estate

8.   Services

9.   Government

10. All others.

   The principal divisions are themselves divided into major groups, such as printing and publishing, or chemicals and allied products, with each major group having assigned to it a two-digit SIC number. Further classification is achieved by means of three- and four-digit numbers. By using the SIC system, industrial markets can be divided into relatively small, medium, or large market segments.

PURPOSE

One basis by which the market can be segmented involves specifying whether a product is to be supplied as a part or subassembly to other manufacturers to be incorporated into a finished product (e.g. brake linings for new cars), or supplied for maintenance or repair purposes (e.g. brake linings for the DIY motorist).

GEOGRAPHIC SEGMENTATION

There are often differences in how regional markets buy and in how they should be approached. This provides a further basis for segmentation.
   Other ways of segmenting include the following.

- **Operating variables** – reflecting the customer technologies employed and the firm's usage rate.

- **Purchasing approaches** – reflecting the different methods and criteria of purchasing employed by the firm – e.g. centralized vs. decentralized.

- **Situational factors** – reflecting speed of service required, size of orders, and specific versus specialized service provided.

- **Personal characteristics** – reflecting such things as loyalty to a supplier, attitude towards risk, and whether the segment companies share the same values as the supplier company.

- **Channel segmentation** – reflecting the sales and distribution channels through which the end-user is reached.

- **Market life-cycle segmentation** – reflecting different stages in the technology life cycle of a product or service.

We have looked at various bases for segmenting both consumer and industrial markets; we now look at segmentation strategy: identifying market segments, selecting segments in which to operate, and managing to operate profitably having made this selection.

SEGMENTATION STRATEGY

PROCEDURE FOR IDENTIFYING MARKET SEGMENTS

There are three stages:

1. survey

2. analysis

3. profiling

Survey stage

At the outset of the task, researchers conduct informal interviews with groups of consumers to find out about their motivation, attitudes and behaviour. Based on this preliminary work, the researchers then collect further data by means of a formal questionnaire served on a sample of consumers. The information sought is as follows.

- The importance and ratings people give to certain attributes of the product.

- The extent to which people are aware of the existence of different brands of the product.

- If brand awareness exists, how people rate different brands.

- How, when, where and by whom the product is used.

- Attitudes towards the product category.

- Demographic, psychographic and mediagraphic profiles of consumers of the product.

Analysis stage

There is a range of statistical methods which can be used to analyse the data in order to categorize the segments based on the identified characteristics.

Profiling stage

Each segment is profiled with respect to its distinguishing attitudes, behaviour demographics, psychographics and media consumption habits. Segment characteristics and make-up vary over time, so the procedures have to be periodically carried out again.

Having identified potential market segments, firms have then to select those which they wish to enter or develop.

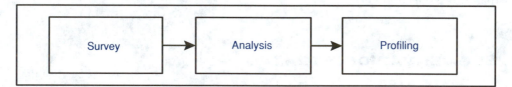

Figure 7.6 Stages for identifying market segments.

SELECTING A SEGMENT IN WHICH TO OPERATE

Market segmentation enables a firm to analyse a market and select those segments in which it thinks it can operate most profitably. Two important questions have to be answered.

- Which are the best market segments for the firm?

- What should be the strategy to effect in entering market segments?

Several factors influence the firm's choice of target markets. These factors will reflect such things as:

- Market size, growth potential and profit potential

- Number, size, strength and resources of competitors serving the segments

- The extent to which there is a good match with the company's strengths, objectives, resources and distribution channels.

Selection of market segments (targeting) is discussed in more detail in the next chapter.

TIMING

It has been found (Abel, 1978, pp. 21–6) that market segmentation may lead to profit opportunities and 'strategic windows' that allow new competitors to challenge established market leaders. The concept of a 'strategic window' implies that there are only limited periods during which the 'fit' between the key requirements of a market and the particular competencies of an enterprise competing in that market are at an optimum. For example, Ever Ready dominated the small battery market until Duracell used lithium technology to replace conventional zinc cells. The new batteries had operating lives two to three times those of Ever Ready, whose market share collapsed (Doyle, 1994, p.20).

The timing of investment and disinvestment of a product or service should coincide with periods during which the strategic window is respectively open and shut. Moreover, as a market develops, new segments become visible and older ones disappear. The marketing strategist is usually primarily interested in those segments which appear to offer the best growth and profit potential. However, it may be possible to operate very profitably in declining segments as competition withdraws.

Expanding market segments intuitively may seem to be the most appealing. However, it should be borne in mind that such segments will also be appealing to competitors. Gaining a good position in such segments will be difficult and it will be expensive in terms of application of resources to maintain a position in an expanding market segment. A successful strategy, however, could have a substantial pay-off.

Static or declining market segments will seem less appealing to a potential new entrant – decidedly less attractive than ones which are expanding in size. Nevertheless, contracting market segments can cause some companies to pull out, thereby not only reducing competition in the market segment but also artificially enlarging the market for those firms remaining in it. Firms may sometimes operate very profitably in a declining market segment provided there is a close fit between the needs of the segment and the firm's own capabilities. Resources and objectives must be considered when selecting segments. The fit between the market needs and the company's capabilities is important.

Some firms place a product within a single market segment. Few resources or a lack of a competitors in the segment may make this strategy attractive. In so doing, a firm may be able to develop a strong market position by gaining an in-depth knowledge of the segment's needs over a long period of time. Operating economies may also result from specialization. Such a strategy is of course risky, since a turn-down in the market, or the sudden emergence of a strong competitor can have a drastic impact on profits. A more conservative strategy is to look for a match between capabilities and the demands of several different segments. This makes it possible to spread the risk so that if one segment starts to become unprofitable there are still others that can bring in cash for the firm.

Firms sometimes concentrate on producing one product or service which is supplied to several different customer groups. In pursuing this strategy a firm can build a good reputation in the specific product area. This can be a risky strategy, since it involves concentrating on a single product or service.

Concentrating on serving the needs of a particular group of customers represents yet another way of segmenting the market. This can involve making available many different products or services. Risk in this case is associated with a downturn in the fortunes of the particular group of customers selected.

SEGMENT SYNERGIES

Firms which decide to serve more than one segment need to pay close attention to synergies between segments with respect to cost, performance and technology. Two or more segments might provide just the opportunity for exploitation because they share common distribution channels, manufacturing facilities, etc. The joint effect of marketing to all segments creates synergy. That is, the overall effect of marketing to two or more segments is to produce greater sales and profits than if each segment had been exploited one at a time in complete isolation from the others.

In international markets it is sometimes a good strategy to use a segment to which one can gain access as a stepping stone to other segments which might otherwise be difficult to access, without a base in the country concerned.

SEGMENT INVASION STRATEGY

Having selected segments to enter, the final strategic decision concerns the method of 'invading' the segments. The question is whether firms should invade all segments at once, or whether they should 'pick them off' one at time. Much depends on the resources that firms have available. A firm is more likely to be successful if it concentrates its efforts on one strategic objective at a time, ensuring that resources are not too thinly spread. It is also more prudent to enter one segment at a time and to conceal the overall plan, as well as being more productive to market goods to selective market segments where synergy can be achieved.

SUMMARY

This chapter has examined the nature of market segmentation and the benefits of using market segmentation. Segmentation is an integral part of marketing strategy; the role segmentation plays within the framework of marketing strategy has been discussed. There are various bases for segmenting both consumer and industrial markets; these were explored in some depth, with examples being drawn from both domains.

Products can be designed and marketed so as to have a more or less general appeal to most members of a market. Since customers have varying wants and needs, however, firms are likely to achieve a greater competitive advantage by producing a number of different offerings to meet the needs of specific segments. Customers are more likely to buy something which fits with their specific wants and needs. While the wants and needs of individuals within segments may not be entirely homogeneous they will be less diverse than those within the market as a whole.

Marketing employs the following steps:

- segment the market

- target the users

- position the products.

Market segments must be:

- clearly identifiable, so that marketing communications can be easily directed at the segment

- large enough to generate the volume of sales and profits that the firm requires.

In the case of consumer products, market segmentation may be based on geographic, demographic, psychographic or behavioural characteristics of customers – or upon any combination of these.

In the case of industrial products a variety of approaches may be used. Commonly adopted ones are:

- demography – type of industry, size of firm

- SIC code

- purpose for which the product is to be used

- geographic location.

The procedure for identifying market segments involves three steps:

- **survey stage** – where researchers collect data from customers to find out about their motivation, attitudes and behaviour

- **analysis stage** – where a range of statistical methods are used to analyse the data in order to categorize the segments based on the identified characteristics

- **profiling stage** – where each segment is profiled with respect to its distinguishing attitudes, behaviour demographics, psychographics and media consumption habits.

Segment characteristics and make-up vary over time so the procedures have to be repeated.

Market segmentation enables a firm to analyse a market and select those segments where it can operate most profitably. Questions which have to be answered are which are the best market segments for the firm, and what should be the strategy for entering market segments? Several factors influence the firm's choice of target markets. These factors will reflect such things as market size, growth potential and profit potential; number, size, strength and resources of competitors serving the segments; and the extent to which there is a good match with the company's strengths, objectives, resources and distribution channels.

Segment selection is part of a systematic plan. Combinations of segments, where obvious synergies exist, might be preferred to choice of detached or isolated segments. Unless considerable resources are available, it may be a better strategy to pick off segments one at a time, rather than trying to enter them all simultaneously.

DISCUSSION QUESTIONS

1. What benefits are to be gained from employing market segmentation, as opposed to treating the market as a single entity?

2. Why should some bases of segmentation be more suitable for some products than others?

3. What factors impact upon a firm's selection of market segments?

4. What stages are involved in identifying market segments?

5. What do you understand by 'segment strategies', and how do these influence a firm's approach to market segmentation?

6. Under what conditions might a firm attempt to penetrate a number of new segments simultaneously?

7. What are 'segment synergies'?

REFERENCES

Abell, D.F. (1978) Strategic windows. *Journal of Marketing*, **42**(2), 21–6.
Abell, D.F. (1980) *Defining The Business: The Starting Point Of Strategic Planning*, Prentice Hall, Englewood Cliffs, N.J.
Burnett, J.J. and Oliver, R.L. (1979) Fear appeal effects in the field: segmentation approach, *Journal of Marketing Research*, May, 181–90.
Corchado, A. (1989) Hispanic supermarkets are blossoming, *Wall Street Journal*, 23 January, B-1.
De Bono, A. (1992), in *Liberation Management* (ed. T. Peters) Macmillan, New York.
Doyle, P. (1991) Managing the Marketing Mix, *The Marketing Book*, 2nd edn (ed. M.J. Baker), Butterworth Heinemann, Oxford.
Doyle, P. (1994), *Marketing Management and Strategy*, Prentice Hall, Englewood Cliffs, N.J.
Haley, R.I. (1991) Benefit segmentation: a decision-oriented research tool, *Marketing Classics*, 7th edn (eds B.M. Enis and K.K. Cox), Allyn and Bacon, Needham Heights, Mass.

Hartley, R.F. (1992) *Marketing Mistakes*, 5th edn, John Wiley, New York.

Joseph, D. and Yorke, D. (1989) Know your game plan: market segmentation in the personal financial services sector. *The Quarterly Review of Marketing*, **15**(1), 8–13.

Larson, E. (1961) *A History of Invention*, Phoenix House, London.

Levitt, T. (1960) Marketing myopia, *Harvard Business Review*, **38**, July–August, 45–56.

Murphy, P.E. and Staples, W.A. (1992) A modernized family life cycle, *Marketing Classics*, 7th edn (eds B.M. Enis and K.K. Cox), Allyn and Bacon, Needham Heights, Mass.

Proctor, T. (1992) *Essential Marketing*, Collins, London.

Trost, J. (1974) The family life cycle – an impossible concept?, *International Journal of Sociology of the Family*, Spring, 37–47.

Walker, H. (1986) *Marketing*, Pan Books, London.

FURTHER READING

Roberts, A.A. (1961) Applying the strategy of market segmentation, *Business Horizons*, Fall, 65–72.

Smith, W.R. (1956) Product differentiation and market segmentation as alternative marketing strategies, *Journal of Marketing*, July, 3–8.

CASE PROBLEM 7.1

THE SWISS WATCH INDUSTRY: SEGMENTATION METHODS

The Elgin watch company has often been quoted as a classical example of a firm which exhibited acute symptoms of marketing myopia on its way to eventually going out of business. The company refused to adapt to the changing demands of the market place and take account of the dwindling number of customers for its long-established product offering to the market. It may seem rather obvious to us today that in order to survive in the market place, a company should adapt its strategy to meet the changing wants and needs of its customers. However, the watch industry possesses a number of quirks and does not necessarily always respond in the way one would expect.

The Swiss watch industry has dominated world markets with its fine clockwork movements, elegant designs and quality image for most of the 20th century. Quality, elegance and accuracy are key features which people look for in a watch, and some people are prepared to pay very high prices in order to obtain what they want. Up until 1970, watches were powered by clockwork movements, and precision engineering dominated an industry where a key dimension of quality reflected accuracy in time-keeping. An 'Officially Certified Chronometer' certificate given by the Swiss authorities was a sure sign that a particular watch met with specific time-keeping standards. Watches carrying such certificates were eagerly sought after and could command high prices. Apart from accuracy, features such as self-winding movements, elegance in design, precious metal casing and sometimes jewel-adorned dials added to the desirability of such watches.

Firms such as Rolex and Blancpain are world renowned for their ability to produce desirable watches of such a quality that only better-off people can afford to own. A major breakthrough in technology, however – invention of the quartz movement – made it possible for accurate watches to be mass produced by anyone. The Swiss industry did not use the invention for fear that it would kill its existing market, but watchmakers in the Far East adopted the quartz movement, and in a single year sales of Swiss watches dropped by 25%.

The Swiss watch industry was rescued by the Swatch. The Swatch gave the signal that telling the time was no longer the most important thing in a watch, since quartz movements had made it possible for all watches to do this to the satisfaction of most customers. The Swatch was not selling 'time telling', so much as fun and costume jewellery. Since then, firms such as Ebel have concentrated almost exclusively on the expensive end of the jewellery-conscious market. In addition watches with famous fashion labels such as Yves St Laurent, Burberry, Next and Benetton have come to stake their claim.

However, some people still think a 'real' watch must have a clockwork movement. Rolex and Blancpain, for example, have stuck with the traditional demands of the market and produce mainly watches with clockwork movements.

So whether it is for fun, jewellery or sheer manufacturing precision it doesn't really matter. In all cases, the market segments reflect the benefits that will accrue to the wearer.

(Source: De Bono, 1992, p.635)

QUESTION

1. Suggest ways of segmenting the market for:

   (a) ladies watches

   (b) gent's watches

   (c) girl's watches

   (d) boy's watches.

CASE PROBLEM 7.2

DAVID BROWN TRACTORS: METHODS OF SEGMENTATION

The David Brown company has roots in and around Huddersfield, West Yorkshire. It was at one time best known for the production of high quality gears for use in machinery in a variety of industries. Later, David Brown, the proprietor, was associated with Aston Martin, the world-famous manufacturer of sports car saloons. The David Brown company's talents, however, were more widely based and it developed expertise in producing agricultural tractors.

The agricultural tractor market is typical of most automotive markets. The majority of sales for products are achieved in export markets throughout the world. The geographic dispersal of markets leads automatically to some form of geographic segmentation. This sometimes disguises the fact that it is the end-use to which the tractors are put, rather than the geographic area itself, which creates the market segmentation. For example, the Canadian and Italian markets are clearly geographically distinct markets, but each of which has a preference for a distinct type of agricultural tractor. The Canadian market requires especially powerful tractors, capable of operating on the prairies with maximum efficiency. In the wine-growing areas of Italy, however, narrow track, low horsepower tractors are required.

David Brown Tractors produces a number of different sized models of varying horsepower capacity. The more powerful tractors are naturally physically larger than the smaller horsepower tractors. Size of tractor required is also associated with the size of fields that tractors have to plough and the number and size of implements which they have to drive, as well as the nature of the terrain which they have to work. Different horsepower tractors, with varying sizes of tracks, are suitable for different uses.

While end-use is clearly the dominant way in which the tractor market is segmented, the market is not without its quirks. The David Brown tractor is very distinctive compared with competitors' product. The David Brown tractor is white in colour, and considered 'the white Mercedes of the cornfields'. Another interesting point is that despite the obviously utilitarian nature of the agricultural tractor in most world markets many farmers exhibit great pride in their 'iron horses'. It is just as much a status symbol to have a brand new large horsepower tractor parked in full view of neighbours in the farmyard as it is to have a new Mercedes parked on the drive of a suburban house.

CASE PROBLEM 7.2 *CONTINUED*

QUESTIONS

1. Given the traditional way in which the tractor market is segmented, what scope do you think there is for using behaviouristic methods which one normally associates with consumer goods marketing?

2. What other bases of market segmentation do you think agricultural tractor manufacturers could employ?

3. Gears are sold to a large number of firms operating in many different industries. What do you consider to be suitable methods for segmenting these markets?

8 MARKET TARGETING AND POSITIONING

This chapter examines the differences between various strategic approaches to targeting, and assesses the nature and importance of positioning in strategic marketing. It describes how a positioning plan and strategy for a product or service should be developed and looks at the factors which influence the choice of positioning strategy. The need for periodic repositioning is discussed, as well as how competitive advantage may be assessed through positioning analysis.

OBJECTIVES

After studying this chapter you should be able to:

- explain the differences between various strategic approaches to targeting – e.g. mass marketing and single segment strategy

- appreciate the nature and importance of positioning in strategic marketing

- comprehend what is involved in developing a positioning plan and strategy for a product or service and be acquainted with those factors which influence the choice of positioning strategy

- understand and appreciate the need for repositioning and how this may be achieved

- understand how competitive advantage may be assessed through positioning analysis.

INTRODUCTION

In the previous chapter we saw how a firm can identify the wants and needs of various sectors or segments of a market as being sufficiently distinct to warrant the offering of individual products or services. Instead of offering one catch-all product or service which is likely to have broad appeal to people generally, it is strategically more beneficial to tailor products and services to individual market segments.

In this chapter the importance of market targeting in strategic marketing is examined and the different approaches to target marketing are described. There is no single best strategy for all firms to adopt, since businesses face different marketing opportunities and have different ranges of resources, skills and competencies at their disposal.

Positioning enables firms to place their products and services within chosen segments so that they stand out from those of their competitors. This chapter examines the process of product positioning, both for single and multiple brands, and concludes by examining the need to reposition from time to time.

TARGETING

A target market is the market or market segments which form the focus of the firm's marketing efforts (Pass *et al.*, 1991). Once segments have been identified decisions about how many and which customer groups to target must be made. The options include the following.

1. **Mass marketing strategy:** offering one product/service concept to most of the market, across many market segments. Although scale economies can be achieved, there is a risk that few customers will be adequately satisfied. The underlying assumption of this approach, referred to as undifferentiated marketing, is that all customers in the market have similar needs and wants and can therefore be satisfied with a single marketing mix – that is, a standard product or service, similar price levels, one method of distribution and a promotional mix which is directed at everyone.

   There are probably only two conditions under which a mass marketing approach is best. The first reflects the demand side of the equation and is the position where there is little variation in the needs of consumers for a given product or service. This is a situation which is becoming increasingly rare, since in both consumer and industrial markets different individuals and organizations have widely varying characteristics, wants, needs and interests. The second condition reflects the supply side of the equation and refers to the ability of the enterprise to develop and sustain a single marketing mix that satisfies all. Where markets are large this capability requires the availability of substantial resources.

2. **Single segment strategy**: concentrating on a single segment with a product/service concept. This is relatively cheap in resources, but there is a risk of putting all the eggs in one basket – if the segment fails, the company's

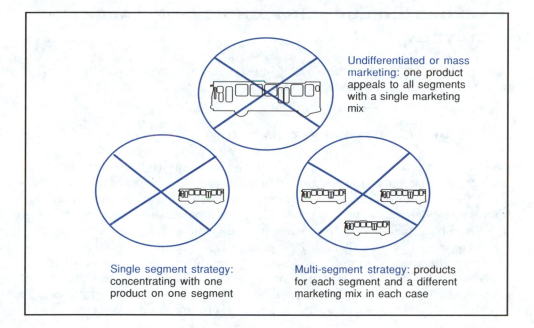

Figure 8.1 Targeting strategies.

financial strength will rapidly decline. Rolex, for example, targets relatively high income consumers with its prestigious wrist-watches. When world economies are buoyant, sales will be good but in times of economic recession even the better off can change their spending patterns.

There is also a problem with regard to flexibility in changing the product-market posture. High quality image companies experience difficulty in terms of moving into product-market segments which have a lower quality image. Rolex, for example, would find it impossible to manufacture and market cheap quartz watches in competition with firms such as Sekonda. Rolex does, however, have its slightly 'down-market' Tudor range of watches, which retail at prices considerably less than the those for the Rolex brand range. But it can only do this by offering a product under a different brand name and ensuring that the product is not too far removed price-wise from the main brand of Rolex. On the other hand, a single segment strategy does permit a firm to specialize, and to concentrate all its energies on satisfying the wants of a particular market segment.

3. **Multi-segment strategy**: targeting a different product or service concept at each of a number of segments and developing a marketing mix strategy for each of the selected segments. Although this approach can reduce the risk of being over-committed in one area, it can be extremely resource-demanding.

Which target segment strategy a company adopts will be dependent on a wide range of market, product and competitive factors. Each of these must be carefully considered before a decision is made about segments to be targeted.

Factors influencing choice of targeting strategy

Having looked at some of the ways of targeting, let us now consider the kind of factors which influence choice of strategy.

Stage of product-market maturity

Segmentation strategies are most critical during the maturity stage of the product-market, because buyer's needs are different. At the introductory stage of the life cycle there are few, if any, product-type competitors; however, competition can occur among alternative product types. If product-type substitution exists, the new market entrant may benefit from targeting one or more segments in the existing product-markets. Where there are no product-type substitutes, a broad or relatively undifferentiated targeting strategy may be appropriate at the introductory stage of the life cycle. This may amount to attempting to identify a broad segment of potential buyers. The nature and intensity of competition at each stage of the product life cycle are important in guiding market targeting decisions.

Extent of buyer differentiation

When buyer wants are similar throughout the product-market, there is less opportunity for extensive segmentation than in markets with buyers with different wants. A product-market made up of a relatively small number of end-users is more suitable for a broad or relatively undifferentiated targeting strategy, particularly if the value of purchases of individual buyers is small. In addition, the more complex the product-market structure with respect to competing firms, variety of product-market offerings, variations in user needs and wants, etc., the more likely it is that a useful method of segmentation can be found.

Market position

A firm's market share in an existing product market plays an important role in determining the target market strategy that it uses. Low market share firms have to compete in segments where their strengths are most highly valued and where large competitors are unlikely to compete. The strength may be in the type and range of products that are offered, the method by which the product is produced, the cost and speed of distribution, or the credit and service arrangements. In these firms management has to spend time identifying and exploiting unique segments, rather than attempting to serve entire industries.

STRUCTURE AND INTENSITY OF COMPETITION

When several firms are competing in an industry, selective targeting is often an appropriate target market strategy. Such selectivity is often essential for small firms in fragmented, transitional and global industries. Large firms may be able to reap the benefits of extensive targeting using a multiple segmentation strategy.

ADEQUATE RESOURCES

The possession of considerable resources can often place an organization in a position where it can consider various target market alternatives. Where resources are limited, however, a company may be forced to adopt a single segment targeting strategy. The ability to analyse market capabilities is a decided asset, particularly where the task of market segmentation is a complex one. Thus possessing both resources and the capacity to undertake such complex analyses provides firms with flexibility in choosing market targets.

PRODUCTION AND MARKETING SCALE ECONOMIES

Choice of target market strategy may be influenced by production and marketing scale economies. The production process, for example, may require large-scale output to achieve necessary cost advantages. The same may also apply to marketing and distribution programmes. In such cases an extensive market coverage strategy may be required in order to gain the sales volume necessary to support large-volume production and distribution.

CHOICE OF SEGMENT(S)

Five factors govern the attractiveness of a segment (Doyle, 1994, p.68.):

- segment size
- segment growth
- profitability of the segment
- current and potential competition
- capabilities of the business.

Deciding whether or not to enter a particular segment depends essentially on the match between the company's capabilities and the characteristics of the segment. While a large, expanding and lucrative market segment must be intuitively appealing, it will attract considerable competition, so a firm must have the capabilities (resources) to compete effectively in such a market segment. Similarly, as segments contract, larger competitors may tend to withdraw, making the segment less competitive and more attractive to firms with lesser capabilities.

In the above case example, many of these issues are highlighted.

MAURICE BEAUFORT: TARGETING

Maurice Beaufort set up in business in January 1994. Up until December, 1993, he had been working as an electrician with a small firm of contractors. He had always wanted to work for himself – but not as an electrician.

Maurice had a hobby which he had spent many years cultivating. This hobby was collecting postage stamps. His interest had begun when he was a boy and he had carried it through to middle age. The opportunity to set up his own business had occurred when a new city centre shopping complex had been opened up. In the basement of the complex, space had been set aside for small businesses wanting to retail antiques, curios and other ephemera. The city council had been keen to encourage people to take space and had offered three months' free rent plus a cash bonus of £1500 to anyone who was prepared to take on a stall during the first three months of operation.

Maurice's experience with stamps had been an active one. Initially, as a boy, he had been given stamps as presents, bought them in packets from market stalls, swapped them with friends at school and, later on, had received stamps on approval from reputable vendors advertising in stamp magazines. In the 1970s, antique and collectors fairs had started to become fashionable and stamp dealers had begun to appear at such fairs. More specialized fairs soon developed, and at the turn of the 1980s fairs dedicated to the sale of stamps were commonplace. Most of the business with collectors at stamp fairs was conducted at weekends, though fairs were conducted during the week as well. The usual venue for such fairs was at a hotel, though occasionally church halls and other outlets were used. Stamp fairs have grown in popularity since the beginning of the 1980s and several fair organizers now operate different circuits of the country.

Dealers in stamps obtain their stock in three ways. They buy at fairs or at their own retail premises direct from collectors; they buy at auctions which are held regularly in different parts of the country; or they buy from other dealers at stamp fairs – usually during the first hour or so, before trading with collectors begins.

Collectors as well as traders can buy at auctions, and this can be done either at the auction in person or by postal bid. Maurice had attended auctions quite regularly for a period of ten years prior to setting up in business and was very conversant with the value of stamps and the whole process of buying and selling

CASE EXAMPLE *CONTINUED*

them. In setting up in business to sell stamps, however, he had encountered the all-important problem of what stock he should keep in order to satisfy callers at his stall.

The market for stamps can be segmented in different ways. Age and income are segmentation variables as are the interests of the collectors. Some people, for example, like to collect 'themes' – birds, animals, trains, cathedrals, saints, religion, paintings, etc. Other people obtain old printed albums covering specific periods – say 1840–1936 – and collect stamps to fill the designated spaces in these albums. Some people collect only British stamps, others only Commonwealth stamps, while others collect everything. Unfortunately, there is not a lot of published information concerning market segment sizes or the behaviour of stamp collectors.

Maurice had observed from the auction brochures that most of the business transacted appeared to be in terms of British stamps, with no particular period predominating. Commonwealth stamps appeared to be next on the list, though trade in certain foreign countries – for instance, the USA – was brisk. Lots at auction rarely fetched more than £2000 and most of the bigger lots ranged between £100 and £600. For this kind of expenditure many thousands of different stamps could be bought. Auction lots varied, from collections in albums to paper accumulations in shoe boxes; often, the latter accumulations were unsorted.

The city centre premises attracted a high volume of passers-by, comprising all ages and income bands. The rental agreement on the stall prevented anyone else from setting up in business in the shopping centre to sell the same products without prior agreement with existing similar businesses.

QUESTIONS

1. What does segmentation and targeting mean to a business such as that run by Maurice Beaufort?

2. Assuming that Maurice has limited resources for investing in the business, say £10 000, how would you advise him to spend this money in terms of buying stock?

POSITIONING

Positioning, it has been suggested (Marken, 1987, p.7), represents the most important decision and action management has to make for the company and its marketing; yet it remains one of the most nebulous and controversial areas of new product development (Davis, 1977, p.1). Targeting and positioning strategies are interrelated. The choice of one or more target markets is based, at least in part, on the feasibility for the organization of designing and implementing an effective positioning strategy to meet the target's needs. Positioning strategies used to pursue target markets may vary considerably, or they may have common features. For example, a firm may have a unique combination of the product offering, distribution approach, price, advertising and personal selling to serve each segment. Alternatively, some marketing mix components may be similar for different segments. An airline service, for example, can appeal to business and holiday makers, although different advertising and sales efforts are aimed at each market niche and fare prices may vary across segments.

What is it that differentiates one product or service from another, even when they are almost identical? The answer seems to reflect the way in which the marketers of the product or service position them in the minds of users. Positioning refers to the decisions and activities intended to create and maintain a firm's product concept in customers' minds. Market positioning amounts to arranging for a product or service to occupy a clear, distinctive and desirable place – relative to competing products – in the minds of target customers.

What is being marketed must be perceived by the selected target customers as having a distinct image, relative to competitors, which meets with their own desires/expectations. The position of an offering is related to the attributes ascribed to it by consumers, such as its standing, its quality and the type of people who use it, its strengths and weaknesses and any other unusual and memorable characteristics it may possess, its price and the value it represents to users.

The whole of the marketing mix is important in developing effective positioning, as attributes of the offering must be closely in line with the targeted customers' expectations and needs, as must the associated price points and channels of distribution. However, promotional activity is one of the fundamental elements of creating an effective positioning as it is through promotion that the positioning is communicated to the target audience.

POSITIONING CONCEPTS

The positioning concept may be functional, symbolic, or experiential.

- The **functional** concept is relevant to products designed to solve consumption-related problems for externally generated consumption needs. Toothpastes aiming to prevent cavities and banks offering convenient service fall into this category.

- The **symbolic** concept relates to the buyer's internally generated need for self-enhancement, role position, group membership, or ego satisfaction. Cosmetics relating to lifestyle, and clothes stressing image or appropriateness of occasion, are examples of this.

● The **experiential** concept is used to position products that provide sensory pleasure, variety or cognitive stimulation. Documentary films and books are examples of this.

Positioning is a systematic process and requires systematic planning. In the next section we move on to look at how this is achieved.

STEPS IN DETERMINING A POSITIONING PLAN

There are seven steps involved.

1. Define the segments in a particular market, as discussed in Chapter 7.

2. Decide which segment or segments to target which the firm thinks it can successfully exploit.

3. Understand what the target customers expect and believe to be the most important factors or criteria when deciding on a purchase. This is the step or part of the process which involves identifying the underlying factors upon which the product/service or brand will be based.

4. Develop a product/service or brand which caters specifically for these expectations. The product/service or brand has to be carefully designed to reflect clearly how it meets with customer expectations.

5. Evaluate the positioning and images, as perceived by the target market, of competing offerings in the selected market segment or segments. Positioning is concerned with how the brand will be perceived in the minds of users with respect to competing brands. The aim will be to differentiate the brand from competing brands, so understanding how competing brands are perceived is very important.

6. With the knowledge of a product/brand, the needs and expectations of the target customers, and their perceptions of competing brands' positioning, select an image which sets the product or brand apart from the competing brands, ensuring that the chosen image matches the aspirations of the target customers. In this respect it is important that the selected positioning and imagery are credible.

7. The marketer must communicate with the targeted customers about the product – the promotional element of the marketing mix – as well as making the product readily available at the right price, along with the full marketing mix.

These are the mechanics of positioning, but positioning must be based upon some underlying strategy. In the next section we address this particular issue.

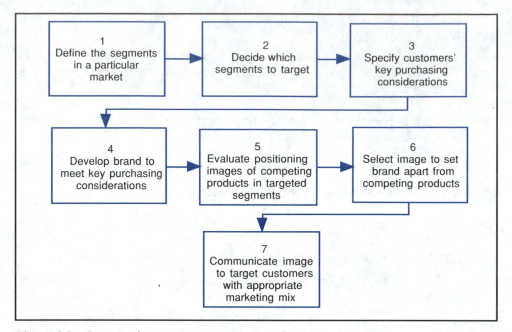

Figure 8.2 Steps in determining a positioning plan.

POSITIONING STRATEGY

Producers of goods and services attach their own label or brand to their particular market offering. For instance, we talk of a 'Mars Bar' or a 'Kit Kat', differentiating one offering from another. In this particular case the products are made by different manufacturers but this does not need to be the case. A single firm may put two or more brands into the market which actually compete with one another. We will discuss this strategy below.

In view of the fact that markets comprise people with different wants and needs, one brand of product or service cannot usually serve the requirements of the entire market segment. The focal point of any strategy is that it should aim to match a brand with that segment of the market where it is most likely to succeed. The brand should be positioned in such a manner that it stands apart from competing brands. A product's positioning indicates what the product represents and how customers should evaluate it.

Positioning is accomplished through the use of the marketing-mix variables, particularly through product design and marketing communications. Positioning to achieve product differentiation applies equally to consumer and to industrial goods. In some cases product positioning can be achieved on the basis of tangible differences (e.g. product features); however, in many instances customer perceptions about products are used to differentiate and position them.

Product positioning is accomplished by using the following procedure.

1. Find out and explore the nature of the product attributes that are considered important by customers.

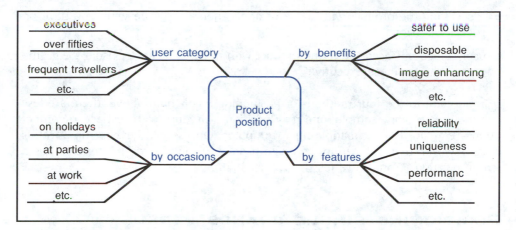

Figure 8.3 Bases of product positioning.

2. Established how the importance of these attributes varies among the different market segments.

3. Examine the best position for the product with respect to each attribute, taking into account the positions of existing brands.

4. An overall position for the brand (based upon the overall match between product attributes and their distribution in the population and the positioning of existing brands) is finally worked out.

For example, the product positioning of a brand of motor cycle to young drivers could be based on price and economy. It could be ascertained that price is the important product attribute in general but that in the case of the younger driver market segment price and economy are the most important attributes. It might be discovered that in the younger driver segment of the market there are already cheap motor cycles, but only one of them is really economical. The task then might be to offer a cheap economical motor cycle which possesses one or more of the following attributes:

● cheaper than the existing product offering

● more economical than the existing product offering

● both cheaper and more economical, plus offering more features than the existing product.

There are a number of different ways of positioning a product (see, for example, Burnett, 1993, p.60). The positioning may be based on (Figure 8.3):

● product features – such as the low calory content of some foods

● product benefits – e.g. a particular model of car being 'the most economical way to get to work by car'

- associating the product with a use or application – e.g. 'the wine you have on special occasions'

- user category – associating the product with a user or class of users – e.g. 'the car for the business executive'.

In addition to the four methods of positioning highlighted above, there are less common ways. For example, one may position a product with respect to competition – e.g. 'an IBM compatible microcomputer'. One should bear in mind in this case, however, that one cannot compete head-on against a competitor that has a strong position (Trout and Ries, 1972, pp. 35–8).

POSITIONING SINGLE BRANDS VERSUS MULTIPLE BRANDS

So far we have assumed that a firm will produce either one product which will appeal to a number of segments or individual products for individual segments. We have not considered the situation where more than one 'brand' or 'label' is offered by one manufacturer to a single segment. In this section we will contrast the positioning of a single brand with that of multiple brands.

POSITIONING A SINGLE BRAND

In order to make the most out of a single brand, a firm should try to associate itself with a core segment of the market where it can play a dominant role. In

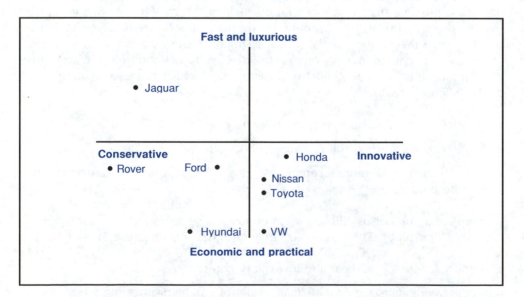

Figure 8.4 Perceptual map of brand images of selected cars – a hypothetical example.

CASE EXAMPLE

POSITIONING HOW MULTIPLE BRANDS CAN LEAD TO INCREASED PROFITS

If a company launches two brands into the same market segment then they will take away sales from each other. However, if they are so positioned so that customers perceive the products as being decidedly different then the combined effect of having the two brands in the same segment can lead to substantial profits.

Alpha markets a soap powder called Cleen which has a 20% share of a soap powder market segment. Five years ago it introduced a new soap powder called Scrub which was perceived by users to be very similar to Cleen. The result was that Cleen's share of the market segment dropped to 10% as Scrub took 10 per cent of the market segment sales. Cannibalisation had occurred – many people who normally bought Cleen had simply shifted their allegiance to Scrub. In this case Alpha actually was much worse off since it had incurred development and marketing costs on the new product Scrub and was now spending more money marketing the two products than it had previously done in just marketing Cleen. In addition there were also extra production costs involved. Altogether this was a marketing fiasco and Alpha quickly rectified the situation by withdrawing Scrub from sale.

Two years ago Cleen had regained its 20% share of the market segment and Alpha decided once again to launch another brand alongside Cleen. This time it made sure that the soap powder was perceived to be significantly different by potential users. The new product's name is Mop and it now has a 15% share of the same market segment as Cleen.

Cleen has only dropped two points off its original share of the market segment which now stands at 18 per cent. Adding the two market shares together now means that Alpha has a 33% share of the market segment. The additional costs of having two brands in the market segment have been more than recovered and the firm's profitability has been increased substantially.

QUESTION

1. How did Alpha ensure that Mop achieved an increase in overall market share?

CASE EXAMPLE

FORD PROBE: REPOSITIONING

'The car you always promised yourself' was the slogan used by Ford in 1969 to launch the Capri in Europe. The design of the Capri was not entirely new, having been inspired by the Mustang which had been launched in the USA some five years earlier. Ford had previously introduced a car with the Capri name earlier in the 1960s, which had proved a complete flop. Launching a new model under the same label might have been considered by some people to have been a unnecessary gamble.

Based on an adaptation of the Cortina chassis, it had a desirable coupé body which resembled a sports car but had four-seater accommodation. The car continued in production until 1987, by which time nearly two million had been sold. However, by then the UK was the only market of any consequence for the car, and projected sales volumes were insufficient to justify developing a model based on the Sierra, the replacement for the Cortina.

For many people, the going of the Capri was a sad loss. Although hot hatchbacks like the Escort XR3i could be bought by those who wanted something faster and more distinctive than the normal run of family saloons, there was an unfulfilled want in the market place. The Capri could not be replaced by the hot hatchbacks, which possessed shorter life cycles and were seen as too expensive to insure, too attractive to young criminals, and too flash for comfort in the politically correct 1990s.

With the demise of the XRs, a smarter, smoother sports coupé was waiting in the wings to make an entrance. Its name, this time, was the Probe and the idea again came from the USA. The Probe is made by Auto Alliance International, a joint venture between Ford and Mazda in Flat Rock, Michigan. The body is styled by Ford of America, though it is in effect a Japanese design. On the mechanical side the engines, transmissions and major mechanical components all originated at Mazda. Technically the Probe is very similar to the Mazda MX6 coupé.

The Probe is quite unlike any of the other cars in Ford's European range and quite different to the old Capri. The Vauxhall Calibra may be seen as its chief rival but the Probe, having been purpose-built as a sports coupé, is substantially different to the Calibra. In the Probe lies Ford's hope of regaining the Capri's old position as Britain's best seller in this class. However, in contrast to the Calibra – a restyled Cavalier with full four-seater accommodation – the Probe is a 2 + 2.

CASE EXAMPLE *CONTINUED*

In designing the Probe all the emphasis has been placed on the driver and front seat passenger – there is very little room in the back.

Some people would argue that the Probe is more like cars such as the Volkswagen Corrado, Honda Prelude, Toyota Celica, the forthcoming Fiat coupé and the Mazda MX6. Whatever the case, the Probe is likely to appeal to a good number of people, since it feels more special than the Calibra and has more aggressive looks and better responses than the Mazda MX6.

The Probe has wide, low-profile tyres that provide plenty of grip. Although its ride at low speed is harsh enough to be uncomfortable on some bumpy roads, cornering on smooth roads is a confidence-building experience and the power steering is excellent.

Under the bonnet the powerful V6 engine is impressive. It comes in two sizes: the 165 bhp 24V engine produces a top speed of 136 mph and a 0–60 mph acceleration time of eight seconds, while the 115 bhp 16V engine produces a top speed of 127 mph and a 0–60 mph time of ten seconds.

Whichever version of the Probe is chosen it will be an enjoyable tourer for two, or even a family with small children. The Probe is priced directly against the Calibra, with a tag of around £16 500 for the 2 litre engine and around £19 500 for the larger engine.

(Source: Hutton, 1994, pp.662–3)

QUESTION

1. Discuss the approach to positioning the Ford Probe.

addition it might also try to attract customers from other segments outside its core. An alternative single brand strategy would be to consider the market as being undifferentiated, and to try to serve it with a single brand. This strategy only tends to work in the short run. In order to gain entry to a market, competitors segment and challenge the dominance of the single brand by positioning themselves in small viable niches.

To protect the position of a single brand a firm may introduce other brands. Its original brand may have been challenged by a competitor with a cut-price alternative product. A solution for the firm might be to increase the price of the original existing brand, thereby taking it out of direct competition with the alternative brand, at the same time introducing a new brand priced to compete directly with the competitor's brand.

There are two requisites to managing a single brand successfully in the market place:

1. the brand has to be positioned in the market place so that it can stand competition from the strongest rival brand

2. its unique position should be maintained by creating the appearance that it is in fact a different product.

POSITIONING MULTIPLE BRANDS

Multiple brands are introduced to the market for two major reasons:

1. to achieve growth by offering varied products in different segments of the market

2. to meet competitors' threats to a single brand.

When a firm is seeking to achieve growth targets, multiple brands have to be positioned in the market so that they do not compete with each other. Failure to do so effectively means that 'cannibalism' can occur – the phenomenon whereby sales of one brand take sales away from another brand marketed by the same company.

Where multiple brands are being offered to the market by the same producer, cannibalism will always occur to some extent, and the aim should be to minimize its effect. As a strategy the positioning of multiple brands, if properly implemented, can lead to increases in growth, market share and profitability.

REPOSITIONING STRATEGIES

Positioning is not a one-time event. A product or service will require its positioning adjusting from time to time. This is referred to as repositioning, and it can become necessary if:

● a competitor's new product or service has been positioned next to the brand and this is having an adverse effect on the product or service's share of the market

● consumer preferences with respect to the product or service have changed

● new customer preference clusters have been identified that suggest promising opportunities

● the original positioning was incorrect.

Whether a firm is engaged in positioning or repositioning a product or service there are always high risks involved. The technique of perceptual mapping can often be used to reduce those risks. A perceptual map is a grid which shows how people perceive products to be positioned in relation to one another. The technique may be illustrated with a hypothetical example relating to the car market

(Figure 8.4). The map helps the marketing strategist in assessing whether the company's cars are on target. The concentration of dots representing competing models shows what opposition there is likely to be in a specific area of the map.

Cars towards the top of the graph, where the stress is on performance and luxury, should fetch a higher price than cars towards the bottom, where the stress is on economy and practicality.

Products may be repositioned in three ways.

1. **Among existing users** – by the promotion of more varied uses of a product. A table wine may have been positioned as a wine for 'special occasions'. Repositioning might suggest its use as 'being suitable for every occasion'.

2. **Among new users** – this requires the product to be presented with a different image to the people who have so far rejected it. In so doing, it is important to make sure that in the process of getting new customers, current customers of the product are not alienated.

3. **For new users** – here one has to search for latent uses of the product. New uses for nylon sprang up in the form of varied types of hosiery, tyres, bearings, etc. It was the new uses that kept nylon on a growth path: wrap knits in 1945, tyre cord in 1948, textured yarns in 1955, carpet yarns in 1959, and so on. Without new uses nylon would have hit saturation level as far back as 1962.

The above case example provides thought-provoking ideas on matters relating to repositioning.

POSITIONING EFFECTIVENESS

Evaluating how successful one had been in positioning a product is of course an essential task. A sustainable competitive advantage results from offering greater value or lower costs than the competition. Evaluating competitive advantage is based on positioning analysis.

Positioning analysis involves looking at how the 'advantage' in the position has been gained. It may be based on cost, value or performance.

COST ADVANTAGE

A positioning advantage comes about when an organization can offer, at a lower cost, a bundle of benefits perceived as equivalent to those of the competition. Most importantly, the targeted buyers must consider this set of benefits as being of positive value to them. Otherwise, what is being offered will not satisfy the targeted buyers' needs and wants.

This can be aptly illustrated by new models of cars which are regularly released onto the market. With each new model, additional benefits are offered at the same cost to the customer. These may take the form of extended warranties, in-car entertainment extras, or mobile communication facilities.

VALUE ADVANTAGE

This kind of positioning advantage is based upon occupying a location in product attribute space that represents for buyers the most preferred combination of attributes and is one that is not currently occupied by any competitor. Much of the work in using perceptual maps is aimed at identifying these exact combinations. In the case of the car market, for example, where one might be combining comfort with performance, the task is to determine just how much of each of these two factors identifiable groups of customers want and what combination is likely to satisfy the greatest number of people.

MANAGEMENT'S PERFORMANCE EXPECTATIONS

This considers the performance of a position. It takes account of whether a particular value advantage is worthwhile in terms of revenues and costs. Performance evaluation is necessary in evaluating the adequacy of an existing position or in considering a repositioning strategy. In this respect, a successful positioning strategy should be evaluated on a regular basis to identify shifting buyer preferences and changes in competitor strategies.

SUMMARY

This chapter has examined the importance of market targeting in strategic marketing. Firms have to identify market segments which they can best serve with the resources they have available and select a combination which will enable them to operate profitably.

There are a number of different approaches to target marketing. One approach, mass marketing, is where a product or service is designed to appeal to most customers in the market. As an alternative, firms can adopt a more selective approach. In the latter case firms may choose single market segments in which to operate, or may choose to operate in a number of market segments where a degree of synergy among the segments can be achieved.

There is no single best strategy for all firms to try to adopt. All businesses face different marketing opportunities and have different ranges of resources, skills and competencies at their disposal. A firm must be able to recognize appropriate targeting strategies for specific business situations.

In addition to targeting market segments firms have to be able to position their products and services within chosen segments such that they stand out from those of their competitors. It is through positioning products and services clearly in the minds of customers that firms are able to establish a differential advantage for their market offerings.

Positioning planning involves:

● defining the segments in a particular market

● deciding which segment or segments to target

● understanding what the target customers believe to be the most important factors or criteria when deciding on a purchase

● developing a brand which caters specifically for these expectations

● evaluating the positioning and images, as perceived by the target market, of competing offerings in the selected market segment or segments

● knowledge of a brand, the needs and expectations of the target customers, their perceptions of competing brands' positioning

● selecting an image which sets the product or brand apart from the competing brands.

Product positioning is achieved by exploring the nature of product attributes that are considered important by customers and establishing how the importance of these attributes varies among the different market segments. One then has to examine the best position for the product with respect to each attribute, taking into account the positions of existing brands. Finally, an overall position for the brand (based upon the overall match between product attributes and their distribution in the population and the positioning of existing brands) is worked out.

In the case of a single brand, a firm should try to associate it with a core segment of the market where it can play a dominant role. In addition it might also try to attract customers from other segments outside its core, or consider the market undifferentiated and try to serve it with the single brand.

Multiple brands are introduced to the market for two major reasons:

1. to achieve growth by offering varied products in different segments of the market

2. to meet competitors' threats to a single brand.

When a firm is seeking to achieve growth targets, multiple brands have to be positioned in the market so that they do not compete with each other. Failure to do this effectively means that 'cannibalism' can occur – the phenomenon whereby sales of one brand take sales away from another brand marketed by the same company. Cannibalism will always occur to some extent – the aim should be to minimize its effect. As a strategy, the positioning of multiple brands, if properly implemented, can lead to increases in growth, market share and profitability.

A product or service will require its positioning adjusting from time to time. This is known as repositioning and it can become necessary if a competitor's new product or service has been positioned next to the brand and this is having an adverse effect on the product or service's share of the market. It can also happen when consumer preferences with respect to the product or service have changed, or new customer preference clusters have been identified that suggest promising opportunities, or if the original positioning was incorrect.

DISCUSSION QUESTIONS

1. What is implied by a mass marketing strategy? How does this relate to targeting?

2. Under what conditions might a mass marketing approach be an appropriate marketing strategy to adopt?

3. What do you understand by a single-segment strategy, and what are the advantages and disadvantages of adopting such a strategy?

4. Explain the concept of a multi-segment strategy.

5. Explain the idea of positioning.

6. Explain the three bases of deriving positioning concepts.

7. What are the steps to be followed in determining a positioning plan?

8. What do you understand by a positioning strategy?

9. How is product or service positioning accomplished?

10. Discuss the factors that influence choice of positioning strategy.

11. How does positioning a single brand differ from positioning several brands?

12. What is repositioning, and why are products and services repositioned periodically?

13. How would you evaluate competitive advantage based on positioning analysis?

REFERENCES

Burnett, J.J. (1993) *Promotion Management*, Houghton Miflin, Chicago, Ill.

Chronoswiss Uhren GmbH, *Fascination of Watchmaking*, Chronoswiss, Munich.

Davis, L. (1977) Grasp behavior before picking target markets, *Marketing News*, 1.

Doyle, P. (1994) *Marketing Management and Strategy*, Prentice Hall, Englewood Cliffs, N.J.

Hutton, R. (1994) Best of the bunch, *Scottish Business Insider*, March, 662–3.

Marken, A. (1987) Positioning key element for effective marketing, *Marketing News*, **21**(4), 7.

Matthews, V. (1994) Pawn again on the high street, *Marketing Week*, 28 January, 19.

Pass, C., Lowes, B., Pendleton, A. and Chadwick, L. (1991) *Dictionary of Business*, Collins, London.

Trout, J. and Ries, A. (1972) The positioning era cometh, *Advertising Age*, 24 April, 35–8.

FURTHER READING

Aaker, D.A. and Shansby, J.G. (1982) Positioning your product, *Business Horizons*, May/June, 56–62.

Ries, A. and Trout, J. (1981) *Positioning: The Battle For Your Mind*, McGraw Hill, New York.

CASE PROBLEM 8.1

HIGH STREET PAWNBROKING: TARGETING AND POSITIONING

Pawnbroking is now a major source of money-lending, along with banks and building societies. There are around 350 pawnbrokers in the UK and between them they have turnover of around £400m. The trend in business transactions is also on an upward spiral, showing an increase in 1993 of about one-fifth on the previous year. More than 10 000 people borrow from pawnbrokers every day, using their valuables as security. Almost 80% of all items pawned are redeemed well within the six months allowed; the rest are sold and any net proceeds are given to the original owners.

There are now a number of pawnbroking chains, and despite the traditional image of the pawnbroker as a collection of tiny, usually backstreet, independent and locally-based family-run operations, the multiple pawnbroker is now a feature of the industry. The largest chain is Harvey & Thompson, which has a string of shops widely dispersed throughout the country.

Pawnbroking is closely regulated by the DTI, which advances pawnbroking's case for recognition as a respectable industry. In addition, the National Association of Pawnbrokers' members, concerned about trade in stolen goods, offers customer compensation insurance schemes and a wide-ranging legal advice. Both of these factors give a boost to the respectability of the industry. The image of poorly lit, dismal shops has been replaced with a new image which is one of a brightly illuminated and prominently placed high street pawnbroker.

One pawnbroker maintains that people prefer to deal with pawnbrokers rather than banks because they do not like having to ask for a loan and having to tell 'some cocky 23 year old bank clerk' what they are going to do with the money. Unlike the bank, pawnbrokers do not expect people to offer anything more than the item being pawned. The pawnbroker said that not only did pawnbrokers have all the subtle lighting and designer decor of the banks, but that they also have something which is more important – the sort of staff who truly value discretion and who will tend to give people the money they require without being awkward.

The image of pawnbroking has changed substantially from the days of the 1920s and 1930s, when it was seen as second only to the Church

CASE PROBLEM 8.1 *CONTINUED*

in terms of its capability to relieve the needs of the poor. Gone are the days when it was seen solely as a place for the needy, where torn bed-linen and cracked chamberpots were often high on the list of pawnable items. Nowadays, pawnbroking is becoming not only a handy way to borrow money, but in more middle class circles is also curiously fashionable.

The nature of the item pledged can provide some surprises. Between gigs, musicians often pawn their guitars or other instruments; most reclaim them for their next booking. On a different level altogether some pawnbrokers take cars, boats and even aeroplanes; in such cases the value of the pledges can amount to thousands of pounds. One pawnbroker is said to be have taken a pledge involving £20 000 and a helicopter but to have somewhat unwillingly refused a race horse and a fishing trawler because of lack of room!

(Source: Matthews, 1994)

QUESTION

1. How would you see pawnbrokers positioning themselves with respect to banks and building societies?

CASE PROBLEM 8.2

CHRONOSWISS: TARGETING AND POSITIONING

In the early 1980s Gerd R. Lang set out to develop and manufacture exclusive mechanical wrist-watches. This could have been viewed as a rather eccentric thing to do, at a time when many people thought that the day of the mechanical watch had passed. However, Gerd was certain that there were people who preferred classical, mechanical wrist-watches and that such people would not be satisfied with the limitations imposed on them by the range available in the used-watch market of collectors' items.

Gerd decided to produce high quality mechanical watches for a small circle of connoisseurs and individualists. He subsequently found that his judgement was right, for the response to the first Chronoswiss watches was stronger than expected. Success encouraged him to continue and eventually resulted in a Chronoswiss Collection. Each of the watches in the collection is a fully mechanical timepiece manufactured in accordance with strict quality standards and intended to provide many years of lasting value.

The idea came to Gerd in 1983, when manufacturers of 'ticking' watch movements were considering stopping production in view of the lack of demand. Gerd's idea was targeted to a market in the knowledge that there would always be people who do not want silent electronic quartz movements in their watches but who prefer the pleasant ticking of classical watches with real mechanical movements.

It was the rebirth of the lunar disk watch that endorsed the company's strategy: the first Chronoswiss wrist-watch was a chronograph showing the date and phase of the moon. This proved very successful and the company soon added additional moon phase models, chronographs and skeleton watches. In 1988 the firm introduced the 'Regulateur', an exclusive, limited Chronoswiss model. This attracted many admirers and was even copied by other watch manufacturers.

In a short space of time, Chronoswiss has been able to establish itself in the market place. Its market profile is based on the philosophy of a firm making high-quality mechanical watches for people who are sensitive to the exceptional, and who wish to have wrist-watches that express their individual lifestyle.

(Source: Chronoswiss)

QUESTION

Explain Chronoswiss's approach to targeting and positioning.

9 MARKETING STRATEGY AND PLANNING

This chapter relates the corporate strategy/plan to marketing planning. Marketing strategies are examined as they relate to the needs of the corporate plan, and the role of new product markets is emphasized. An appreciation of the usefulness of the concept of the product life cycle and the main product/service portfolio models is presented. Attention is then given to strategy selection; finally, the chapter looks at how marketing plans are developed.

OBJECTIVES

After studying the chapter you should be able to:

- understand the nature of corporate strategy and the role of the corporate plan

- appreciate the kind of financial goals that an organization sets for itself and how these are in turn related to marketing planning

- appreciate the usefulness of the concept of the product life cycle

- understand that firms need to have a balanced product/service portfolio with elements at different stages in the product life cycle to ensure long-term survival and growth

- describe the stages in the marketing planning process.

INTRODUCTION

Both corporate and marketing planning entail setting objectives, setting goals, auditing resources, undertaking gap analysis, writing down plans, implementing plans and evaluating their implementation. In the first instance, overall corporate financial goals are set and these are then translated into goals for marketing planning. Marketing strategies aimed at achieving stated goals and objectives are based on an analysis of marketing strengths, weaknesses, opportunities and threats and their impact on the organization.

Gap analysis is used to identify the difference between aspirations and likely achievements with the current product-market portfolio. Choice of marketing objectives and strategy is aided by skilful analysis to identify strengths and weaknesses of the organization, and opportunities and threats that exist in the environment. Through a careful matching process and creative thinking, strategies emerge.

Central to the success or failure of a business is the health of its product mix. This chapter first considers theoretical notions relating to the product life cycle concept. This is a useful conceptual framework within which to study how firms should apply their marketing strategies. At different stages in the product life cycle some strategies are more appropriate than others. The life cycle concept also points to the different earning patterns through the various stages and suggests that it is necessary to have a balanced portfolio of products/services to ensure steady sales and profits at all times. This means that the firm has to prune its product lines and introduce new products to stay on course.

Examining the nature of the product life cycle concept acts as a good introduction to product portfolio models. Several product portfolio models – perhaps the best known of which are the BCG (Boston Consulting Group) matrix and the GE-McKinsey matrix – were developed to help firms assess the balance of the product mix. This chapter examines the use and limitations of such models.

The portfolio models are useful diagnostic tools, but more formal and detailed planning mechanisms are required to evolve and evaluate detailed strategies. The chapter looks at the TOWS matrix, a development of SWOT analysis, in this context.

Finally, plans in themselves are not sufficient to ensure that an organization achieves its desired objectives. Marketing budgets have to be established to provide specific targets to achieve and resources to allocate.

In this chapter we will start off by looking at the nature of the corporate plan and corporate strategy and then look more specifically at the marketing plan.

CORPORATE STRATEGY AND THE CORPORATE PLAN

The corporate strategy of an organization reflects its objectives and goals and produces the principal policies and plans for achieving those goals. The corporate strategy normally defines the nature of the business the organization must pursue, which in turn has a bearing on the kind of economic and human organization it needs to possess. Goals and objectives are usually set within a time framework.

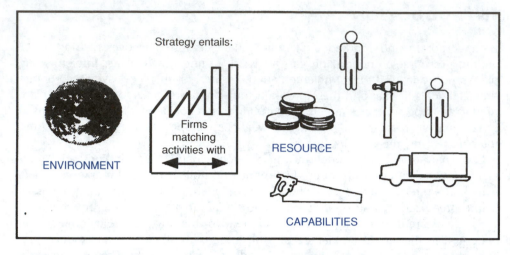

Figure 9.1 What strategy entails.

Strategy entails matching the company's activities to its resource capability. There is little point in trying to take advantage of some new opportunity if the resources needed are not available or cannot be made available. An organization must formulate strategy within the boundaries of the resources that are likely to be made available. This is a fundamental consideration that must be addressed when formulating corporate strategy.

Strategy is also to do with matching the activities of a company to the environment in which it operates. Since the environment is continually changing, strategic decisions necessarily involve coping with change. The extent and speed of environmental change will vary and the pace at which strategy must change will necessarily vary too.

THE CORPORATE PLAN

The corporate plan is the plan for the company as a whole. It defines the business in which the company operates, indicates financial objectives that have to be accomplished, specifies how revenues are to be generated through various marketing programmes and assesses the various costs that will be incurred in achieving these objectives.

The corporate plan answers the following questions.

- Where are we now?

- Where do we want to go?

- How do we organize resources to get there?

Defining the nature of the business in which the firm operates is crucial. For example, if Cunard had not seen its business as being that of transportation it is

THE BLUE LAGOON CLUB: ESTABLISHING A CORPORATE STRATEGY

Comino is a small island lying between the larger islands of Malta and Gozo. Both Malta and Gozo are popular holiday destinations for Europeans, and Malta in particular has a well-established commercial infrastructure and a highly developed hotel .and holiday trade. Gozo, by contrast, is smaller, quieter and much less commercially developed. In recent years tourists have started to visit Gozo in much larger numbers and the island now has two five-star hotels and a number of less prestigious hotels.

Comino lies only a short distance away from one of Gozo's chief towns – Mgarr. It is a quiet island with only a handful of local inhabitants and only one or two buildings. The island, however, does have one very notable feature: a lagoon in which the sea water is crystal clear, Mediterranean blue in colour and teaming with all forms of aquatic life.

The blue lagoon is an attraction to all visitors to the Maltese archipelago. Throughout the spring, summer and autumn thousands of tourists visit the lagoon, either to admire its natural features or to participate in aquatic activities.

Early in 1995 two Sicilian brothers, with wide experience of commercial ventures in the Maltese Islands, were looking into the possibility of developing leisure facilities near to the Blue Lagoon. One idea was to develop an exclusive club offering a wide range of recreational facilities – such as a tennis court, mini-golf course, gymnasium, etc. along with residential accommodation for up to 100 guests.

The brothers argued that Comino was close to Gozo, which tended to attract the richer and more sport-active holiday-makers. These kind of individuals tended to take accommodation in Mgarr and made regular forages across the channel to Comino to enjoy its splendour and recreational pursuits.

QUESTION

1. What do you think should be the corporate strategy of the Sicilian brothers in this case? Explain.

less likely that the company would have moved into containerization from its position as a provider of a passenger liner service. The above case example poses the question regarding selection of an appropriate corporate strategy.

GOAL SETTING

Goals must be realistic, and an organization has to be aware of where it stands in relation to competition and the various markets it serves. It also has to be reasonable in terms of specifying what it wants to achieve. For example, it may not be realistic for a small electronics firm to expect to grow to the size of a multinational company within five years. Nevertheless, in the Far East there are now some giant international corporations competing successfully which did not exist 25 years ago.

The first phase of corporate planning entails setting long term goals in terms of sales turnover, profit before tax and return on capital invested.

AUDITING

Next comes a management audit. All of the functional areas of management are audited: marketing, production, finance and personnel. We will restrict ourselves to examining the marketing audit here.

A marketing audit amounts to an evaluation and assessment of all factors which affect the firm's marketing performance. The factors can be internal to the firm or be part of the external environment.

The internal marketing audit

The internal audit comprises a detailed analysis by product/service of the market share and profitability of the various lines. In addition, strategies relating to marketing mix elements are reviewed and studied, together with the use made of marketing research data. At the same time an examination is made of marketing budgets and how they were drawn up and related to previously agreed objectives.

The external marketing audit

The external audit examines the organization's external environment. It commences with a review of the general economy and then makes an assessment of the prospects for the firm's markets. The external audit attempts to estimate what should be the appropriate course of action, taking into account economic and market indicators.

Many factors have to be considered. Economic, fiscal, social, business, legal and technological developments all have a substantial impact on the business. In addition, market segments, channels, products, end uses, needs, tastes, attitudes, stocks and profits have to be considered. Attention must also be paid to the activities of competitors and potential competitors.

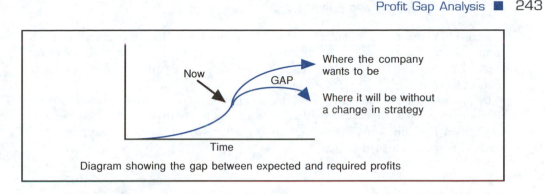

Diagram showing the gap between expected and required profits

Figure 9.2 Classical gap analysis.

PROFIT GAP ANALYSIS

Forecasting what is likely to happen in each business sector in the immediate and longer-term future is important. The organization must make predictions that take into account factors which are external to the firm, such as market trends, economic trends, competitive trends, socio-cultural trends and technological trends.

The implications of these trends are then compared with the likely performance of the company based on internal factors such as product strengths, material costs, technical ability, productivity prospects and financial capacity. The next step is to project earnings from existing business over the timescale of the forecasts and to make comparisons with the required objectives.

For example, a manufacturer of wrist-watch batteries would recognize that technology and the market demand for cells with longer life are likely to have an impact on future product requirements. The next step is for the firm to examine its current position. It would see that if it carried on producing the current type of battery, using existing technology, it would start losing sales sometime in the foreseeable future as competitors introduced larger capacity cells or an alternative technology. It has to predict when the changes are likely to occur and what impacts these will have on its sales and profitability.

Factors arising from such things as the technology and product life cycles often indicate the existence of a potential profit gap. That is, a gap between what the firm wants to achieve in terms of profit and what it is likely to achieve on the basis of its existing portfolio of activities (see Figure 9.2). A firm has to relate the expected profit to the amount of resources employed to achieve that profit. The measure it needs to consider is the return on investment generated by new actions it may take. Return on investment for individual products can be linked to the overall rate of return on capital employed earned by the business. Performance of the firm in the latter respect is reflected in the general confidence of other firms and financial institutions in dealing with the firm in the market place and in the firm's ability to attract and retain shareholders' investments.

Firms strive to maintain their existing rate of return on invested capital. In pursuit of such an objective they should only accept new projects which promise a return on investment potential which is at least equal to the current rate of return on capital employed. Of course, even then, as its more profitable offerings start to decline, it still may not actually maintain the existing rate of return on invested capital.

In practice, of course, firms have to accept the best available projects. These may generate less than the required rate of return, with an inevitable negative impact on medium/longer-term profitability. Next we will look at ways in which firms can try to close the 'gap'.

STRATEGIES FOR REDUCING THE GAP

Ansoff's product/market expansion grid (Figure 9.3) provides a useful though not exhaustive framework for looking at possible strategies to reduce the gap (Ansoff, 1987). All four of the strategies suggested by Ansoff are discussed below, along with others.

Market penetration strategy of existing markets

Here the strategy amounts to increasing sales of existing products while at the same time trying to maintain current margins of profitability on sales. When the market is expanding this may be accomplished with nominal outlays of marketing expenditure by getting more first-time users to buy the product. In a saturated market, extra sales may only be generated as a result of increased market share.

Increasing market share puts heavy pressure on marketing resources and can impact negatively on short run profitability. However, if economies of scale or the impact of the 'experience curve' are felt as a result of increased supply to the market, then this may more than offset the impact on profitability of any additional marketing expenditure.

Market development strategy

Finding new markets does not guarantee long-term or short-term profitability, but economies of scale in producing for the market or in supplying the market will

Figure 9.3 Ansoff's product/market expansion grid.

contribute to profitability. However, there may well be barriers to entry to the market which mean that neither short-run nor long-term contributions to overall profitability are attractive.

Product development strategy

The introduction of new products can have a positive impact on sales growth. Initially, profitability may not increase since there may be substantial research, development and launching costs associated with the venture which have to be recouped.

Longer-term rates of return on investment which are at least equal to the current rate of return on capital employed are required from new products. This may not be possible, and firms may have to accept the possibility or even certainty of lower profitability, just to stay in business. Predicting demand for new products can be difficult and hence the estimation of profit potential.

Diversification

Diversification involves moving simultaneously into new products and new markets. It is a risky strategy, but with careful selection of the right kind of business, considerable improvements in profitability can be experienced. Diversification can take place into related or unrelated products. A firm in microcomputer production might move into making personal telecommunications equipment. This might be seen as diversifying into related products, since both products make use of microelectronic technology and the experience gained in one field might be usefully employed in the other. The same firm diversifying into shoe manufacturing would be moving into unrelated products.

Moving into areas where a firm does not have any prior experience is highly risky, and firms may prefer to move into related markets. Moreover, there may be some synergy to be gained from moving into related markets. The synergy may be in marketing or even in production.

Vertical integration

Vertical integration can take two forms: forward integration, as when a producer takes over a distributor, or backward integration, as is the case when a manufacturer takes over a supplier. Integrative strategies enable firms to gain greater control over the chain of production and distribution. For example, a manufacturer may have difficulty in obtaining vital components from a supplier. This may be because the supplier is also selling the same component to other firms and cannot produce enough to satisfy everyone. Under such circumstances the manufacturer may be tempted to try to buy out the supplier (i.e. become the owner of the supplier's business) to ensure that it will always have supplies of the key component.

Reducing costs

Reducting the costs of running the organization is another way of reducing the gap. It involves the better use of materials or labour, or the reduction of distribution or management costs or of other overheads. There is often scope for this kind of cost saving in organizations.

Adjusting prices

The adjustment of prices and discounts to propel the firm to new higher gross profits without losing sales revenue can enable a firm to close an identified profit gap. Such a strategy could imply repositioning the products or services, or even modifying them in one way or another.

JOINT VENTURE/STRATEGIC ALLIANCE

While many of the above approaches can be implemented by a firm without outside assistance, most of them can be assisted by co-operation with other organizations. This may take the form of acquisition of firms operating in markets to which entry is desired, or acquiring firms at different stages in the production and marketing chain for the purpose of assuring vertical integration. However, there is now a trend towards forming joint ventures and strategic alliances between two or more firms.

Joint ventures involve inter-organizational pooling of strengths for the effective delivery of product market strategies. Franchise arrangements such as those used by Coca-Cola and McDonald's are examples of one type of joint venture. There are many reasons for joint ventures but they revolve around a beneficial exchange of resource strengths (the franchiser provides the systems, products, marketing material and image, for example, and the franchisee provides local knowledge and expertise, human resource inputs and cash).

There are various kinds of strategic alliance. Some are new ventures formed between sellers and customers to ensure a smooth flow of raw materials, components, or services into the customers' manufacturing operations. Others alliances may be found between potential competitors in order to cooperate in the development of related or convergent technologies, or in the development of a new product or close products, or in the development of a new market.

The following case example provides challenging questions regarding the choice of an appropriate strategy.

THE PRODUCT LIFE CYCLE

The above strategies highlight the need for new products and product-markets as a centrepiece of strategy formulation. This is because there is evidence to show that most products have life cycles and progress through recognized stages. Every stage in the life cycle brings with it environmental threats and opportunities that

CASE EXAMPLE

CALYPSO FERRY: CORPORATE STRATEGY AND COMMUNICATIONS

The Calypso Ferry company is facing a crucial decision with regard to how it should improve its long-term profitability prospects. The company is based in Dover on the English Channel and for many years has operated various passenger ferries across the English Channel to France. The opening of the Channel Tunnel has posed threats of a new form of competition, which Calypso fears will have an adverse effect on its profitability.

Competition between cross-channel operators has been fierce for many years. Somehow, the ferry operators have managed to survive the impact of various technological breakthroughs such as air travel or the hovercraft. Air travel obviously appeals to people wanting to travel extensive distances into Europe, but for residents living south of London, or visitors from France to the South of England resorts, the Ferries have always offered an attractive alternative. In addition many holiday makers take their car abroad (either to Britain or to the Continent), and for these people the car ferries are clearly essential.

For business travel without a car, air travel is usually preferred because of the speed with which distances can be covered. Freight transport, however, has depended very heavily on the ferry services.

The advent of the Channel Tunnel poses a direct threat to the operation of Calypso. People with cars, and freight traffic, can switch to use the faster rail service with its drive-on and drive-off facilities for cars and its ability to capitalize on containerized freight.

QUESTIONS

1. How might Calypso try to meet the competition from the Channel Tunnel rail link?

2. How is this reflected in its corporate strategy?

require changes to be made in marketing strategy and have implications for marketing planning. In general, life cycles exhibit the following features:

- products have a finite life span

- the typical product life cycle curve, as reflected in the sales history of a product is S-shaped, until it eventually levels off; at this point, market maturity occurs and when the maturity phase has run its course a period of decline follows

- in general terms the stages in the life cycle are known as introduction, growth, maturity and decline or decay

- the life cycle of a product may be prolonged by finding new uses or new users for the product, or by getting present users to increase the amount they use

- during its passage through the life cycle the average profitability per unit of the product sold at first increases and then eventually begins to decline.

A typical life cycle of a successful product appears in Figure 9.4.

THE LENGTH OF THE PRODUCT LIFE CYCLE

Product life cycles can vary enormously in length. Large sailing ships appeared centuries ago and only disappeared from regular service after the beginning of this century. One can still, of course, find enthusiasts using them in the 1990s. In contrast, clothes change fashion with the seasons, so they appear to have relatively short life cycles. However, fashions come back in vogue again from time to time, and old products are introduced as new ones.

One difficulty in trying to make use of the product life cycle concept as a management tool is that many products do not appear to act as it suggests they should. They seem to bypass some stages, while getting stuck in other stages. Moreover, they may even bounce back after a period of downturn. These observations have drawn criticism of the usefulness of the product life cycle as a concept.

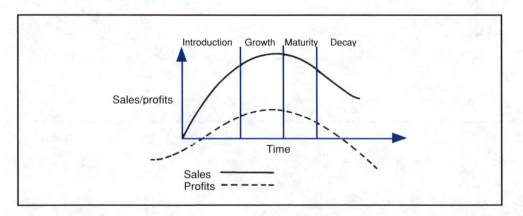

Figure 9.4 The product life cycle.

Sales and profitability vary at every stage in the life cycle. Moreover the comparative significance of, nature of, and interrelationship between price, promotion, distribution and the actual specification of the product itself change over the life cycle. The quality of the product is often important during the introductory stage, as inadequacies that appear during the trial of a product can end in long-term buyer lack of interest in the product. Advertising and marketing communications in general need to be informative during this period. Later, widening distribution or price reductions may become more important.

Awareness of the product life cycle concept can help a firm to take better advantage of the market position of the product or service. It can provide indicators of when new launches should be considered, when moving to new markets should be on the agenda, and the need for diversification.

The product life cycle concept can be used to analyse:

● product category (e.g. microcomputers)

● product forms (e.g. desk-top microcomputers)

● product brand (e.g. IBM).

The most useful application of the product life cycle concept is with respect to product forms.

THE INTRODUCTORY STAGE

Losses, or at best low profits, tend to be incurred during the introductory stage. This is mainly because sales are low and promotion and distribution costs are high. Gaining distribution for a product requires substantial amounts of cash, and promotional costs are at their highest in relation to sales during the introductory stage.

In addition, extensive advertising is required to secure distribution at the retail level. High margins can provide the cash required for heavy promotional expenditure; this in turn produces high initial prices that may discourage rapid adoption of the product by certain customer segments.

GROWTH STAGE

Growth is rapid and new competitors enter the market attracted by the prospect of large-scale production potential and the large profits to be made as the market grows in size and economies of scales come into effect. There is little change in prices and promotional expenditure from the introductory stage, though both may be slightly reduced. There is also a decline in the promotion to sales ratio, the amount of money spent on promotion in relation to the amount of sales generated, since sales are expanding during this stage. The net result of all this is that increased profits are generated as costs are spread over a larger volume and unit manufacturing costs decrease in line with the effect of the experience curve.

Growth eventually decelerates, as fewer first-time buyers enter the market. This often means that a firm has to employ one of several strategies to keep up market growth as long as possible. These include:

- continually looking for new ways to improve product quality

- adding new features to a product or service

- refining the styling of a product

- introducing new models and flanker products

- entering new market segments

- switching the emphasis of advertising away from creating product awareness to producing conviction and purchase

- lowering price to entice price-sensitive buyers.

MATURITY STAGE

The maturity stage ensues from the onset of the decline in the rate of sales growth. The latter produces overcapacity in the industry, which in turn leads to increased competition. It is a stage in which profits decline. During the maturity stage firms implement frequent price reductions and increase advertising and consumer promotions. There is an emphasis on research and development to come up with product improvements and flanker brands. While the well-established competitors do well, the weaker competitors may quit the market. Cash earned by strong competitors at this stage can be put into products that are at earlier stages in their life cycles.

DECLINE STAGE

For several reasons, sales of most products eventually start to decline. These include technological progress, shifts in consumer tastes, and increased domestic and foreign competition. Overcapacity in the market is thus produced, along with price-cutting and lower profits. It is a time when some firms may withdraw from the market and those remaining reduce the number of products that they have to offer, pull out of smaller market segments and weaker trade channels, cut the promotion budget, or reduce prices even further.

Thought has to be given to dropping products during this stage, unless there are good reasons for keeping them. Weak products tend to occupy a disproportionate amount of management's time and resources. The products often require frequent price and inventory adjustments, short production runs and expensive set-up times. Moreover, they may need the kind of advertising and sales-force attention which if it were to be spent on more lively products could produce greater profitability.

THE PRODUCT/SERVICE PORTFOLIO

While some products or services produce considerable amounts of cash, others do not. Where considerable cash is generated, it is often more than necessary for operational expenditure and for additional investment in facilities and staff. In other cases, however, the cash generated may be insufficient to cover operational expenditure. As we shall see below, products which are not satisfactorily contributing to profits and overheads of the firm may well be dropped from the product mix. However, there may well be particular reasons why some products are such poor cash generators at a particular moment in time. Indeed it may well be that such products go on to become the big cash earners for a company in the future. Product portfolio models provide a means of rating products and/or services in order to assess the future probable cash contributions and future cash demands of each product or service.

PORTFOLIO MODELS

Portfolio analyses start by examining the positions of products. They consider the attractiveness of the market and the ability of the business to operate competitively within the market. The first of the portfolio models to be used extensively was the growth/share matrix – sometimes referred to as the cash quadrants model or BCG matrix. In this model, market growth rate was employed as an indicator for market attractiveness and relative market share was used to indicate competitive position.

There have been a number of variations on the portfolio approach, but they all rely on the work of the Boston Consulting Group for theoretical and empirical underpinning. Here we will examine three such approaches in some detail and comment on a number of others.

The Boston Matrix

The illustration here maps products onto a two-dimensional matrix. The method applies equally well to services or any form of strategic business unit.

According to the Boston Consulting Group, the two most significant factors which govern the long-term profitability of a product are the rate of growth of its market and the share of the market that the product has relative to its largest competitor. The Boston Consulting Group presented the model in the form of a simple two-dimensional matrix (Henderson, 1970). The two axes of the matrix are relative market share and market growth rate.

As previously indicated, the relative market share of a product is assessed with respect to that of its largest competitor. The cut-off between high and low market share was originally judged to be equality with the leading competitor, and in the case of market growth rate was originally put at 10% p.a. Both these dividing points were subsequently revised and the matrix was defined less mechanistically.

One interprets the strength or limitations of a product by its position in the matrix.

Products falling into the high growth, high market share quadrant are termed 'stars'. They are tomorrow's cash-earners. Being high market share businesses, they will be highly profitable and generate a lot of cash, but at the same time their high growth will also mean that they will require a lot of cash, both to finance working capital and to build capacity. Thus, though profitable, stars might have either positive or negative net cash flow.

Products positioned in the low growth, high market share quadrant are designated 'cash cows'. These are the real cash generators, being profitable as a result of their high relative market share. It is quite likely that they will also create surplus cash not required to finance growth.

Products falling into low growth, low relative market share quadrant are designated 'dogs'. These are inherently unprofitable and seem to possess no future, though their cash requirements are low.

Products in the high growth, low market share segment have been referred to as 'wild cats', 'problem children' or simply '?'s. They are unprofitable as a result of their low market share, and they consume a lot of cash merely to maintain their market position because of the high growth rate of the market.

The overall strategy is defined simply with regard to the management of cash flows in order to achieve a balanced portfolio over time. Cash is obtained from cash cows and invested in stars to convert them into tomorrow's cash cows. Dogs are divested and problem children are either converted into stars or liquidated. In this way a balanced portfolio should be achieved with an adequate succession of stars ready to take over from today's cash generators, the cash cows.

The BCG matrix is shown in Figure 9.5.

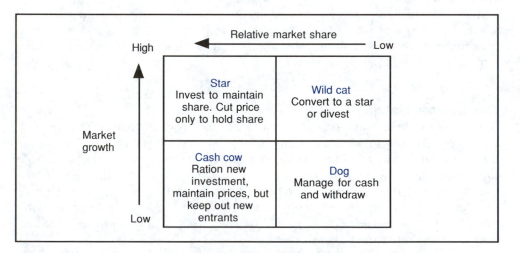

Figure 9.5 The Boston Consulting Group matrix.

While the matrix is intuitively appealing, it has significant shortcomings which limit its value as an analytical tool.

The Boston Consulting Group's original work from which the matrix resulted was founded on an analysis of 24 different commodities. While this work has been replicated many times with other commodities, it has not been replicated with differentiated or branded products. Its empirical foundations rest entirely on an analysis of commodity products selling at market prices, while the substance of marketing is concerned with differentiating products for customers prepared to pay higher than base prices to satisfy their particular needs and wants.

The model is based on an implicit assumption that costs fall with experience and that the business which gains the most experience will have the lowest costs. In a young and rapidly growing market, experience is rapidly acquired, thus increasing the benefits of cost reduction and making it attractive to have a large market share. However, in low-growth, mature markets the cost benefits accruing from experience are low and the benefits from increasing market share in order to gain cost advantages are small. The experience curve should not therefore suggest continuous cost reductions, but reductions during the growth phase, with cost increases occurring during the maturity stage.

A firm's relative market share was measured as share relative to its largest competitor, and the division between high and low relative share was therefore set at unity. Thus in any industry there could only be one business with a high relative market share. Where industries are experiencing low growth, all but one competitor would fall into the low growth, low share 'dog' quadrant, for which Boston's prescription was simply to divest.

The Boston prescriptions are restricted to versions of the buy, sell or hold type of decision. There is no qualitative substance in these statements and little to assist strategic management apart from investment/divestment. Nevertheless, the model has been used far beyond the strictly defined investment portfolio application. Corporate strategists have used the Boston portfolio to guide their investment decisions between businesses. Marketers, too, have misused the matrix to maintain a balanced portfolio of products, and for them the limitations of the model are even more profound.

The Boston model has, of course, been widely criticized by strategists and marketers alike (Proctor and Kitchen, 1990). Strategists have objected to the fundamental proposition that the strategic success of a business can be determined by just two quantifiable factors – market growth rate and market share. This seems too simplistic and could only be true if it were assumed that management itself could not make a difference.

Product life cycle portfolio matrix

To deal with specific criticisms aimed at the BCG matrix Barksdale and Harris (1982) designed their own matrix. The specific criticisms of the BCG that they sought to address were:

● that the BCG ignored products or businesses that were new, and

● that the BCG overlooked markets with a negative growth rate.

As will be seen from the matrix in Figure 9.6, there is a specific focus on the growth and maturity stages of the product life cycle.

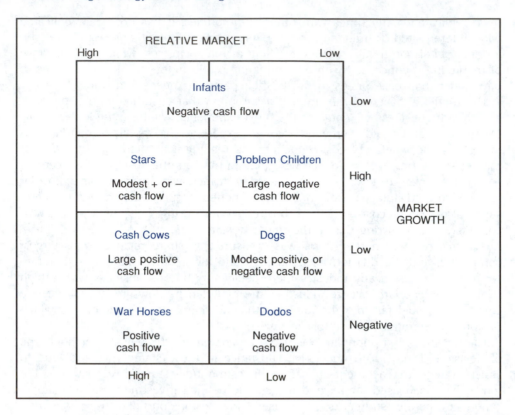

Figure 9.6 The product life cycle portfolio matrix.

Using the same assumptions as are inherent in the BCG matrix, Birksdale and Harris bring out the additional issues which arise from introducing new products (infants) and products in declining markets.

- **Warhorses**   Cash cows develop into warhorses when an established market enters decline. Such products still exhibit a high market share and can still be substantial cash generators. Marketing expenditure may still have to be reduced, or, market segments selectively withdrawn from, or certain models eliminated.

- **Dodos**   Such products possess a low share in declining markets and there is little opportunity for growth or cash generation. Usually they should be removed from the portfolio, but if competitors are in the course of withdrawing from the market and look as if they will all have withdrawn fairly soon, it may be profitable for 'Dodos' to remain.

- **Infants**   These are high-risk products, not earning profits and using up considerable cash.

As with the BCG, there are still problems in defining products and markets, or even rates of growth. Other criticisms of the BCG can also be levelled at this matrix too.

The GE/McKinsey Matrix

A nine-celled multifactor portfolio matrix was designed by General Electric working with McKinsey and Company to overcome some of the limitations of considering only market share and market growth in accomplishing strategic marketing management. Once again, services or other forms of business unit can be plotted in place of products.

The GE/McKinsey multifactor matrix (see *Business Week*, 1975) has two dimensions. Across the horizontal axis is industrial attractiveness and along the vertical axis, business strength. Both, as with the BCG matrix, increase toward the upper left corner of the matrix. The general categories of industry attractiveness and business strength, permit additional factors to be considered in positioning product groupings in the matrix.

For example, GE originally considered size, market growth, pricing, market diversity, and competitive structure as the major factors to describe industry attractiveness. In the case of business strength attention was focused on size, growth, share, position, profitability, margins, technology position, strength/weaknesses, image, pollution, and people. However, a company can use different factors in either the business strength or industrial attractiveness category, depending on the situation.

In order to construct a GE/McKinsey Matrix the factors have to be rated by their importance, each product has then to be rated on each factor and the evaluations combined into a summary measure. Summary measures are obtained for each dimension of the matrix and thence plotted within the matrix.

The position of products or product groupings within different cells implies different strategic actions. For example, product groupings falling in the upper left

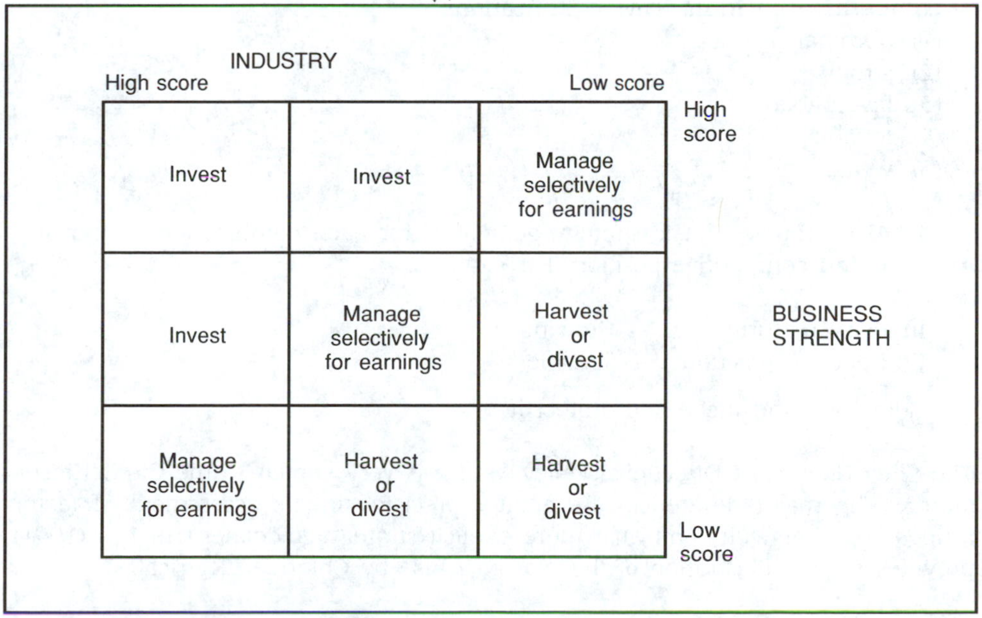

	INDUSTRY		
High score		Low score	
Invest	Invest	Manage selectively for earnings	High score
Invest	Manage selectively for earnings	Harvest or divest	BUSINESS STRENGTH
Manage selectively for earnings	Harvest or divest	Harvest or divest	Low score

Figure 9.7 The GE/McKinsey matrix.

three cells define those that should be invested in for growth; those falling in the lower right three cells of the matrix are harvested or divested. This leaves three cells, starting from the upper right corner down to the lower left corner of the matrix. The general instructions for these three cells are to manage those products selectively for earnings.

Although the GE/McKinsey Matrix offers a greater number of prescriptions than the Boston Consulting Grid, the general outcome is not very different to that produced by the latter. In all cases, products exhibiting a low share of a low growth market should be divested, those exhibiting a high share of a low growth market should be milked, and those exhibiting a high share of a high growth market should receive investment.

Other portfolio models

The ADL (Arthur D. Little) multifactor portfolio model is another widely used model (Patel and Younger, 1978). It is a hybrid of the BCG growth share matrix and a multifactor matrix. The two dimensions used to evaluate each business or segment are:

- **Industry maturity** – four classifications
  (1) embryonic
  (2) growing
  (3) mature
  (4) ageing

  and

- **competitive position** – five classifications
  (1) dominance
  (2) strong
  (3) favourable
  (4) tenable
  (5) weak.

The ADL proposes basic strategy guidelines for each combination of industry maturity and competitive position. For example:

Industry maturity   – Growing
Competitive position – Tenable

Guideline: find niche and protect it

The Shell Chemicals Directional Policy Matrix is very similar to the GE/McKinsey Matrix. The major differences are greater precision in the assessment of factor ratings, together with somewhat more explicit strategy guidelines. Hughes (1991) provides a good illustration of the matrix in use by Chloride Electrical.

COMMENTS ON PORTFOLIO MODEL USAGE

Portfolio models are easy to use and the benefit of using such models is to gain some idea of the profile of strong/weak products or services in the mix. They may, however, cause an organization to put too much stress on market share growth and entry into high growth businesses. They may also cause firms to pay insufficient attention to managing the current business.

Another problem is that the results produced by using the models are responsive to the weights and ratings and can be manipulated to produce desired results. Since an averaging process is taking place, several businesses may end up in the same cell location, but vary considerably in terms of their ratings against specific factors. Moreover, many products or services will end up in the middle of the matrix, which makes it difficult to suggest an appropriate strategy. The models do not accommodate the synergy between two or more products/services and this suggests that making decisions for one in isolation from the others may be short-sighted.

THEORY OF CORE COMPETENCE

Arguably, the theory of core competence offers perhaps a better alternative to that provided by the portfolio models (Pearson and Proctor, 1994). Core competence is more than the possession of a particular technological or managerial capability. Core competence has been described by Prahalad and Hamel (1990) as a 'combination' of such capabilities which provide the firm with a leadership position in the development of certain generic or core products. It is this that gives a business a sustainable competitive advantage.

Core competencies can be identified in the following ways:

- a core competence provides potential access to a wide variety of markets. Competence in display systems, for example, enables a company to participate in such diverse businesses as calculators, miniature TV sets and computer monitors

- a core competence should make a significant contribution to the perceived customer benefits of the end product

- a core competence should be difficult for competitors to imitate.

Core products are the tangible link between identified core competencies and end products. Honda's engines, for example, are core products, Linchpins between design and development skills that ultimately lead to a proliferation of end products. Core products are the components or subassemblies that actually contribute to the value of the end products. By thinking in terms of core products, a company is forced to distinguish between the market share it obtains in end product markets and the manufacturing share it achieves in any particular core product.

Strategy formulation itself requires a more detailed approach in which specific attention is given to the strengths and weaknesses of enterprises and the opportunities and threats which exist in the market place. in the next section we look at ways of doing this.

SWOT AND THE TOWS MATRIX

SWOT (strengths, weaknesses, opportunities and threats) analysis is a technique specifically designed to help identify suitable business strategies for an organization to follow. It involves specifying and relating together organizational strengths and weaknesses and environmental opportunities and threats. The TOWS matrix (Weihrich, 1982) represents a mechanism for facilitating this linkage and a framework for identifying and formulating strategies. Implementing the TOWS matrix requires that the following steps are taken:

1. identify and assess the impact of environmental factors: economic, political, demographic, products and technology, market and competition on the organization

2. make a prognosis about the future

3. undertake an assessment of strengths and weaknesses in terms of management and organization, operations, finance and marketing

4. develop strategy options.

Product: Plastic Bags		
	Strengths	**Weaknesses**
	1. Brand name 2. Distribution 3. Low costs	1. Exports 2. Sales force
Opportunities 1. Need for robust rubbish disposal bags 2. European markets 3. Scented bin-liners	Use existing distribution and brand name to market scented bin-liners (S1,S2,O3)	Strengthen sales force and export skills. Look to European markets (W1,W2,O2)
Threats 1. Substitute materials 2. Imports	Capitalize on brand name, distribution, and low costs to meet competition from imports (S1,S2,S3,T2)	Develop capability in substitute materials particularly for products that can be sold to export markets (T1,W1)

Figure 9.8 An example of the TOWS matrix.

CASE EXAMPLE

NHS: USING THE TOWS MATRIX

A health service enterprise applied the TOWS matrix extensively in its analysis of the corporate strategy it might follow (Wheeler and Proctor, 1993). Internal strengths of the enterprise included spare surgical capacity, a good stock of buildings built in the 1970s and 1980s, a strong management team, good hotel services (including laundry and catering) and an active League of Friends of the hospitals.

Internal weaknesses included problems in recruiting and retaining staff, a lack of resident junior medical staff, the poor state of some of the buildings, industrial relations problems, and the continuing under-utilization of some surgical facilities.

The enterprise identified growth in the size of the ageing local population as an opportunity and also the fact that there was a lack of provision to meet certain needs in the district. These included the need for a rehabilitation unit for the younger physically disabled and a wide range of psychiatric facilities to replace those provided in unsatisfactory conditions. There was also the opportunity to utilize government-provided 'waiting list initiative moneys' to reduce the very long waiting lists that existed in the district.

The threats facing the unit included competition for patients arising from other provider units (both NHS and private), competition for staff from other local employers (who could afford to pay higher salaries and wages), and an unknown factor, the power of the GP fundholders. Another important threat was related to problems associated with mental handicap services. This took the form of resistance to change among the relatives of the client group, and the continuing downward pressure on funding for community services.

QUESTION

1. Can you suggest appropriate strategies for the enterprise to consider?

Working through this process enables internal and external factors to be entered on a grid and different combinations to be studied. For example, the entry to one cell of the grid could involve maximizing opportunities and strengths. This would amount to putting together at least one strength and one opportunity to produce a strategy that capitalizes upon this combination.

There is no limitation as to the type of organizational unit that can benefit from this type of analysis. Moreover, any situation that involves strategic decision-making can benefit from this approach. Weihrich discusses a conceptual application of the TOWS matrix to the strategic dilemma which faced Volkswagen in the USA during the 1970s. The discourse illustrates the usefulness of the TOWS matrix as a structuring device for strategic problems. Experience also shows that the use of the TOWS matrix can lead to the identification of appropriate strategies for an organization. An example of the use of the TOWS matrix is provided in Figure 9.8.

One of the most powerful applications of TOWS analysis is to generate strategies based upon identified strengths, weaknesses, opportunities and threats in conjunction with brainstorming.

Brainstorming helps to overcome the restrictive nature of evaluation that takes place in most business meetings. Social pressures inhibit individuals from stating their ideas, but this can be remedied through the medium of structured meetings at which ideas are freely expressed prior to evaluation.

THE MARKETING PLAN

The final step involves developing the marketing plan so that objectives which have been identified and decided upon can be systemtically pursued. The plan will vary from organization to organization and situation to situation. However, the composition of the overall marketing plan is such that it is built up from separate sub-plans. Sub-plans comprise the following.

- **A product mix plan** This indicates product deletions, product modifications, product additions, when they are to occur, and the volume, turnover and profit objectives, broken down by product groups and even product items. Products may be grouped together and each grouping should have its own set objectives.

- **A sales plan** The sales plan specifies desired servicing levels for existing accounts, together with targets relating to new accounts. Targets are broken down by area and even by individual representative.

- **An advertising plan** Where advertising is deemed important, there should be an advertising plan. This plan should specify the timing, nature, and amount of advertising to use by media. It should also include information appertaining to communications objectives, such as increasing the level of interest in a brand, or achieving new users for each main brand.

- **The sales promotion plan** This is assembled in a similar fashion to the advertising plan.

Other sub-plans could include physical distribution, market research and research and development, pricing and even regional plans.

FORMULATING THE PLANS

With the exception of advertising and certain expense items, goals need to be established by region, district and salesman's territory. Territory goals should be undertaken jointly by the salesperson and his or her manager. Sales goals are then broken down by weeks, taking into account seasonal variations. These then become budgeted figures against which subsequent performance is measured.

At the next stage, strategy selection and tactics feature predominantly. Strategy selection involves working out the best way to attain specific objectives. Tactics appertain to the specific action that must be taken, by whom it should be taken, when, and within what constraints. Taken together they specify how the plan is to be put into effect.

Control procedures are incorporated into a plan and are concerned with specifying those measures in the organization which have to be monitored to assess how well a plan is succeeding. Control establishes the standards, measures the activities and results, compares the measurements to the standards, and reports variances between the measurements and the standards. This enables a plan to be kept on course and facilitates the kind of decisions that need to be made with regard to modifying the original plan, if the need arises.

Contingency planning is undertaken to specify what action will be taken if key objectives cannot be accomplished subsequent to implementing the plan. One must also be on the look-out for cases where achievements greatly exceed planned expectations.

Following implementation, plans have to be reviewed in the light of what has actually taken place or been achieved. On the basis of these reviews corrective action, if need be, can be taken. The subject of control and evaluation is dealt with in detail in Chapter 18.

SUMMARY

Marketing planning may be seen as part of the corporate planning process in which a firm reviews its current situation, decides where it would like to get to and specifies how it is going to do so. The marketing planning element refers to how the firm is going to use its marketing resources to achieve specific objectives which contribute to the overall corporate objectives.

The planning process involves setting corporate objectives, setting goals, auditing marketing resources, undertaking gap analysis, setting marketing objectives and strategy based on assumptions, writing down the marketing plan, implementing the marketing plan and evaluating the marketing effort. An organization sets itself overall financial goals that have to be attained and these are then translated into goals for marketing planning.

Gap analysis is undertaken to identify the nature of the likely financial requirements, assuming that the organization carries on with its present strategy and does not undertake any changes. An organization can pursue various strategies to reduce the 'gap' – for example, by increasing sales of existing products, by looking for new markets, by looking for new products, through diversification, etc.

The product life cycle presents a useful conceptual framework within which to study how firms should apply their marketing strategies. At different stages in the cycle some strategies are more appropriate than others. The life cycle also points to the different earning patterns through the various stages and suggests that it is necessary to have a balanced portfolio of products/services to ensure steady sales and profits at all times. This means that the firm has to prune its product lines and introduce new products to stay on course.

Several product portfolio models, perhaps the best known of which are the BCG (Boston Consulting Group) matrix and the GE/McKinsey matrix, were developed to help firms assess the balance of the product mix. The BCG approach has limited applicability in so far as it can only be applied in those instances where there is a definite correlation between market share and profitability. The GE/McKinsey matrix overcomes such difficulties.

In order to develop marketing strategies which will enable stated goals and objectives to be achieved, an organization has to analyse marketing strengths, weaknesses, opportunities and threats and evaluate their impact on the organization. Choice of marketing objectives and strategy can be aided by skilful application of the TOWS analysis to identify strengths and weaknesses of the organization and opportunities and threats that exist in the environment. Through a careful matching process and creative thinking, strategies will emerge.

Plans in themselves are not sufficient to ensure that an organization achieves its desired objectives. Marketing budgets have to be established to provide specific targets to achieve and resources to allocate. Control has to be effected to ensure that the organization keeps to the specified plans.

DISCUSSION QUESTIONS

1. What do you understand by the term 'corporate strategy'?

2. What role does the corporate plan play in an organization?

3. Discuss the kind of financial goals that an organization sets for itself and how these are in turn related to marketing planning.

4. What do you understand by 'gap analysis'?

5. What strategies can be used to reduce the 'gap'?

6. Differentiate between joint ventures and acquisitions.

7. In using SWOT analysis, how would one set objectives and strategy?

8. Discuss the usefulness of the concept of the product life cycle.

9. Explain why firms need to have a balanced product/service portfolio with elements at different stages in the product life cycle to ensure long-term survival and growth.

10. Explain how the Boston Consulting Group (BCG) model might be used to assess the health of a firm's product mix and to suggest strategies.

11. What are the limitations of the BCG model?

12. How might the GE/McKinsey matrix be used to assess the health of a firm's product mix and to suggest strategies?

13. What are the limitations of the GE/McKinsey model?

14. Describe the stages in the marketing planning process.

REFERENCES

Ansoff, H.I. (1987) *Corporate Strategy*, revised edn, Penguin Books, Harmondsworth.

Barksdale, H.C. and Harris, C.E. (1982) Portfolio analysis and the product life cycle, *Journal of Long Range Planning*, **15**(6), 35–64.

Business Week (1975) The GE portfolio matrix, 28 April.

Henderson, B.D. (1970) The product portfolio, in *Perspectives* (The Boston Consulting Group), No. 66, Boston, Mass.

Hughes, M. (1981) Portfolio analysis, *Long Range Planning*, February, 101–3.

Patel, P. and Younger, M. (1978) A frame of reference for strategy development, *Long Range Planning*, **11**, April, 6–12.

Pearson, G.J. and Proctor, R.A. (1994) The modern framework for marketing planning, *Marketing Intelligence*, **12**(4), 22–6.

Prahalad, C. and Hamel, G. (1990) The core competence of the corporation, *Harvard Business Review*, May–June, 74–93.

Proctor, R.A. and Kitchen, P.J. (1990) Strategic planning: an overview of product portfolio models, *Marketing Intelligence and Planning*, **8**(7), 4–10.

Weihrich, H. (1982) The TOWS matrix: tool for situational analysis, *Long Range Planning*, **15**(2), 54–66.

Wheeler, N. and Proctor, R.A. (1993) Strategy analysis in the health service, *Journal of Marketing Management*, **9**(4).

Woudhuysen, J. (1994) Marketers in the UK must consider a Far East alliance, *Marketing*, 27 January, 5.

FURTHER READING

Day, G.S. (1986) *Analysis for Strategic Market Decisions*, West Publishing Company, St Paul, Minn.

Hambuck, D.C. and Macmillan, I.C.(1982) The product portfolio and man's best friend, *California Management Review*, **25**(Fall), 84–95.

Johnson, G. and Scholes, K. (1989) *Exploring Corporate Strategy*, Prentice Hall, Hemel Hempstead.

Levitt T, (1965) Exploit the product life cycle, *Harvard Business Review*, October–November.

Proctor, R.A. and Pearson, G.J. (1994) Strategy and marketing: an interlocking relationship, *Working Papers in Management*, Keele University.

CASE PROBLEM 9.1

JAPANESE MARKETS: OPPORTUNITIES FOR WESTERN FIRMS

Getting to grips with the dynamics of far eastern markets and industries represents a challenge for any company. Some seem to cope with the peculiarities and complexities well, while other fare less well. In 1993 Rolls-Royce increased sales of its cars to the far east by 60%, although the number of cars and the revenue involved were comparatively small. By contrast, British Aerospace had to sack hundreds of skilled plane makers in part because a large order for business jets failed to come through from Taiwan.

Japan is renowned for its role in world exports. It has been particularly successful in marketing its products to developed countries in Europe and North America. Over recent years, however, the inflow of world foreign direct investment into Japan has increased considerably. The UK has invested around £200m. a year, but the amount which the rest of the world puts into Japan is only about 5% of what Japan sends out.

Japanese companies manufacturer in many Pacific Rim countries, making TVs and audio tape in Thailand (JVC, TDK), air conditioning units and VCRs in Malaysia (Hitachi), and compact cameras in China (Canon). The Japanese are making their business culture a pan-Asian one.

However, arranging mergers and acquisitions in Japan is difficult.

(Source: Woudhuysen, 1994)

QUESTIONS

1. What do you consider to be the best ways for UK firms to gain access to Japanese markets? Why?

2. In which sectors could the UK most productively join the Japanese rather than attempting to beat them? Explain.

3. Are your suggestions the same if one considers what is likely to happen in the future?

CASE PROBLEM 9.2

JOHN PRICE: A FIRM THAT DID NOT SURVIVE

John Price, the owner of a small business, set up as an upholsterer in an eastern suburb of Manchester, some two miles from the city centre, in the early 1950s. Living standards were poor for many people in the United Kingdom during the early post-war years, particularly suburban parts of cities. Many goods were rationed on account of shortages in supply, and many possessions which today people might readily discard were zealously maintained, renovated and repaired.

Good quality suites of furniture were much prized possessions in the immediate post-war years, and people sought to have such suites reupholstered since it was either too expensive or not possible to replace the suites with new ones. There was a boom in the re-upholstery business in the late 1940s and throughout the early 1950s. The company fared well during this latter period and opened premises in most of the towns and suburbs on the east side of Manchester.

Reupholstery is a craft, but there was no shortage of skilled craftsmen at the time. A typical reupholstery shop was sited in the midst of a large collection of poor to middle quality terraced houses, often away from the town centre. Such premises were cheap to rent and in close proximity and highly visible to the customers who made use of the service.

The business enjoyed considerable success throughout the 1950s.

Although rationing had come to an end by the middle of the 1950s, reupholstery of old suites was still popular with the bulk of lower to middle income families.

The 1960s heralded a shift in the distribution of disposable income, a growth in the demand for new goods, and considerable changes in consumer tastes, wants and needs. Towards the end of the 1950s people had begun to move into modern houses, with smaller rooms. While they made do, where possible, with old, larger furniture for a short while, they saw the acquisition of more compact, modern-looking furniture as a priority purchase. The growth in demand for such products was matched by a supply of newly fledged furniture companies eager to satisfy the new wants of consumers.

In the years that followed, the demand for reupholstered furniture began to decline and by the early 1970s was a mere fraction of its original size. In line with the decline in demand the firm suffered a similar fate, and by the end of the 1980s it had disappeared altogether. The owner had failed to respond to changes in the marketing environment. Yet there had been a clear strategy open to this firm, if it had only recognized it. The mass reupholstery market had disappeared but there still remained

CASE PROBLEM 9.2 *CONTINUED*

very profitable market niches. The slum clearance programmes of the 1960s had shifted many people *en masse* to different kinds of dwellings and many of the areas served by the reupholstery firms had disappeared. However, in the outskirts of large suburban areas, where larger and better housing existed, there were high income earners who valued quality furniture. A niche existed for the reupholstery of Edwardian and Victorian furniture which had become fashionable with the 'better offs' during the 1960s and 1970s. To this date, this market niche still remains a profitable opportunity. Had the premises of the reupholstery firms been sited in the town centres as opposed to local neighbourhoods, the owner of the business might well have observed the new market possibilities. Unfortunately he did not.

QUESTIONS

1. Why do you think that John Price went out of business in the 1980s?

2. If John Price had made use of concepts such as product portfolio matrices, core competencies, product life cycles, strategic intent, Ansoff grid, etc. how might they have helped him stay in business?

10 PRODUCT STRATEGY

A product (or service) is a complex entity, characterized by quality, features, options, style, brand name, packaging, sizes, services, warranties, and returns. This chapter considers the various ways in which a firm can alter the nature of the product (or service) mix. The use of design as part of the product strategy and the problem of product liability are also considered. Finally, branding is discussed.

OBJECTIVES

After studying this chapter you should:

- understand that a product (or service) is a complex entity, characterized by quality, features, options, style, brand name, packaging, sizes, services, warranties and returns
- know how marketers can alter the nature of the product mix
- know how firms make use of design as part of their product strategy – especially how they use standard and customized products
- know how firms deal with the risk of product liability
- be able to describe how marketers use branding as a strategy to market their goods and services.

INTRODUCTION

When making product decisions one is involved in such things as decisions regarding quality, features, options, style, brand name, packaging, sizes, services, warranties, and returns. In the first part of this chapter each of these kinds of decisions is explored in depth. Product or service quality, for example, is reflected in such things as performance, features, reliability, conformance to specifications, durability, serviceability, product finish and appearance.

Firms rarely offer one product or service alone, and determining what products or services to offer is a key decision area. Marketers can change the nature of the product mix by adding new lines and thereby widening the product mix; by lengthening existing product lines; by adding new product variants to deepen it, or by altering product consistency, depending upon whether a firm wants to acquire a strong reputation in a few or many different areas.

Profitability can often be improved by discontinuing certain products. This can take the form of harvesting, line simplification and line divestment

Product design can have a substantial impact on both sales and profitability. Getting the right mix between standardized and customized products is the key. Value analysis is a useful tool for ensuring that costs of manufacture are optimal.

Customers may misuse product in a way which can have unfortunate or dangerous consequences. The onus is on the producer of the products to ensure that they are properly labelled, to ensure that users know the dangers of misuse.

Branding is an important aspect of product strategy. Important decisions relate to whether to make use of multi-brand products or multi-product brands and where appropriate providing distributors with their own brands. Part and parcel of the branding issue is the question of brand names and trade marks.

THE PRODUCT AS A COMPLEX ENTITY

The products or services of an organization help to create the image of the firm in the mind of the customer. This will be reflected in customers' perceptions and feelings about its products or services. This is important, since experience with only one of a firm's products or services can affect a person's attitude to the firm's other products or services. This can apply even if the customer has never used the other products.

Products are more than tangible objects, and services are more than a visible activity. People purchase products and services to satisfy needs or wants. As a result of the satisfaction of these needs and wants, consumer experience benefits. Organizations have to understand the nature of the needs and wants in order to appreciate the kind of benefits people expect to obtain.

Among the different kinds of benefits that people can obtain from buying goods and services are:

- good value for money

- novelty

- availability

- good design

- ease of use

- safety

- economy in use.

CASE EXAMPLE

PRODUCT BENEFITS: HOW TO CAPITALIZE ON THEM

There are occasions when a person may buy a car to suit his or her personality. Through the car purchased, the person is able to express their personality. It is the ability to express that personality which is the benefit. The use of the 'personal analogy' technique can sometimes enable researchers to uncover the relationships between people's personalities and their potential purchases such as a car.

All of us possess emotions and feelings. The personal analogy mechanism harnesses the use of our emotions and feelings in order to obtain insights into how people perceive decisions or problems. The idea is to identify oneself with a non-human object which is the subject of the problem. One has to transfer one's own feelings into the entity and imagine how it might feel and act in the problem situation.

One might, for example, be asked to imagine what it would feel like to be a new BMW car. Answers might be:

'I feel powerful'.

'I feel extremely fit and raring to go'.

'I feel ready for my new executive owner'.

Based upon such an analysis it might then be possible to develop advertising themes to aim at specific customer groups. It is through such a technique that we are able to release ourselves from looking at a problem in terms of its previously analysed elements.

QUESTIONS

1. Can one associate benefits with all kinds of products and services?

2. Is it possible to use the personal analogy technique with all kinds of products or services?

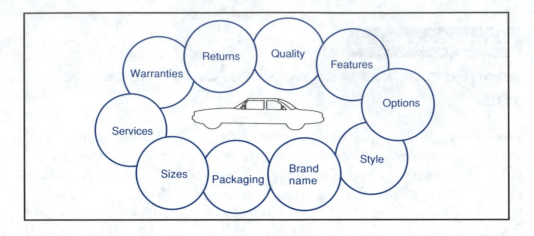

Figure 10.1 Product attributes.

Benefits enter into the equation when a customer decides to buy one product in preference to another. Similarly, when marketing a product or a service, an organization should give attention to the benefits it creates for the user. It is the benefits which make a product or service attractive to a customer. Organizations have to communicate these benefits to the user, directly or indirectly, in order to persuade the latter to make a purchase.

The capability of a product or service to produce the kinds of benefits desired by the user is exhibited in various characteristics of the product or service.

'Product decisions' have to be made with respect to these various attributes. When a producer of goods or services makes decisions about 'the product' he or she is making decisions about:

- quality
- features
- options
- style
- brand name
- packaging
- size
- services
- warranties
- returns.

Each one is considered in turn in the sections below.

QUALITY

Quality is something which reflects differences among products or services. As long as it is possible to create differences among products, then it should be possible to create differences in quality. Even in cases where it is difficult to create differences, producers can still try to promote their products through 'perceived' quality differences – that is, the way in which they are perceived by the customer.

Quality is a relative value that people attribute to things. It reflects people's expectations concerning a product or service and how well it will provide the various benefits they require from using it. Fortunately, large groups of people have common ideas about quality and it is possible to produce and market products and services that will meet with the perceptions of large groups of customers. Groups of customers sharing a common perception of a particular level of quality form market segments. A firm can direct its promotional messages to these groups of customers, provided that it knows how to reach them.

We can contrast notional ideas about product quality with similar ideas about service quality.

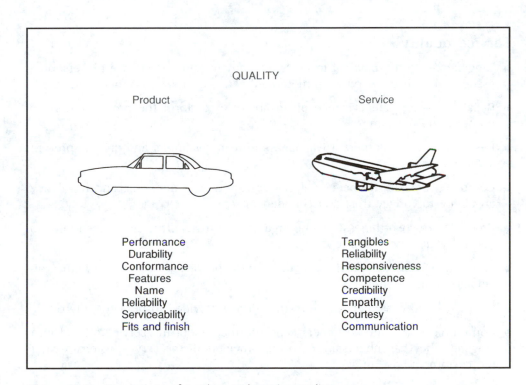

Figure 10.2   Dimensions of product and service quality.

Product quality

- Performance – how well does a product perform the task it is designed to do?

- Durability – how long will the product last?

- Conformance with specifications – what is the incidence of defects found in the product on delivery; what is the incidence of defects which cannot be remedied?

- Features – what special features does the product have which make it superior to competitive offerings?

- The name – can one associate the image of the firm and the brand name with concepts of quality?

- Reliability – can the same kind of quality be expected every time the product is used?

- Serviceability – is the service system efficient, competent, and convenient?

- Fit and finish – does the product look and feel like a quality product?

Service quality

- Tangibles – do the physical facilities, equipment and appearance of personnel associated with the service promote confidence in the quality of the service?

- Reliability – is there evidence of an ability to perform the promised service properly the first time?

- Responsiveness – is there a willingness to help customers and provide prompt service?

- Competence – do the personnel possess knowledge and skill, and have they an ability to convey trust and confidence?

- Credibility/trustworthiness – is the organization trustworthy, and does it always deliver what it promises to deliver?

- Empathy – does the provider of the service provide its customers with individualized attention?

- Courtesy – do customers perceive the service provided to be a friendly one?

- Communication – are customers kept informed about the service offered in a language they can understand? Do the providers of the service listen to what the customers have to say?

Product quality contributes to business profitability. It has been found to be positively related to market share and return on investment over a wide range of products and in different market situations. Moreover, high quality is usually associated with premium prices. The ways in which product quality can be improved are shown in Figure 10.3.

CASE EXAMPLE

TA CENC: QUALITY AT ITS BEST

Sometimes referred to as an 'island within an island', the 'Ta Cenc' hotel at Sanat, on the Maltese island of Gozo, is no ordinary five-star hotel. An air of quality meets guests as they arrive at the reception from the taxi laid on from the heliport. Smiling helpful staff, all speaking English greet one on every corner. Many staff speak Italian and some German too.

Perhaps the quality of the hotel is most in evidence in its restaurant. Waiters and waitresses are properly attired and neat and tidy in their appearance. Orders are taken promptly and the service is extremely friendly. Breakfast is served either to residents' rooms or in the beautifully appointed breakfast room, where a waitress is constantly on hand to see to customers' extra wants and needs.

Facilities at the hotel are excellent – two luxurious swimming pools, tennis courts and bar facilities that are difficult to surpass. The design of the hotel is quite unique, comprising linked bungalows with plush interiors.

Courtesy and empathy are very much a feature of the hotel. Gozo is an island where the Roman Catholic Church has deep roots. On Saturday evenings there is an invitation for those who would like to celebrate Mass in a quiet corner of the lounge.

QUESTION

1. Discuss the kind of qualities you would expect to find in a five-star hotel in a major city such as London. What similarities and dissimilarities are there between the Ta Cenc and the city hotel?

Product quality can be enhanced in a number of ways e.g.

- by improving product performance
- by including new improved product features
- by increasing product reliability
- by ensuring that a product corresponds closely with its specification
- by making a product more durable
- by improving the serviceability of a product
- by improving the product finish and appearance

Figure 10.3 Ways in which product quality can be improved.

A business has to build sufficient quality into its goods and services to satisfy customer requirements. If quality levels are set too high or too low – under- or over-engineering, as it is called – this can result in leaving customers disgruntled.

FEATURES

Features relate to specific characteristics of a product that may provide different benefits to users. There are diesel-engine cars and petrol engine cars. Diesel-engine cars are usually more fuel economic than their petrol-driven counterparts and diesel fuel is often cheaper than petrol. Diesel-engine cars may appeal to those people who seek economy in running a car.

Products are made to appeal to different customer groups by producers incorporating different features into their products. These, in turn, produce different benefits in recognition of the fact that people have different requirements. This is known as the strategy of product differentiation and is a means of gaining a competitive advantage in the marketplace.

OPTIONS

Options are non-standard product features. Producers may consider that it is not worthwhile incorporating certain features into the standard product because there will be too few people requiring the specific feature. In addition, since including special features usually involves additional costs, this will push up the price to the customer, who may then be deterred from purchasing. On the other hand, additional groups of customers may be persuaded to buy the product because optional features are available. By offering options a firm may put itself in the position where it can obtain the best of both worlds. The strategy is to strike a balance between permanent product features and optional extras.

The car market is a good illustration of where one finds examples of product features and options in operation. Many modern cars have built-in safety features and the specification is standard in all such cars. The object is to satisfy the wants and needs of the target market – the safety conscious motorist. Car makers also provide optional extras for cars – a sliding roof, variations in engine size, etc.

STYLE

Style usually refers to the appearance of a product or the way in which a service is given. Often style is something that goes out of fashion with the passing of time, though it may very well come into fashion again. Style is most applicable to consumer goods, though it can be found in industrial products as well. We associate style mostly with goods such as fashion clothes and motor cars, but it is equally applicable to holidays, the theatre or cinema, and to many other products. Style relates to the image that the producer wants to associate with the goods or services. The image of the goods, in turn, has to fit in with the users' self-perceptions. The symbolic action that a user puts on the product can be used to good effect by the producer in promotional strategy.

BRAND NAME AND LOGO

Two important strategic marketing tools, the brand name and the company logo, are at the disposal of marketing management. They take up little promotional space and can have a very significant effect. If you ask a person at random in the street to name the major chocolate companies operating in the UK the likelihood is that they may not be able to tell you all the names. Ask the same person to name a chocolate bar brand, and immediately Mars Bar and Kit Kat will be recalled.

So that they can be easily remembered, it is recommended that brand names should be short and snappy. Ideally, brand names should capture the 'spirit' of the product in the name. Logos, on the other hand, should be very distinctive and easily recognized, preferably incorporating the name of the organization. ICI, Ford, Shell and IBM have instantly recognizable logos. Any one of these firms could issue an advertisement incorporating its logo and the company would be instantly recognized, even if the firm's name were not specifically mentioned.

A firm adopts the strategy of branding to ensure that people can always rely on obtaining a particular quality in the products purchased. If a customer purchases a Ford car then he or she can expect a particular level of performance from that machine – this is guaranteed. Moreover, if the product fails to live up to expectation and is faulty, then the customer knows how to have the product corrected or how to obtain a replacement product. With unbranded goods, one can never be sure of the quality of the product and it may be almost impossible to obtain a replacement for an unsatisfactory product, or one that fails in use after the lapse of a period of time.

PACKAGING

In addition to protecting a product, packaging is also an important form of promotion. In the first instance, it calls shoppers' attention to the product in retail stores – particularly important in supermarkets. Second it carries messages and other items of information to assist the shopper in buying decisions.

Package design has to be capable of attracting the shopper's attention away from an enormous selection of other products and brands also competing for attention. Good package design involves a proper blend of colour, design and style which suits the situation.

For some products the packaging is effectively the product. One of the best illustrations of this is to be found in the packaging of perfumes. Often perfumes come in specially designed dispensers, bottles or other forms of packaging which are instantly recognized on shelves in shops.

Through cleverly designed packaging marketing management can play on the perceptions of people. People often buy goods which add to their appearances because they fit with their self-images. The packaging of goods can be designed to reflect the self-images that people seek.

SIZE

Products can vary in size to meet the individual requirements of consumers. Size can reflect the quantity purchased, as in the case of raw materials purchased for industrial use, or family pack size in the case of domestic washing powder or frozen foodstuffs. Alternatively, it may be related to the technical specification of the product, reflecting the power or capacity of the product, such as in engine size of a vehicle or memory capacity of a desktop computer. An important marketing strategy decision is working out the best combination of sizes to offer and the quantities of each size to produce and market.

PRODUCT SERVICE

The complex nature of some products means that the customer cannot use the products until they have been properly installed.

In some cases, customers also need to be instructed in their use. In addition, some products require after-sales service to ensure that they function correctly. Dealers offer different forms of maintenance contracts to businesses and individuals who have purchased products from them. A full service is required by some customers, whereas others are prepared to manage without but expect to pay a lower price for the product.

In the case of goods supplied to firms for business use, maintenance contracts are often regarded as essential. This is particularly the case with computer hardware and software, where firms cannot afford for machines not to function properly and where it is inappropriate for the firm's own staff to attempt to maintain machines. The same is also true of cars used for business purposes, but a firm may prefer to employ its own mechanics to maintain lorries and other large delivery vehicles.

WARRANTIES

When someone buys a product or a service, one needs to have some assurance that it will perform in accordance with its specifications. Legal obligations on manufacturers and suppliers demand that goods are fit for the purpose for which they are intended. For example, a company which sells a portable computer with a dud battery to an unsuspecting buyer would clearly be in breach of the law, and the customer would demand reparation. However, the scope of the law is somewhat limited and does not extend to products that have been in use by the customer for more than a given length of time.

Warranties are guarantees by the provider that the product or service supplied will perform satisfactorily for a given minimum period of time. For example, a wrist-watch may be guaranteed to function correctly for up to two years. What this means is that the purchaser can return the product during the guarantee period if it turns out to be faulty, in which case it will be repaired or replaced free of charge.

In some cases, determining the length of warranty period to offer needs very careful consideration. Car batteries, tyres and exhausts are cases in point.

A guarantee is a statement or promise to the customer that a product being offered for sale is fit for the purpose being claimed by the producer. The promise indicates what the seller will do if the product performs below expectations, or is defective.

The provision of guarantees accomplishes several things. It:

- provides lower risks for the user

- signals high product reliability

- reduces buyer complaints and dissatisfaction with the product

- generates feedback on products or services from the user

- indicates an emphasis on product quality within the company

- signals to the market the company's belief in customer satisfaction

- provides an additional incentive for the customer to use the product correctly.

RETURNS

Faulty products have to be replaced and a producer should develop a policy for dealing with this.

Having looked at the complex nature of individual products and the problems they pose, we will now examine how a firm manages all the products or services that it provides in the most efficient way. We refer to the collection of products that a firm has to offer as the 'product mix'.

PRODUCT MIX

Except in the case of very small firms, it is rare to find a firm offering a single product or service. It is much more common to find firms offering a mix of products or services.

The product mix has:

- width – quantity of lines the firm carries, e.g. radios, TVs, videorecorders, etc.

- length – quantity of items in the product mix, e.g. three kinds of radio and four kinds of TV

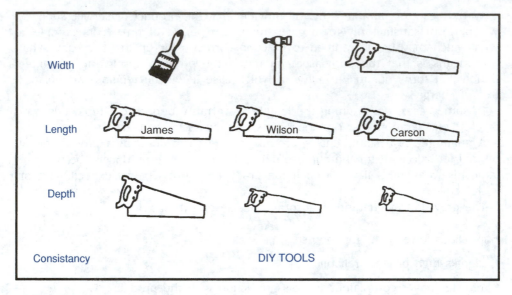

Figure 10.4 Dimensions of the product mix.

- depth – number of variants of each product offered in the line, e.g. clock radios, car radios, pocket radios, etc.
- consistency – how closely related the various product lines are in terms of the use to which they are put, e.g. all electrical leisure/entertainment goods.

The above examples, and those shown in Figure 10.4, provide a basis for defining the company's product strategy, since the company can increase its business in four ways.

1. New lines can be added to widen the product mix – e.g. a manufacturer of radios could introduce a line of cassette players.

2. The length of existing product lines can be increased by introducing additional items – e.g. the radio manufacturer may introduce larger or smaller radios than are currently being offered.

3. New product variants can be added to deepen the product mix – e.g. the radio manufacturer can add new models which are the same size as existing items but which have different features.

4. Product consistency can be increased or decreased, depending upon whether a firm wants to acquire a strong reputation in a few or many different areas.

PRODUCT LINE DECISIONS

The various items within a product line make different contributions to sales and profits. In cases where a couple of items make up the bulk of the contribution this means that a product line is vulnerable in the event that competition increases, since sales of these items could fall substantially. Where products are making very low contributions it would probably be better to drop them from the product line, unless there are good reasons for doing otherwise.

Attention needs to be paid to what competitors are offering. Gaps in the product line may become apparent when product offerings are compared to those of competitors.

If a product line is too short a firm may be able to increase its profits by adding items to the line. On the other hand if it is too long, profitability may be increased by dropping products.

There is a tendency for product lines to grow longer over time. This may result from excess production capacity at various times and the need to introduce new items to take up this excess capacity and increase overall profitability. However, as items are introduced to the line, costs may rise. When eventually a product line is reviewed for its profitability, it may become apparent that profits can be improved substantially by pruning less profitable or unprofitable products and shortening the line.

Three broad categories of action can be taken with respect to a product or service. It can be introduced to the market, it can be given a 'face lift' and it can be withdrawn, discontinued or eliminated. The first two of these are discussed in the next chapter. They relate to the introduction of entirely new product lines into the product mix, to the introduction of new items within a product line and to major changes to existing product items within a line. Here, we will briefly review the third option of discontinuation/elimination/withdrawal.

PRODUCT ELIMINATION

Recalling the discussions of the BCG matrix and other portfolio models, it will be recognized that there can be benefits to a firm from discontinuing a product/service or line of products/services. For example this may free up resources which can be assigned to more viable or profitable products. The resources comprise money, staff and machine time. Warning signals that indicate that a product should be withdrawn are shown in Figure 10.5.

There are three courses of action which can be taken with respect to the product elimination strategy.

1. **Harvesting** This involves getting the most from the offering while it lasts. Efforts should be made to cut costs to help improve cash flow. Alternatively, prices may be increased without a simultaneous increase in costs. Harvesting produces a slow decline in sales; when the business no longer provides a positive cash flow, it should be dropped.

2. **Line simplification** Here a line is trimmed by pruning the number and variety of products or services on offer. The aim is to keep the falling line stable and to restore the health of the line. It is a strategy which becomes especially relevant during times of rising costs and resource shortages.

3. **Total line divestment** In this case the whole product line is discontinued.

- Absolute decline in sales volume
- Sales volume declining as a percentage of total sales
- Declining market share
- Volume sales not meeting with anticipated projections
- Future sales projected lower than what is wanted
- Return on investment falling below minimum acceptable
- Variable costs more than sales revenues
- Consistently rising costs as a percentage of sales
- Products taking up more and more executive time and attention
- Regular cut in price required to maintain sales
- Regular increase in promotional budgets to maintain sales

Figure 10.5 Warning signs that a product should be withdrawn.

In the next section we will introduce the notion of product design strategy and value engineering. These concepts can be most effective when incorporated into marketing strategy.

PRODUCT DESIGN STRATEGY

A firm can offer standard or customized products; between these two extremes it may also offer standard products with modifications.

STANDARD PRODUCTS

Standardization limits a firm's product and component range as a means of controlling production and marketing costs. By limiting the production range the firm can mass-produce each product and achieve economies of scale through long production runs.

Producing standard products has two benefits. Firstly, standard products benefit from the effects of the 'experience curve' more than customized products, giving the firm a cost benefit. Secondly standard products can be marketed nationally much more efficiently. However, there is always the danger with such an approach that it pushes management thinking toward concentrating on per unit cost savings so much that even the requirement for small changes in production design because of shifts in market requirements may be ignored.

There is considerable evidence to suggest that larger firms derive greater profits from standardization by taking advantage of economies of scale and long production runs. They are thus able to produce at a low price. Small companies fare better as job shops, doing customized individual work where there are higher profit margins. By and large, small firms cannot obtain the advantages of economies of scale of the larger companies, but do have the advantage of greater flexibility.

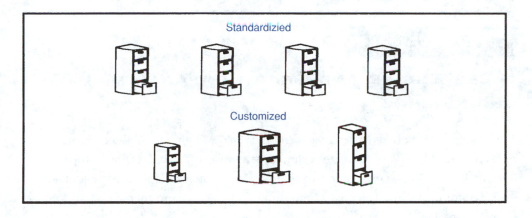

Figure 10.6 Standardized versus customized products.

Standardization can lead to loss of sales because a firm is constrained in terms of the number of market segments that it can serve. However, by introducing interchangeability of components it may still be possible to maintain product variety and avoid loss of sales.

CUSTOMIZED PRODUCTS

Customized products are marketed on the basis of the performance of the finished product. Performance reflects the extent to which the product meets the customer's specifications. The producer works closely with the customer, monitoring the progress of the product until completion. Unlike standard products, price is not usually an important factor. Customers anticipate paying a premium for customized products.

Customized products may be produced by large firms. This varies considerably with the nature of the product. A spin-off from developing customized products can also occur, in that it sometimes may lead to the development of new standard products.

STANDARD PRODUCTS WITH MODIFICATIONS

Here, the customer is offered the standard product but is able to specify a limited number of options or modifications. By producing a standard product, a firm can obtain economies of scale; by allowing modifications (colour, size, packaging, etc.) the product is individualized to meet the particular requirements of the customer. Such a strategy enables the firm to keep in close contact with market needs and to identify how those needs may be satisfied through product improvements and modifications. The organization's reputation for flexibility is also enhanced by being able to meet more customers' requirements.

CASE EXAMPLE

MILES ENGINE AND GEAR COMPANY: VALUE ENGINEERING

By chance, the production manager of the Miles Engine and Gear Company observed that the material cost of cylinder head inserts for one of the company's line of V8 diesel engines seemed very high. Further investigation, in conjunction with the company's metallurgist, showed that the inserts were manufactured from stainless steel.

It was then that the metallurgist began to question why stainless steel was being used at all. It was clear that other engines in the line did not use the material, nor did competitors' engines. Where inserts were used, they were made of cast iron.

The answer as to why stainless steel inserts were used could be explained by the allegory of the seventh soldier standing to attention while the artillery was fired (because years ago he had held the mule reins). The reason why stainless inserts were used was lost in the annals of the company's history. As a result the production manager directed that some inserts should be cast out of an inexpensive grade of iron.

Subsequent testing of several hundred engines with the experimental inserts over a period of a year demonstrated no difference in performance as compared with the engines which had the stainless steel inserts. The modification resulted in a substantial saving in materials costs.

(Source: Marquis, 1969)

QUESTION

1. Suggest ways in which value engineering could be applied to fast moving consumer goods.

VALUE ANALYSIS

Value analysis is an important aspect of product management and is concerned with finding the most economical and cost-effective method of producing a product or service. In effect, the specifications of a product or service are considered in minute detail and management looks for more cost-effective ways of performing the same function. For example, a piece of equipment may be made up of all-metal parts which are relatively expensive to produce. Substitution by parts made from other materials may lower the cost of the equipment but without impairing performance, including its reliability. When properly carried out, value engineering should prevent over- or under-engineering from occurring. A good example of value analysis is to be found in the case example on the previous page.

Not only do products have to be designed so that they help to maximize a firm's long-term profitability, but they have to be designed so that they can be used with safety. Marketing products which are unsafe can have disastrous consequences for a firm.

In the next section we will look at problems which can arise from marketing unsafe products, and what steps can be taken to avoid such problems in the first place.

PRODUCT LIABILITY

'Let the buyer beware' was a catch phrase much banded about not all that long ago. Today, however, matters have changed, largely as a result of product liability suits which have gone in favour of the plaintiff. Inherent design faults in a product or service which result in injurious or harmful effects can produce claims from users for substantial damages. There are many examples of such claims; examples include unforeseen side effects experienced as a result of using pharmaceutical drugs and death and injury caused by design faults in motor vehicles (Examples of product liability cases are given in Hartley (1992) and Proctor (1993). See also Manley (1987).) A wide range of products have the potential to produce unfortunate results if they are used incorrectly, and the labelling and packaging of a product must clearly specify how the product should be used.

WHAT IS A DEFECT?

Defective products fall into three classifications:

1. defects in the manufacturing process

2. defects in design

3. failure to give adequate instructions or warnings concerning products that cannot be made totally safe.

Defects in the manufacturing process

These occur when the product is not manufactured to the design specification. For example, take the case of a person who falls from the top rung of a ladder and is badly injured. Subsequent examination of the ladder shows that while the welds on most of the rungs had been stressed to the degree required in the design specification, the top rung had only been stressed to withstand 20 kilos. In this case the ladder would be held to have been defective as a result of the manufacturing process.

Defects in design

There are three different instances where design defects can occur.

1. **Where the design creates a dangerous condition** Suppose a bulldozer reverses into and kills a man. The design of the bulldozer is such that the operator, while driving the machine in reverse, cannot see a distance within 48 feet behind him, although inexpensive side-view mirrors would have reduced the distance to ten feet. In such a case the design creates a dangerous condition.

2. **Where the design fails to supply a safety device** Here, someone might be badly burned in bed while using an electric blanket. The person falls asleep and the blanket overheats, setting the bed on fire. For a small amount, the manufacturer could have installed an overheat cut-off switch which would have prevented the accident from occurring. In this case the design fails to supply a safety device.

3. **Where the design calls for inadequate materials** A car manufacturer knowingly uses a steering wheel made out of a material that degenerates with use. A 12-month old car is involved in an accident and the steering wheel disintegrates upon impact, causing severe chest industries to the driver. Here, the design called for inadequate materials.

Failure to give adequate instructions or warnings concerning products that cannot be made safe

A manufacturer produced a box of fireworks on which were printed the instructions, 'Do not relight the touchpaper'. A purchaser of the fireworks did relight a firework and was badly injured as a result of the firework exploding in his hand. The manufacturer failed to provide a separate warning as to what would happen to the person if the touchpaper was relighted and, therefore, was held responsible.

PREVENTING PRODUCT LIABILITY CLAIMS FROM ARISING

To overcome potential problems, firms have instigated a variety of action plans. Some refer to actions which can be taken by the firm's employees to ensure that goods leaving the factory are safe. Others refer to actions that can be taken to monitor how the products are used by customers. Actions which can be taken include:

- producing a list of legal safeguards and making sure that employees know about them

- ensuring employees are aware of their potential culpability which results from improper product modifications, unsafe packaging, absence of warnings to users, etc.

- ensuring that all products in stock are safe products

- checking all doubts with legal advisors

- setting up and reviewing risk management policies to ensure that products needing disclaimers and warnings about misuse and abuse are identified and properly catered for

- telling salespeople to investigate reported product use that could lead to potential risks

- arranging seminars for customers on the use of hazardous equipment and materials.

In the next section we will move on to examining the important topic of branding. So important is this topic that manufacturers' makes, models and products are often referred to simply as 'brands'.

BRAND STRATEGY

Branding is a major marketing tool that a firm can use to its advantage in the market place. Creating an instantly recognizable brand name for a product or service is a decided benefit in gaining a competitive advantage – particularly when the brand name can be associated with a high-quality image.

A brand name is a name given by a producer to one or a number of its products or services. It could be the producer's own name, or it could be a name unconnected with the producer. The British Alcan company, for example, uses the Alcan name with many of its industrial aluminium products but uses the brand name Bacofoil with aluminium food wrapping foil for consumer markets.

Firms use brand names to differentiate their products from those of their competitors. In addition a given level of service or quality comes to be associated with a brand name, thereby enabling people to buy in the confidence that the same quality or service will be purchased on every occasion.

The ability of branding to enhance a product's saleability does tend to vary along with the product and the company. Where price is almost the only factor upon which firms compete, then branding is not an important issue. However, where a firm is trying to develop consumer preference for a product by differentiating and promoting it, then branding becomes an issue.

Having a brand name is necessary for the firm which wants to differentiate its product from competitors' products. It can provide the company with some control over the resale and marketing of the product by wholesalers and/or retailers, and simultaneously enhances promotional effectiveness. In making use of brand identification a company is taking important steps towards competing on a non-price basis.

Branding is most effective where it is possible to differentiate the product effectively with respect to benefits that consumers consider important. It also has potential pay-offs where products or services have benefits for which shoppers are actively searching. The time shoppers have to spend in finding products or services with the desired features is reduced.

MULTIPRODUCT BRANDS

In the case of a firm which is offering more than one product or service, a choice has to be made between whether to sell each one under a separate brand, or to use a 'family brand' to cover all offerings. There are benefits associated with both approaches. In deciding which approach to adopt, the nature of the product line, the promotional policy and the desired market penetration should be taken into account.

The nature of the product

The main factor to consider is the nature of the product line. There are considerable benefits from family branding where products are perceived as being similar to one another in the mind of the customer. Nevertheless, a family brand name may sometimes have negative effects. All items carrying the family brand must conform to consumers' standards of acceptance and there has to be a similar level of quality across all the products being marketed. Consumer acceptance that the quality the manufacturer has achieved with one product can be carried over into another is essential. For example, Sony originally manufactured televisions before producing camcorders. Since both products rely upon the same 'core competencies', then credibility should be assured.

Promotional policy

The amount of money spent on promotion is generally less where family branding has been implemented. Promotional expenditure can be spread over the entire line. Moreover, promotional expenditure on a single item can increase recognition or demand for the whole line. Family branding, however, can restrict opportunities for emphasizing individual differences in items.

Market penetration

Desired market penetration is important because individual items in a product line meet with varying degrees of competition. Where the same degree of market penetration does not exist for all items in the line, individual branding permits greater promotional flexibility. In addition, individual branding can enable a producer to achieve greater market penetration by marketing similar but differentiated products which appeal to different market segments.

MULTIBRAND PRODUCTS

Speciality goods are often marketed through a limited number of selected retail outlets in order to gain dealer co-operation in aggressively promoting the goods. This can impose a limitation on the total sales potential, because in any one market no single retailer or small group of retailers can attract all the buyers. In such a case, market penetration can be increased by offering identical merchandise under a different brand name to a second group of selected retailers.

It may also be appropriate to market separate brands where products or services have been developed and positioned in clearly defined target market segments and where marketing policy is directed towards developing a clear and identifiable brand/segment relationship.

Multiple brands often result from mergers between firms. The retention of the brands depends on the extent to which they have distinct images that appeal to separate market segments.

MANUFACTURER'S BRAND AND RETAILER'S OWN BRAND

Sometimes distributors (usually retailers) market goods under their own labels. These are called private brands. For example, a manufacturing firm may produce a product and sell it through retailers under its own brand name. The same manufacturing firm may also sell the same product to the same retailers, to be offered for sale under the brand name of the retailer (the private brand).

From the producer's point of view, accepting private brand orders can lead to additional sales and profits. However, the producer does have to take into consideration the effect that the private brand will have on sales and profits of its own branded products. The situation is somewhat complicated by the fact that a large retailer may not be prepared to place orders at all with a firm unless it can sell at least some of the goods that it purchases under its own brand name.

In addition to the extra sales and profits generated, accepting private brand orders can also facilitate stable production planning and longer production runs, because of the extra volume of sales that is generated and the fact that demand is assured. Moreover, such transactions can then take place without incurring much marketing or promotional expenditure.

Supplying own brands puts the retailer in a powerful position, since the retailer controls the marketing of the product. In addition, the manufacturer will have to conform to the specifications, stock levels and delivery patterns laid down with the retailer. There is a danger for the producer that in addition to losing control over the marketing of the product, it can also lose control over the running of its whole business if it becomes too dependent on the retailer, particuary where a private brand accounts for all or a large part of the production of the producer. Should the firm suddenly decide to go elsewhere for the product, the producer will have problems.

CASE EXAMPLE

CHINESE COSMETICS: BRAND NAMES

In 1988, an exhibition in a northern Chinese city produced information which revealed that a cosmetic was required that would both moisturize the face and whiten it. To meet this requirement, a new product 'Xiafei Gold Brand Special Whitening Honey' was developed and introduced to the market, breaking the sales record with 20 million items sold in four years.

'Xiafei' and 'Olice' feature among the most best-known brands of cosmetics in China. Both products were introduced to the market by Cao Jianhua, who subsequently introduced yet another new product, 'Chaotian'.

The success of 'Xiafei' is attributable to its middle-price position and suitability for a wide range of people.

'Olice' was formulated by adapting a product and adding a biological ingredient known as SOD, supposed to protect middle-aged women from signs of age. With the name 'Blue Noble', the packaging was given an image of elegance in order to satisfy customers' desire for fashion and modernity; the product was an immediate success.

'Chaotian Beauty Treasure' was introduced in 1993 into the top 10 department stores in Shanghai and this too has been an immediate success.

The brand names, supportive of the positioning strategy adopted, were considered very important to their success. The names sound bright and modern in Chinese – 'Xiafei' means 'the brightening of a colourful morning glow' and names such as 'Whitening Honey', 'Blue Noble' and 'Beauty Treasure' give the impression of safety, nutrition and grace associated with expected levels of product quality.

(Source: Xiong, 1994)

QUESTION

1. Discuss the use of brand names in this case.

PRODUCT NAMES

Products may have product names as well as brand names. Ford may be the brand name, but 'Mondeo' is the product name for a particular range of cars. The use of such a name reinforces the product differentiation value of the brand and makes it easier for the customer to recognize and recall the product.

A product's name has to be appropriate for the product and the image it is trying to communicate to a potential purchaser. The name should suggest the benefit to be gained from purchasing the product. Sometimes imagery or benefits associated with product names are not obvious from the name, and the benefits of the product have to be more fully communicated through advertising and promotion.

Companies that market their products in international markets face a difficult problem sometimes when it comes to choosing a brand name. For instance, the brand name for Snickers chocolate bars was changed to 'Marathon' when it was first introduced into the UK. This was because the company was concerned that Snickers sounded too much like 'knickers'. However, the name was later changed back to Snickers so that the product could be sold with the same name throughout Europe (*Wall Street Journal*, 1992). In another instance, early sales results of Nissan's 'Fair Lady' sports car in the USA were disappointing. As a result, the company decided to investigate the reason for this: it turned out that 'Fair Lady' was not perceived to be 'sporty' enough; the name was changed to 240Z, whereupon sales picked up and the product became a big success (Ricks, 1993, p. 36).

Product names in an oriental setting are the topic of the case example on the previous page.

TRADEMARKS

To protect brands and product names from unauthorized use, they have to be registered as trademarks. Names that deliberately confuse or mislead customers are not acceptable, and there are also other restrictions.

SUMMARY

Product decisions involve such things as quality, features, options, style, brand name, packaging, sizes, services, warranties, and returns.

Depending upon whether a firm wants to aquire a strong reputation in a few or many different areas, marketers can change the nature of the product mix by:

- adding new lines and thereby widening the product mix
- lengthening existing product lines
- adding new product variants to deepen it
- altering product consistency.

Product design can have a substantial impact on both sales and profitability. Getting the mix between standardized and customized products is the key. Value analysis has an important role to play in keeping manufacturing costs down.

Customers may misuse products, with unfortunate or dangerous consequences. The onus is on the producers of products to ensure that they are properly labelled and to ensure that customers are aware of the dangers of misuse.

Profitability can often be improved by discontinuing products. This can take the form of harvesting, line simplification and line divestment.

Branding is an important aspect of product strategy. Important decisions relate to whether to make use of multi-brand products or multi-product brands. Part and parcel of the branding issue is the question of use of brand names and trademarks or, where appropriate providing distributors/retailers with their own brands.

DISCUSSION QUESTIONS

1. What are the major characteristics of products and services?

2. What is meant by product or service quality?

3. How can product quality be changed?

4. Differentiate between product or service features and options.

5. What is product style?

6. Why do firms use brand names?

7. Why is product packaging important?

8. How would you interpret 'size' with respect to a product? Give examples of where it may be strategically desirable to offer different sizes of a product.

9. Under what circumstances might competitive advantage be obtained with respect to the following? (a) services (b) warranties (c) returns.

10. How can marketers alter the nature of the product or service mix?

11. Differentiate among harvesting, line simplification and line divestment.

12. How do firms make use of design as part of their product strategy?

13. Differentiate between standard and customized products.

14. Discuss role of value analysis in product management.

15. How might firms deal with the risk of product liability?

16. How do marketers use branding as a strategy to market their goods and services?

17. What are the essential characteristics of good brand names and trademarks?

REFERENCES

Hartley, R.F. (1992) *Marketing Mistakes*, 5th edn, John Wiley, New York.

Manley, M. (1987) Product liability: You're more exposed than you think, *Harvard Business Review*, September–October, 28–41.

Marquis, D.G. (1969) The anatomy of successful innovations, *Innovation*, November.

Proctor, R.A. (1993) Strategic windows and entrapment, *Management Decision*, **31**(5), 56–61.

Ricks, D.R. (1993) *Blunders in International Business*, Blackwell, Oxford.

The Wall Street Journal In pursuit of the elusive Euroconsumer, 23 April, B1ff.

Xiong, R. (1994) Moving towards market economy and marketing application in China, MBA dissertation, Keele University Management Department.

FURTHER READING

Aaker, D. (1991) *Managing Brand Equity*, Free Press, New York.

de Chernatony, L. and McDonald, M.H.B. *Creating Powerful Brands*, Butterworth Heinemann, Oxford.

Hendon, D.W. (1992) *Classic Failures in Product Marketing*, NTC Business Books, Chicago, Ill.

McBurnie, T. and Clutterbuck, D. (1988) *The Marketing Edge*, Penguin, London.

CASE PROBLEM 10.1

SAINSBURY: OWN LABEL PRODUCTS

Sales figures reported by the AGB Superpanel for Classic, Sainsbury's new own label Cola drinks, showed that it took 15% to 20% of the market within Sainsbury during the launch week, in contrast to 2.5% to 3% for the normal private label cola. During the same period Coke's share fell by almost half from 63% to 33%, while Pepsi sales dipped two-thirds.

Sainsbury agreed to a request to redesign its Classic soft drink, following insistence from Coca-Cola that this be done. It was agreed to change the typeface on cans, bottles and all signs from an italic to an upright style, and to remove the wavy line under Classic. Sainsbury refuted any suggestion that consumers had been confused by the similarity of the packaging, indicating that the company had decided to make the changes to maintain goodwill between itself and Coca-Cola. However, global brand leader Coca-Cola had a different view. A spokesman for Coca-Cola said that the company had conducted consumer research which showed that there was extensive confusion among customers.

There are many interesting questions to answer. For instance, why did the switch occur? Was it because the new version launched by Sainsbury was dressed in the well-known red, white and gold livery? Or was it because it was cheaper and a good drink? Could the consumer have been confused and thought that the two types of Cola came from the same manufacturer? Did the outer likeness support the inner resemblance?

(Source: The Grocer, 14 May 1994, pp 4–5).

QUESTIONS

1. What reasons do you think caused consumers to switch to the new Sainsbury brand?

2. Do you think that Sainsbury should have changed the packaging? Why, or why not?

CASE PROBLEM 10.2

A.H. ROBINS: PRODUCT LIABILITY

The view held by Roger L. Tuttle, a former A.H. Robins attorney, was that the firm panicked. Encountering a disaster with very severe consequences, it simply resorted to the defence mechanism of denial. After the product had been put on the market and problems began to arise, it seemed that pressures on the decision makers from various sources precluded the possibility of any form of rational decision making, and panic set in.

A.H. Robins was a long-established company – well known for cough syrup, chap stick lip balm, and flea and tick collars – when it took on a new product, an intrauterine contraceptive device. In the course of time, the product turned out to be potentially dangerous and many lawsuits for damage to persons and death caused by the use of the product ensued.

Although the product was introduced in 1970 it was not finally removed from sale in all countries until 1975, when the economics of meeting law suit claims began to look very unattractive. Ten years later the firm filed for bankruptcy following successful claims for very substantial damages. Many women fitted with the device had continued with its use for years after it was officially withdrawn from sale.

There is no doubt that the firm showed a lack of sound business sense by entering a market in which it did not have any previous experience at all – without even a gynaecologist on its staff. Moreover, the company neglected to carry out any testing of the product itself and subsequently, it ignored reports of major problems with the product years after its intro-duction.

(Source: Hartley, 1992)

QUESTION

1. What do you think are the principal lessons to be learned from this case?

11 NEW PRODUCT STRATEGY

This chapter examines why new products succeed and fail, along with what can be done to prevent failure. How firms get hold of or generate new product ideas, and the various stages involved in the new product screening process, are also described. Finally, attention is given to the process of consumer-adoption of innovations.

OBJECTIVES

After studying the chapter you should be able to:

- understand what constitutes a new product
- understand what is meant by a new product failure and appreciate the factors which contribute to failure
- know how firms get hold of or generate new product ideas and systematically screen and evaluate them
- describe the consumer-adoption of innovations process.

INTRODUCTION

The ability of organizations to survive can be influenced by a continuous supply of new products. Where a firm fails to innovate and market products which meet with the expectations of customers, it risks going out of business. Firms need to be continually on the look-out for new products – the nature of the product life cycle is such that new products are needed to replace existing ones. This chapter examines how firms can try to make sure that good, profitable new products are found.

Consideration is given initially to the task of defining what is a new product.

Many new products 'fail' in the market place; attention is given to explaining exactly what failure means in this context, and what factors contribute to new product failures.

If firms get hold of good ideas and have the necessary resources and skills to design, produce and market them, then there is a good chance that the ideas will become a commercial successes, provided that there is strong demand for them. The acquisition of good ideas is of paramount importance, as are the means for facilitating idea acquisition.

All ideas need to be systematically screened against a variety of criteria reflecting the firm's resources and capabilities. Those that satisfy these criteria may move on to the next phase in the new product development process. Those that fail are eliminated from further consideration.

Having successfully negotiated the various screening devices the next stage is product development. It is at this stage that substantial costs may be incurred.

The launching of new products can also be an extremely costly affair – even when the product is successful. While a firm may feel confident that it has developed a new product with success potential, it still cannot be sure that this is the case. Before launching a new product nationally (or internationally) it is better to test market the product beforehand – if this is possible.

The chapter concludes by examining the nature of the process of consumer-adoption of innovations.

DEFINITION OF A NEW PRODUCT

A 'new product' can be defined in several different ways. A product can refer to a physical entity or a cluster of expected customer benefits, depending on whether the perspective adopted is that of the business or that of the market. From the point of view of a business, a product innovation may represent a change in, or addition to, the physical entities that make up its product line. From a market perspective the term refers to a new or revised set of customer perceptions about a particular cluster of benefits. Thus, that which is considered a product innovation by a business enterprise may not be recognized as such by its customers. Here we will adopt a business perspective. More generally, a new product is one that is new in any way for the company concerned. (McCarthy and Perreault, 1993, p.299).

Let us consider a new product in terms of it being new to a company. Creda, for example, was not the first company to bring washing machines to the market, but the product was certainly new to Creda at the time. Additions to existing product lines and improvements of an existing product may also be thought of as 'new products'. In practice, few new products are actually new to the firm and new to the market.

CASE EXAMPLE

UNITED DISTILLERS: DEFINING A NEW PRODUCT

Following considerable speculation, United Distillers declared its intention to intro-duce Gordon's Gin and Tonic in a single serve can. United Distillers indicated that the new product had been the focus of a great deal of consumer research and sampling operations. The product would be sold in a ready-mixed conve-nience drinks sector which is growing in size.

(Source: The Grocer, *12 February 1994, p. 27).*

QUESTION

1. How does the product here satisfy the definition of being a new product?

IMPORTANCE OF NEW PRODUCTS

Theodore Levitt (1960) stressed the importance of innovation in the market place almost 30 years ago when he warned against the dangers facing firms which did not respond to new developments in the marketplace and which lurked in the shadow of product obsolescence. Two important trends in the market place have been of major importance in stimulating product innovation: the increasing instability of consumer preferences and the growing intensity and sophistication of competition.

Changes in consumer and competitor behaviour are not the only external forces affecting product innovation. Technological advances have an equally significant impact, often leading to radical changes in size and characteristics of established product markets. A good example is the impact of the microchip on the world market for wrist-watches. This was initially dominated by Swiss manufacturers, with their mechanical movements, but latterly manufacturers in the Far East have moved in using microchip technology. Moreover, improvements in product and process technology are often introduced simultaneously to a wide range of product markets.

New products can account for a substantial proportion of a firm's sales and profits over a relatively short time period. A good illustration is provided by Lever, which between 1968 and 1984 introduced 12 new brands of soaps and soap powders to UK national markets. Five of these introductions became brand market leaders and three others became sectional leaders (Hardy, 1987).

A company develops new products for one of two reasons:

1. to replace or supplement its existing offerings in their existing markets

2. to serve new markets, defined in terms of customer benefits or geography.

It can develop new markets without new products, by making appropriate adjustments in the pricing, promotion and/or distribution policies associated with an existing offering.

While new products are essential to companies, much expense can be incurred and squandered in developing and launching unsuccessful ones. In the next section we look at why new products fail.

NEW PRODUCT FAILURES

While innovation may be thought of as the corner-stone of success in many industries, not all innovations are in fact successful. Indeed, the incidence of failure in introducing new products is extremely high. Of course what is a failure for one firm may very well be a successful product for another firm. It all depends upon the financial expectations of the firm. Failures are never absolute entities in themselves.

The usual measure taken when evaluating the comparative success of a new product is the return on investment it generates. But of course what will satisfy one company will not necessarily satisfy another. A company that is accustomed to earning an overall after-tax rate of return on capital employed which exceeds 30% per annum will on average need to introduce new products which will generate at least this level of after-tax return on investment in order to maintain long-run profitability. Firms with different rates of return on capital may have different expectations, reflecting the nature of the industries in which they operate. In addition, firms of substantially different size, yet considering the same product market opportunity, will also have different expectations.

Forecasting sales, profits and costs for new products is difficult and the estimates made can sometimes be widely inaccurate. Potential new product opportunities which are likely to incur heavy R. & D. costs need to be screened out at a very early stage to avoid unnecessary losses. In the early 1980s spending in the early phases of new product development accounted for 10% of the total cost of bringing out the product. By 1990 this figure had risen to 20%. In the face of uncertainty and soaring costs, firms would definitely benefit from examining ways of screening new product opportunities.

During the early stages of the product life cycle of the tumbler drier the larger firms, such as Philips, were deterred from entering the market because they considered they would be unable to generate sufficient profits in order to earn the level of return on investment they required. It was only later when the market had increased in size that they felt the market was attractive (Proctor, 1989).

Large firms working on the frontiers of technology often come up with good ideas, but because the initial market size or even long-term market size is small they may not choose to develop the product. Instead they may 'transfer the technology' to a smaller firm, for a royalty payment. The smaller firm is better able to exploit the opportunity. Of course the reverse can happen, too; when a small firm lacks the resources to exploit a new product idea it may call upon the help of a larger firm which has the resources required.

REASONS FOR FAILURE

There are many different reasons why new products can fail to meet up with the expectations of the firms which launched them. Some major reasons for new product failure are as follows.

- Products lack useful/meaningful uniqueness.
- Planning is poor during the introduction phase.
- The introduction is badly timed – the market is not yet ready for the product.
- Key important points are sometimes overlooked in the enthusiasm to go ahead.
- Poor marketing and failure after launch.

CASE EXAMPLE

AMERICAN MOTORS CORPORATION: NEW PRODUCT FAILURE

When American Motors Corporation decided to introduce the 'Pacer', another model in its line of small cars, it was essential that the car was economical on fuel. In the event, this just did not happen. The car turned out to be 'heavy and clunky', and heavy on fuel.

In putting the car onto the market the company had taken a calculated risk, since it had failed to obtain the engine on which the fuel economy was dependent. The original idea had been to mount the General Motors Wankel rotary engine in the car, but the Wankel engine was never produced. In its place, AMC used a big, old AMC-designed engine which added considerable weight to the car and increased the car's price substantially.

The car was dead before it was launched.

(Source: Hartley, 1992)

QUESTION

1. What steps could the company have taken to avoid this disaster?

CASE EXAMPLE

SONY: TIMING WITHDRAWAL FROM A PRODUCT MARKET

Commenting on Sony's one-time entry into the electronic calculator market, Akio Morita (Sony's chairman) said that he soon realized that several dozen Japanese companies had done the same thing and that he knew some would exit the market sooner or later because they would be unable to cope with a very brutal price war.

What he predicted turned out to be correct and it became obvious that competitors would be discounting dangerously to get a share of the market. It was that which made Sony get out of the calculator business. When the big discounting came, many calculator makers actually went bankrupt while others just left the market incurring a large financial loss.

Looking back, Akio Morita felt that the decision at Sony to get out of calculators was probably too hasty, and that the company's action had shown a lack of technical forethought. He argued that had Sony remained in the market, it might have developed early expertise in digital technology, for later use in personal computers and audio and visual applications. This, he felt would have provided Sony with a competitive advantage.

(Source: Morita, 1987)

QUESTIONS

1. Do you think that withdrawal from the market constituted a miscalculation on Sony's part?

2. What steps might it have undertaken to have been more sure about its deci-

---

- The top management in the organization does not provide adequate support for the product.

- Company politics – e.g. between various brand managers.

- Unforeseen high product costs.

A firm's inability to use common sense reasoning, or inattention to the management task of marketing the product are often factors in new product failure (see, for example, Proctor, 1993).

It is much easier with hindsight to evaluate the reasons for the success or failure of a new product. The case example on the previous page highlights the difficulty of evaluating success and failure at a particular point in time.

In the next section we will look at how firms can try to avoid new product failure by adopting a systematic approach to finding, screening and evaluating new product ideas.

A METHODICAL APPROACH

In order to prevent costly failures, firms need to adopt a methodical approach to finding and evaluating new product ideas. To this end firms can benefit enormously from having aids that structure thinking and analysis. A first step to structured thinking about new products is the adoption of a six-phase development programme (Figure 11.1).

Costs accumulate as firms progress through the six phases; the earlier that potentially poor product ideas are screened out, the better it is for the company.

CASE EXAMPLE

FORD: PRODUCT TEAR-DOWN

There would seem to be something almost sacrilegious about taking delivery of a shiny, new car and then dismantling it piece by piece. Yet this exactly what competitors do to each other's new products. 'Product tear-down' is a way for a business to improve its own product strategies by finding out how its competitors' products are manufactured. Indeed, the Ford Motor Company frequently strips down its competitors' products to discover how they are put together, and the nature of their likely cost structure.

There are five steps involved in product tear-down.

1. Obtain the product.

2. Tear the product down – literally.

3. Reverse-engineer the product – this amounts to making detailed drawings of parts and producing part lists, together with analyses of the production processes that seem to have been involved.

4. Build up costs – this entails costing out parts, taking into consideration whether they should be made by the firm or bought in from suppliers. The

CASE EXAMPLE *CONTINUED*

number and variety of components and assembly operations are also detailed. Production costs are then derived from both direct labour and overheads, taking account of the probable cost structure of the competitor.

5. Establish economies of scale. Guides to economies of scale are then developed, taking into consideration the volume of cars produced by the competitor and the total number of its employees. The last step involves working out model-run lengths and volumes needed to achieve break-even and specified amounts of profit.

As a result of regularly tearing down the Leyland Mini over a number of years, the technical and production people at Ford came to the conclusion that Leyland was not making money on the Mini at its current price. As a consequence Ford decided against entering that market, as long as the current prices prevailed.

(Source: Leaf, 1978)

QUESTION

1. Product tear-down can obviously be applied to a large number of manu-factured consumer and industrial products. Can it be applied to services, or to fast moving consumer goods such as cosmetics? Why, or why not?

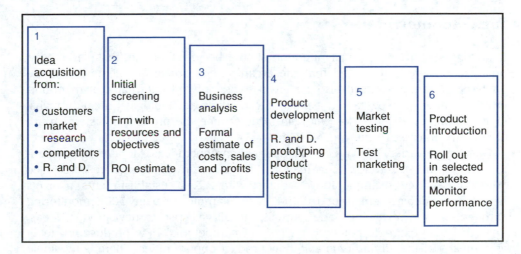

Figure 11.1 Six phases of the new product development programme.

CASE EXAMPLE

PRINCES: CONSUMER RESEARCH FOR NEW PRODUCT IDEAS

'Lunch Breaks', from Princes, represents one of the most innovative launches into the canned food sector for some time. There is a trend towards eating on the move and snacking, and this in turn is producing a growth in the demand for single-portion meals. From research studies, Princes discovered that customers were dissatisfied with available 'tuna in sauce' variants and would respond favourably to a self-contained, nutritious tuna-based meal. Consumers desired products that were healthy, different to the extent that they could be considered adventurous, and which at the same time represented good value for money. In addition the research discovered that more convenient packaging formats, which allowed consumption to take place away from the home, would be appreciated.

(Source: The Grocer, *May 14th 1994, p 30.)*

QUESTION

1. The product concerned here is relatively simple in its concept and make-up. How might user research studies like these produce useful ideas for more complex products such as cars and domestic appliances?

IDEA ACQUISITION

It is suggested that particular attention should be given in the first place to an organization's resources, and that the organization's major problems should be analysed. Attention should also be given to identifying external growth opportunities ready for exploitation – expanding markets, technological breakthroughs, or rising profit margins. This will help to determine the product fields which are of primary interest to the organization.

There are a variety of ways of obtaining new product ideas. Monitoring competitors' new product development, feedback from customers, market research (see 'The Princes' case example above) contact with R. & D. establishments, a firm's own R. & D. department (see 'The 3M' case example on page 303), monitoring competition and reviewing trade journals can all give rise to new product ideas. The Ford case example points to analysis of competitors' new products in detail as a means of identifying profitable new product opportunities. There is no single best method – firms should try all methods, wherever possible.

CASE EXAMPLE

3M: R&D/MARKETING INTERFACE

'Post-it' notes are taken for granted these days, both at home and at work, yet the invention appears to have come about purely by chance. A researcher at the American company 3M, Dr Spencer Sylver, was conducting research into an entirely different area when he found an adhesive which 'sticks without sticking'. Enthused by his discovery he sent samples to other laboratories in the 3M group, but none of them were able to find any application for the idea at the time.

A decade later, Arthur Fry, another research worker in the 3M group, did find a use for what was to become the 'Post-it'. His discovery also occurred purely by chance. Arthur Fry was a member of a choir and he wanted to mark the pages of his music book without ruining the paper. He applied a thin layer of Dr Sylver's adhesive onto the page-markers of his score and, of course, it did exactly what he wanted it to do.

From these beginnings the small pastel coloured pieces of paper which stick, unstick, and can be re-stuck at will, were created. 'Post-it' was born in 1981.

(Source: Giscard d'Estaing, 1992)

QUESTION

1. 'Chance discovery is a fine thing, but it takes a practical mind and a good filing system to turn such ideas into saleable products'. Discuss.

The use of a creativity technique such as morphological analysis (see, for example, Majaro, 1991) can help executives to generate many new product ideas. The basic premise behind using this technique is the idea that a product is an entity which has different dimensions. It may come in different shapes and sizes, appeal to different target markets, be made of different materials, etc. It is the combination of attributes of these different dimensions which creates the product entity itself. For instance, a desk may be made of wood, be relatively large with respect to comparable products, be styled in the classical mould and appeal to the user at home. It is even possible to go beyond tangible dimensions.

Morphological analysis entails recognizing the most important dimensions of a product – usually two, three or four – and then generating a list of attributes relating to these dimensions. The next stage involves taking combinations of the attributes listed (one for each dimension) and deciding whether or not this kind of product is already marketed by the firm.

For example, taking fast foods as an example, one combination might be:

Dimensions

Type of dish:		Target market:
Attributes:	curry	late-night supper callers

A two-dimensional example for gloves is illustrated in Figure 11.2

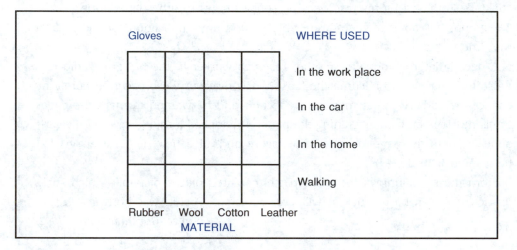

Figure 11.2 Morphological analysis with 'gloves' as the subject.

The technique can be elaborated and 'computerized' by making use of a random word generator to suggest possible attributes (Proctor, 1989).

If the combination generated does not represent a current product offering and it is felt that it could constitute an attractive product market opportunity then it could be retained as a possible idea to be progressed to the next of the six phases – screening.

An organization needs to establish a programme for planned idea generation. This could involve identifying idea-generating groups and giving them a clear concept of the organization's interest fields. Conducting exploratory technical research can also be productive.

SCREENING

Usually, ideas for new products arise sequentially, one at a time, and cannot be compared and evaluated along with a large set of alternative ideas for new products, unless a technique such as morphological analysis is used. Benchmarking against important criteria is thus an important procedure to follow.

Clearly, the likely financial performance and implications of developing and/or adopting a new product idea are the key factors that need to be taken into account. However, without undertaking desk and/or field research it is difficult to quantify what might be expected to sell, although pooled estimates of subjective expert opinions, can sometimes provide remarkably close estimates. Members of the firm who might have some idea of the quantities of the various new product ideas that the firm might expect to sell should be consulted. With such estimates it should then be possible to make rough financial estimates of likely profits to be generated. These rough estimates are turned into more precise estimates at the third phase, business analysis, where a full quantitative analysis and evaluation is made.

The initial screening stage is characterized by a checklist of benchmarks which new products must satisfy before they can be moved on to the next phase in the six-step process. For example:

- Is the product compatible with present distribution channels?

- Is the product complementary to current products?

- Can it be priced competitively alongside products of a similar quality?

- Will promotion of the product be easy?

- Will there always be uses for the product?

- Is there a wide variety of potential customers?

- Are existing resources sufficient to facilitate production and marketing of the product?

- Will the product fill an unsatisfied need in the market place?

- Is the market likely to grow in size?

Such a checklist can of course be extended and modified. Experience seems to indicate that successful products fit well both with the internal functional strengths of the business and with the needs of the market. New product ideas can be rated against the items on the checklist and those satisfying key criteria moved on to the next phase – business analysis.

BUSINESS ANALYSIS

At the business analysis phase sales, costs and profit projections have to be made in order to determine whether adoption of the new product into the product mix will satisfy company objectives. The phase involves predicting sales and cost behaviour, so that profitability of the product can be estimated. This can be done in a variety of ways – it is always advisable to use as many different ways as is feasible. Approaches include:

- examining sales histories of similar products

- surveying market opinion

- using expert opinions

- statistical models (see Chapter 5).

Irrespective of the approach taken, minimum and maximum sales estimates need to be obtained to provide an idea of the degree of risk involved. The method of forecasting depends on whether the product is a one-time purchase, an infrequently purchased product, or a frequently purchased product. In the case of infrequently purchased products, attention has to be given to predicting first-time sales and replacement sales. In the case of frequently purchased products, attention has to be given to first-time buyers and repeat purchases. In using any of the identified methods of forecasting it is essential to gain separate estimates of:

- first-time purchase

- replacement purchase

- repeat purchase.

Costs also have to be estimated, and these may change over the timespan of the sales forecast. This has to be taken into account when estimating profits and likely sales, since costs do have uncertainties attached to them. Escalating prices of raw materials or bought-in parts can stifle the sales growth of a new product, because of the need to continually adjust its price upwards.

Placing a value on the financial appeal of a new product is of course very important. However, it does have to be borne in mind that a large degree of uncertainty surrounds any estimates that are made. Moreover, there is always the danger that once numbers are put down on paper, they will be treated as if they represent certainties. It is therefore a good idea to keep in mind the more qualitative aspects of evaluation, as defined in the checklist of criteria used at the screening stage.

Financial evaluation of new product ideas should examine the following:

- estimated after-tax return on investment

- payback period

- variance in the estimates of return on investment and payback between the best scenario and the worst scenario – to indicate risk.

Surveys of market opinion can be particularly helpful at the business analysis phase, since in addition to helping to quantify potential demand they can also help to provide other information as well. It may be possible that with some adjustment to the product or service it will sell better. It is important to get this right at the outset. The kind of qualitative questions to ask here relate to whether:

- the benefits of using the product are clear to the user

- the product solves a problem or fills a need

- other products already fill this need and give satisfaction

- the price is right in relation to the perceived value.

One should, of course, choose an appropriate group of target customers. Where the new product is only a concept it can be presented symbolically. At this stage a word or a graphic description will suffice.

Products which satisfy the criteria set for this phase can then move on to the product development phase.

EVALUATING THE FINANCIAL ASPECTS OF A NEW PRODUCT

Discounted cashflow (DCF) return calculation recognizes the time value of money and allows choices to be made among alternative courses of action. A pound of today's money invested in a facility has a higher value than a pound received in, say, five years' time from now. The DCF return is the interest rate which brings the present worth value of the cash inflows (profit, depreciation, tax effects, etc.) for a project exactly equal to the present worth values of the cash outlays (investment, research programme, engineering studies, etc.). A decision whether to accept or reject the proposal will be influenced by whether the DCF return is greater or less than the investor's minimum acceptable return standard for the investment opportunity.

Here is a simple illustration to show how a DCF return is calculated. Assume the cash outlay is £100 000 in year one. In addition, assume that the cash inflow over the life of the project (say four years) will be as shown below:

	£ '000
Year 2	45
Year 3	40
Year 4	35
Year 5	30
Total cash inflow	150

From a handbook of present value factors we obtain the additional figures shown below on the following page.

In this simple example, the interest rate at which the present value of the cash inflow exactly equals the present value of the cash outlay is 20%. That is, we can expect a 20% return on investment. We can also observe that the payback period is between three and four years.

PRODUCT DEVELOPMENT

Product development is the stage at which a new product proposal is developed into a physical entity and plans are put together for its production and introduction to the market place. Some products are obviously more complex than others. Product development can therefore be an extremely lengthy business, or it can be reasonably brief. Nevertheless, as a stage in the new product development process it is important for all products.

Year	Current year cash flow £'000	Present value of cash flow @ 10%		Present value of cash flow @ 20%	
		Factor	Discounted-cash flow	Factor	Discounted cash flow
Cash outlay					
1	−100	1.000	−100	1.000	−100
Cash inflow					
2	45	0.9091	40.9	0.8333	37.5
3	40	0.8264	33.1	0.6944	27.8
4	35	0.7513	26.3	0.5787	20.3
5	30	0.6830	20.5	0.4823	14.4
	150		120.8		100.0
Net cash flow	50		20.8		0

When a product moves into R. & D. and Engineering (in the case of a complex technological product) the really heavy costs can start to mount up. Work is directed at trying to turn the idea into a technically and commercially feasible product. This involves what is known as prototyping. The objective is to develop a physical version of the product (a prototype) which:

● will meet with consumers' expectations

● will perform safely under normal use and conditions

● can be produced for the budgeted manufacturing costs.

Developing a prototype can take days, months or years, according to the nature of the product. Commercial aircraft, for example, take years to develop. When completed, the prototype is subjected to rigorous functional and consumer tests. Such tests are carried out both on the bench and in the field, to ensure that the new products will perform safely and effectively.

There is a variety of approaches to consumer testing. These include bringing consumers into the laboratory to try out the product or providing them with samples or models to try out in their own homes.

TEST MARKETING

Where launch costs are high it would seem common sense to test market new products before embarking on commercialization on a national or international scale. However, not all products are test marketed. It is possible under certain circumstances that test marketing the product may provide important business knowledge to competitors. Nevertheless, test marketing can avoid disasters, perhaps saving a firm millions of pounds.

The amount of test marketing to be given to a product reflects investment cost and risk on the one hand, and pressure of time and cost of research on the other. Clearly the greater the investment, the more need there is to proceed with thorough testing. The same is also true of high-risk new products.

A variety of test marketing methods exist and there are differences between test marketing industrial and consumer goods.

TEST MARKETING OF CONSUMER GOODS

- **Simulated store technique** This technique consists of inviting a large group of shoppers to a brief screening of a number of well-known advertisements, along with a number of new ones. One of the advertisements promotes the new product, but this is not specifically brought to the attention of the audience.

  Members of the audience are provided with money to spend and are invited into a simulated store where they may buy items of their choice .Alternatively, they are allowed to hold on to the money. A note is made of how many people buy the new product and how many buy competing brands.

  The audience is asked to explain their reasons for purchase or non-purchase. Some weeks later group members are contacted by telephone to assess their attitude, usage and satisfaction with the product. They are also offered the opportunity to repurchase products (Shocker and Hall, 1986).

- **Sales wave research** In this form of research people are persuaded to try a product at no cost and are then re-offered the product, or a competitor's product, at a reduced price. They may be re-offered the product as many as three to five times (sales waves). Researchers note how many customers pick the product again. People are also asked to report their level of satisfaction with the product and this also is noted. From the data, researchers estimate repeat purchase rates in settings where consumers spend their own money and choose among competing brands.

- **Controlled test marketing** In this case a number of stores agree to carry a new product. The firm supplying the product oversees shelf location, number of facings, displays and point of purchase promotions, and pricing. Subsequent sales are determined by observing movement off the shelves and from inspecting diaries which are kept by a consumer panel who buy goods from the stores. At a later date, a sample of consumers are interviewed to obtain their impressions of the product.

  This kind of test marketing can be criticized for not being realistic, because the firm with the new product does not have to sell to the stores in the first instance. Moreover, opportunity exists for competition to intervene and distort the results.

- **Actual 'test marketing'** Here, the usual procedure is that a few representative towns and cities are selected and the company sells to the trade, just as it would do following a national launch. Full advertising and promotion campaigns are conducted in the places involved. While test marketing can be expensive, its costs are a mere fraction of the amount involved in a full scale national launch. As well as enabling companies to predict sales, it allows firms to test out various different marketing plans.

TEST MARKETING OF INDUSTRIAL GOODS

Test marketing of industrial goods is uncommon. It is often too expensive or even impractical to produce a sample of many industrial products.

However, product use tests are commonly used by producers of industrial goods. This is similar to in-home use testing of consumer products, but in this case the manufacturer selects potential customers who agree to use the product for a limited period of time.

The manufacturer's technical staff then observe how the the product performs in use and how the customer uses it. Unanticipated problems of safety and servicing can be uncovered in this way. In addition, it gives the manufacturer an idea of the amount of customer training and servicing that is necessary to ensure proper use of the product.

Occasionally, controlled test marketing is used and in this case a limited supply of the product is produced and the sales force is instructed to sell it in a limited geographic area. The sales effort is accompanied by full promotional support. Failures that occur in the testing stage are not as expensive as commercialization failures, but they do involve significant financial losses.

COMMERCIALIZATION

This is the last phase of the product innovation process. At this point a successfully developed and tested product is introduced on a full scale basis to the entire market. The introduction has to be carefully planned, with special reference to the response characteristics of potential buyers and competitors.

For the manufacturer then it is likely that commercialization will incur the heaviest expenditure of the whole process of introducing a new product. The costs of production and marketing can be huge. Introducing major new consumer goods into the market can involve costs amounting to millions of pounds, accounting for as much as half the sales earnings during the first year of operation.

The timing of the introduction of a new product can be critical. The firm has to monitor competitors' actions and change its strategy accordingly. It also has to bear in mind the effect of a new product on its other products – the introduction must be timed so that sales of a similar product are not suddenly stifled.

Much attention has to be given to deciding where to launch a new product. Few companies launch a product into full national or international distribution. A planned market roll-out over time is the normal approach. In the case of smaller companies, one city and surrounding area at a time is selected and a blitz campaign is mounted. Once these have been secured the programme moves on to new cities and surrounding areas. Larger companies tend to operate on a region-by-region basis. Where a company has a national distributor network then it may introduce its product nationally.

SOLEIL CYCLING COMPANY: SCREENING NEW PRODUCT IDEAS

The Soleil Cycling Company, based near Rouen in northern France, claim to have invented the world's first solar-powered bicycle. Powered by two solar-charged batteries the machine is capable of moving along a flat surface carrying a 60 kg person for a distance of 20 miles when fully charged. The batteries are charged by the action of light on solar panels mounted above batteries on the rear mudguard. A powerful dynamo also provides a trickle charge to the cells when the bicycle is in motion, and the batteries can be recharged from the mains supply. The framework and the wheels of the bicycle are constructed from an ultra light non-rusting aluminium alloy.

The company has been working on the product for the last five years and a company executive points out that much time, effort and money has gone into developing what it regards as a major technological breakthrough. The firm has yet to decide on a price for the machine, but anticipates high volume sales if the price can be kept at a reasonable level.

QUESTION

1. How should the Soleil company proceed from this point onwards?

At the commercialization stage, failures should rarely occur in well managed and adequately developed companies, because such companies know how to produce and sell. Where failure does occur it may be traced to an earlier stage and reflects weakness in the product concept itself.

While having effective screening and evaluation procedures is clearly an effective way of avoiding products that are unlikely to prove successful, there also has to be a suitable organizational structure for new product development. In the next section we will address the question of organizing for new products.

AN ORGANIZATIONAL STRUCTURE FOR NEW PRODUCTS

Effective innovation is helped by good organization. Conventionally, innovation is associated with production departments in the course of carrying out research and development functions, where prototypes are produced and shown to top management for approval. This procedure is still followed in many companies. However, the problem with this kind of approach to organization is that it only rarely emanates from market-oriented planning, and the products developed may not be directly related to consumer needs.

Many firms recognize the dangers inherent in leaving innovation entirely in the hands of the R. & D. department and seek to redress the situation by giving responsibility for new product development to a committee. Usually, the committee is made up of people representing the major functional areas of the business. Unfortunately, because the members of the committee are usually very senior staff and have other commitments, this sort of arrangement may not be very effective if many new product ideas have to be considered.

An alternative approach adopted by many UK firms entails putting responsibility for the development of new products with product managers in marketing departments. While this is an improvement on the structures outlined above, difficulties may arise in that since product managers are responsible for existing products, they may not have the time to attend to new products. A logical extension to cope with inadequacies of having product managers in charge of new product development is to have a new products department. In this case departments usually have line responsibility for the new products until the test market stage.

Monitoring how well a new product is faring after launch can easily be neglected. It is too easy to assume that having developed and launched a new product successfully, it needs no further consideration. Of course how a new product is received by the user is of vital interest to the company. Action is needed if the product does not meet with expectations. An understanding of the consumer adoption process is required in order to monitor progress effectively. This is discussed in the next section

THE CONSUMER ADOPTION PROCESS

The consumer adoption process is a descriptive model of how potential customers learn about new products, try them, adopt them or discard them. Knowledge of this process is of paramount importance to marketing management engaged in launching new products.

Adopters of new products are considered to move through the following stages.

- **Awareness** – people are aware of the innovation but are lacking in information about it.

- **Interest** – people want information about the innovation.

- **Evaluation** – people are considering whether to try the innovation.

- **Trial** – people try out the product on a limited basis to assess its desirability.

- **Adoption** – people decide to use the innovation regularly.

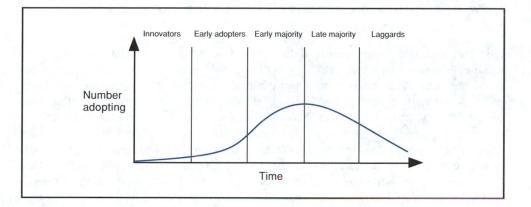

Figure 11.3 The diffusion of innovation.

Rogers (1962) looked at how people adopt innovations. He came up with the following typologies who were active at different stages in the adoption cycle.

● Innovators – those who were willing to try out new ideas and take risks.

● Early adopters – opinion leaders in their social sphere who take on innovations.

● Early majority – people who adopt new ideas early in the cycle but are not usually opinion leaders.

● Late majority – sceptical people who tend to adopt an innovation only after a majority of people have tried it.

● Laggards – people who seem suspicious of change and only take on an innovation when it has been tried and tested.

The implications of the Rogers typology seem to indicate that in launching new products a firm should research carefully the personal characteristics of innovators and early adopters, along with the characteristics of the media they peruse. Unfortunately, it is not quite as simple as this since people may fall into one typology for one product and another typology for a different product.

Rogers argued that there was a tendency for early adopters to be younger in age, to have a higher social status, a more favourable financial position and a different type of mental ability from later adopters. He saw them as making use of a greater range of more impersonal and cosmopolitan information sources that were in closer contact with the origin of the new ideas. He also saw them as being more cosmopolitan in outlook.

HOW THE ADOPTION PROCESS IS RELATED TO THE PRODUCT LIFE CYCLE CONCEPT

One can link the theory of the diffusion and adoption of innovations with the product life cycle concept. When launching a new product a company seeks to stimulate awareness, interest, trial and purchase, but during the introductory stage only a relatively few people will buy it (the innovators). Later on, provided that people find the product satisfactory, larger numbers of buyers will start to purchase the product (the early adopters). The emergence of competition speeds up the process by increasing awareness and causing prices to fall, and the 'early majority' are drawn in. This corresponds to the growth phase in the product life cycle. Eventually the growth rate of the market declines as new buyers approach zero and sales become steady at the replacement rate – the maturity phase. It is here that the late adopters begin to purchase the product. After sales start to decline, as new product categories, forms and brands appear and cause the consumer to shift allegiance, the laggards are purchasing the product.

COMMUNICATION AFFECTING THE DIFFUSION OF INNOVATION

These are of two types: informal and formal. Informal communications lie largely outside the sphere of the marketer and consist of reference groups and family influences. While one might suppose that people who first adopt a product are the ones who influence others to purchase, interpersonal influence of relations do seem to be more complex.

Formal communications can be influenced by marketers. These influences comprise advertising, personal selling and various other forms of reseller support. When control of communication is possible one has to decide which types of media are most likely to transmit messages to persons who are first adopters of an innovation. In particular, the question arises as to which media are considered to be the most authoritive and what messages are most likely to influence new product acceptance.

The diffusion of innovation is a social phenomenon. The interest of diffusion research focuses not only on the characteristics of a decision-making unit (individual or family) but also on the environment of diffusion provided by the social setting.

SUMMARY

There are various ways of defining new products. Perhaps the simplest is to consider them as being anything which is new to an organization and which amounts to more than a simple modification of an existing product.

Defining a new product failure is not a simple matter, since it depends upon the criteria adopted to evaluate success or failure. Put in simple terms, a new product failure is anything that fails to live up to the organization's expectations (usually expressed in financial terms). This being the case it follows that what may constitute a failure for one firm could well be a success for another firm.

Many factors contribute to new product failures. If, however, an organization carefully states its expectations on key criteria in the first instance and then evaluates new product ideas against this criteria, there is a possibility that failures may be avoided.

Ideas for new products arise in many ways. Suggestions may come from competitors, distributors and the organization's own staff. There are also a number of creativity techniques which can be used to help generate new product ideas. One of the best known of these is morphological analysis.

The new product screening process is intended to help to eliminate from further consideration those new product ideas that are not likely to be successful in the firm's terms. Initial screening amounts to constructing a checklist against which to rate any new ideas that arise. Those that pass the checklist stage then go on to further analysis.

Business analysis is part of the new product screening process. It is here that estimates are made about the feasibility of developing and marketing a product to meet with the firm's required sales and profit targets. Costings and market research data, where available, are used to make projections and reach conclusions.

If firms are reasonably sure that a product idea is a good one, they can then go on to the product development stage. This can vary enormously in length and cost according to the nature of the product.

It is generally advocated that all products should be test marketed prior to commercialization on a national or international basis, unless there are strong grounds for not doing so. Test marketing cannot prevent heavy R. & D. expenditure, but it can obviate the necessity of wasting money on expensive marketing and production of initial stocks if it proves that products are unlikely to be successful in their current form.

New products are at the very first stage in the product life cycle. To get new products off the ground one has to understand the process by which new products come to be adopted. Key people in the adoption process are the innovators and the early adopters. Organizations need to be able to identify these people and persuade them to adopt the product to stand the best chance of getting the product off the ground.

There are two types of communication that influence the adoption of innovations: informal and formal. The former is largely outside the sphere of the marketer and consists of reference groups and family influences. Formal communications, however, can be influenced by marketers, and comprise advertising, personal selling and various other forms of reseller support. The diffusion of innovation is a social phenomenon and the environment of diffusion provided by the social setting must also be studied.

DISCUSSION QUESTIONS

1. How might one define a new product?

2. Examine the difficulties in providing an exact definition of a new product failure.

3. Discuss the various factors which contribute to new product failures.

4. How might new product failures be avoided?

5. Outline the various ways in which ideas for new products arise.

6. What items might be included in a checklist to be used in the initial screening of new product ideas?

7. What is involved at the business analysis stage of the new product screening process?

8. Why does the product development stage vary enormously in length and cost? Find some illustrations.

9. Explain what is involved in test-marketing a new product.

10. Under what circumstances might a decision be taken not to test-market a new product?

11. What is the consumer innovation adoption process? Why is it important for marketers of new products to understand this process?

REFERENCES

Giscard d'Estaing, V.A. (ed.) (1992) *The Book of Inventions and Discoveries*, Macdonald, London.

Halstead, R. (1994) The emperor has no clothes, *Business Age*, February, 22–3.

Hardy, L. (1978) *Successful Business Strategy*, Kogan Page, London.

Hartley, R.F.(1992) *Marketing Mistakes*, John Wiley, New York.

Leaf, R. (1978) How to pick up tips from your competitors, *Director*, **30**, February, 60–2.

Levitt, T. (1960) Marketing myopia, *Harvard Business Review*, **38**, July–August, 45–56.

McCarthy, E.J. and Perreault, W.D. (1993) *Basic Marketing*, 11th edn, Irwin, Chicago, Ill.

Majaro, S. (1991) *The Creative Marketer*, Butterworth Heineman, Oxford.

Morita, A. (1987) *Made in Japan*, Fontana, London.

Proctor, R.A. (1989) Innovations in new product screening and evaluation, *Technology and Strategic Management*, **1**(3), 313–23.

Proctor, R.A. (1993) Product innovation: the pitfalls of entrapment, *Creativity and Innovation Management*, **2**(4), 260–5.

Rogers, E.M. (1962) *Diffusion of Innovations*, Macmillan, New York.

Shocker, D. and Hall, W.G. (1986) Pretest market models, a critical evaluation, *Journal of Product Innovation Management*, **3**, 86-107.

FURTHER READING

Majaro, S. (1991) *The Creative Process*, Allen and Unwin, London.

Urban, G. and Hauser, J. (1990) *Marketing of New Products*, Prentice Hall, Englewood Cliffs, N.J.

Von Hippel, E. (1988) *The Sources of Innovation*, Oxford University Press, New York.

CASE PROBLEM 11.1

ASTON MANOR BREWERY: PRODUCT INNOVATION

Widgets are continuing to revolutionize the packaging of beer. Wanting to ride on the back of the success of a new form of canned beers including widgets, the Aston Manor brewery in Birmingham has come up with a small gadget which is inserted into the neck of beer bottles immediately after they have been filled. This device, the brewery reckons, will enable it to produce a draught style beer with high potential sales. The brewery considers it is offering a good proposition because consumers receive, at no extra cost, a widget in the bottle that produces a quality of product comparable to that of the major brewers.

The non-return valve allows little air back into a bottle once it has been opened. The device not only makes the beer last longer, but it also produces a good head for the beer. The beer is 'poured' by squeezing the bottle and forcing it through the valve in the neck. Once it has been squeezed, the bottle stays compressed, only gradually regaining its shape as the air creeps in. Aston's beer can keep its sparkle for at least five days.

Trade customers have responded enthusiastically to the innovation and if the idea takes off it could boost sales, even though the sector is in decline. The trade will also benefit from a strong healthy profit margin. In comparison with Guinness's new widget brand, Cherry, it was claimed that in volume terms, Draught at Home (Aston's comparable product offering) would be £1 a case cheaper.

Aston Manor brewery has no canning facilities of its own and depends very much on bottled sales for its off-trade business. The company could reap considerable benefit from the new device. While the firm lacks the resources to market the technology, sales of the beer should benefit from the interest which has been aroused for canned widget beers in general. Already, the new technology has been accepted by customers, who now know what to expect from a packaged product with such a device.

The firm estimates that it will be under six months before other brands hit the market making use of a similar widget.

(Source: The Grocer, *12 February 1994, p. 27)*

QUESTION

1. How should Aston seek to evaluate this new product?

CASE PROBLEM 11.2

EUROTUNNEL: ASSESSING FINANCIAL VIABILITY OF A PROJECT

In the Eurotunnel project one is reminded, though on a much larger scale, of the Brighton Marina disaster of the 1970s. In that particular case, rational people invested £60 million in a project that could only hope to generate a million pounds revenue a year at the most. The venture was sold later for £11 million and it made a return for the new owners at that level of investment.

Even assuming that the cross-Channel tunnel takes all the available business until the year 2000, it is estimated that it will still lose £200m. a year. Over a longer period of time, however, there is optimism that Eurotunnel will be a financial success, but it seems that if Eurotunnel was a small start-up company approaching venture capitalists or banks for seed money, its business plan would be rejected. With a start-up cost of £2 billion, Eurotunnel could make a useful return, but at £10 billion there seems to be no possibility.

It is suggested the Eurotunnel will expand the market, attracting extra freight, extra passengers from the airlines, and many more motorists. But even if the market doubles in six years and trebles within 12 years, and Eurotunnel obtains a two-thirds market share of it, Eurotunnel will only break even in 12 years' time. Moreover, it can be argued that that is the best it will do, and prior to that it will have piled up around £4 billion of new losses. Unless there is a huge restructuring of its debt, Eurotunnel will not make money.

From a marketing viewpoint, Eurotunnel's pricing strategy seems disastrous. With fares of up to £310 for a passenger car at peak hours, many people will be discouraged from using the service. It had been expected by industry analysts that fares would perhaps undercut the ferry service, which offer on-board cinemas, restaurants and duty-free shopping. It is clear that prices will have to fall, but one does have to bear in mind that while the marginal cost of laying on extra trains is comparatively small, capital investment costs have been very high, with interest payments alone amounting to as much as Eurotunnel hopes to turn over in its first year from car-carrying trains. The market has to expand, but at high prices people will not be rushing to cross the Channel in this way.

The enterprise is pinning its hopes on six million cars using the service by 1996, around half of the predicted Channel-crossing market, bringing in about £1.2 billion. Along with the revenue from freight and Eurostar, the passenger rail service, it expects to generate an extra £200 million, and according to Eurotunnel it will be on course to pay dividends on time and start tackling the debt mountain. However, these things are by no

CASE PROBLEM 11.2 *CONTINUED*

means certain. Freight operators will have to be convinced of the tunnel's convenience – especially as lorry drivers now use the ferry crossing to take their mandatory rest periods. Eurostar will have to undercut cheap airfares (currently £79 return to Paris). Moreover, motorists will have to quit using the ferries *en masse* for a service that is only slightly faster, no cheaper, and doesn't possess a duty-free supermarket.

(Source: Halstead, 1994)

QUESTION

1. Is it possible to tell whether the Eurotunnel venture is likely to be a success or a failure? Why, or why not?

12 PRICING DECISIONS

Economic ideas about pricing, and their limitations, are explored in this chapter, along with a variety of practical price-setting methods. Attention is given to the relationship between price and quality. The nature of price leadership and its ramifications is discussed, as well as the dangers of price wars.

OBJECTIVES

After reading this chapter you should be able to:

- appreciate when pricing is most important
- appreciate elementary economic ideas about pricing and their limitations
- describe a variety of practical price setting approaches
- understand how pricing can be used strategically
- appreciate the nature of price leadership and its ramifications
- understand the dangers of price wars.

INTRODUCTION

This chapter explores different dimensions of pricing. After defining price, the conditions under which price takes on its greatest degree of importance are examined. Next, the classical economic theory of pricing is considered, along with what it does and does not explain about pricing in reality. Pricing in practice is then considered and a variety of practical price-setting approaches outlined. Special attention is given to the principles of competition-oriented pricing and the psychological aspects of pricing. The relationship between price and quality is then considered.

Lastly, the nature of price leadership and its ramifications are introduced, along with the dangers of price-cutting and price wars.

THE IMPORTANCE OF PRICE

All members of the production and distribution chain – buyers, distributors and producers – are interested in price. As an element of the marketing mix, it has a strategic value to all firms. Price can be looked upon as the amount for which a product or service is exchanged, or offered for sale to potential purchasers, irrespective of value or worth.

There are market conditions under which organizations can exert some control over the level at which price is set. If an organization cannot exert any control over the setting of pricing then it has to accept whatever the market determines will be the price.

Perfectly competitive markets specify that there is a homogeneous product, complete information among buyers, rational buyer behaviour, and large numbers of producers. In a perfectly competitive market a producer has almost no control over prices. They are determined by market forces brought about by competitive pressures and patterns of consumer expenditure. There are extremely few such markets in reality. Most markets are imperfect, and some control over the setting of prices is possible.

Pricing is most important in a business under the following circumstances.

- **When a new product is being introduced** There are often very few guidelines as to the level at which the price should be fixed. Moreover, it is difficult to assess exactly how people will respond to various price settings without actually launching the product into the market place, since people's attitudes and behaviour are not always predictable.

- **When a competitor increases or reduces prices** When the price of a competitor's product is changed, some kind of response may be required. Action may centre upon changing one's own price to match that of the competition, or alternatively undertaking other competitive marketing strategies. Whatever the case, pricing becomes an important issue.

- **When a change arises in the economy that will influence demand** The demand for some goods is relatively unaffected by changes in the economic climate. However, most goods are affected in one way or another. Even the demand for food items may change with people switching their consumption patterns from one type of food to another. As we will show below, demand for products can influence the level at which prices are set. Thus any change in demand has an impact on the level at which prices may be set.

- **When there are shifts in the price of substitute products** The price of substitute products will have an important effect on the price level set for a specific product. The extent to which products are substitutable and the speed with which substitution can occur are also additional factors. People may be able to switch between using the train and the bus with relative ease but may experience greater difficulty in changing central heating from electricity to gas. The relative price differential may also only be temporary, and the extent to which this is perceived to be the case is also important.

- **When there are changes in government regulations** Safety regulations and moves to protecting the environment can increase the costs of producing some products. Such increases in costs are inevitably passed on to the user. Some prices may also be controlled by the government, and may be frozen or even reduced if this is felt to be in the public interest.

- **When there is a technological breakthrough which influences production costs** Technological innovation is an accepted feature of the modern business environment. Improvements in technology almost inevitably mean an improvement in either the product itself or the way in which it is produced. These changes influence the price to be charged for the product and hence the importance of pricing for that product, as far as the organization is concerned.

- **When the firm changes its strategy or tactics** A change in strategy is almost inevitably linked to reconsidering the various elements of the marketing mix. Pricing therefore becomes an issue.

Over time various ideas have been expressed as to how prices should be set. These range from theoretical ideas of economists through to ideas of modern-day practitioners who are concerned with earning revenue for their organizations. In the next section we will start to explore these various perspectives by looking at some of the ideas suggested by the theoretical economists.

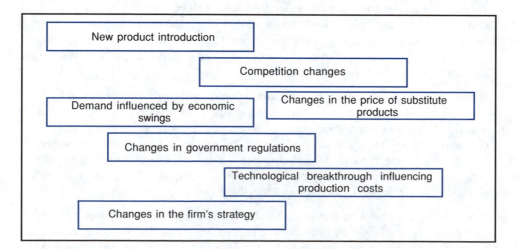

Figure 12.1 Factors causing price to become more important.

Price elasticity of demand	Effect of a change of price on total revenue
1	None: demand rises (falls) by the same percentage that price falls (rises)
>1	Demand rises or falls at a greater percentage rate than rate of price change
<1	Demand rises or falls at a lesser percentage rate than rate price change

Figure 12.2 Price elasticity of demand.

PRICING FROM AN ECONOMICS PERSPECTIVE

Pricing has traditionally been a topic of considerable interest to economists. Indeed, the relationship between the supply and demand for goods and price has figured predominantly in a good deal of the economic literature. Classical economics takes the view that price determines both the supply and the demand for goods and services in the marketplace, formulating the 'law of demand' to explain this phenomenon.

THE LAW OF DEMAND

The law of demand states that the quantity demanded per period of time is inversely related to price. That is, as the price increases, demand will fall, and as price falls then demand will increase.

Of course, the law assumes that a consumer is rational and has full knowledge of the price and availability of goods and their substitutes. It is also assumed that a consumer has a limited budget and motivation to maximize utility. This means that if relative prices of goods and services change, the consumer will normally substitute less expensive for dearer goods and services, thereby increasing his or her utility.

A key concept in understanding how demand shifts with respect to changes in price is **price elasticity** (see Figure 12.2).

Price elasticity is defined as **the ratio of the percentage change in demand to a percentage change in price.** While, by definition, the ratio usually has a negative sign – this is because as price rises, demand usually falls – it is customary, in illustrating elasticities, to drop the sign. A price elasticity equal to one signifies that demand rises (falls) by the same percentage that price falls (rises). In this case, total revenue is not affected by price changes. However, when the elasticity is above or below one, then total revenues will be affected by changes.

Knowing the price elasticity of demand for its products or services enables a firm to determine whether its price is too high or too low. Assuming that a firm is trying to maximize its revenue, then the price for a product or service is too high if demand elasticity at that price is greater than 1, and it is too low if demand elasticity at that price is less than 1.

Unfortunately it is not possible to generalize this rule to profit maximization, since we have to take into account the behaviour of costs.

The concept of elasticity can be extended to consumer income. If a substantial reduction in price occurs on an item then this in effect adds up to an increase in real income for those households consuming the item in large quantities. As a result, because they have additional purchasing power, these households may elect to change to buying more expensive products instead of consuming more of what they usually purchase. In this case the effect on income outweighs the substitution effect.

For example, if a poor family consumes a lot of rice and if the price of rice falls, then this family might use the increase in real income to buy other foods and reduce its consumption of rice. As is the case with price **elasticity of demand**, there is also a measure called income elasticity of demand (IE):

$$IE < 1 = \text{normal goods}$$
$$IE > 1 = \text{superior goods}$$
$$IE < 0 = \text{inferior goods}$$

In the case of 'inferior goods', a decline in future sales can be expected when consumer affluence increases. In response to this a producer might hold back on investment plans for the inferior goods and bring forward plans to produce goods with positive income elasticity coefficients (superior/normal goods). The firm might also change the image of the inferior goods by providing them with an up-market appeal in order to attract more well-off customers. Where 'superior goods', usually luxury items, are concerned, rising consumer affluence increases the demand for these products and additional investment is encouraged. 'Normal products' are necessities, and the demand for such goods changes relatively little with respect to income changes.

The relationship between the price of one good and the quantity demanded of another is another important measure. It is known as the **cross-price elasticity** of demand (CPE). In this case:

Products are substitutes for one another if $CPE > 0$
Products are complements to one another if $CPE < 0$

Price elasticity alters with time and according to the stage in the product life cycle. Moreover, there is a tendency for price elasticities to be different for price increases to what they are in the case of price reductions. Price elasticities are also influenced by the amount a given price diverges from the average market price.

Elasticity is central to economic notions about price. Sales of products with a high price elasticity of demand fluctuate the most with price changes. Elasticity also varies at different prices and revenues are maximized when it is equal to (–)1.

THE CLASSICAL MODEL AND ITS LIMITATIONS

From the point of view of practical applicability, some key assumptions limit the usefulness of the model. These include:

- a firm's objective to maximize short-run profits
- immediate customers are the only concern
- price is set without regard to other marketing variables
- demand and cost equations can be estimated with some degree of precision
- the firm has control over price
- the market response to price changes is well understood.

Let us now consider each one of these in turn.

Objectives

There is an assumption in the classical economic model that a seller sets the price for a single product which maximizes immediate rather than long-run profits. It also assumes that costs do not change over time. In reality, demand and costs do change over time because of changes in taste, population and income on the one hand, and in technology and input prices on the other. In addition to the foregoing, account has to be taken of the position of the product in its life cycle.

Theories of the firm suggest that firms seek long-term profit maximization. In so doing they may pursue any of a number of pricing objectives at any one time. The price may be set low to stimulate sales growth or to discourage new entrants to the market, or even to speed the exit of marginal firms from the market. Quite apart from profit maximization, small family businesses may aim for a profit that provides a comfortable lifestyle (Rappaport, 1978).

Prices may also be set at such a level as to avoid government investigation or control (*Wall Street Journal*, 1983); to maintain loyalty of distributors and get their support; to enhance the image of the firm; or to be regarded as 'fair' by customers. Prices may be set to create interest and excitement about an item; to help in the sale of weak items in the line; to discourage others from cutting prices; to make a product 'visible'; or, simply to 'build traffic'.

Multiple parties

In setting the price for goods and service in the real world there are other people to consider than just the firm's immediate customers. There are intermediate customers, with whom a variety of relationships may exist. On the one hand, the producer may set a price to the distributor and allow the latter to charge whatever price it likes. On the other hand, the producer may determine the final price to the consumer and the distributor margin that is necessary to create an incentive for the distributor.

There are competing firms, and the pricing policy adopted by a firm has a profound influence on the rate of entry of new competitors and the pricing policies of existing competitors.

Finally, there is the government, which may periodically intervene to control prices. Price controls can be targeted specifically to benefit particular groups of buyers or suppliers, or can be controlled more generally in the context, for example, of an anti-inflation policy. In the former case, price controls may be used to benefit consumers by preventing suppliers from charging monopoly prices where essential products are concerned. Occasionally, the government may wish to encourage the greater supply of a product (benefiting the supplier) by setting minimum prices which are higher than the free market price (the common agricultural policy within the EC is an instance of this).

Interaction with other elements in the marketing mix

Price is often taken as an indication of product quality. Users associate a high price with high quality. In the case of consumer goods a high price, signifying high quality, is often accompanied with advertising in up-market glossy magazines and distribution through selected quality image retail outlets. All of these factors influence the level of demand for the product. Price, though important, is not the only variable in the equation.

A substantial failing and a cause for criticism which can be made against the classical economics approach is that it pays no attention to the role of the other marketing mix variables. The approach assumes that these other variables remain constant.

Estimation of demand and cost functions

An essential part of the classical economics approach is the supposition that demand and cost functions can be measured. Indeed, much of the economics literature makes use of mathematical equations which assume that measurement of the relevant variables is possible.

Demand functions are very difficult to estimate and, of course, must be based on historical data or survey estimates. In the case of cost data, econometric analysis is used but the reliability of the estimates in making future projections has to be questioned.

Price discretion

The extent to which a seller can vary the terms of the price set is largely influenced by the concerns of the buyer with price and the amount of product differentiation that exists in the market. Where there is considerable product differentiation and the buyer shows little concern over price, then the firm will have considerable discretion in setting the price. Where product differentiation is low and the buyer's concern is high, fewer options are open to the firm.

Varying buyer reactions to price changes

Classical economic theory indicates an inverse relationship between price change and demand for goods and services. A reduction in price is identified with an increase in demand, and an increase in price with a fall in demand. In reality, however, this may not necessarily be the case. A price decrease, for instance, could signal to the market any of the following things:

● the product is about to be supplanted by a later version

● the product has bugs in it and is not selling well

● the firm is in financial trouble and may not stay around to provide spares when they are needed

● the price will come down more and it will pay to wait

● there has been a decline in product quality.

All of these may lead to a fall in demand, rather than an increase. Equally, a price increase might suggest:

● the product is in strong demand and may soon become unobtainable

● the product represents exceptionally good value for money

● the seller may charge more if the buyer waits too long.

These factors may of course lead to an increase in demand.

In addition, there is an expected range of prices which people anticipate having to pay for a product. If the price lies outside the range – above or below – then it is likely that purchases will not be made.

In the next section we will look at price setting in practice.

PRACTICAL PRICING

The classical economic approach to price setting provides an interesting theoretical framework within which to consider the setting of prices in practice. Putting theory into practice, however, is fraught with many difficulties. Economic pricing models over-simplify reality and cannot be readily implemented. Nevertheless, pricing rules of thumb and guidelines used in practice also tend to emphasize one factor, such as cost, demand or competition, to the neglect of other factors. What is really required is a consideration of all of the practical and theoretical guidelines available when setting prices.

Pricing should have objectives, and these should result from marketing and company objectives. Some possible pricing objectives are shown in Figure 12.3. The objective of maintaining position predominates when the total market is not growing. At other times pricing may be geared to expanding market share or just growing sales. Alternatively, the prime objective may be to achieve given levels of

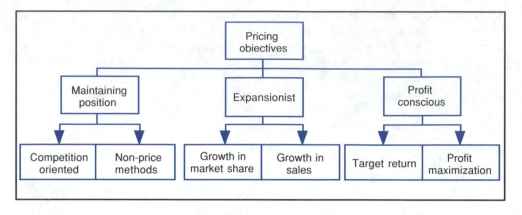

Figure 12.3 Some general pricing objectives.

profitability. Below, we look at the various methods firms use to set prices. One can observe how these methods relate to the various objectives which have been suggested above.

COST-ORIENTED PRICING

Cost-oriented pricing attempts to be profit conscious, but of itself is unlikely to lead to profit maximization or the obtaining of a target return, since it does not take into account the demand for a product at different price levels.

A lot of firms set prices mainly or even completely on the basis of their own costs. It is common practice to count all the costs, including an arbitrary allocation of overhead made on the basis of expected levels of operation. The most common and the most basic types of cost-oriented pricing are standard cost pricing and mark-up pricing. In applying both methods a fixed percentage is applied to the unit cost to arrive at a preliminary price. A comparison is then made between the preliminary price and the going market price for a similar product, and an adjustment is made if it is considered necessary.

Figure 12.4 The cost plus approach to pricing a bicycle.

A cost-oriented price approach to pricing a bicycle might proceed as follows.

Costs:

frame £70 + handlebars £30 + handlebar grips £5 +
wheels £50 + tyres £10 + gears £40 + gear change £25
+ chain £5 + pedals £20 + seat £20   = £275

General overhead

£ 15 000

The manufacturer assumes that it will sell 1000 of the bicycles. It wants to make £100 000 profit from the proceeds, or £100 per bicycle sold. Hence the final price asked is :

fixed cost/number to be sold + variable cost per bicycle +
profit per bicycle or £15 000/1000 + £275 + £100   = £390.

Of course, the basic assumption is that the firm will be able to sell 1000 bicycles at this price. In reality, the demand may only be 500 at this price, in which case having made 1000 bicycles and assuming nothing can be done with the bicycles if they remain unsold, the manufacturer will make:

500 × £100 – £15 000 = £35 000 on the bicycles sold

but incur a loss of

500 × £275 = £137 500 on the unsold bicycles,

that is a net loss of £102 500.

Another possibility is that the manufacturer may be able to obtain more than £390 for each bicycle. If the price that customers were willing to pay was, say, £415, then an opportunity loss of £25 per bicycle might be incurred. In addition, more than 1000 customers might have been willing to pay this price, in which case the total opportunity loss would increase.

The complexity of the issue is compounded by the fact that it is assumed, in the illustration here, that unit costs of components are fixed, irrespective of output. In reality, costs of components would vary with the level of output. Thus a frame might have a unit cost of £70, assuming that 1000 frames were produced, but the unit cost could drop as the number of frames produced increased. Similarly, if fewer frames were produced, then the unit costs would increase.

Assuming that the going market rate is, say, £400 for similar bicycles, then the price of £390 is not far out from what other manufacturers are charging. This being the case, the manufacturer may well choose to bring the asking price slightly more in line with the figure of £400.

STANDARD COST PRICING

Standard cost pricing is best explained through an example.

A camcorder manufacturer estimates that the average variable costs and fixed costs associated with producing a particular model of a given specification, assuming unit sales of 100 000 over five years, amount to £410 per unit.

The average cost per unit is found by adding up all fixed and variable costs and dividing by the number of units to be produced. The following costs are included:

- design and development costs

- production costs

- depreciation

- overhead

- rent

- insurance

- handling and packaging

- storage

- cost of inventory

- advertising

- delivery

- installation

- warranty service

- patent royalty.

Selling, merchandising and administration expenses usually add another 40% to the costs and the firm would want to make £200 profit per machine. The preliminary price then becomes:

$$£410 + (0.40 \times 410) + 200 = £774$$

The manufacturer notes that dealers would normally expect to pay around £799 for such a machine, so it adjusts the price up to that level.

MARK-UP PRICING

A different cost oriented approach is known as mark-up pricing. Again it is illustrated by an example.

In this case the manufacturer would proceed as above but would desire a specified percentage mark-up on sales for profit. Let us assume this to be 30%. Then the price to the dealer would be calculated as:

$$\text{Mark-up price} = \frac{\text{Unit costs}}{(1 - \text{desired return on sales})}$$

Unit costs were initially estimated at £410 but £150 has to be added for selling, merchandising and administration. Hence the preliminary mark-up price to dealers would be:

$$\frac{(410 + 150)}{(1 - 0.30)} = £800$$

Such an approach does not really make for sound practice. Any approach that leaves out demand elasticity in setting prices is unlikely to lead, except by chance, to profit maximization, either in the long run or the short run. As demand elasticity changes – as it is likely to do, seasonally, cyclically or over the life cycle – the optimum mark-up should also change. If the mark-up remains a fixed percentage of the cost then it is unlikely under normal conditions to lead to profit maximization.

There are conditions when a rigid mark-up at the right level may produce optimum profits. These are when:

● average unit costs are fairly constant for different points on the demand curve, and

● costs are constant over time.

Both of these prerequisite conditions – constant costs and constant elasticity – have been found to exist in many retailing situations. This could account for why moderately inflexible mark-ups are in broad use in retailing and why they may well lead to optimal pricing requirements.

TARGET RETURN PRICING

Yet another commonly applied cost-oriented approach is that of target return pricing, where a firm tries to determine a price which will give a specified rate of return on its investment. Like the above approach, it takes no note of demand and other than by chance cannot lead to profit maximization.

$$\text{Target return price} = \text{Unit cost} + \frac{\text{Desired return} \times \text{Invested capital}}{\text{Unit sales}}$$

Approaches to pricing which involve adding up the costs and putting on an amount for profit are easy to calculate and are often practised in business. Even

CASE EXAMPLE

TARGET RETURN PRICING: SETTING A PRICE TO EARN A SPECIFIC RETURN ON INVESTMENT

A washing machine manufacturer has £4 000 000 invested in the business and wants to set a price to earn a return on investment of 30% – that is, £1 200 000. The washing machine manufacturer estimates unit costs to be £260 and thinks that it can sell 40 000 units. Using this information we can see that the target return price, using the formula in the text, would be:

$$= £260 + 0.30 \times £4\,000\,000/40\,000$$
$$= £290$$

As we can see from this example, the manufacturer does not try to establish the relationship between price and demand and then set a price afterwards. At the price of £290 it may very well be able to sell many more units of the product, or of course it may sell less than it expects. In either case it is unlikely to maximize profits, except by chance. A higher price may generate fewer sales but it could generate larger profits. A lower price could generate more sales and more profits. However, unless the firm tries to establish the relationship between price and demand, it cannot really expect to maximize profits.

QUESTION

1. What price should be set to earn a return on investment of 40% in this case?

when prices are adjusted to take account of what other firms are charging, however, they still may not take account of demand.

BREAK-EVEN ANALYSIS

Break-even analysis is a useful technique for helping to set prices for new products. The production and marketing of every product acquires a cost on the one hand, and yields revenue on the other. As long as revenue exceeds cost the product is profitable.

Two kinds of costs are associated with a product. There are those which are readily identifiable and which can be costed against definite output of the product.

CASE EXAMPLE

BREAK-EVEN ANALYSIS: IMPACT OF VARYING COSTS

A new product being put on to the market has fixed costs of £40 000 associated with it and unit variable costs of £4 per unit. The selling price is to be £8 per unit.

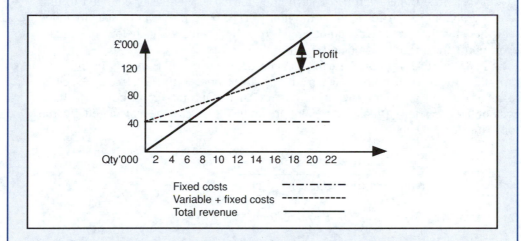

Fixed costs —·—·—·—·—
Variable + fixed costs -----------
Total revenue ————————

The chart indicates how sales revenue and profits for this product will vary with the amount that is sold. Break-even point can be ascertained from the graph to be sales of 10 000 units, which give a sales revenue of £80 000.

QUESTION

1. Assume variable costs were £6 pounds per unit. How would this affect the calculations? Show this graphically.

These tend to be costs such as labour and materials put into producing the products. Many firms have sophisticated costing systems and can easily allocate such costs to individual products. These are usually alluded to as variable costs, since they vary in magnitude with the amount of the product produced and marketed.

The second kind of costs are fixed costs which do not vary according to the output of a product. If the firm only produced one product then clearly all of the fixed costs could be charged to the one product. Since firms usually produce many products, however, spreading or allocating the fixed costs tends to be rather arbitrary. Fixed costs are also known as overheads, and do not vary with output. Rent, heat, interest, executive salaries, etc. are examples of fixed costs.

In setting the price for a new product we are interested in two things: whether the product will cover its variable costs, and what contribution it makes to fixed costs and profits. Product and services which cover their variable costs and then make large contributions to fixed costs and profits are regarded as the more desirable.

In applying break-even analysis the idea is to estimate how much sales revenue is needed to recover the fixed costs associated with the product and at the same time cover variable costs. The sales revenue amount at the point where this occurs is known as the break-even point (in money terms) – it is easily changed to unit sales by dividing sales revenue by the unit price. Above the level of sales revenue indicated by the break-even point, the firm is in profit, while below the break-even point the product is not recovering all its costs.

Rather than use a graph we can calculate break-even point and profit by using formulae. Break-even point is where the total revenue = the total cost. A selling price of £8 and an average variable cost of £4 results in a contribution to fixed cost of £4 per unit. Break-even point in units (BPU) can be calculated by the following formula:

$$BPU = \frac{\text{Total fixed cost}}{\text{Per unit contribution to fixed cost}}$$

Given that total fixed costs are £40 000 then:

$$BPU = \frac{40\ 000}{4} = 10\ 000$$

We can calculate the break-even point in money terms (BP£) by applying the following formula:

$$BP£ = \frac{\text{Total fixed cost}}{1 - \text{variable cost per unit/price}} = \frac{40\ 000}{1 - 4/8}$$

$$= £80\ 000$$

It will be remembered that profit is the excess over break-even point.

Profit = selling price – unit cost × quantity sold in excess of break-even point

With sales of 12 000 units the profit is:

$$(8 - 4) \times (12\ 000 - 10\ 000) = £8000$$

Break-even analysis can be applied to test out different assumptions. Various prices, costs and sales figures can be assumed and corresponding associated levels of break-even, profitability and loss determined.

The following assumptions have to be made when applying break-even analysis:

- a fixed relation exists between sales volume and returns
- accurate prediction of the demand curve is possible
- the costs remain stable.

Break-even analysis is a useful tool to use when considering the setting of prices for new products. It enables a firm to associate various levels of profits with different prices, assuming different costs and volumes of sales.

MARGINAL PRICING

Another important cost-oriented approach is that of marginal pricing. Suppose a firm manufactures widgets which carry a fixed overhead charge of £100 000 and variable costs of £0.50 per widget. The firm currently supplies 1 000 000 widgets to breweries in the UK at £0.75 each and has considerable spare capacity. An enquiry has come in from a company in the Far East which is interested in using the same widgets for a different purpose. The interesting question is: at what price should it offer to sell the widgets to the firm in the Far East, assuming that additional production capacity is not required?

Common sense tells us that the firm will have already recovered the fixed overhead on the widgets it supplies to the brewery industry. One million widgets at £0.75 generate £750 000 of revenue. One million widgets at a unit cost of £0.50 per widget generate a variable cost of £500 000. This leaves £750 000 - £500 000 = £250 000 to cover the fixed costs and the profit. With fixed costs at £100 000 this means that the firm is already making a profit of £250 000 - £100 000 = £150 000.

The price to be charged to the company in the Far East need only take account of the variable costs and additional transportation and delivery costs. This may mean that in theory the price charged to the firm in the Far East can in fact be lower than that charged to brewery firms at home, and the firm will still be generating profit! This is what as known as marginal pricing.

The key point, however, is whether the two markets supplied know that a price differential exists and that essentially the products supplied are identical. If such information is available to both parties then a marginal pricing strategy may be impossible to implement, since the UK customers will argue for equal treatment. The application of a marginal pricing policy does require that no new fixed costs have to be incurred – which would seem to be satisfactory in the foregoing case. The following case example provides some points for discussion.

CASE EXAMPLE

AMELUK CORPORATION: MARGINAL PRICING

Ameluk Corporation is a large firm operating in the metals industry in the UK. It produces metal, metal semi-finished goods, and metal finished goods at various stages of the production and manufacturing process. Initially the firm was a smelting company but over the years, through acquisition, it has achieved a high degree of vertical integration.

The firm is made up of over 100 different smaller companies, each of which operates as an autonomous unit. There is considerable trading between the companies which make up the larger corporation.

In trading with one another the firms have always accepted a policy of charging the market price – the going rate price which they charge to other customers who are not members of the group. Recently, one of the companies has developed spare capacity on one product line because of the loss of a contract with one of its major customers outside the group. While the company is still able to recover its fixed costs from the remaining sales of the product line, profits have been adversely affected on this particular product line.

The company has recently received two enquiries to supply material which would take up the spare capacity available. One is from another company which is a member of the group and the other is from another UK-based customer. In both cases the enquiries stipulate an expectation that the price will be 10% lower than the current going rate in the market place.

QUESTION

1. What action should the company contemplate?

APPROACHES THAT ARE NOT JUST COST-ORIENTED

Moral pricing

All of the practical approaches considered above have been cost-oriented with the specific aim being to add a margin of profit to identified costs. 'Moral pricing' moves away from this principle, and while it is a very special form of pricing, it could be deemed to be taking account of demand since attention is paid to what people can afford to pay.

Moral pricing is a term which is often given to the kind of pricing approaches adopted by non-profit making organizations. Charity organizations often price their products and functions at a low level for their regular customers, but when they put on a special event to attract the wealthy then they price tickets to their special attractions very high indeed. This is because in this case they are in fact appealing to wealthy people who can afford to pay. Pricing is therefore related to ability to pay.

Demand-oriented pricing

A demand-oriented approach to pricing takes account of the strength of demand. Firms ask a high price when or where demand is strong, and a low price when or where demand is weak, even if there is no difference in costs in either case. Differences in the strength of demand in the market enable firms to charge different prices in different market segments. The ability to practice this kind of price discrimination requires:

- different levels of demand in market segments

- inability of buyers to resell at a higher price

- that competitors will **not** undersell the firm in the segment being charged the higher price

- the cost of segmenting and policing the market not to exceed the extra revenue obtained

- that price discrimination is legally permissible

- that customers are prepared to pay more when demand is high, and do not react negatively.

Such an approach is commonly referred to as charging what the market will bear. Price discrimination helps suppliers to increase sales and profits, improve market share and contribute to the full capacity utilization of manufacturing plant. However, when it is adopted by a firm in a dominant position in an industry or a market, it is sometimes used to remove troublesome competition or as a means of exploiting buyers.

OTHER DIMENSIONS TO PRICING

PRICE SQUEEZE

Discriminatory prices may sometimes be charged by a firm which is vertically integrated, for the supply of inputs to non-integrated rivals, in order to put the latter at a competitive disadvantage. This can occur when the integrated firm produces both the input and the finished product, while its customer produces only the finished product, and is dependent on the integrated firm for supplies of the materials, sub-assemblies or parts.

A 'squeeze' occurs where the integrated firm charges the non-integrated firm a high price for the input, but sells its own finished product at a low price. This allows the non-integrated firm only minimal profits, or may even force it to make a loss.

It is common for there to be many suppliers of partly finished goods in an industry, so that the power of any one supplier to effect a price squeeze is limited. However, as a result of acquisitions, takeovers and mergers, it is not beyond the bounds of possibility for a group of companies to come to dominate the supply side for certain materials and components and thence to exert a price squeeze on an industry. Such a practice may be regarded as anti-competitive, and in the UK such cases may be referred to the Monopolies and Mergers Commission.

PENETRATION VERSUS SKIMMING PRICING STRATEGIES

Penetration and skimming policies are most often encountered when dealing with new products, but they are sometimes used in other situations.

Penetration strategy

When introducing a new product the objective may be to achieve early market penetration. The strategy may amount to setting a comparatively low price to instigate market growth and capture a large share of it. The effect of the experience curve will cause long-run profitability to rise as a result of gaining a large market share or a growth in market share. A penetration strategy may be appropriate if the market seems to be highly price sensitive, or if a product is favoured by economies of scale in production, or where a low price discourages actual and potential competition.

Skimming strategy

A skimming strategy contrasts with a penetration strategy and is used to take advantage of the fact that some buyers are prepared to pay a much higher price because they want the product very much. Firms adopting this strategy may initially set a high price to gain a premium from such buyers, and may only reduce it progressively to bring in the more price-elastic segments.

This strategy is appropriate where there exists a large number of buyers whose demand is relatively inelastic. It may also be used where the unit production and distribution costs associated with producing a smaller volume are not so much higher that they cancel out the advantage of charging what some of the market will buy, or where little danger exists that a high price will stimulate the emergence of competition.

COMPETITION-ORIENTED PRICING

In this case, a firm makes sure that the prices it sets are in keeping with those charged by competitors. This is referred to as going-rate pricing and is often used in homogeneous product markets where the market structure ranges from pure competition to pure oligopoly. In a purely competitive market the firm has little flexibility in setting its price. In the case of pure oligopoly it has more choice, and firms can charge the same price as their competitors. In such markets there are only a few firms, each one of them knows the others' price and buyers are also well abreast of prices.

Pricecheck, published by the William Reed Publishing Company, provides monthly information on retail prices of a wide range of grocery items such as cigarettes/tobacco, confectionery, dairy and delicatessen products, frozen foods, groceries, health, beauty and chemist lines, household products and drinks. The publication gives updated benchmark prices that are based on typical wholesale prices, plus a built-in profit margin.

PSYCHOLOGICAL DIMENSIONS TO PRICING

Goods are often priced at £2.99 or £4.99, rather than £3 or £5, reflecting the fact that people tend to round down prices in their minds, so that the prices in fact are perceived to be £2 and £4 respectively.

Another interesting point is that putting up prices can actually increase sales, price often being seen as a surrogate for quality. In the absence of information to the contrary, people tend to assume that goods or services are of better quality if they carry a higher price tag. This can lead to nonsenses whereby two products which have the same intrinsic value may fetch vastly different prices because the consumer considers one to be more 'special' than the other. A good example is to be found in the purchase of jewellery. Rings, in particular, can carry exactly the same gems in terms of size, and be of the same carat gold. However, because of the differing ways the gems are cut and the rings are set, there can be large differences in the price which is asked.

PRICING POINTS

Retailers like to sell goods in stores at specific pricing points. Pricing points may, for instance, always end in the number 9. That is 9 pence, 19 pence, 29 pence, etc. The retailer may argue that these are the prices which consumers prefer to pay. A producer and a retailer may agree on a point of sale shop price of say 89p. The retailer is obtaining a satisfactory margin on the product at this price and the producer is also happy with the price. Were the producer to require extra shelf space, then it would probably have to offer the retailer more promotional discount so that the retailer could sell the product at 79p. The retailer will not agree to sell it at 80p or 85p, because these prices do not correspond with pricing points. The producer then has to determine whether this would be worthwhile. One way round this problem, of course, is to produce products in different packet sizes to correspond with retailers' specific pricing points.

INCREASING PRICES WITHOUT INCREASING PRICES

Sooner or later organizations have to adjust their prices. When it is in a downward direction this usually pleases the customer and the firm does not need to disguise its actions. However, when an upward adjustment in price is required, consumer resistance is often expressed quite strongly.

Organizations can seek to disguise price rises, in any one of the following ways.

- The discount structure can be altered so that the total profit to the company is increased but the list price to customers remains the same.

- The minimum order size is increased so that small orders are eliminated and overall costs thereby reduced.

- Previously free delivery and special services can be charged for.

- Repairs on purchased equipment can be made more expensive.

- Charges can be increased for engineering, installation and supervision.

- Customers are made to pay for overtime required to get out rush orders.

- Interest is collected on overdue accounts.

- Lower margin models in the product line are eliminated and more profitable ones sold in their place.

- Escalator clauses which allow the price to be increased in the light of unforeseen circumstances, e.g. rise in world market price for raw materials, are built into bids for contracts.

- The physical characteristics of the product are changed – e.g. it is made smaller.

RELATIONSHIP BETWEEN PRICE AND QUALITY

Products of a higher quality can fetch higher prices, and many firms base their prices on a product's perceived value to the buyer. In addition, the non-price variables in the marketing mix are employed to build up the perceived value in the mind of the buyer.

Perceived value fits in well with the modern approach to product-positioning. Key dimensions upon which the product will be judged by end-users are identified. For example, let us consider a camcorder. The price may be:

£400   if it is only equivalent to the competitors' camcorder
+ £100   is the price premium for superior performance
+ £100   is the price premium for superior service
+ £100   is the price premium for longer warranty on parts
———
£700   is the price to cover the value package
———

This kind of pricing strategy requires information about how much customers are willing to pay for these additional characteristics.

PRICE LEADERSHIP STRATEGY

This is the position where a particular supplier is generally accepted by other suppliers as the 'lead' firm in introducing changes in market prices.

There are two principal forms of price leadership. The first occurs when the largest firm in terms of market share, and/or the lowest cost producer, leads on prices changes and where other firms are prepared to follow because the price change yields them adequate profits.

The second form of price leadership, sometimes referred to as barometric price leadership, is where a particular firm, often a smaller firm, is 'adopted' as the price leader, having demonstrated itself capable of spotting changes in market conditions.

In theory, a market leader enjoys all the advantages over competitors that are associated with higher volume sales. The leader should be able to set the price structure for the market. In the event that the market leader decides to take a low unit profit margin, then because of the volume of sales achieved, profits generated should still be substantial. This profitability will not be enjoyed by competitors who do not have the same high volume of sales, however. In fact, these competitors will have higher unit costs, higher distributor margins and probably lower selling prices to the trade.

A market leader which takes a higher unit profit margin gives the whole market a form of price umbrella. Since all firms can charge higher prices, profitability all round can be increased. This allows competitors to introduce product improvements, funded by retained additional profits. Competitors can also invest in more aggressive marketing. The net result will probably be to weaken the market leader's position.

Price leadership is often viewed by suppliers as a way of co-ordinating pricing policies so as to limit price competition and avoid the problems of price wars.

THE LEADER'S STRATEGY IN RELATION TO THE STAGE IN THE PRODUCT LIFE CYCLE

If the market is in the growth stage of the product life cycle then extra sales volume is available. The leader will want to take a major share of new business and so it will want to keep competitors' actions under control and persuade other firms not to enter the market. By keeping the unit margin of profitability low, the leader can make progress to this end.

As volume sales of a market increase, the effects of the experience curve are felt and product unit costs should decline. The dilemma facing the market leader concerns reducing prices and the speed with which this should be effected, if at all. The answer is to be found in the leader's designs with respect to the next stage in the product life cycle – the maturity stage. If it is the market leader's intention to lead in this phase, then it will have to maintain its leadership through the transition phase. It must ensure that its prices move downwards as volume moves ahead and unit costs decline. If it does not do this then there is always a chance that competitors will take advantage of the position and increase capacity and market share. It is usually advantageous for the leader to maintain its position, since the additional volume of sales generated can mean that total margins will increase despite the lower selling prices.

Other firms will not enjoy the same cost advantages as the leader; operating on tight profit margins, they are not in a position to achieve great improvements in differentiation. Potential entrants may consequently feel deterred from entering the market.

During the market maturity or the decline phases the horizon for the market leader can be altogether different. There will be little chance of a new competitor entering the market, and brand loyalty will have been established. In such circumstances the leader should be able to take higher margins without taking excessive risks.

Firms with a lower level of market share should follow the leader when it comes to changes in prices. Marketers of low-share brands will not want to engage the leader in direct price competition. Direct and indirect costs of production of these competitors are higher than the leader's, and price to the trade is probably lower.

PRICE WARS

Price wars arise from time to time and involve general price cutting within a market. Haphazard price wars may materialize from gossip and slip-up. Others may be introduced intentionally. In neither case does the end result bring about an improvement for any of the parties involved. Once in a while a price war can work to the aggressor's advantage. It is clearly an advantage in a price war to have lower unit costs than competitors. In such a position the aggressor may fare well from the experience.

The following case example suggests that consumers prefer price cuts; it poses some interesting questions for consideration.

CASE EXAMPLE

PRICE PROMOTION: CONSUMER ATTITUDES

Consumers seem to prefer 'money off' when it comes to sales promotion. Many marketing people are afraid of price promotion, however, because they fear that over time it will gradually erode a brand's equity. If price promotion is used continually with a brand because it has nothing convincing to say about itself, then it could be that people will conclude that the argument for buying the brand is based on price. Not surprisingly, under such circumstances, if the product is not price promoted people do not buy it. Of course, that is because of the brand's inadequacies and is not the fault of price promotion.

Strong brands backed with confident advertising are a totally different proposition. When consumers are hard up, price-cutting does not suggest weakness in a product but simply acknowledges the reality of the situation. Low prices do not have to be associated with low quality. If the price of a poor quality product is reduced, consumers will probably think that the price reduction has been made because nobody is willing to buy at a higher price. However, where a high-quality brand is involved then today's consumer will quite likely recognize it as a bargain not to be ignored.

(Source: Toop, 1994)

QUESTION

1. How can one reconcile price-cutting with a high-quality product image?

SUMMARY

Pricing is an important element in the marketing mix. It takes on its greatest importance, however, when a price change is instigated. Pricing has received considerable attention over the years by writers on economics. A good deal of basic microeconomic theory is devoted to the relationship between price and demand. While many of the principles which have been developed have relevance to what happens in the real world, there are nevertheless many other factors that have to be taken into account. In reality, then, many differences can be found between theory and practice.

In practice firms use a variety of price-setting methods. These may be cost-oriented, profit-oriented, demand-oriented or competition-oriented. Pricing also has its psychological aspects.

Consumers perceive price to be an indicator of product quality. Getting the price-quality right and in line with what competitors are offering is related to product positioning and establishing a differential advantage.

Price leadership brings with it many advantages, not the least of which is high volume turnover and good profitability based on low margins. Firms exercising price leadership need to be wary of raising price margins since this can provide an umbrella for competitors to develop a differential advantage for their products.

Firms are advised to avoid price wars, since these can lead to a stalemate position for all parties involved and all firms can lose out as a result. Nevertheless, where competition is keen, products are fairly homogeneous and economic times are gloomy price-cutting may be the order of the day. This can, however, lead to price wars.

DISCUSSION QUESTIONS

1. Define price.

2. Under what conditions does price take on its greatest degree of importance?

3. What do you think are the main limitations of economic theory in trying to explain pricing?

4. Discuss the relevance of the law of demand to marketers.

5. Differentiate between a cost-oriented approach to pricing and a demand-oriented approach to pricing.

6. A manufacturer estimates that the average variable costs and fixed costs associated with producing a particular product, assuming unit sales of 500 000 over three years, will be £500 per unit. Other overhead expenses usually add another 30% to the costs and the firm wants to make a profit of £300 per unit. What price should the firm seek to charge for the product? What other factors would it need to take into account?

7. Outline the principles of competition-oriented pricing.

8. What do you understand by 'moral pricing'?

9. What is price discrimination?

10. Under what circumstances might a 'price squeeze' occur?

11. What do you understand by the psychological aspects of pricing?

12. What are 'pricing points'?

13. How might a firm seek to increase prices without actually increasing them?

14. Examine the relationship between price and quality.

15. What are the principles involved in calculating break-even point, and how does this relate to price setting?

16. What is price leadership and how does it occur?

17. Discuss the dangers of price wars.

18. Discuss the consequences of price competition.

REFERENCES

Macleod, A. (1994) Prices drop, value increases, *Business Age*, February, 66.

Rappaport, A. (1978) Executive incentives versus corporate growth, *Harvard Business Review*, July–August, 81–8.

Toop, A. (1994) Price promotion bolsters brands in harder times, *Marketing*, 10 January, 10.

The Wall Street Journal (1983) Price policy on space shuttle's commercial use could launch – or ground – NASA's rockets, 19 April, 8.

FURTHER READING

Winkler, J. (1983) *Pricing for Results*, Heinemann, London.

CASE PROBLEM 12.1

HOTEL ACCOMMODATION: ESTABLISHING A WORKABLE APPROACH TO PRICING

Business class hotels are becoming good value for money – especially outside London. For an overnight stay the average price has dropped by 7% since 1991. As well as being able to drop prices, hotels have managed to maintain a high level of quality. The movement to lower prices has been accompanied by complex and bewildering pricing systems used by the major hotel groups. No standard pricing structure exits and the terminology varies from chain to chain. Even within the same chain and the same city, prices can be different.

Even the smartest business traveller has difficulty with the system and is likely to resort to haggling. Indeed, many hotels now use the haggling approach themselves in an attempt to segment customers. Guests can easily be confused, however, if they don't understand the system and those who learn to work the system add to the problem from the hotelier's point of view.

Marriott seem to have got to grips with the problem by dispensing with the haggling system and replacing it with 'rational pricing'. Rates are categorized into corporate rates and clear discounted rates, with restrictions based on advanced purchase, non-refundable prices. It is similar to booking an Apex airline ticket: the discounted rates are available during periods of slack demand, but they offer less flexibility.

The complexity of the pricing system has boosted the business of firms such as Expotel. Set up in 1972 to arrange hotel accommodation for corporate clients, Expotel is now one of Europe's leading specialist in worldwide hotel reservations. The firm can negotiate reduced rates with all of the world's major hotel groups, as well as with many independents, and promises the customer the room he or she wants at the lowest rate.

(Source: Macleod, 1994)

QUESTION

1. Suggest ways in which pricing of hotel accommodation could be improved.

CASE PROBLEM 12.2

PLUMB-IT: PRICING STRATEGY

Plumb-It is the leading producer of plumbing materials in the UK. In the major market segments the company has steadily increased its share to around 45%. The firm guarantees delivery by 8.15 am of all orders received by 4.30 pm the previous day. This has meant that plumbers can virtually eliminate stocks and avoid problems of pilferage and damage. It also means that retailers and merchants can carry smaller stocks. None of the other manufacturers have their own warehousing and direct distribution organization, so all use wholesalers for the bulk of their output.

During the recession of the late 1980s and early 1990s demand for plumbing materials reduced. Smaller producers started cutting their prices in order to achieve a higher sales turnover. Plumb-It followed suit and in January 1995 prices stood at only 80% of their 1988 levels. Plumb-It's sales turnover had been maintained throughout the period, but fixed costs amounted to £30 million; with a mark-up of only 50% on variable manufacturing costs, profits were down to £1.6 million.

In late January 1995 the company learned that a competitor was offering another price reduction of 2% on plumbing materials.

QUESTION

1. What action should Plumb-It take? Should it offer a price reduction? If so, by how much?

13 OVERVIEW OF MARKETING COMMUNICATIONS

This chapter addresses the basic concepts of communications theory, along with their relevance to marketing. Objectives that can be set for marketing communications are discussed. The design of marketing communications and media choice is considered, along with the role of marketing research in providing feedback.

OBJECTIVES

After studying this chapter you should be able to:

- describe the basic concepts of communications theory and understand the relevance of the various elements to marketing communications

- appreciate the kind of marketing communications objectives that can be set

- describe how marketing communications have to be designed; specifically matters relating to the format and structure of the message and the information source

- know how the most appropriate media are selected

- understand the role of marketing research in providing feedback in the marketing communication process.

INTRODUCTION

Marketing communication is concerned with giving out facts about a product or service in such a way that people or business will eventually be persuaded to adopt or use the promoted item. Advertising and personal selling are some of the ways in which this can be achieved. Marketing communication should be viewed within the broader context of general communication, and it is the purpose of this chapter to provide such a framework.

First we introduce the general concept of communication and how marketing communication can be viewed within such a framework. A general context for understanding ideas about communications is first outlined. This includes the role of both the sender and the receiver of information, the channel selected, noise/distortion in the channel, and feedback. Attention is then given to the step-wise models of communication and promotion which have been developed to relate to communication and influencing behaviour.

The setting of objectives for marketing communications is explored, and this is then related to how marketing communications have to be designed to facilitate the achievement of such objectives. It involves paying specific attention to the structure of the message and the choice of the information source. An overview of factors that have to be taken into account when selecting the most appropriate media is then presented. This is followed by an appreciation of how the importance of specific elements of the promotional mix varies across firms and industries, and an appreciation of the factors which cause it to vary.

The importance of word-of-mouth communication is stressed and an appreciation of the theory surrounding the 'two-step flow' of communication from message sender to opinion leader, along with its limitations, is given.

Finally, the role of marketing research in providing feedback in the marketing communication process is presented.

A GENERAL MODEL OF COMMUNICATION

People communicate face to face, over the telephone and in writing. In face-to-face situations, communications can be verbal or can be inferred from gestures, postures or numerous other clues which occur in the course of interaction. There is less opportunity for non-verbal cues when communication is by telephone or in writing. Nevertheless, voice intonation in the former case, and 'reading between the lines' in the latter case, can often provide us with additional information that is not apparent in the main communication itself. It is easy for communications to become confused and ambiguous unless the communicator and the recipient of the information have a clear understanding of the intended message.

Effective communication is a two-way process. Messages are sent by the communicator and received by the other party, who returns some kind of confirmation that the message has been received and understood. However, if the targeted receiver fails to attend to an intended message, then communication has not been effective. A person wanting to communicate must do so at the time and in the way that best suits the targeted receiver, and must communicate the intended message clearly and persuasively.

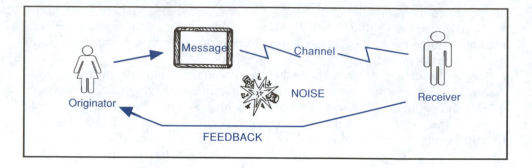

Figure 13.1   The communication process – a descriptive model.

A DESCRIPTIVE MODEL OF THE COMMUNICATION PROCESS

The communication process is aptly illustrated in Figure 13.1 (Severin and Tankard, 1979).

A message is sent through a channel of communication to its destination. The receiver of the message provides feedback to the originator, to show that the message has been understood. The clarity of reception and feedback is distorted somewhat by 'noise' in the system (Mortensen, 1979). Noise is produced by a variety of factors, including other messages being sent to the recipient, and communications between other people. Imagine the situation in the bar of a pub where you are talking with a friend. Noise is present in the form of other people round about talking, perhaps a television set that is switched on, the sound of a telephone ringing, and waiters and waitresses interrupting your conversation to ask for payment for drinks with which you have been served.

There can be a variety of competing stimuli which distract the recipient and prevent him or her from grasping the full impact of a communication. In the case of mass communication it is commonly accepted that the average individual is exposed to several hundred marketing communications stimuli in the course of a typical day. This means that it is quite easy for any given marketing communication to be lost and to fail to register as intended. People are inundated with all kinds of messages – visual, audio, sensual and olfactory (e.g. advertisements, announcements, incidents in the street or in the home, etc.) and may not receive an intended message.

The reasons for this are that people possess the following attributes.

● **Selective attention** – people do not pay attention to everything that is going on around them. A great deal of what is happening round and about is ignored, otherwise people would be so overwhelmed that they would be unable to cope with it all. On the other hand, attention is given to something and they stand out – e.g. red traffic lights – but not to others – e.g. stationary cars near red traffic lights. We learn to pay attention to things which are important and upon which we rely for direction or information. In Figure 13.2 it is a small package.

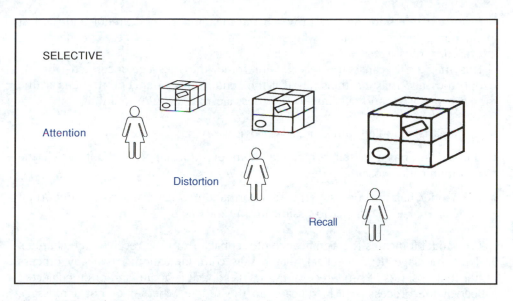

Figure 13.2 Selective attention, distortion and recall.

- **Selective distortion** – all messages are subjected to selective distortion in one way or another. People interpret messages in terms of what they want to hear. In Figure 13.2 the package is perceived to be large.

- **Selective recall** – relatively few of the messages received can subsequently be recalled. In addition people may often recall a face but may have difficulty in fitting a name to the face. Recall is therefore quite selective. In advertising, where the visual image may well be recalled but not the brand name of the product, efforts have to be directed at getting people to associate the two. Much effort is put into doing this. In Figure 13.2 the package is recalled as being large.

A person wanting to send a message starts off with both an intended content for the message and an intended effect for the message. In order to create a meaningful message, the communicator has to be able to understand the nature of the external and internal stimuli that affect the recipient. Good effective communication depends upon empathy between the communicator and the recipient of the message.

For a person to receive and grasp the point of a message two requirements have to be met:

- the message has to be designed to gain attention

- the message should be oriented as closely as possible to the receiver's background, interest, needs and psychological dispositions.

The channel denotes the medium through which the message is sent. This is usually the spoken or written word. In addition there is non-verbal communication, such as body movement, voice qualities and the use of dress and cosmetics.

Distortion refers to the way in which the meaning of a communication is lost in handling. It occurs mainly when encoding, creating messages, and decoding, interpreting messages.

This may be because the receiver interprets the message incorrectly, or the wrong message may be transmitted if the sender fails to encode the idea in the message precisely and accurately. The message may also be faulty if:

● the idea is muddled, ambiguous or illogical

● the sender has omitted some vital item of information without which the communication loses its effect

● the sender has included superfluous information which obscures the important item or makes it difficult to assimilate the message.

The model indicates the significance of feedback from the receiver, the channel, and the message. It is feedback that makes communication a two-way process rather than a series of send–receive events. Feedback is a vital and often neglected aspect of the process, which indicates to the sender whether or not a message has been successfully received, understood and interpreted.

Marketing communication is a straightforward adaptation of this model. A company is the originator, source or sender of the message. The message itself consists of ideas, suggestions or requests. The channel is the medium used to transmit the message and can take the form of TV, journals, newspapers, billboards, etc. The destination or receiver in this instance is potential customers, or the target.

The main task for a communicator is to create a message that will gain the person's attention and subsequent action, despite the amount of noise in the system.

Having looked at a general model of communication we will now move on to examine how communications can influence people's behaviour. This is explained by looking at various descriptive models of the process.

HIERARCHY OF EFFECTS AND OTHER MODELS

Attempts have been made to construct a descriptive model of the process by which a person comes to buy or adopt a product as a result of receiving information about that product. These are known as 'hierarchy of effect' models (also known as response hierarchy models) and they suggest a simple relationship between the promotional message and the purchase of goods. In the marketing world, it has traditionally been thought that advertising was a method to get the product known to the customer, and that as long as one delivered enough advertising to the right consumers, the results could be measured in sales. The stepwise models, however, suggested something else altogether.

The idea of a descriptive model to relate promotional messages to actual selling of goods was first suggested by E. St Elmo Lewis in 1898. Lewis suggested four

attracting	ATTENTION
maintaining	INTEREST
arousing	DESIRE
getting	ACTION

Figure 13.3 The AIDA model.

stages of consciousness through which a customer must pass prior to effecting a purchase. Lewis reached the conclusion that a sales talk must be planned to enable a sales person to guide a prospect through these stages of consciousness.

E.K. Strong suggested the AIDA model in 1925 (Kotler, 1991) (see Figure 13.3). The AIDA model argued that there were four stages which the communicator had to put into effect when trying to bring about action in someone.

Lavidge and Steiner (1961) developed the 'hierarchy of effects' model many years later, in 1961. This reflected many of the ideas discussed above and was directly related to advertising. The model, shown in Figure 13.4, suggests a six-stage process which the customer progresses through.

In using this model, different promotional activities are considered appropriate to move customers through the various stages. To create **awareness**, teaser campaigns, sky-writing, jingles, slogans and classified advertisements are considered appropriate. In order to convey **knowledge,** announcements and descriptive copy are suggested. Image advertising and status or glamour appeals are seen as ways of developing a **liking**, while competitive advertisements and argumentative copy are seen as ways of developing a **preference**. Finally, price appeals and testimonials are seen as ways of developing **conviction,** while deals, last-chance offers and point of purchase retail store advertisements are seen as ways of bringing about a **purchase**.

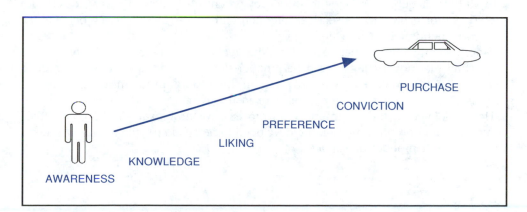

Figure 13.4 Lavidge and Steiner's model.

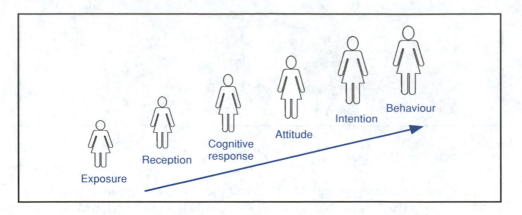

Figure 13.5 A general model of behaviour change.

In the same year, Colley (1961) produced a model called DAGMAR (standing for defining advertising goals, measuring advertising results). This model expressed the view that a communication must take a prospect through four levels of understanding:

awareness → comprehension → conviction → action

A year later, the 'Innovation Adoption' model was put forward by Rogers (1962):

awareness → interest → evaluation → trial → adoption

The various models seem to fit with the more general communications model shown in Figure 13.5.

This model of communication suggests that people have to be exposed to a message and receive it. The cognitive response stage is similar to becoming aware and informed about the topic of the message – awareness and comprehension. The attitude stage corresponds to the development of a liking, interest, desire or preference for a product or service. Intention comes just before actual behaviour, and corresponds with conviction or trial.

More recently, interest has focused on the qualitative dimensions of advertising suggesting that advertising should be emotionally appealing and novel in nature.

The following case example provides an interesting problem. The material discussed so far in the chapter is relevant in this case.

Having looked at the communication process, we now examine how effective communication programmes can be developed to persuade people to buy or otherwise acquire a product or service.

APEX COMPANY: UNDERSTANDING HOW COMMUNICATION WORKS

The Apex company sells screwdrivers to the general public through small hardware, handicraft and tool shops. As part of its continuous programme of consumer advertising to pull sales through retail outlets the company placed a number of advertisements in area evening newspapers featuring the firm's screwdrivers and the addresses of the local dealers who could supply the product.

Despite regular placing of these advertisements over a period of six months, no noticeable new enquiries appear to have been generated at any of the retail outlets concerned and very few people who have asked for screwdrivers at the outlets have been able to recall seeing the advertisements.

Sales of the screwdrivers through the outlets concerned are reasonably buoyant and the retailers concerned are insisting that Apex continues to provide the same kind of advertising support.

QUESTION

1. Do you think that Apex should continue advertising in the way in which it is currently doing? Why, or why not?

DESIGNING MESSAGES TO COMMUNICATE

In this section we will first look at communication objectives. We will then look at how messages should be designed to facilitate the attainment of these objectives, looking particularly at message structure, content and source.

COMMUNICATION OBJECTIVES

In developing an effective communications programme the basic steps involved are:

- identifying the target audience
- determining the communications objective
- designing the message

- selecting the communications channels
- allocating the total promotions budget
- deciding on the promotions mix
- measuring the results of the promotion.

We have already discussed targeting, in Chapter 8, and will therefore start with communication objectives. Marketing communications efforts can have different communications objectives. Some of these are listed below:

- to create awareness of a product or service
- to provide information about a product or service
- to generate enquiries
- to build recognition of a company name
- to reach those people who are beyond the reach of salesmen
- to evoke desire for a product or service
- to make the selling task easier
- to overcome prejudices
- to remind people about a product's benefits
- to allay cognitive dissonance.

It will be seen that some of the objectives match with some of the stages in the hierarchy of effects models described above.

DESIGNING THE MESSAGE

Effective communications need to appeal to the needs and wants of the recipients. They should give the recipient a motive or incentive to act. They also need to generate involvement with the message on the part of the recipient by asking questions which leave the message incomplete. In addition they should spell out exactly what course of action it is expected that the recipient will follow.

Getting people to consider purchasing a product or service can be achieved through appealing to their cognitive processes. One needs to arouse desire, indicate a need, or offer a logical reason why a product or service offers the best means of satisfying a need. In so doing the message becomes implanted in the recipient's memory and can be triggered by future needs, motives and associations. However, one does have to bear in mind that the rational approach may not be so effective for less educated recipients, or in situations where there is likely to be less involvement in the purchase – i.e. little search behaviour. In these cases emotional appeals may be used.

Promotion through mass media requires that the story be told in such a way that it will communicate to groups of prospects an inflexibility that may cause the message to miss the mark with some individuals. The salesperson, by contrast, is free to vary the message to meet each situation; this is a powerful advantage of personal selling.

The appeal, theme, idea or unique selling proposition is what the communicator has to get over to the target audience in order to achieve the desired response. Benefit, identification and motivation are all concepts that can be built into the message.

Messages can be built around rational, emotional or moral appeals, themes, ideas or unique selling propositions. Economy, value and performance are used in messages with a rational content. This type of message is often directed at industrial buyers and consumers making expensive purchase items such as cars, houses and substantial consumer durables.

Emotional appeals make use of both positive and negative emotional appeals. On the negative side this involves fear, guilt and shame while on the positive side it comprises humour, love, pride and joy. Too much fear in a message may cause the audience to reject it. The use of humour may generate 'noise' and interfere with the message.

Moral appeals concern people's sense of what is right and just. They can be used in 'green' advertising or in promoting social causes, or even in items for children, such as books and safety prams.

MESSAGE STRUCTURE

The overall context and readability of a message provides its structure. There are a number of dimensions to message structure, and these include:

- whether it is verbal or non-verbal
- readability
- order of ideas
- repetition
- the presence or absence of counter-arguments.

VERBAL VERSUS NON-VERBAL COMMUNICATION

According to a study by Ogilvy and Mather, in a given message words create 15% of the impact, tone of the message 25% and the remaining 60% is attributable to non-verbal cues (Burnett, 1993, p.255). Weitz (1977) has suggested five categories of non-verbal communication:

1. facial expression and visual interaction

2. body movement and gestures

3. loudness, tremor and pitch of the voice

4. proximity of communicating people to one another

5. multichannel communication – e.g. simultaneous interaction between various factors operating in a particular communication.

In making persuasive appeals it is considered that the most effective non-verbal cues are facial and vocal behaviour and timing of phrases (Burnett, 1993, p.255).

READABILITY

The readability of a message is influenced by the arrangement of words in the core message, the word frequency and the length of sentences. The number of ideas used in the core message should be kept to a minimum, and should be restated throughout the message (MacLachlan, 1983/4). Other mechanisms include (Percy, 1985, pp. 75–98):

- metaphorical expressions
- concrete words
- rhyme
- commonly used words
- no synonyms, homonyms or negative constructions
- maximum headline length of five to eight words.

ORDERING EFFECT

Research (Hovland, 1957) shows that if people already feel a strong need for a product or service, supportive information should be provided first. Furthermore, points that are most valued by the receiver should be listed first and unfavourable information should be placed last. Overall it would seem that the earlier the key message points are got over, the better they will be remembered.

REPETITION

There is research evidence to indicate that repeating a message increases its believability, regardless of its content (Ray and Sawyer, 1971). There is still, however, no consensus of opinion on the optimum number of repetitions. Repeating a point within a single message does appear to have a positive effect on persuasion. Research indicates that it facilitates retention and increases believability, irrespective of any evidence to the contrary (Gelb, Zenkhan and Stewart, 1988).

ARGUING AND COUNTER-ARGUING

One-sided arguments are considered to reinforce any decision that the recipient may have already made. Two-sided arguments, in which the counter-argument is put, work better with well-educated audiences who believe that putting both sides of an argument is more honest. In addition, where the audience has multiple opinions on related topics, putting both sides of the argument improves persuasiveness (Gelb, Zenkhan and Stewart, 1988).

MESSAGE CONTENT

Rational appeals tend to be factual and follow a prescribed logic, whereas emotional appeals are directed towards people's feelings and are intended to produce a certain mood, such as guilt, joy, anxiety or self-pride.
The major appeals used are as follows.

- **Fear** Fear tends to be effective up to a certain level, beyond which its use tends to have negative results. In addition, demographic characteristics such as age, sex, race and education all seem to influence the effect (Janis and Feshback, 1953).

- **Humour** The results of research on the positive effects of humour are inconclusive, despite suggestions that it enhances source credibility, attracts attention, evokes a positive mood and increases persuasion (Sternthal, 1973). On the negative side use of humour has been found to hinder recall and comprehension, as well as persuasion or source credibility (Madden and Weinberger, 1982). Humour has also been found to be effective for only a limited period and people may eventually become irritated by the humour in a particular advertisement (Beggs, 1989).

- **Pleasantness** This can be expressed in the form of fun and entertainment – showing people dancing or singing and having a good time. Warmth, nostalgia and loving relations portray the effect of pleasantness. Babies, puppies and kittens are usually accepted symbols of pleasantness. There is considerable evidence to support the effectiveness of pleasant appeals (Gelb, Zenkhan and Stewart, 1988).

- **Sex** Sex, as expressed through portrayals of nude and semi-clothed models, does appear to be attention-getting for both sexes. But there is inconclusive evidence to show that in general use it produces any other useful effects, and it can even be detrimental. Used in a correct context, however, it can be effective: for example, fantasy fulfilment (such as in travel holidays) or functional fulfilment (such as in fashion).

- **Music** There is little empirical evidence to support the effective use of music in promotional messages. However, music can aid learning and persuasion by creating an atmosphere of excitement, relaxation, news and imagery (McGuire, 1961).

MESSAGE SOURCE

The credibility of the information source is an important influence on whether a message is likely to receive attention and be recalled. Expertise, trustworthiness, likeability, physical attractiveness, articulateness and charm are the descriptors most associated with the credibility of the information source (Frieden, 1984).

On an interpersonal basis people are more likely to be influenced by a source they like. Such a source often has a similar background or personality to the person being influenced. Indeed, if a person has a positive attitude towards the information source and the message is contrary to the receiver's attitude the receiver is quite likely to adjust his or her own attitude, in order to overcome this dissonance. Other things being equal, where a positive source of information recommends the use of a product or service, the receiver of the communication is likely to take notice.

Where mass communications are concerned, presenters need to simulate inter-personal communications. An attractive, down-to-earth presenter or a charismatic celebrity can be most effective. An alternative approach involves establishing positive attitudes towards the organization acting as the message source. Here the strategy is to ensure that products or services do not disappoint buyers and that the organization becomes associated with appealing celebrities and symbols. There is also the strategy of selling a positive corporate image through PR, sponsorship, charitable donation, etc.

The credibility of an advertising or any other commercial message may reflect the receiver's perception of the reputation of the originator of the message, the retail outlet selling the product, or the actor endorsing the product. The authority a person can command in promoting a product or service will be greatly enhanced if he or she is acknowledged to be an expert in the use of the product or service in question. It can even help recipients of the message to overlook the fact that the message may be commercially motivated. Even dressing someone up to look like an expert can achieve similar effects.

Over time, the credibility effects of a communication source are eroded. Immediately after exposure to the message, the credibility of the information source has an impact on response. However, with time this becomes less and less effective. This 'sleeper' effect is attributed to disassociation in the receiver's mind of the message itself from the positive or negative feelings about the source. Indeed, experience seems to indicate that people forget the source of the message more quickly than they forget its content. Reiterating the message seems to stimulate memory and the effects of the source's credibility rating recur. Messages from positively-rated sources need to be repeated in order to reinforce the source credibility.

Credibility is the theme of the following case example.

In the first sections of this chapter we have provided an introduction to the nature of communication, how the communication process results in persuasion and how messages might be structured so as to be most effective in creating persuasion. In the next section we will outline the various communication vehicles in marketing which can be used to get messages over to the intended audience, and how choice is effected amongst them.

CASE EXAMPLE

DRINK AND DRIVE PREVENTION: GETTING OVER THE MESSAGE

Every year thousands of people die on the highways as a result of road accidents. In many cases drink is associated with the crash, and prosecution under the law follows.

Festive seasons such as Christmas are times when drivers of cars and other users of vehicles and highways are most at risk from drink related accidents. Every Christmas, extensive communication programmes are undertaken both on TV and elsewhere to try to persuade travellers on the highway to leave drink well alone.

Despite many efforts, the problem still exists and there are still accidents throughout the year which are drink related. In this case, it would seem, the marketing of ideas has failed.

QUESTION

1. How would you attempt to communicate the powerful message of 'don't drink and drive' to all road users?

COMMUNICATION IN MARKETING

At one time, all promotion was undertaken on a face-to-face basis through personal selling. Nowadays there are other more cost effective ways of communicating with target markets. However, personal selling provides lessons in communication that are relevant to other forms of marketing communication.

From a communication point of view, personal selling involves the interaction of a communicator, the salesperson, and the recipient of the message. In personal selling the salesperson 'feels out' the prospect and thereby determines the proper communication content, in view of the customer's background and psychological influences. The salesperson can then phrase the message so that effective communication takes place; if the message somehow misses its mark, the availability of direct and immediate feedback permits the salesperson to try again. The customer, in turn, can usually express his or her needs and thereby procure necessary information in a direct and expeditious fashion. Both parties therefore engage in mutual role-taking, and the communication difficulties, while they should never be minimized, are less than those presented when the mass media are used.

SELECTION OF COMMUNICATION MEDIA

A mass market is reached through a variety of media, such as television, magazines, newspapers, direct mail, display of a product on a shelf, and point of sale advertising. All these media share the common characteristic that one message or appeal is used to reach more than one prospect. Selection of appropriate media is a difficult task but there are many sources of data which document the characteristics of the audience reached by a given medium. If market segments are properly defined and classified, it is possible to select media which reach the desired target audience. The objective is to minimize waste coverage so far as possible.

THE PROMOTIONAL MIX

There are a number of promotional vehicles available to a firm:

- advertising
- publicity
- sales promotion
- personal selling.

The proportion of a firm's marketing communications budget that is spent on each of these activities varies somewhat across organizations and industries. There is a tendency, for example, in the case of industrial and business goods, for more effort to be put into personal selling, while advertising features prominently in the case of fast moving consumer goods. Despite these broad generalizations considerable variation exists within product classes. In the case of advertising there is also the complicating factor that there are a number of advertising vehicles which can be used to communicate the product: television, radio, newspaper, magazine, mobiles, posters, etc.

The most appropriate marketing mix for a product will be influenced by a number of factors.

- **The available budget** The amount of money available for expenditure on promotion is obviously a critical factor. Small firms have comparatively small budgets for promotional expenditure and hence have to select the most cost-effective means of communicating with the market. TV advertising for such firms, for example, may be prohibitively expensive.

- **The promotional message** The nature of the message, as influenced by the objectives which have been set for the communication, will exert considerable influence over the choice of mix. Where a product is to be demonstrated, either face-to-face selling or a visual medium such as television or cinema advertising will be most appropriate. In addition, if we take the hierarchy of effects communication model into consideration, it will be recalled that at the various stages of the step-by-step process different messages are deemed appropriate.

- **The complexity of the product or the service**   In some cases a large amount of service support is required and in this case the only appropriate communication method is personal selling. Where this kind of support is not required, as is the case in fast moving consumer non-durables firms, then advertising is more appropriate.

- **Market size and location**   Large dispersed markets tend to favour mass communication coverage such as advertising. Local markets or small numbers of buyers may favour direct mail, specialist press or even personal selling.

- **Distribution channels**   The key to successful marketing of a product often lies in obtaining suitable distribution for the product. Distributors therefore can exert considerable influence over the choice of promotional medium used to communicate with the ultimate customer.

- **Life cycle**   In the same way that application of the hierarchy of effects models suggests that different messages may be appropriate, so too does the stage in the life cycle a product has reached. If the service or product is in the introductory stage of the life cycle, building awareness is the main aim. If it is in the growth stage, the requirement is to persuade customers to change their buying patterns and switch brand loyalty.

- **Competition**   Matching or beating competition is obviously a key component in determining the strategy behind the formulation of the promotional mix. Where a firm does not have the financial resources to match competitors in terms of expensive promotional campaigns, for example, it must find some other mechanism.

The problem of choosing an appropriate communications mix is posed in the case example on the following page.

WORD OF MOUTH COMMUNICATION

Personal influence is a major information source in consumer decision making. Some people even think that it is the most important marketing element there is (Bayers, 1985). Those who perform the important role of information dissemination through this channel are referred to as opinion leaders. Opinion leaders do not differ greatly in terms of characteristics from the recipient of information. However, much research has been carried out regarding the motivations and other distinguishing features of opinion leaders. Gregariousness appears to be the main distinguishing characteristic of the opinion leader.

For a long time it was felt that there was a two-step flow of communication. The belief was that influences and ideas flowed from the mass media to opinion leaders, and from them to the less active members of the population. The mass media were thought to influence opinion leaders in the first place, who then

CASE EXAMPLE

JOHN SEWELL AUCTIONS: PROMOTING A SERVICE

John Sewell decided to set up in business as an auctioneer in used camcorders, home/desktop/laptop computers and hi-fi equipment. This was a unique venture, since to his knowledge no one else in the UK was operating a similar business. He had noticed that specialist auctioneers existed in used computer equipment of the kind he had in mind, but no one operated in either of the other two areas.

John was able to acquire premises on a small industrial estate some ten miles to the west of Manchester. The premises were five minutes' drive away from the M62 motorway which is part of the main UK motorway network. On account of easy and rapid access to his premises, he felt that his target market, for both buyers and sellers stretched from the northern fringe of Birmingham, some 70 miles to the south to Preston in the north. At the same time he saw clientele coming from Liverpool in the west to Leeds in the east. The target market was thus substantial and dispersed over a wide area.

Auctions were to be held once a month to begin with, but could obviously increase in frequency if sufficient volume of business could be developed. John noted that weekends were popular times for such auctions to be held. However, he was unsure as to what communication mix he should use in order to reach the target market.

QUESTION

1. How do you think John Sewell should set about communicating with the potential target market?

influenced others. This two-step flow idea is not now thought to be accurate: its greatest error was that the audience was viewed as a passive recipient of influence, whereas in fact a large proportion of word-of-mouth communications are initiated by people seeking information. Mass media can perform the important function of stimulating word-of-mouth communications from both leaders and non-leaders or seekers.

A more comprehensive model of mass communication includes the influence of opinion leaders, reference groups, role models and word of mouth. The model

CASE EXAMPLE

WATFORD MAIL ORDER CATALOGUE: USE OF WORD-OF-MOUTH COMMUNICATION

The Watford Mail Order Catalogue company set up in business in 1993 to market directly to the consumer a large variety of consumer durable goods, including clothes and a variety of household furnishings and fittings. The goods are purchased by letter or telephone, and it is common practice for a customer who holds a catalogue to place orders on behalf of neighbours and friends as well. The customer who holds the catalogue is thus in a position effectively to act as an agent for the company and run a small business operation of their own.

The majority of catalogue holders tend to be women with young children who live on large housing estates within a 50-mile radius of the firm's headquarters in Watford. The area in question contains many large conurbations and the proportion of one-parent families is quite high. Restricted incomes of these families means that for many people the ability to pay on a weekly basis for goods from a reliable provider is an essential service.

The company is keen to expand its coverage but is not quite sure how it should do so.

QUESTION

1. Word of mouth communication would appear to be relevant in this instance. How do you think it might be applied with good effect?

suggests that information can be directed to influencers, or opinion leaders, whose interpersonal communication, with its greater persuasive potential, then reaches a wider target audience, reinforcing the message to those who look to them for more information and evaluation. However, even this model is incomplete, because of the complexities of social influence.

The importance of word-of-mouth communication is obvious. The difficulty lies in developing suitable strategies to capitalize on it. The most difficult problem is in identifying the opinion leaders – often they do not form a discrete market segment, and cannot be reached through appropriate media. Where identification is possible several strategies can be applied. In the first place, advertisements can be directed at them, in the hope that they will use the product and talk to others. Second, the opinion leader tends to be an innovator, so monitoring of their behaviour can be an advance notice of consumption trends. Third, products can be given or loaned to these individuals with the objective of stimulating interest among the non-leaders. An alternative is to stimulate interest among the public at large, and hopefully encourage them to talk to others who might be leaders or influential.

Whatever the strategy adopted, the importance of word-of-mouth communication must not be ignored. Interpersonal channels are most influential, in that most buyers accept that their friends have no commercial motivation in making a specific recommendation about a product or service (see the case example on the previous page). On the other hand, friends and neighbours may be perceived as lacking the competence to provide detailed information, and advertisements are consulted for this purpose.

In the final section of this chapter we will examine the role that marketing research plays in the marketing communications process.

CASE EXAMPLE

CORPORATE CONSULTANTS: BODY LANGUAGE RESEARCH SERVICE

People communicate how they feel through body language. Their postures and gestures communicate what they are thinking. This belief has helped Corporate Consultants decide to create and develop a new approach for testing service quality, named Talisman. The Talisman service is devised to quantify and analyse people's physical cues.

The theory behind the Talisman approach is that while spoken words are often censored, non-verbal communication is not and people are not aware of their non-verbal behaviour. People wanting to understand body language need to have the information it provides summarized and analysed, and this is where Talisman comes in. A vast array of body language expressions can be interpreted and coded through this new software system. The system then summarizes the messages in the form of an easily understood conclusion.

(*Source:* Marketing, 1994)

QUESTION

1. How might this service be operationalized in practice?

MARKETING RESEARCH AND FEEDBACK OF INFORMATION

Information on marketing communications is provided by marketing research studies. In the case of advertising these are usually carried out by an advertising agency and fall under the general heading of advertising research. Advertising research is examined in depth in chapter 14, and chapter 6 provides an insight into how qualitative data on the relative merits of other forms of marketing communication may be obtained.

Essentially, research tries to:

- identify target audiences and their characteristics

- design appropriate messages with which to address target audiences

- pre-test the perceived comparative effectiveness of messages to achieve their objectives

- post-test the comparative effectiveness of messages in achieving their objectives.

The kind of research involved is therefore both qualitative and quantitative. It is qualitative in the sense that it helps to identify what should be the message and to whom it should be directed. It is quantitative in the sense that it helps to define the comparative success of a communication or series of communications in terms of achieving their objectives. Research into communication can take on innovative and novel dimensions, as the case example the previous page illustrates.

SUMMARY

This chapter has examined the general concept of communication and how marketing communication can be viewed within such a framework. The framework within which to understand the process of communications includes the role of the sender and receiver of information, the channel selected, noise/distortion in the channel, and feedback. The need for the message to be designed to gain attention was stressed, along with the importance of its containing symbols referring to common meaning. This means that the message should be oriented as closely as possible to the receiver's background, interest, needs and psychological disposition. Communication is facilitated when the communicator and the recipient are as much alike as possible, from the point of view of knowledge, experience, needs, social influence and so on. The accuracy of communication is influenced by noise which enters into both the message and the channel. Noise refers to any extraneous factor which can interfere with the reception of the message. There can be a variety of competing stimuli which distract the recipient and prevent him or her from grasping the full impact of a communication.

Attention was then given to the stepwise models of communication and promotion which have been developed over time to explain these processes. The stepwise models relate to general communications, selling and to advertising. The idea behind such models is that people move through a series of stages on their way to making a decision to purchase a product, and that marketing communications can be used to move people through these different stages. The implication of this is that different forms of communication are appropriate in moving people through the various stages, and that it can be difficult to relate expenditure on marketing communications to direct sales. Performance measures should be related to the particular communication objectives that have been set.

Following this theoretical analysis, the setting of objectives for marketing communications was examined. This was then related to how marketing communications have to be designed to facilitate the achievement of such objectives. The latter involves paying specific attention to the structure of the message and the choice of the information source. Marketing communications have to be designed carefully and matters relating to the format and structure of the message and the credibility of the information source require special attention. Since the process of marketing communications is a multi-stage one, objectives can be set for marketing communications which relate to each stage in the process – for example, to create awareness or evoke interest.

An overview of how the most appropriate media are selected was then presented and an appreciation of how the promotional mix varies and the factors which cause it to vary. The promotional mix is made up of advertising, publicity, sales promotion and personal selling. The proportion of a firm's marketing communications budget that is spent on each of these activities varies somewhat across organizations and industries. Moreover, in the case of advertising there is also the complicating factor that there are a number of advertising vehicles which can be used to communicate about the product: television, radio, newspaper, magazine, mobiles, posters, etc. The most appropriate marketing mix for a product will be influenced by the budget that is available, the nature of the promotional message, the complexity of the product or the service, the market size and location, the nature of the distribution channels, the stage in the product life cycle and the nature of competition.

The importance of word-of-mouth communication was stressed, and an appreciation of the theory surrounding the two-step flow of communication, along with its limitations, was given. A comprehensive model of mass communication includes the influence of opinion leaders, reference groups, role models and word of mouth. The model suggests that information can be directed to influencers, or opinion leaders, who then use interpersonal communication with its greater persuasive potential to reach a wider target audience and to reinforce the message to those who look to them for more information and evaluation. However, even this model is incomplete because of the complexities of social influence.

The importance of word-of-mouth communication is obvious but the difficulty lies in developing suitable strategies to capitalize on it. The most difficult problem lies in identifying the opinion leaders, as often they do not form a discrete market segment and thus cannot be easily reached through appropriate media. Interpersonal channels are most influential, in that most buyers believe that their friends do not have any commercial motivation in making a specific recommendation about a product or service despite the fact that friends and neighbours may be perceived as lacking the competence to provide detailed information, and advertisements are consulted for this purpose.

Finally, the role of marketing research in providing feedback in the marketing communication process was presented.

DISCUSSION

1. Explain the roles of the sender and receiver of information, the channel selected, noise/distortion in the channel and feedback in the communication process.

2. What is meant by 'symbols referring to common meaning'?

3. How might the accuracy of communication be influenced by noise or distortion which enters into both the message and the channel?

4. Explain the nature of the stepwise models of communication and promotion.

5. Suggest some of the kinds of objectives that might be set for marketing communications. How might some of these be related back to the step-wise models?

6. How might the design of specific communication messages be related back to objectives that have been set? Give some examples.

7. What factors affect the make-up of the marketing communications mix?

8. What factors influence choice of communication media?

9. What is the 'two-step' theory of communication? What is the role of 'opinion leaders' or 'gate-keepers' in this theory? What are the major limitations of the theory?

10. Given the importance of word-of-mouth communication, what are the difficulties in developing suitable strategies to capitalize on it? How might one try to overcome these difficulties?

11. Comment on the role of marketing research in providing feedback in the marketing communication process.

REFERENCES

Bayers, L.B. (1985) Word of mouth: the indirect effects of marketing efforts, *Journal of Advertising Research*, **25**(3), 31–9.
Beggs, W.B. (1989) Humour in advertising, *Link*, November–December, 12–15.
Burnett, J. (1993) *Promotion Management*, Houghton Miflin, Boston, Mass.
Campaign (1994)Govt to start ad drive for blood donors, 28 January, 4.

Colley, R.H. (1961) *Defining Advertising Goals for Measuring Advertising Effectiveness*, Association of National Advertisers, New York.

Frieden, J.B. (1984) Advertising spokesperson effects: an examination of endorser type and gender in two audiences, *Journal of Advertising Research*, **24**, 33–41.

Gelb, H., Zenkhan, C.P. and Stewart, D.W. (1988) Advertising repetitions: a critical review of wearin and wearout, *Current issues in research in advertising* (eds J.H. Leigh and C.R. Martin) University of Michigan, Ann Arbor, Mich.

Hovland, C (1957) *The Order of Presentation in Persuasion*, Yale University Press, New Haven, Conn.

Janis, I.L. and Feshback, S. (1953) Effects of fear arousing communications, *Journal of Abnormal and Social Psychology*, **48**(1), 78–92.

Kotler, P. (1991) *Marketing Management: Analysis Planning and Control*, 7th edn, Prentice Hall, Englewood Cliffs, N.J.

Lavidge, R.J. and Steiner, G.A. (1961) A model for predicting measurement of advertising effectiveness, *Journal of Marketing*, **XXV**, October.

McGuire, W.J. (1961) Resistance to persuasion confirmed by active and passive prior to refutation of the same and alternative counter arguments, *Journal of Abnormal and Social Psychology*, **63**, 326–32.

MacLachlan, J. (1983/4) Making a message memorable and persuasive, *Journal of Advertising Research*, **23**(6), 58–9.

McNulty, M. (1994) Agencies intensify bra war, *Campaign*, 28 January, 2.

Madden, T.J. and Weinberger, M.G. (1982) The effects of humour on attention in magazine advertising, *Journal of Advertising*, **11**(3), 8–14.

Marketing (1994) Expert view, 27 January, 36.

Mortensen, C.D. (1979) *Communications: The Study Of Interactions*, McGraw Hill, New York.

Percy, L. (1985) A review of the effects of special advertising elements upon overall communication response, *Current Issues and Research in Advertising*, (eds J.H. Leigh and C.R. Martin), University of Michigan, Ann Arbor, Mich.

Ray, M. and Sawyer, A. (1971) Repetition in media models: a laboratory technique, *Journal of Marketing Research*, **8**, 20–9.

Rogers, E. (1962) *Diffusion of Innovations*, Collier Macmillan, London.

Severin, W.J. and Tankard, J.W. (1979) *Communication Theory: Origins, Methods, Uses*, Hastings House, New York.

Sternthal, B. (1973) Humour in advertising, *Journal of Marketing*, **37**, 12–18.

Weitz, S. (1979) *Nonverbal Communication*, Oxford University Press, New York.

FURTHER READING

Coulson, T.C.J. (1983), *Marketing Communications*, William Heinemann, London.

CASE PROBLEM 13.1

NHS BLOOD SERVICE: EVALUATING PROMOTIONAL METHODS

Every year some two million donors give blood in England. Altogether, some 11 % of the population has given blood, but around 20 % of the list of donors has to be replaced each year because of age, health or moving house. The National Health Service has to attain a daily target of 10 000 units – one unit being the amount given by one person. In October 1993 supplies fell below the minimum level of 20 000 units which is estimated necessary to cope with a major emergency. The aim is to have 30 000 units – three days' supply – always in stock.

In place of appealing for donors, Euro RSCG is to demonstrate the need for more blood by producing a daily 'blood index' indicating the level of supplies available. The new drive to persuade people to give blood involves a £250 000 press campaign. The press work will include a telephone number so that donors can find out when and where they can give blood. The Junior Health Minister is to launch the campaign and it will run for three months.

Euro ESCG's target audience is ABC1 men and women aged between 18 and 44.

(Source: Campaign, 1994)

QUESTION

1. Evaluate the method employed to promote blood donations.

CASE PROBLEM 13.2

PLAYTEX AND GOSSARD:
APPROPRIATENESS OF COMMUNICATION

'Hello boys'
'Look me in the eyes and tell me that you love me'
'Or are you just pleased to see me?'.

These are the one-liner messages Playtex is employing in the war of the plunge bras with rival Gossard. The next battle commences on Valentine's Day, but the Playtex Wonderbra is likely to benefit more from the body of a supermodel, Eva Herzigova, than the aura of the chosen day.

The advertising agency handling the account is understood to have declined to use some of the more enthusiastic one-liners for fear of appearing too alluring. These included such phrases as: 'Lost your tongue?', 'Get down shep'.

Susanna Hailstone, the account director at TBWA, described the £1 million campaign as 'raunchy but fun'. She claimed that it was not remotely sexist. She said that it was the way women talk to each other about sex and it is the look women who buy the Wonderbra want to create.

(Source: McNulty, 1994)

QUESTION

1. Do you agree or disagree with Susanna Hailstone? Explain.

14 ADVERTISING

In this chapter, creative advertising is examined, along with the relation-ship between positioning and advertising strategy. Attention is give to how advertising budgets are put together, and to the work of adver-tising agencies. The advantages and disadvantages of the different advertising media are discussed, together with how the cost-effective-ness of advertising is determined. Finally, the nature of advertising research is examined.

OBJECTIVES

By the end of this chapter you should be able to:

- appreciate the nature and purpose of advertising
- appreciate how advertising budgets are put together
- know what advertising agencies do and how they work
- understand the advantages and disadvantages of using newspaper, magazine, television, commercial radio, outdoor and cinema advertising
- appreciate how the cost-effectiveness of advertising is determined
- appreciate the nature of advertising content research and advertising media research.

INTRODUCTION

This chapter will look first at the nature of advertising and advertising objectives, followed by the nature of its role as an element of the communications mix. The need for creative advertising and how this can be achieved is considered next, followed by positioning, appeals and the tone of advertisements within the context of creative advertising.

Advertising is used to create a variety of different responses in a target audience. The degree to which people respond to advertising messages varies, and can be represented by a mathematical curve referred to as the advertising response curve. This chapter examines the nature and interpretation of the advertising response curve. There is another mathematical curve, which reflects how the effects of advertising decay over time.

Advertising can be expensive, and care has to be taken to work out a budget which will provide just sufficient promotional effect to bring about the desired level of sales. We examine the way in which such advertising budgets can be formulated.

Firms rarely advertise for themselves in the media. Instead they hire the services of an advertising agency. We shall look at what advertising agencies do.

There is a variety of advertising media available and each has its advantages and disadvantages. Newspaper, magazine, television, commercial radio, outdoor, and cinema advertising are all explored.

Expenditure on advertising varies considerably over a wide range of products and services, for a variety of reasons. Some idea of the extent of this variation is presented in the text.

The choice of advertising medium is a complex decision and the steps involved in making such decisions are explored. In doing so one has to appreciate how the cost-effectiveness of advertising is determined. Cost effectiveness is partially determined by media scheduling and this, too, is examined.

The chapter concludes by examining the breadth and make-up of advertising research and its major constituents: advertising content research and advertising media research. Attention is also given to how advertising effectiveness in relation to sales may be estimated.

THE NATURE AND PURPOSE OF ADVERTISING

Advertising is any paid form of non-personal presentation and promotion of ideas, goods or services by an identified sponsor. It includes print and broadcast advertisements, packages, motion pictures (films), mobiles and billboards.

Advertising provides customers with information about products and services which helps to create attention, interest and desire in a product or service. In some circumstances an advertisement may directly result in a sale.

ADVERTISING OBJECTIVES

A variety of different objectives can be set for advertising. These may include the following.

- To create awareness of a brand, company or organization.
- To keep a product or brand name constantly in the mind of a customer.

CASE EXAMPLE

AUDI: ADVERTISING CAMPAIGN OBJECTIVE

Car-maker Audi sees itself as being about innovation, individuality and modernity. In an attempt to portray the personality of the marque and excite people about what Audi represents, in early 1994 Audi returned to television, following a two-year absence. The phrase 'Vorsprung Durch Technik' was retained in the new advertisements, while to raise awareness of the Audi symbol, the four intertwined rings were to receive more emphasis.

There were two one-minute tinted black and white commercials. In one, a woman was featured, in the other a man, both talking indirectly about their cars. The target audience was 25 to 45 year olds. Forming the larger part of a £12 million above the line budget for Audi that year, the campaign lasted for five months.

(Source: Cole, 1994)

QUESTION

1. What do you think were the objectives of the advertising campaign in this case?

- To stimulate interest in a product or brand.
- To give out information about what a product or service can do for the customer.

Advertising can take place at the corporate level, where it is used to promote the company name, or at the level of a product or brand. There can also be differences in terms of the target audience. It can be directed at the final consumers, or alternatively it can be aimed at selected distribution channel members.

Advertising has an image of being expensive, but this need not be the case. Large firms can spend considerable amounts of money on advertising campaigns, while small firms think in terms of modest sums spent to best advantage. Large firms use national newspapers, television and posters, while small firms may be well served by local newspapers, local radio and trade journals. In addition there is a tendency for large firms to deal with well-known advertising agencies, while small firms use local agencies.

Differences also exist between industrial and consumer goods firms in their use of advertising. Consumer goods firms seek to address very large audiences with their marketing communications, and advertising is an excellent means of communication to achieve this purpose. Industrial goods producers, on the other hand, tend to communicate with smaller numbers of buyers and there is less need for using mass communication channels – although use is made of trade journals

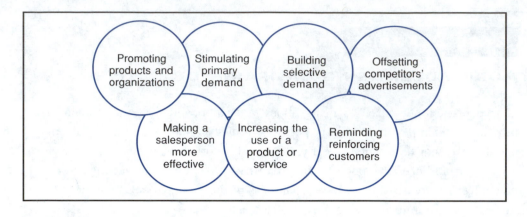

Figure 14.1 Purposes of advertising.

and other magazines to communicate with people who influence the buying decision. Regardless of whether consumers or industrial firms are involved, to be effective, advertising has to target the right message to the right people.

Setting advertising objectives is the theme of the case example on the previous page.

WHAT ADVERTISING IS USED FOR

Promoting products and organizations

Advertising is used for promoting organizations, ideas, products or services. For example, the government makes use of advertising to give out information on health issues such as drink driving, smoking, AIDS, etc. Other organizations use advertising to create positive images for themselves in the minds of the public. In this case the corporate advertising 'rubs off' on the products or services that the organization markets. However, advertising is perhaps most closely associated with the promotion of individual products and services.

Stimulating primary demand – pioneer advertising

When an innovation is first launched into the market place, potential purchasers have to be made aware of the existence of the product and have to be encouraged to make a purchase. Often, one firm will pioneer a product or service that is an innovation and will create the primary demand for that product. Xerox is a case in point – Xerox created the primary demand for photocopiers.

The cost of creating primary demand can be very high. Not only does the firm have the hard task of moving people through all the stages from awareness to action, but it has to do so quickly and build up its market share position ahead of the competition. Advertising is therefore an expensive investment cost and has to be taken into account when looking at the profitability, potential or actual, of an innovation.

Much of the effort that is put into creating primary demand can very easily benefit competitors who enter the market at a later stage and capitalize on the unsatisfied demand that exists at the time of entry.

Building selective demand – competitive advertising

Advertising has not only to create primary demand for new products but it has to create demand specifically for the firm's own products and services. This it must do by showing how the firm's offering has a differential advantage over those of competitors.

Offsetting competitors' advertising – defensive advertising

Naturally, all competitors in the market place are trying to build up demand for their own product or service at the expense of competitors. Since all firms may be advertising, much of the advertising has to be 'defensive' to simply match that of the competition. For example, if Ford is mounting regular TV commercials extolling the virtues of its range of cars, then competitors such as Vauxhall must do likewise. Failure to do so means that customers will come to accept the Ford point of view, in the absence of contradictory information provided by Vauxhall.

Defensive advertising was at the heart of the famous 'soap wars'. Here the two detergent manufacturers Procter & Gamble and Unilever, duelled over whose soap powder was best. In the true tradition of the Cold War they stockpiled weaponry – in this case millions of pounds of investment in defensive advertising expenditure on TV. Of course, everyone knew that the overall level of expenditure could have been cut by as much as 50%, that both firms would still retain the same market share, that primary demand would not be reduced and that both companies would be the richer by incurring less expenditure on advertising. But who was to make the first move? If Unilever reduced its expenditure by only a small amount and Procter & Gamble did not reduce its expenditure at all, then Unilever could lose millions in lost revenues. Fortunately the situation was resolved by a government directive which forced both firms to reduce their advertising expenditure simultaneously.

Making a salesperson more effective

If distributors know that the producer is advertising direct to the next business or person in the chain of distribution (i.e. the distributor's customer) then the distributor will be more disposed to stock the product and the producer's sales representative will have an easier time making a sale.

Increasing the use of a product or service

Strange as it may seem, people do not always know what to do with a product. Take for example a camcorder. It may seem obvious what one does with a camcorder, but it is not quite so obvious what use a typical buyer actually makes of a camcorder. It is even less obvious what use a typical buyer will make of a camcorder when the product reaches the maturity stage of the life cycle – at the time of writing it is still in the early stages of the life cycle. Advertising is a mechanism which can give out information on the kinds of things a person can do with a product. It is by giving out this information that new users can be attracted, since they can be shown how possession of a given product can create desirable benefits.

Reminding and reinforcing customers

Forgetfulness is a basic human failing. We all forget to do things, or forget experiences we have had, unless they are things which have been very forcibly and graphically entered into our memories. We may remember a specific moment from 20 or 30 years ago when something traumatic happened to us – such an experience is likely to be lodged indelibly in our memories. On the other hand, it is quite likely that we will not be able to remember exactly what we were doing at 8.45 on a particular evening several weeks ago.

Since people forget mundane and relatively unimportant things so easily, marketers of goods and services have to keep reminding them of their product or service.

THE NEED FOR CREATIVE ADVERTISING

For a product or a service to be successful in the market place it has to be noticed, and it has to be trusted by the customer. This means that the advertising will have to stand out from the crowd. Advertising faces a major challenge, in so far as much of the information provided to the customer is ignored. Advertising has therefore to catch the customer's attention and deliver the message in an original way that will enable the customer to remember and identify with the message and the brand.

In addition to its key function to inform, advertising is also expected to entertain. Following on from this, advertising has to rely heavily on emotions and images to attract the customer's attention and interest. The emphasis is therefore on images. Images have the capacity to capture the essence of a thousand words. They can be absorbed and remembered with much less effort by a viewer. Images also have much more power to satisfy viewers' needs for entertainment.

Advertising will need to become increasingly emotional in tone as it becomes even harder to base a competitive advantage merely on the functional attributes of a brand. Differentiation will be achieved through emotional attributes of a brand.

All this means that advertising will have to become more creative.

A MODEL FOR CREATIVE ADVERTISING STRATEGY

Creative advertising strategy is operationalized into 'what is said' and 'how it is said'. This in turn is reflected in the positioning, appeals and tone of advertising.

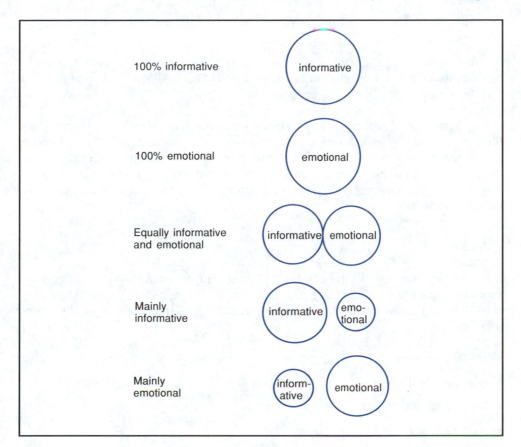

Figure 14.2 Five positioning appeals.

Positioning

Positioning reflects what the product stands for in the minds of customers in reference to competition. This is effectively what functions, physical or emotional, the product performs for people. The functional and emotional elements of the position depend upon the customer's awareness of a need and knowledge about available products. A positioning strategy can therefore be both informative and emotional in its appeal.

There are five positioning alternatives (Kroeber-Riel, 1990):

1. 100% informative positioning – the advertisement includes information about the product or its use

2. 100% emotional positioning – the advertisement contains only emotional appeals

3. Equal information and emotional positioning

4. mainly informative positioning – the advertising provides information for the most part, but this is supported by strong emotional appeals. The purpose of

such an approach seems to be to provide information enveloped in an emotional context

5. mainly emotional positioning – the advertisement is used to convey mainly emotions, but some information is included. The idea is to link emotions to the product.

The particular appeal used varies according to the stage reached in the product life cycle. As the product moves towards the decline stage, people's information requirements become trivial. The positioning tends to be informative in the introductory stage and becomes increasingly emotional in the growth and maturity stages. In the decline stage, however, both information and emotional appeals may be necessary.

Appeals

An advertising appeal is the reason embedded in an advertising message that should motivate a person to buy a product or service. Applebaum and Haliburton (1993) list 24 different appeals used to advertise food and beverages. Amongst these are:

● relief from stress

● nostalgia and security

● friendship and togetherness

● romance and sex

● fashion

● convenience

● value for money

● country of origin.

For an appeal to work, of course, it must have cultural or subcultural value for the target audience at whom the message is addressed.

Tone

Tone refers to how the message is expressed and, in conjunction with the format of an advertisement, is sometimes referred to as the 'advertising concept'. Together, the elements of tone and format create the image surrounding the product or service on offer and help to provide credibility. There are many ways in which the tone of an advertisement can be set. These include the following:

● **The use of humour** Ray (1982) considers this to be effective only when the objective is to attract attention and create awareness.

- **The use of argumentative versus narrative material** Argumentative material tries to address the recipient of the message at the rational level, and is informative in nature. Narrative material, in contrast, takes the form of a story in which no explicit statement is made to the recipient. The recipient is more involved and has to actively interpret the material. Such an approach is more emotional in nature.

- **Hard versus soft sell** Mueller (1987) identifies the soft sell approach in which mood and atmosphere are conveyed through imagery or the development of an emotional appeal. Human emotional sentiments are given preference to product-related appeals. In the case of a hard sell the emphasis is on brand name, comparison with other products and the product's performance.

- **Using words or images as the prime communication mechanism** Providing the prime message through image does carry the risk that the message may be misunderstood by the recipient.

ADVERTISING RESPONSE CURVE

The advertising response curve is upward-sloping for the most part (Figure 14.3), generally indicating that the greater the amount of money spent on advertising, the greater will be the customer response in terms of increased awareness, interest, desire or even action. Of course, this means that all other factors, for example, the price, distribution, product and other promotional variables, have to be held constant. It also assumes that 'quality' of advertising is held constant. If the quality is unsatisfactory then the response may be poorer than say a very good advertisement which receives only a modest financial backing. This brings out two

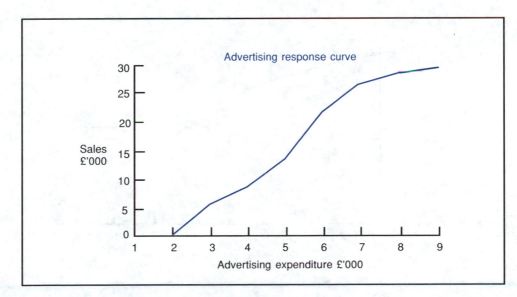

Figure 14.3 Response and threshold effects.

important dimensions of advertising – the frequency with which an advertisement is displayed to members of the public, and the quality of the advertisement. In the first instance the more often an advertisement is placed in the media, then the greater will be the advertising expenditure. One may also pay more for quality advertisements, but the quality will be achieved by the advertising agency and it is not always certain that the more one pays, the better will be the quality.

There are a number of other features about the response curve which are worth noting. In the first place the exact slope of the curve will vary from firm to firm, and even from situation to situation. Moreover, after a given point there will be diminishing returns to scale. Advertising may be effective in terms of creating awareness, for example, for the first 80% of the target audience, but to create awareness among the remaining 20% may be much harder to achieve. There can be a variety of reasons for this. For example, the last 20% may be less receptive to media advertising, or they may simply be exposed much less frequently to the chosen media than the bulk of the target audience, and hence harder to reach.

Another interesting feature of the response curve is what is known as the threshold effect (Figure 14.3). People will not respond at all to advertising unless the message is expressed with a minimum degree of force. A one-off advertisement, for example, may not be seen by customers who would have been interested in the product or service. Thus the effect of spending money on a single advertisement in this instance is to produce no audience response at all. In Figure 14.3 a company sells through direct mail advertisements to members of the public and hence can relate advertising to sales in this instance. It will be noted, however, that unless the firm spends a minimum of £2000 on advertising, no sales will be generated. This illustrates what is meant by the threshold effect.

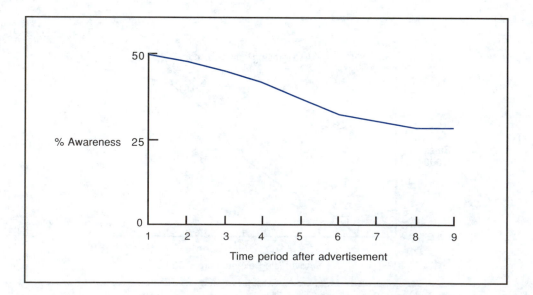

Figure 14.4 Fall-off in awareness following advertisement.

ADVERTISING DECAY EFFECT

Using a different example where an advertisement was designed to create awareness, we can see that although the advertisement may be successful in generating a given level of awareness immediately, this generally falls back over to time to a lower level. The existence of the decay curve lends credence to the argument that advertisements need to be repeated time and time again to keep the message in customers' minds and maintain levels of awareness, interest and desire, etc. The decay curve for the example is illustrated in Figure 14.4.

Having looked at the nature and purpose of advertising, we will now move on to the important question of setting the advertising budget. We explore this in the next section.

THE ADVERTISING BUDGET

Since advertising can have varying objectives, and it is relatively difficult to measure the relationship between advertising expenditure and the attainment of advertising objectives, the method of setting budget expenditure is not very precise. There are several different approaches.

1. Deciding how much the organization can afford to spend on advertising in total and then assigning expenditure for different purposes on a 'best guess' basis.

2. Forecasting sales for the coming year and allocating a fixed percentage of expected sales as the amount to spend on advertising.

3. Taking the previous year's expenditure and adding a fixed percentage to it for inflation.

4. Allocating an amount which is a fixed percentage of the previous year's sales.

5. Systematically working through all the advertising objectives that have been set and trying to determine, as objectively as possible, exactly what is required in terms of advertising and hence expenditure in order to achieve the objectives.

6. As 5, but also taking into account what competitors spend on advertising.

Advertising is only rarely handled entirely by firms themselves. Designing advertisements is a skilled task and knowledge of the media industry a specialized one. Advertising agencies exist to help firms design and place their promotions and make the best use of the money firms have set aside for this purpose. In the next section we will look at what advertising agencies do.

ADVERTISING AGENCIES

Small firms may do some advertising for themselves in local media, though to a much larger extent they will make use of local advertising agencies. Larger organizations make use of large advertising agencies. Users of advertising agency services liaise with an account executive who is responsible for ensuring that all of a client's requirements are dealt with by the various departments in the agency. A typical agency employs a number of staff to work on the various requirements of the client. For example, the creative section prepares the text and layout of advertisements; the studio deals with the artwork; media staff plan bookings and purchase space in appropriate media. In addition there are also staff who try to assess how successful advertising has been in terms of achieving the objectives that were set for it.

Agencies receive payments in two ways:

1. Commission from the media on the advertising they place.

2. Charges for copy preparation (text of an advertisement), artwork and campaign planning advice which they levy on the customer.

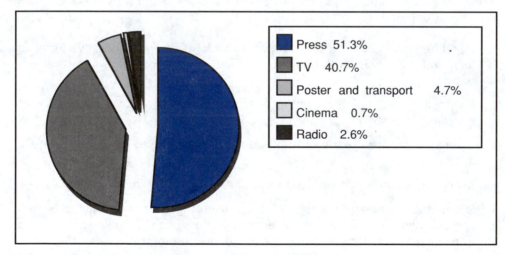

Press 51.3%

TV   40.7%

Poster and transport   4.7%

Cinema 0.7%

Radio 2.6%

Figure 14.5   Display advertising expenditure, 1991.

Display advertising expenditure by medium 1991 (£m.)

Press	2893
TV	2303
Poster & transport	267
Cinema	42
Radio	149

(Source: The Marketing Pocket Book, *1993, p.73)*

Central to the task of the agencies is the problem of selecting the right media for a given client's promotion. Below we look at the media in more detail.

THE MEDIA

Figure 14.5 and the table below it on the previous page give some idea of the amount of money spent on advertising in different media.

NEWSPAPERS

In the UK and many other countries, newspapers have a wide circulation. In the UK there are both national and local newspapers. This has obvious implications for the catchment areas they cover and hence the purpose of advertising in one or other of these types of media. In addition, different national newspapers attract different kinds of readers. This has to be taken into account when selecting a newspaper to reach a target audience.

Circulation figures of selected national and regional newspapers in 1991 ('000)

Nationals:	*Daily Express*	1519
	Daily Mail	1684
	Daily Mirror	2881
	Daily Record	760
	The Star	838
	The Sun	3665
	Today	460
	The Daily Telegraph	1058
	Financial Times	287
	The Guardian	410
	The Independent	372
	The Times	387
Regional:	*The Evening Standard* (London)	502
	Bristol Evening Post	105
	Birmingham Evening Mail	203
	Express and Star (Wolverhampton)	228
	Liverpool Echo	184
	Manchester Evening News	241
	Yorkshire Post	86
	The Scotsman	85
	Belfast Telegraph	129

(*Source:* The Marketing Pocket Book, *1993*)

In the UK, local evening newspapers, such as the *Liverpool Echo* and the *Bristol Evening Post*, tend to be bought by people within roughly a 30-mile radius of the city centres from where they are published. They are particularly useful for firms wishing to promote their goods in those particular areas. It is possible to place advertisement at relatively short notice and the size of the circulation audience provides good penetration of the target audience. The free weekly newspapers can also provide a good advertising inroad into local markets.

Newspapers will often publish news stories in their editorial review columns, provided the firm places some advertising with the newspaper. This is particularly useful when a firm is introducing new products or moving to new premises.

MAGAZINES

Magazines are used for advertising purposes by both consumer and industrial goods producers. General interest magazines and specialist magazines covering particular topics such as computers, cars, DIY, etc. are available for advertisers of specialist goods. A company which advertises in these magazines can be reasonably sure that the message is reaching the target audience.

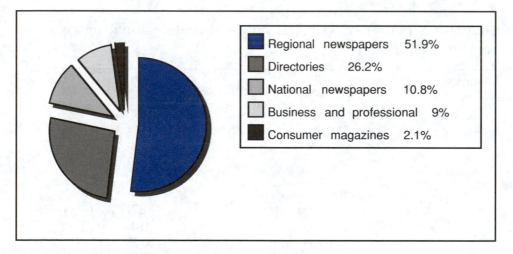

■ Regional newspapers	51.9%
■ Directories	26.2%
■ National newspapers	10.8%
□ Business and professional	9%
■ Consumer magazines	2.1%

Figure 14.6 Classified advertising expenditure by medium, 1991.

	£m.
National newspapers	208
Regional newspapers	996
Consumer magazines	41
Business and professional	174
Directories	504

(Source: The Marketing Pocket Book, *1993, p.73)*

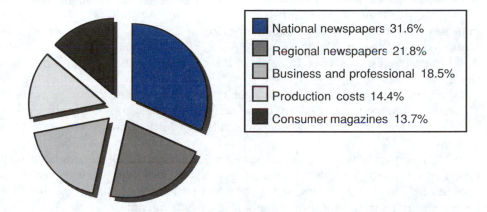

National newspapers 31.6%
Regional newspapers 21.8%
Business and professional 18.5%
Production costs 14.4%
Consumer magazines 13.7%

Figure 14.7 Press display advertising expenditure by medium, 1991.

	£m.
National newspapers	914
Regional newspapers	632
Consumer magazines	397
Business and professional	534
Production costs	417

(Source: The Marketing Pocket Book, *1993, p.73)*

Since many consumer goods are distributed through intermediaries, the availability of retail and trade magazines provides an excellent means of communication for producers who want to advertise to distributors.

In the case of producers of industrial goods there are many magazines which are read by people who exert an influence on the buying process in different industries. Purchasing officers and buyers in firms, as well as technical specialists, read these magazines to gain current information about what is going on in the industry. These magazines also carry advertising and they represent a good means of bringing informative advertising to the attention of potential decision makers in industrial buying groups.

TELEVISION

Television is watched by millions of viewers throughout Europe and in many other developed regions of the world. In the UK, TV advertising operates on a regional basis so that it is possible to aim advertising through this medium at homes in specific geographical areas.

TV offers colour, sound and movement to illustrate promotional messages. In the UK the two commercial channels attract large viewing audiences, but research indicates that these tend to be confined to particular social groups – upper and middle class social groups show a preference for watching the BBC channels. Another problem is that many viewers of the commercial networks do not watch the advertisements.

TV advertising has many benefits over other types of media. For example, a TV advertisement is couched in a pre-defined manner and hence the possibility of reaching the target audience in a different form to that intended cannot occur.

In 1991 display advertising expenditure on TV totalled £2303m compared with £2303m for press (excluding advertising in directories but including financial notices and display advertising in business and professional journals), £267m for poster and transport, £42m for cinema and £149m for radio.

COMMERCIAL RADIO

Commercial radio stations operate world-wide. In the UK local radio stations tend to be situated in cities and provide local news and entertainment for the surrounding area. Reception varies, but generally speaking is very good within a radius of 20 miles, and local radio stations can be heard up to 30 miles away.

In comparison to TV advertising, commercial radio represents a cheap way of addressing target market groups. Research seems to indicate that the prime listeners are women at home, people driving to work, and younger people, and are not therefore representative of the population as a whole. An obvious weakness of this form of promotion is that there is no visual stimulus.

OUTDOOR ADVERTISING

Under the heading of outdoor advertising come posters, hoardings, neon signs, mobiles on buses, taxis and tube trains. The principal use of outdoor advertising is that of reminding people of a product or an advertising campaign or to reinforce a detailed TV or newspaper message. They are also used by firms to introduce their names to consumers for the first time.

This type of advertising is considered to be an inexpensive form of promotion.

CINEMA ADVERTISING

Following a period of substantial decline in popularity, attributed to the growth of TV ownership in the 1950s and 1960s, cinemas staged something of a recovery in the 1980s.

Audiences tend to be in the younger 15–24 age range, and advertising tends to concentrate on items which appeal to this age group.

OTHER ADVERTISING MEDIA

Other advertising media comprise:

- aerial banners
- airships
- balloon displays, tethered
- balloon releases
- electronic outdoor advertising display
- golf tee signs
- hot-air balloons
- inflatable porta-boards
- litter bins
- motor posters
- post office nu-media (graphic display)
- post office continuous video tape
- post office leaflet dispensing
- taxi cabs
- teleguide (telephone recordings)
- video tapes.

ADVERTISING EXPENDITURE BY PRODUCTS AND SERVICES

Expenditure on press and TV advertising varies considerably across a wide range of products. The table on the following page gives some idea of the variation.

The variation in expenditure can be attributed to several factors, such as the size of industry and the number of buyers in the market.

Having looked at the characteristics of different types of media we will now examine how media decisions are made and how the cost-effectiveness of the media is assessed.

MEDIA DECISIONS

In choosing media in which to advertise, organizations seek to discover the most cost-effective way to deliver the desired exposure to the target audience. This involves examining the reach, frequency and impact of advertisements that are placed in different media.

Annual adjusted register-meal advertising expenditure by product category

Press and TV in £m 1991	
Agriculture & horticulture	19.9
Charity and educational	25.5
Drink	200.4
Entertainment	100.2
Financial	312.5
Food	526.0
Government	84.8
Holidays, travel & transport	159.7
Household appliances	82.2
Household equipment	63.9
Household stores	212.2
Institutional and industrial	123.8
Leisure equipment	164.1
Motors	323.4
Office equipment	78.2
Pharmaceuticals	99.5
Publishing	122.2
Retail & Mail Order	434.9
Tobacco	42.9
Toiletries and cosmetics	183.5
Wearing apparel	38.2
Other	24.7
Total	3422.6

(*Source:* The Marketing Pocket Book, *1993*)

● **Reach**   When we refer to 'reach' we mean the number of persons who are exposed to a media schedule at least once during a specific time period. Reach is most important when a firm is trying to create initial awareness of a product.

● **Frequency**   Frequency is the number of times within a specific time period that an average person is exposed to a message. Frequency is most important for a complex product or when the aim is to create a brand image.

● **Impact**   Impact is the qualitative value of an exposure through a given medium.

The media planner has to be familiar with the reach, frequency and impact of the major media types. Each type – newspapers, TV, direct mail, radio, magazines and outdoor – has advantages and limitations in terms of reach, frequency and impact. Media planners match limitations and advantages with the requirements of the message. For example, a message announcing that a sale is taking place today may be given over the radio. Obviously, the nature of the product, the nature of the message, the cost and the type of audience accessible through the medium are key factors in the process.

ASSESSING THE COST EFFECTIVENESS OF MEDIA VEHICLES

The size and composition of the target market and the cost of reaching that audience are indicators of the effectiveness of the media and are studied carefully by planners. Circulation and type of audience are other important measures taken into account by the planners. They calculate the cost per thousand of the target group reached by a particular vehicle. One should bear in mind that this is not simply the same thing as the cost per thousand people reached with respect to users of the media. Many of these people may not be in the target group. Other things being equal, a planner prefers media vehicles that have the lowest cost per thousand reached of the target media group. Other considerations are the quality of the editorials and the extent to which people pay attention to the advertisements.

MEDIA SCHEDULING

A firm can vary its advertising expenditure to suit the seasonal pattern, or it can advertise throughout the year. Most firms do the latter. Kuehn (1962) showed that the appropriate pattern of timing should reflect how much advertising carry-over effect exists and the degree of habit in customers' choice of brand. Where both are low it is appropriate to use a seasonal pattern and it is better to time the advertising so that it coincides with the seasonal pattern. Where carry-over effects and habits are high, it is better to time the advertising to lead the sales curve. The higher the carry-over, then the greater should be the lead time. Steady advertising expenditure should be used when habitual purchase patterns are greatest.

Having decided how to vary its advertising expenditure, a firm has then to look at advertising over a short period of time so as to obtain the maximum impact. More continuous advertising should be used when the rate at which new customers appear in the market is high. This should also be the case when the frequency with which people make purchases is high or the rate at which people 'forget the brand' is high.

Advertisers tend to use continuous advertising when the market is expanding. Concentrated advertising in a single period of time occurs when the product is sold in a single period. In the case of seasonal or infrequently purchased items, or when funds are limited, bursts of advertising are used. An alternative is to use continuous advertising at low weight levels, reinforced periodically by waves of heavier activity.

All marketing mix decisions benefit from the availability of relevant information. Advertising is no exception to this. In this case information can help to suggest the content that should go into advertisements, the media to use and finally should provide feedback on the effectiveness of advertising. Information is provided though advertising research; we explore this topic in the following section.

ADVERTISING RESEARCH

Advertising research comprises advertising content research, advertising media research and advertising effectiveness research.

ADVERTISING CONTENT RESEARCH

This kind of research examines an advertisement's ability to project the desired message to the target audience. The design and layout of an advertisement must be tested in detail along with the basic theme – the copy platform. Alternative kinds of appeal to the target audience are tested in this kind of research. For example, when advertising a new desktop computer, should the main appeal be size, speed of operation, memory capacity, etc?

In 'content' research measurements can be taken at two stages: pre-publication and post-publication. At the pre-testing phase emphasis is placed on ideas and methods of publication, whereas in the case of post-testing the emphasis is on measuring how effectively communication concepts were received by the intended audience.

There are a number of ways of pretesting advertisements.

- **Direct rating** involves showing a consumer panel alternative advertisements and getting them to rate the advertisements. Ratings are made on the attention-getting power of an advertisement, whether it encourages the recipient of the message to listen, watch or read further, the clarity of the message, the effectiveness of the appeal and whether it suggests follow-through action.

- **Portfolio tests** provide the consumer with a collection of advertisements and ask them to recall their content. Recalling the advertisement indicates its ability to be understood and remembered.

- **Laboratory tests** are used to measure consumers' physical reaction to advertisements. Pupil dilation tests, changes in heartbeat, etc., reflect an advertisement's ability to command attention.

Post-testing relies on measuring recall and recognition of advertisements. Measuring both verbal and visual recall of advertisements may be either aided or unaided. In the case of unaided recall, people are shown a series of advertisements and then questioned to see exactly how much of the advertising messages, etc. that they can accurately recall. In the case of aided recall, people are questioned as to whether they have seen a particular advertisement, and if this is the case they are asked to state what impact it has had on them.

Since campaigns will have a number of objectives advertisers are interested to find out how effective they have been in reaching these objectives. Changing awareness, knowledge and preference about a brand may be objectives for campaigns. One measure of post-testing to measure effectiveness is to draw a random sample of consumers in the target market and to ask them suitably phrased questions about the brand to ascertain such information.

We will recall, from the previous chapter, the hierarchy of the effects model proposed by Lavidge and Steiner in 1961. Using this model we can specify the kinds of advertising research that are appropriate, according to the different advertising objectives that have been set. In other words, researchers try to assess how successful an advertising campaign has been in terms of say creating an awareness of a product or giving people information about a product or service that will move them further along the ladder of purchase intent. Similar measures are taken for creating a liking, developing a preference, bringing about conviction, and, where relevant, actual purchase.

It is also, of course, quite possible to use any of the other models listed in the previous chapter, such as AIDA and DAGMAR, for the same purpose. However, despite the obvious attractiveness of the 'step-by-step' persuasion models, they have not been without their critics. Several writers, including Palda (1966) have dismissed them as superficial and unconvincing.

Today, four elements are generally regarded as highly important.

1. **Awareness** A variety of studies of assessing awareness point to its importance. Studies by the Dutch organization NIPO (Stapel, 1990) through their brand monitor system demonstrate a high correlation between brand-loyal buying behaviour scores and aggregate brand awareness. They also found a high correlation with brand awareness and the numbers of people who claim that their next purchase of a durable will be a given brand.

2. **The customer liking or finding an advertisement appealing** The Advertising Research Foundation's Copy Research Validation study suggested that the 'likeability of a commercial was the single best predictor of sales effectiveness'. The use of a likeability scale, it was claimed, predicted sales winners 97% of the time (Biel, 1989). Factors such as ingenuity, meaningfulness, energy, and warmth were found to underpin likeability. The relative importance of each of these factors appears to vary across products.

3. **Interest** Finding an advertisement really interesting is suggested as being even more important than liking the advertisement (Stapel, 1991).

4. **Enjoyment** The extent to which an advertisement is enjoyed has been found to be a better pre-test measure than short-term recall (Brown, 1991a,b).

These are advertising effectiveness predictors that are used today by market research companies under the direction usually of the advertising agency. The predictors are linked to the emotional thoughts of the customer.

ADVERTISING MEDIA RESEARCH

This type of research sets out to eliminate waste in advertising by systematically looking at the media available for promoting products and services.

- **Press research**   In the main, this kind of research concentrates on readership surveys, for example, the National Readership Survey which is based on a stratified random sample of 28 500 adult interviews over a continuous period of 12 months. Subscribers to this survey obtain breakdowns by demographic characteristics, regional distribution, television viewing, cinema attendance, commercial radio listening, special interests, etc. Average issue readership is provided for each publication, along with a regional analysis. The National Readership Survey is administered by the Joint Industry Committee for National Readership Surveys (JICNARS).

- **Television advertising research**   The Joint Industry Committee for Television Advertising Research (JICTAR) appoints a research organization to provide a research service based on a television panel of UK households. The service provides information on the size of audiences at different times of the day and week by projecting the viewing patterns of the sample panel. A measure is also taken of audience appreciation of TV programmes.

- **Radio research**   A Joint Industry Committee for Radio Audience Research (JICRAR) follows the pattern set by JICNARS AND JICTAR. The JICRAR survey is based on seven-day diaries distributed among random samples of persons aged 15 or more within a radio station's designated area. Diaries are placed and collected by interviewers.

- **Cinema audience research**   This is covered mainly by the National Readership Survey mentioned above.

- **Poster research**   The Joint Industry Committee for Poster Advertising Research (JICPAR) commissions a research organization to estimate both pedestrian and vehicular audiences for all posters. Information is also provided on types of area, shops and commercial characteristics, so that posters can be sited strategically.

ADVERTISING EFFECTIVENESS RESEARCH

Effective advertising involves three essential ingredients:

1. good copy – the wording and layout of the advertisement are critical
2. correct media selection
3. advertising at the right time and with the right frequency.

Most of the money spent on measuring advertising effectiveness goes into pretesting advertisements rather than trying to evaluate its effects afterwards.

MEASURING EFFECTIVENESS IN RELATION TO SALES

Many factors influence sales besides advertising. The other factors include all the elements of the marketing mix, along with availability of the product and the effect of competitive activity. One might try to relate advertising expenditure to market share. Except in the case of new products one might expect advertising expenditure and market share to be directly proportional to one another. Where imbalance exists with respect to established products then advertising is less effective for those firms which spend disproportionately more on advertising than their market share would suggest. In the case of new products, disproportionate spending on advertising is to be expected.

Various attempts have been made to analyse historical data with sophisticated statistical tools, and other researchers have tried experimental methods. Advertisers seeking to sell goods direct to consumers often ask them to indicate which advertisement they are responding to, in order to gauge the effectiveness of different advertisements.

It is perhaps only in the case of people who place orders in response to advertisements, however, that one can be reasonably sure about its effectiveness in terms of producing sales.

SUMMARY

Advertising gives out information about products and services which helps to create attention, interest and desire in a product or service and even a sale. A variety of different objectives might be set for advertising. These include:

● creating awareness of a brand, company or organization

● keeping a product or brand name constantly in the mind of a customer

● stimulating interest in a product or brand

● giving out information about what a product or service can do for the customer

● promoting products and organizations

● stimulating primary demand

● building selective demand – competitive advertising

● offsetting competitors' advertising

● making a salesperson more effective

● increasing the use of a product or service

● reminding and reinforcing customers.

Advertising takes place at the corporate level or at the level of product or brand. It is directed at the final consumers or at selected distribution channel members.

Consumer goods firms often address large audiences, and advertising is a means of communication to achieve this purpose. Industrial goods producers, on the other hand, tend to communicate with smaller numbers of buyers and there is less need for using mass communication channels – although use is made of trade journals.

Advertising needs to become increasingly emotive as the difficulty of gaining a competitive advantage on the basis of the functional attributes of a brand alone become ever greater. Differentiation can be achieved through evoking emotional attributes of a brand. This means that advertising will have to become more creative. Creative strategy is operationalized into 'what is said' and 'how it is said'. This in turn is reflected in the positioning, appeal and tone of advertising.

The advertising response curve generally indicates that the greater the amount of money spent on advertising, the greater will be the customer response in terms of increased awareness, interest, desire or even action. This assumes that all other factors have to be held constant. After a given point, however, there will be diminishing returns to scale. Another interesting feature of the response curve is what is known as the threshold effect.

The existence of the decay curve lends credence to the argument that advertisements need to be repeated quite frequently to keep the message in customers' minds and maintain levels of awareness, interest and desire, etc.

Advertising budgets may be set through any of the following methods:

- on the basis of deciding how much the organization can afford to spend
- forecasting sales for the coming year and allocating a fixed percentage of expected sales as the amount to spend on advertising
- taking the previous year's expenditure and adding a fixed percentage to it for inflation
- allocating a fixed percentage of the previous year's sales
- systematically working through all the advertising objectives that have been set and trying to determine, as objectively as possible, exactly what is required in terms of advertising and hence expenditure in order to achieve the objectives
- as the last method but taking into account what competitors spend on advertising as well.

Larger organizations make use of large advertising agencies. Users of advertising agency services liaise with an account executive who is responsible for ensuring that all aspects of the client's requirements are dealt with by the various departments in the agency. A typical agency employs a number of staff to work on the various requirements of the client.

In the UK and many other countries, newspapers have a wide circulation. Different newspapers attract different kinds of readers. This has to be taken into account when selecting a newspaper to reach a target audience.

Magazines are used for advertising purposes by both consumer and industrial goods producers. There are specialist magazines which are directed at specific audiences in both cases.

Television is watched by millions of viewers throughout Europe and many other countries. In the UK, TV advertising operates on a regional basis, so that it is possible to aim advertising through this medium at homes in specific geographical areas.

Many different commercial radio stations operate throughout the world. In the UK they tend to be situated in cities, providing local news and entertainment for the surrounding area. While radio is a relatively cheap medium for reaching audiences, listeners to commercial radio are not truly representative of the population as a whole.

Under the heading of outdoor advertising are posters, hoardings, neon signs, mobiles on buses, taxis and tube trains. The principal use of outdoor advertising is that of reminding people of a product or an advertising campaign, or to reinforce a detailed TV or newspaper message.

Cinema audiences tend to be in the younger age range of 15–24 years. Advertising tends to concentrate on items which appeal to this age group.

In choosing media, organizations seek the most cost-effective way to deliver the desired exposure to the target audience. This involves examining the reach, frequency and impact of advertisements that are placed in different media.

Advertising research comprises advertising content research, advertising media research and advertising effectiveness research. Advertising content research examines an advertisement's ability to project the desired message to the target audience. Advertising media research sets out to eliminate waste in advertising by systematically looking at the media available for promoting products and services. Most of the money spent on measuring advertising effectiveness goes into pretesting advertisements, rather than evaluating its effects afterwards.

Various attempts have been made to analyse historical data with sophisticated statistical tools and other researchers have tried experimental methods. It is perhaps only in the case of people who place orders in response to advertisements, however, that one can be reasonably sure about its effectiveness in terms of producing sales.

DISCUSSION QUESTIONS

1. Explain the nature of advertising.

2. What kind of objectives might be set for advertising campaigns?

3. How might advertising be used along with the other elements of the communications mix?

4. Suggest why there is a need for creative advertising. How can this need be satisfied?

5. Explain the relationship between positioning and advertising strategy.

6. How might different advertising appeals be used in promoting motor cars?

7. What do you understand by the tone of an advertisement?

8. Explain the nature and interpretation of the advertising response curve.

9. Can you account for why the effect of advertising decays over time?

10. Outline the different approaches to how advertising budgets are put together.

11. Explain the role and functions of an advertising agency.

12. Compare and contrast the advantages and disadvantages of using newspaper, magazine, television, commercial radio, outdoor and cinema advertising.

13. Can you account for why expenditure on advertising varies considerably over a wide range of products and services?

14. What steps should be followed when media choice decisions are made?

15. How is the cost-effectiveness of advertising determined?

16. What is media scheduling and what is its purpose?

17. What are the constituents of advertising research?

18. Write notes on:
    (a) advertising content research
    (b) advertising media research.

19. How might advertising effectiveness in relation to sales be assessed?

REFERENCES

Applebaum, U. and Halliburton, C. (1993) International Advertising Campaigns: the example of the European food and beverage sector, *International Journal of Advertising*, **12**(3).

Biel, A. (1989) Love the advertisement, buy the product? *ADMAP*, October.

Brown, G. (1991a) Modelling advertising awareness, *ADMAP*, April.

Brown, G. (1991b) Big stable brands and advertisement effects, *ADMAP*, May.

Cole, T. (1994) BBH takes Audi back to TV, *Campaign*, 28 January, 8.

Kroeber-Riel, W. (1990) *Strategie and Technik der Werbung: Verhaltenwissenschaftliche Ansatze*, Kohlhammer, Stuttgart.

Kuehn, A.A. (1962) How advertising performance depends on other factors, *Journal of Advertising Research*, March, 2–10.

Marketing (1994) Making sense of the invisible to create the irresistible, 11 June, 32.

Mueller, B. (1987) Reflections of culture: an analysis of Japanese and American advertising appeals, *Journal of Advertising Research*, June–July, 51–9.

Palda, K.S. (1966) The hypothesis of a hierarchy of effects: A partial evaluation, *Journal of Marketing Research*, February.

Ray, M. (1982) *Advertising and Communication Management*, Prentice-Hall, Englewood Cliffs, N.J.

Stapel, J. (1990) Monitoring advertising performance, *ADMAP*, July/August.

Stapel, H. (1991) Like the advertisement but does it interest me? *ADMAP*, April.

FURTHER READING

Burnett, J.J. (1993) *Promotion Management*, Houghton Mifflin, Boston, Mass.

Douglas, T. (1988) *The Complete Guide to Advertising*, Macmillan, London.

Rossiter, J.R. and Percy, L. (1987) *Advertising and Promotion Management*, McGraw-Hill, New York.

Weilbacher, W.M. (1984) *Advertising*, Macmillan, New York.

CASE PROBLEM 14.1

NEW ZEALAND LAMB: EVALUATION OF A PROMOTIONAL THEME

Demand for various cuts of lamb depends on the time of the year. During the winter months necks and shoulders are popular for stews and casseroles. Legs sell particularly well at Christmas and Easter, when consumers are looking for roasting joints, though demand for these is fairly buoyant all year round. In the summer, chops and boneless loins are in demand, reflecting the seasonal swing towards cuts that can be used for barbecues. Boneless loin has the added appeal of being an economic alternative to sirloin steak. In addition, by adding a marinade to diced New Zealand lamb or chops, something different and exciting to include on the barbecue can be offered.

However, consumers are likely to change their buying patterns in preference for foods that are more readily available, if lamb is not kept in retailers' cabinets all year round. Following the GATT negotiations, there are higher annual imports to the EU of New Zealand lamb and this will ensure consistency of supply throughout the year. Having stocks available in itself is not sufficient, however; demand has to be actively stimulated. To ensure sales in shops, eye-catching point-of-sale and in-store promotions are crucial. In addition, it is important for retailers to be sensitive to their customers' requirements and to be able to adapt to changes in their buying patterns.

It was proposed that an advertising campaign would be mounted throughout the year along with a public relations campaign. The campaign would lend support to the advertising and underline its key message that the natural environment and green pastures of New Zealand produce tender lamb. In addition, brand exposure on radio, in the national press and the influential women's interest magazines would be created through a series of promotions and masterclasses.

(Source: The Grocer, *11 June, 1994, p.60)*

QUESTION

1. Evaluate the promotional theme produced by the New Zealand lamb producers.

CASE PROBLEM 14.2

DCG: EXPLORING THE MEANING A BRAND HAS IN CONSUMERS' LIVES

Mac Cato, chairman of advertising agency DCG, maintains consumers are increasingly making value judgements and purchase decisions based on highly emotional thinking and feelings. DCG searches for the invisible part of the brand to find out what triggers an emotional response. This is done with the aid of SENSE (an acronym for Sensory Exploration, Need State Evaluation). DCG explores the meaning a brand has in consumers' lives. Cato argues that we purchase many brands because they say something about us, and although the typical example is a car, it also applies to certain groceries.

The Gillette series 'the best a man can get', made use of DCG's research methods. Over a three-year period Gillettte and DCG focused on the essential personality of the brand to help maximize Gillette's marketing potential. DCG researched men's likes and dislikes in detail. This included their toys (things like cars, for example!); what sports they play; their hi-fi equipment and all other aspects of their life. DCG discussed bathroom rituals, and even filmed men's gestures and expressions while 'getting ready'. From their research, DCG were able to discern what men expect in a toiletries range. The steel and black look is reminiscent of a car; the grips of sports rackets and the blue offers refreshment of the senses.

(Source: Marketing, 1994)

QUESTION

1. How generalizable is the approach of DCG?

15 SELLING

In this chapter the role of selling in the marketing communications mix is considered. The different roles of the salesperson, the different kinds of selling situation that are to be found, and the different kinds of selling skills and strategies that are required are all examined. Consideration is also given to the various ways of providing incentives to sales staff, and to determining the right size of sales force and how it should be organized. Finally, telemarketing and direct selling are discussed.

OBJECTIVES

After studying this chapter you should be able to:

- appreciate how selling fits in as part of the marketing communications mix
- understand the nature of the different roles of the salesperson
- describe the different kinds of selling situations that are to be found
- appreciate the nature of the different kinds of selling skills and strategies that are required
- understand the various ways of providing a basis for sales staff to be motivated
- understand how sales managers can determine the size of the sales force and organize it in the most effective manner, particularly with respect to assigning people to territories
- appreciate the nature and advantages of telemarketing and direct selling.

INTRODUCTION

This chapter looks at selling within the communications mix, and how the weight given to selling varies with the type of product being marketed. The selling task is complex, and salespeople have different roles and tasks to perform – different selling situations exist, and these require different kinds of selling skills.

Selling effort has to be managed, and the chapter examines the ways in which a sales manager can provide a framework within which sales staff can be motivated in their work. The manager's job also includes organizing the sales force in an efficient manner.

Finally attention is given to telemarketing and direct selling.

SELLING IN THE MARKETING MIX

Selling involves:

- creating positive attitudes towards a product or service

- motivating people to want to purchase a product or service

- convincing people that they will be acting wisely if they do buy

- clinching a sale

- reassuring people that they have acted wisely in making a purchase.

Selling can influence any or all of the various stages in the purchase decision-making process. Earlier, we saw that advertising creates awareness, interest and desire, but only rarely produces action. Selling, too, can involve the first three stages, but it is most frequently associated with the action stage. Salespeople are often paid, at least in part, by results, and results inevitably means action in the form of purchase by the customer.

Selling is a face-to-face encounter with the customer. It is time-consuming, puts considerable emotional strain on the salesperson, and is a relatively slow way of influencing the purchase process. Where it is possible to achieve the same effect with other promotional tools, such as advertising, for example, selling will not be preferred, since it will be less cost-effective in terms of time and money. However, it is possible to use selling as a marketing communications tool in niche market situations where advertising would be wasteful. For example, there is a niche market which comprises people who like to shop at home, for one reason or another. Direct selling is involved when salespeople call on people in their own homes to sell them products which they might normally purchase at retail outlets in towns and cities.

The amount of marketing effort that firms put into personal selling varies according to the types of goods and services that are being sold. The magnitude of the effort often reflects the nature of the target market which is being addressed, though as pointed out above, there are exceptions to the rule. Industrial goods

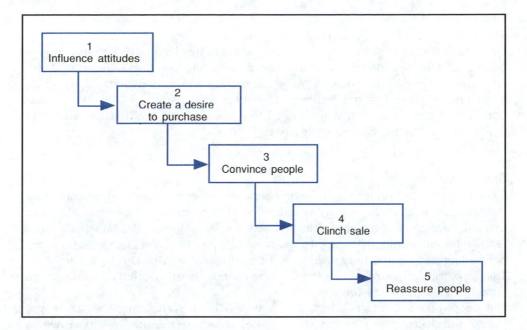

Figure 15.1 Steps in the selling process.

manufacturers put a greater financial emphasis on selling in the marketing mix, whereas large consumer goods producers tend to spend more on other forms of promotion.

THE TASK OF THE SALESPERSON

The selling task is influenced by the nature of what is being sold and to whom it is being sold – e.g. whether it is a consumer product, an industrial product or a service.

Consumer goods

Fast moving consumer goods salespeople often must negotiate with professional buyers who have responsibility for a large number of sales outlets. In such a situation, the retailer's buyer expects that the account manager will be very familiar with the retailer's operations. Large retailers, such as multiples, expect to be consulted in advance about manufacturers' new product plans, including pack and package design, and expect co-operation!

In addition to informing the buyer about new lines and persuading the buyer to stock quantities of the products, the salesperson has to persuade the retail management staff, with the aid of the buyer, to ensure that the product is stocked and displayed in an eye-catching manner at the point of sale.

Industrial goods

The selling task of an industrial goods salesperson is somewhat different. In this case the first task is to identify the people who are involved in the often complex process of purchase decision making, and then to find ways of influencing them. Sometimes the decision making may incorporate recommendations by outside consultants. Because of the technical and specialized nature of the selling situation, salespeople in such a market need to have the skills and the knowledge to negotiate with these kinds of specialists.

Services

Selling can be important in marketing services either to industrial or consumer markets. Because of the intangible nature of services, some people take the view that they are more difficult to sell. Products are tangible and the benefits can be readily demonstrated – this makes the selling task easier. With services, however, persuading people that they need or want a particular service can be a hard task. This is particularly so with services which do not seem to offer any immediate benefits, such as life assurance policies.

If people do not attach a high personal priority to something, they may well put off the decision to purchase, even if they recognize that it is a service which they need. Moreover, from the salesperson's point of view it may be difficult to relate long-term benefits to the cost of the service.

TYPES OF SELLING SITUATION

Not all selling situations are the same; correspondingly, the demands upon a salesperson vary considerably. These situations can be classified according to a number of different typologies (Enis, 1979).

- **Order takers and those who respond to requests** Some situations require salespeople who do little more than take orders or respond to requests. Sales assistants in shops, van salespeople and manufacturers' salespeople calling on the retail trade usually fall into this category, for instance in food, confectionery or soft drinks marketing, where salespeople simply check shops for their stock levels and take orders to replenish stocks whenever necessary. This kind of 'sales' job should not be confused with that of 'key account managers' who negotiate with retail managers at a very high level, discussing very large quantities, and very competitive terms and promotions.

- **Missionary salespeople** Missionary salespeople adopt a low-key approach and primarily seek to provide information and advice about a product. A good example is to be found in the selling of pharmaceutical products, where missionary salespeople call on general practitioners. It is unusual for these people to take orders. It is their job to create awareness so that the benefits of a specific product or service will eventually receive favourable consideration.

- **Technical salespeople** Technical sales representatives possess technical competence as well as selling skills. They offer technical advice to clients as well as helping to supply goods or services to meet their wants and needs. Technical salespeople abound in the marketing of industrial products, where technical knowledge of the product and the purposes for which it is to be used are of paramount importance.

- **Creative salespeople** Creative sales personnel have to actively persuade people to purchase. This is the most difficult job to do, since the customer may not actually be aware of the need for the product or service, or how it can satisfy their needs better than others that are currently available.

Although these different types of selling situation occur, one does find examples where a salesperson is expected to be a missionary, a technical expert and creative as well!

- Compiling a list of prospects

- Researching potential buyers/customers to identify needs, etc.

- Identifying benefits in which the customers are likely to be interested

- Examining and evaluating competitors' offerings

- Ascertaining the benefits the user would derive from using the product or service

- Planning sales interviews

- Arranging to visit a prospect's premises

- Travelling to the prospects premises

- Conducting a sales interview

- Recording an order

- Progressing an order back at the firm

- Reassuring customers that an order will be delivered on time

- Checking to make sure that when an order is delivered everything is as it should be

- Checking up some time later to ensure that no problems have arisen since the order was delivered

---

Figure 15.2 Stages of the selling process.

SELLING CHORES AND SKILLS

In view of the fact that there is a variety of types of selling situation, the selling skills and strategy that are required will vary. Except in the case of the order taker and those responding to requests (to whom the comments that follow in this chapter do not apply) the selling task is complex.

A salesperson will do many things as part of his or her job. For example, apart from clinching actual sales, salespeople have also to collect information on competitors' activities and identify any unfulfilled wants and needs that customers may have. The task of selling itself is divided into a number of stages (see Figure 15.2).

COMPETENCE REQUIREMENTS

Denny (1988) notes that there are six basic areas where a salesperson should be able to demonstrate competence.

- **Business knowledge** A person who is selling must be *au fait* with the overall climate of business and its environment. He or she must be able to talk to clients about marketing trends, changes in business climate and how national and international politics are influencing business. This means that the person has to keep up with current affairs in the newspapers and on television. Demonstrating this kind of knowledge to prospective customers helps to create an impression of competence.

- **Industry knowledge** Being informed about the industry in which one operates is an essential requirement. In particular, salespeople should be familiar with competitors' products, prices and positioning, and, as far as possible, any new developments in the pipeline. They should also be able to demonstrate awareness of other people and particular personalities within the industry. In addition they should know their competitors' main selling points and new product releases. This kind of knowledge is readily available in the trade press and can be obtained from societies, organizations and professional bodies in the industry; a lack of such knowledge may reduce personal credibility.

- **Company knowledge** It goes without saying that a representative of the firm should be well versed in company policy and scheduled events, particularly in the marketing area. They have to know the right people in their own organization and should have good departmental contacts. This kind of personal knowledge can be extremely useful in putting customers, actual or potential, into contact with the right people within the organization who can help them with specific problems.

- **Product knowledge** Prospects want to know all the 'ins and outs' of a product or service. They expect the sales representative to have all the relevant information at his or her finger-tips, or to be able to find out very quickly for them. Ignorance of the product or service means that the selling job will be more

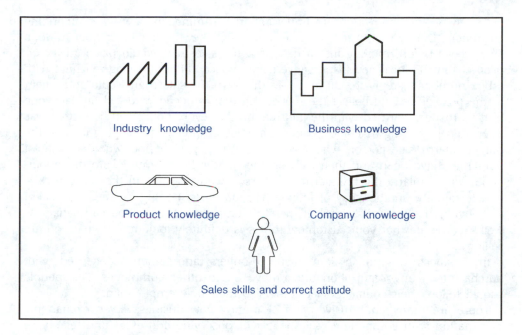

Figure 15.3 Competence skills of a salesperson.

difficult – it is hard to persuade people how the product will benefit them if you don't really understand what the product will do yourself. Again, a lack of this kind of knowledge will impair the credibility of the sales representative.

● **Sales skills** Selling is a skill that has to be learned. Sometimes we forget what we have learned, and the way we act suffers as a result. It is important that the salesperson constantly tries to remember those skills and that he or she exhibits a degree of professionalism in his or her approach to prospective customers.

● **Attitude** Having a positive attitude to everyone and everything is part of the job of selling. It reinforces the corporate image of the company and demonstrates that both are trying to act in everyone's interest.

OBTAINING BUSINESS

Finding new business is one of the prime aims of the salesperson (Thompson and Evans, 1969). There are a number of ways of setting about the task. A good start is to look at the past customer list. Selling to a person who has already bought from the company and who has been satisfied with the purchase is always easier than selling to someone who has never bought from the company before. One of the best sources of new business is to be found in the firm's customer base.

Creativity and innovation are important in dreaming up new ways of finding customers. Denny (1988) tell of a salesman selling sewing machines door to door. Two weeks before moving into a new area the salesman would place an advertisement in the local newspaper, advertising a second-hand sewing machine with a box number to reply to. On arrival in the town the salesman would go straight to the post office and collect the replies. He then proceeded to call on each one of the prospects, armed with the information that every household he visited was interested in sewing machines. Other examples of intelligent foraging include the burglar alarm salesperson who reads the local paper to find where the latest burglaries have been and then calls on the houses in the immediate neighbourhood, and similarly the fire alarm salesperson who operates in the same way.

Referrals are another way of finding new business. Having satisfied one client the obvious next step is to ask if there is someone else that you can satisfy as well – someone that your customers thinks is definitely looking for what you are selling.

In business or industrial marketing, buyers and others concerned with purchasing in an organization often move on to other companies. Salespeople should follow their contacts or customers to their new employment.

There are many unobtrusive ways of finding new business. Even exchanging information with competitors' salespeople or observing addresses and telephone numbers on delivery vehicles can be productive.

GETTING A SALES INTERVIEW

Here we are assuming that the salesperson is selling to another business – i.e. a retailer, wholesaler, manufacturer, etc. – and is making a first approach. The first step is to identify the contact in the target firm with whom to seek an interview. This can be done by telephoning the switchboard of the company and ascertaining who is responsible for making buying decisions. Having obtained this information the next step is to approach the person concerned, either in writing or over the telephone, with respect to an interview.

SALES INTERVIEWS

The sales interview is the focal point of selling. It is where the salesperson encounters the potential customer and tries to persuade the latter to buy the product or service.

Various people have suggested how a sales interview should be conducted. This is a relatively personal matter and much depends on the people and the situational factors which surround the sales interview. Personalities, experience and familiarity with the persons involved influence the outcome of the encounter. Getting the prospect to pay attention to what one has to say, promoting interest and then desire, and finally obtaining action, are key elements of the process.

There are certain guidelines which might be followed. We can summarize these as follows.

- Every sales presentation has to be different because no two prospects will ever be identical.

- A salesperson should set about selling herself or himself as a first step towards selling the product or service.

- Asking questions is the most important skill in selling. Armed with the answers to key questions, a sale can be more easily obtained.

- Listening carefully to what people have to say is another very important element in the selling process. It helps to identify key points in the customer's mind that need to be satisfied before a sale can be clinched.

- The features of a product should be linked to its benefits. Features can readily be seen and can often be demonstrated. Benefits on the other hand may be more obscure, and possibly not demonstrable. Building on what the customer can see and leading towards what he or she wants to know – the benefits – is the correct approach to take.

- Benefits are obtained as a result of using the product or service. When selling perfume one is selling attractiveness, when selling tickets for a boxing match one is selling the opportunity to play out one's inner emotions by identifying with the combatants.

- People do not necessarily buy for 'logical' reasons. Many decisions are made on the basis of emotions and not logic, and appeals to prospects which make use of this approach are often successful. One has to differentiate between when it is appropriate to use logical appeals and when emotional appeals are more appropriate.

- All businesses have unique selling points which establish their competitive advantage in the market place. Being able to communicate this to the prospect helps to win business in the face of strong competition. The unique selling points will be found in both the product and the company.

- Price is an important factor in gaining a sale, but it is not the only factor. It is the price/quality ratio which is important. Being able to demonstrate that the product gives good value for money is more important than actually being able to quote the lowest price.

- It is important not to 'knock' the competition, but on the other hand one should be able to show that one is concerned about the competition.

Along with the above guidelines there are a number of points to be borne in mind with respect to the conduct of the interview. In the first instance, sales interviews have more chance of success if objectives are established for each call and a plan of how to achieve these objectives is laid out. As with other forms of communication, the AIDA model clearly has applicability in this case. The salesperson has to get the prospect's attention, arouse interest in what he or she has to say and then move on to desire and action with respect to buying or ordering the product.

CASE EXAMPLE

RETAIL SELLING: SELLING WHITE GOODS

Jack and Jill Hill wished to purchase a new dishwasher, so they visited a local white goods retailer. After waiting patiently for ten minutes they managed to find someone to ask about dishwashers.

'Good morning' said Jack, to a smartly dressed sales assistant.

'Indeed – I hope it stays that way.'

'We want to buy a dishwasher.' Jill spoke in a firm voice, knowing what in principle she wanted to do, but hiding beneath that firmness was lack of certainty as to exactly which model she would prefer.

'Yes, there are six very good models over there.' The assistant wafted his hand in a south-westerly direction, looking more like a policeman on casual traffic duty than a salesman keen to help a client with an important problem.

'Yes, we know,' John replied, 'But we're not sure which one we ought to buy.'

'Well, that's up to you really. they're all pretty much of a muchness. And they do all have good guarantees.'

'Yes, but they all have different prices,' Jill said with some surprise. 'Why is that?'

'Different brands,' the assistant said. 'Like cigarettes, some are just more expensive than others.'

'Yes, but surely dishwashers are not quite the same thing as cigarettes? There must be some substantial differences among the various models, given the wide variation in price?' Jack asked, incredulously.

'Oh, I don't think so. They are manufactured in different countries and I guess some cost more to produce than others. The price simply reflects this, I think. They all wash dishes and we give the same guarantee with them all. The white one over there is popular with people. We have sold several of those.' The salesman pointed to one with a middle of the range price tag attached to it.

'I see,' said Jack. 'Well perhaps we'll shop around a bit first and come back to you again in due course.'

'See you then' the assistant said, and promptly disappeared into the back of the shop.

QUESTION

1. Analyse the above encounter, indicating where the retailer could have provided more help to the prospective customers.

It must always be borne in mind that it is not a product or service that is being offered for sale, but a set of benefits. It is these benefits which interest the customer, rather than the features of the product or service itself. Having a knowledge of how the product will benefit the customer is extremely important. Three types of benefits can be demonstrated:

- those that arise from the product itself
- those that arise from it being offered by the salesperson's company
- those that differentiate it from competitors' products

Benefits satisfy felt needs; the salesperson has to identify these needs and indicate to the prospect how the product or service will satisfy them. For example, a prospective purchaser of a dishwasher may have a felt need for 'something which is compact and easy to operate'. If the dishwasher is compact then the salesperson can stress that it is relatively small and will fit into most modern kitchens very easily.

DEALING WITH OBJECTIONS RAISED IN SALES INTERVIEWS

In the course of a sales interview a prospect often raises objections when a need for the product or service on offer is not perceived. The objections may relate to price, delivery schedule or certain products or company characteristics. Objections are met by the salesperson:

- keeping a positive approach
- requesting clarification of the the objection
- putting the prospect in the position where he or she has to answer his or her own objections
- objecting to the objection
- making the objection a reason for buying.

Keeping a positive approach
'I don't have any need for that.'
'Of course, and that is what many of our clients say until they appreciate what it can do for them. Would you like a demonstration?'

Requesting clarification
'Plastic components, you say? No, they would not be strong enough.'
'I see. Perhaps you could give me some examples so that I can refer them back to our technical people for their advice?'

Answering objections

'We've done it that way before and couldn't get it to work.'

'You'd better tell me exactly what you did and then perhaps we can see what went wrong.'

Objecting to objections

'I can't believe that it really will do what you say it will do.'

'Look – here are reports of it being used by the 4M international engineering conglomerate.'

Making the objection a reason for buying

'I really think the price is too much.'

'Well that of course is because it is better than inferior competitive products.'

CLOSING A SALE

The sale is 'closed' when an order is obtained. A good approach is to attempt trial closures throughout the length of the sales interview. Positive cues denoting interest or desire on the part of the prospect should be followed up with an attempt to close the sale.

Attempting to close a sale

Sales assistant talking to young woman:

'Many women like yourself prefer this particular model.'

'Yes, this brooch is pretty and will match a number of my outfits well. It's very nice.'

'All these brooches have special safety chains. Did you notice?'

'No, I didn't notice that. That is good. It makes it a good buy.'

'We can offer it to you on good terms if you would like, madam. Would you like me to get you the details? It doesn't take long to fill in the form.'

A final sale will only be obtained if the salesperson asks for an order.

WHY SALES INTERVIEWS CAN FAIL TO PRODUCE RESULTS

There are many reasons why a sales interview may not produce results.

There may be too many interruptions so that both the salesperson and the prospect tend to lose track of what the sales argument is all about. Under these circumstances it may be preferable to terminate the interview early, suggesting that another call is made at a less busy time.

The salesperson may talk about features of the product instead of its benefits. This is a basic flaw in selling technique and can be prevented by adequate training.

The sales argument may have nothing new in it and the prospect may have heard it all before. To get the interest of a prospect it is important to inject something new into the sales argument.

The prospect may not be given the opportunity to say whether he or she fully understands the sales argument. Continuing in these circumstances is futile. Interpersonal communication often produces misunderstandings and a message has often to be repeated in several ways before its recipient really understands what is being communicated. The selling situation is no different.

The sales pitch may be over the prospect's head – usually this means it is too technical, or too difficult to understand. This can often occur when the salesperson mistakenly keeps talking about product features and loses the prospect in a stream of jargon. The answer is KISS – keep it simple, stupid (but not so simple so that the prospect feels if he or she is being talked down to).

The sales presentation may lack enthusiasm. If the salesperson does not show some enthusiasm for the product or service he or she is selling, then it is difficult to expect the prospect to show any enthusiasm. Indeed, in the art of selling the idea is to sell oneself in the first instance, which must mean that enthusiasm has to be displayed.

A prospect's objections to the sales argument presents problems to which only rather superficial answers are given. As a result, the objections remain unanswered and a sale does not therefore ensue. Objections and problems must be dealt with effectively.

A salesperson may irritate the prospect by disagreeing with him or her personally, instead of citing the opinions or the experiences of third parties. Selling oneself as part of the process gets one personally involved in the situation. However, having gained the confidence of the respondent, one has to take a detached view of the prospect's objections and not express one's personal views on the matter.

Many prospects enjoy the opportunity to argue with a salesperson, seeing the encounter as a form of gamesmanship. Sometimes the salesperson is unable to distinguish phoney objections from genuine ones. Failure to do this, of course, can lead to a loss of credibility on the part of the salesperson and thence to a lost sale.

When selling to businesses or industry, the salesperson may fail to identify the true decision maker and present the sales argument to a person who cannot make or even influence the decision. This demonstrates a lack of diligence on the part of the salesperson. Researching the prospect is a critical element of the selling process.

All salespeople should be familiar with the products they sell. Moreover, they must put themselves in a position where they are familiar with how the product benefits the prospect. A lack of knowledge on the part of the salesperson, regarding how the benefits of the product or service would meet the needs of the prospect, usually leads to a lost sale.

A salesperson **must** ask for a sale. Many prospects will not voluntarily agree to buy, but persistence can reap rewards. Nevertheless, the novice or inexperienced salesperson may give up too readily after the first 'no'. What has to be realized is that a prospect may say 'no' but really mean 'maybe'. The salesperson has to try more than once to ascertain if this in fact is not the case.

A salesperson may talk too much and fail, in so doing, to gain an accurate impression of the prospect's attitude. A lack of interest may too easily be discerned when in fact there is no such lack of interest.

Finally, if the salesperson does not believe that a sale can be achieved from the outset, then there is a risk of a self-fulfilling prophecy. A sale will not be made.

A company often employs a substantial number of salespeople and they have to be managed and given motivation to do their jobs. In the next section we will look at the role of management in selling.

MANAGING A SALES FORCE

Co-ordination, organizing and control are the main activities in managing a sales force. This involves agreeing and setting targets for the sales force and arranging provision of the resources that the sales force will require to successfully pursue its targets. Sales managers can only be successful if they recognize that they themselves are no longer selling, but are teaching and leading other salespersons. The sales manager has to develop the selling skills of his or her sales staff.

SALES COMPENSATION AND MOTIVATION

People have different ideas of what they consider important in a job. Many people consider interesting work, where they are able to make the best use of their skills, to be important. Other important matters are job security, convenient working hours and good pay. Clearly, much depends upon the particular circumstances of an individual and the good manager has to be able to identify the key motivating factors for the people he or she manages (O'Hara, Boles and Johnson, 1991; Cron, Dubinsky and Michaels, 1988).

Financial compensation

More or less everyone will accept that financial reward is a prime motivator to work (Pradeep and Block, 1983). This may be slightly modified by accepting the principle that for some people there may not be any motivation to earn more than a certain amount of money.

Some firms pay their sales staff on a salary only basis, while other firms have more elaborate schemes involving both a basic salary and an incentive payment. Salary-only schemes are most commonly found where there is little persuasion involved in the sales job – e.g. order-taking. This kind of system offers no positive reinforcements to really good sales staff, since they are not provided with better benefits than the weaker sales staff.

In contrast, there are situations where people are compensated on a commission-only basis. Such an approach seems appropriate where there is a lot of creative selling. Here financial rewards are related directly to achievement. This is useful where the entire selling role is to achieve a sale and nothing more than that.

Where technical advice and assistance are required the compensation system has limitations since the salesperson, having obtained a sale, is really only motivated to move on to the next prospect.

The above are two extremes, in between which there is a whole range of selling situations where some form of commission and salary are appropriate. This is particularly the case in selling industrial products where a technical salesperson is employed who can provide advice to the customer with respect to using the product.

There are other forms of motivation than money; these are discussed below.

Opportunity for advancement

A job promotion policy can be used to motivate salespeople to do a good job. While not everyone wants to be promoted, for some people promotion prospects are a very important factor.

Personal status

Providing someone with a special job title may well affect the way he or she performs. Many people, for example, relish manager status. Some organizations use the titles 'executive' and 'manager' so freely that the terms have quite different connotations to what is customarily associated with them. The genuine value of such organizational nomenclature within the firm is doubtful, since everyone knows their relative importance, but it certainly enhances the status of the individual when dealing with customers and clients.

Job security

Security of tenure is not a hallmark of selling. Job security, however, is important in motivating personnel. There is always an improvement in performance when a person is not immediately concerned with the fear of losing his or her job.

Positive feedback on performance

Telling a salesperson that he or she is doing a worthwhile job is important. Selling can involve a lot of rejection from potential customers on whom unsuccessful calls have been made. Continual refusals and rejections can be demoralizing so firm support from the sales manager is beneficial.

Other incentives

There are other motivating factors. These include such things as giving salespeople personal authority when it comes to dealing with customers and permitting staff some degree of autonomy. People do not like to be told what they should do and how they should do it. In addition, people like to feel that they are receiving fair and personal treatment.

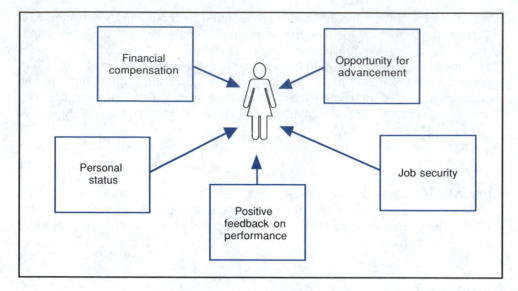

Figure 15.4 Some major factors that motivate salespeople.

Discipline

There is a whole range of penalties or sanctions that can be used as a basis for motivation. Discipline involves setting minimum standards of performance and establishing appropriate penalties for failure to attain them. Penalties can range from private warnings to public reprimands with the ultimate penalty for breaking a rule being termination of employment.

Discipline in selling tends to be the exception rather than the rule, but it is advisable to establish the managerial prerogative of using negative incentives when necessary. Discipline is required for good morale; failure to enforce it can jeopardize an entire marketing operation.

DETERMINING THE SIZE OF THE SALES FORCE

Another key decision-making area for sales management concerns the size of the sales force. In this instance we are considering a sales force which makes contact with other organizations. We are not examining the case where sales staff are working as sales assistants in shops.

It is expensive to maintain a large sales force, on account of the high salaries that have to be paid and sizeable expense accounts. There are many approaches to determining the best size of a sales force; one such approach is to estimate the extent of the selling task and divide this task by the amount that a single salesperson can handle.

For example, assume a firm sells to both end users and retailers and that there are 2000 end-users and 400 retailers. Assume also that the requirement is for the necessary number of salespeople to make 12 calls on each of the end-users and 24 calls on each of the retailers in the course of a single year.

We need to have some idea of the number of calls that an average salesperson can make in a single year. Suppose we estimate from past experience that this amounts to 600 calls per year. We can then use a simple formula to find the best number of salespersons:

$$N = 1/K \times [F1(C1) + F2(C2)]$$

where N = desired number of salespeople
Fn = call frequency required for a given customer class
Cn = number of customers in a given class
K = average number of calls a salesperson can make during a year

In this case it works out to be:

$$N = 1/600 \times [12(2000) + 24(400)]$$

$$= 56$$

CHANGING THE SIZE OF THE SALES FORCE

Sales managers need to make adjustments to the size of their sales force from time to time. The general principle is that if one decides to do without a salesperson then it is to be expected that the total sales will diminish, as will selling expenses. If one decides to hire an additional salesperson then the salesperson has to contribute more in gross margin than he or she will cost. Of course, if a salesperson is not replaced and the cost that is saved exceeds the gross margin, then the company is better off with fewer salespeople.

Consider the situation where a firm employs 20 salespeople and its selling costs are £500 000. Suppose also that its salespeople produce £1 000 000 in gross profit contribution. Imagine that one of the sales staff has decided to leave the company. The sales manager has a number of options. He or she can:

● decide not to replace the salesperson who is leaving (this reduces the sales force to 19)

● hire one person to replace the one who is leaving (keeping the sales force size at 20)

● hire more than one person (increasing the size of the sales force to more than 20 staff).

The sales manager also produces estimates of how much gross profit contribution will be produced by 19, 20, 21, 22, and 23 salespeople respectively.

The figures show that hiring two people is most beneficial. Initially, if one replacement is not made then gross margin will drop by £60 000 while a saving of only

Marginal approach to changing the size of the sales force

No. of sales people	Profit contribution		Selling cost	
	Total	Marginal	Total	Marginal
19	940 000		475 000	
		60 000		25 000
20	1 000 000		500 000	
		50 000		25 000
21	1 050 000		525 000	
		30 000		25 000
22	1 080 000		550 000	
		20 000		25 000
23	1 100 000		575 000	

£25 000 will be achieved. Taking on additional people over and above the replacement is worthwhile. Hiring two people including the replacement will increase profit by £30 000. The hiring of a further person will **not** increase total profit, since although profit contribution will rise, the cost of the additional salesperson is greater than the additional profit generated (£25 000 > £20 000).

SALES FORCE ORGANIZATION

Sales teams can be organized along one of several lines. The organization can be based on product lines whereby some salespeople and their respective managers are responsible for one part of the product line, while another group of salespeople are in charge of other products. This method of organization is common when a company serves two or more types of customers, for example consumer and industrial markets.

A sales force may also be organized along geographic lines. In this case the sales manager manages a territory; this works well in companies with short or homogeneous product lines, or where extreme market segmentation is not encountered. However, where a territory incorporates several different types of industries, it may not be possible for the salesperson to be familiar with the special needs of each. This often leads to the assignment of salespeople on a customer or market basis, where one group of people deals with one type of client while another group handles others. Customers may even be divided on the basis of size where large and small customers tend to demand different services. Another basis for assignment can be the level or type of customer. Here, we would expect to find different salespeople calling on manufacturing wholesale and retail accounts.

It is quite possible to find various combinations of these methods of sales organizations.

ASSIGNING SALESPEOPLE TO SALES TERRITORIES OR SALES TERRITORIES TO PEOPLE

A firm may choose to develop its territories around its salespeople. This is often done when there is a small sales force. For example, if a firm has 30 salespeople, it can proceed in one of two ways.

Either:

1. First, the manager determines approximately how many territories the sales force can handle effectively (based on geographic size of the territory and the number of potential customers in the territory). Let us assume this to be 30 territories. Then the manager divides the total market into this number of geographical areas – i.e. 30 areas.

Or

2. The manager determines the optimum size of territory for a single salesperson (based on geographic size of the territory and the number of potential customers in the territory).

   The manager then divides the total market by the optimum size of territory for a single salesperson. This may produce more territories than there are salespeople – e.g. 35 territories. The manager then sets out the territories in order of attractiveness to the firm and assigns people to the territories at the head of the list.

Employing the first approach can result in a thin coverage of the market, while in the second case a lack of representation may occur. This is a dilemma that all sales managers face. While assigning too large an area to a sales representative means that fewer calls can be made, on the other hand not covering some markets will lose sales. However, it may then be possible to develop the other markets intensively. It has to be recognized, however, that not covering part of a market may allow competitors to establish a foothold, with serious long-term consequences.

DETERMINING THE SIZE OF TERRITORIES

Territories should be about equal – both in terms of sales potential and in terms of difficulty of servicing. This makes it easier to compare the performance of individual salespeople. In addition, the morale of sales staff is improved, since complaints and requests to renegotiate over territorial assignments are minimized.

Achieving equality in terms of potential and workload is hard. Since customers are unevenly distributed it is inevitable that there will be pockets of high potential concentration which will favour one salesperson over others. For instance, a single customer in the Greater London area may have as much business potential for a product or service as one who serves the whole of Wales. There is no ready solution to this problem – it has to be solved by compromise. For example, a single large customer may be handled by the sales manager as a 'house account'. Alternatively, someone who is asked to cover a very large area may be paid a more attractive salary.

SETTING OBJECTIVES FOR SALES STAFF

Quantitative sales objectives should be derived from the sales plan, which is a sub-plan of the marketing plan. This will stipulate the kind of objectives shown in Figure 15.5.

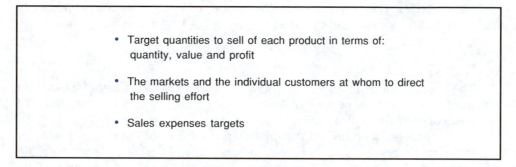

- Target quantities to sell of each product in terms of: quantity, value and profit

- The markets and the individual customers at whom to direct the selling effort

- Sales expenses targets

Figure 15.5 Objectives that are set for salespeople.

Sales staff should be encouraged to keep to the targets which have been set and not to oversell one product at the expense of another. If this were to happen then it might well be that the firm would be unable to meet the demand for particular products, while carrying unsold stocks of other products. To exceed target on a particular product may create as many problems as underselling on another.

Other quantitative objectives which can be set include targets for:

- point of sale displays
- letters written to prospects
- telephone calls to prospects
- sales reports produced
- trade meetings attended.

It may also be possible to set qualitative targets/objectives, though it might be more difficult to assess how well these have been pursued. For example, assessing how well a sales interview has been conducted is not easy because of the many situational variables involved. However, a salesperson's product knowledge, or how well he or she plans out his or her work are easier to evaluate.

SALES SUPPORT STAFF

The task of the sales representative goes beyond selling, involving such activities as drawing up a list of contacts, etc.

However, there is no doubt that there are considerable benefits to be gained from having marketing staff and sales office staff working alongside the sales team. Indeed, lists of possible contacts and sales leads can easily be identified by the back-up team, and this can increase the effectiveness of the sales operation.

TELEMARKETING AND DIRECT SELLING

In this section we look at two rapidly developing areas of marketing in which selling features prominently – telemarketing and direct selling.

TELEMARKETING

Telephone selling is not a new innovation. In fact, it has been around for many years. Although it tended to be used by sellers of financial services and insurance in the first instance, today it is used by providers of a large variety of products and services. While it is a more economical way of approaching prospects than personal selling, as a means of interpersonal communication the telephone suffers from several limitations.

CASE EXAMPLE

ITS: TELEMARKETING

ITS was set up to run the first TV-advertised, big money telephone quiz game, Telemillion. To enable Telemillion to operate, research undertaken indicated there would be a need to handle 2000 or more calls simultaneously. ITS entered the market having the biggest automatic call-handling capacity in Europe, being able to take nearly 2300 calls simultaneously, or up to 750 000 a day.

Nigel Linacre, ITS marketing director, envisaged three main activities for the business: direct response television advertising, sales promotions and charity appeals. TV shopping was another distinct possibility.

(*Source:* Marketing, *3 February 1994, p.21*)

QUESTION

1. How would you envisage ITS's future services being operationalized?

People are often influenced by non-verbal cues when interacting with others. These are clearly absent when using the telephone. Nevertheless, the proof of its usefulness as a selling method is to be found in its take-up rate amongst users. At the present time this still appears to be increasing.

A recent innovation in telemarketing has been the advent of the freephone service. Here, instead of firms making personal calls to prospects, prospects are encouraged through advertising to find out more about a product or service by using a freephone service. This method at least goes part way to reducing the wastage rate in unsuccessful sales calls, since by and large it will only be used by interested people. It is open to abuse, however, and a potential target for commercial vandals. Some idea of the use of telemarketing can be obtained from the case example on the previous page.

DIRECT SELLING

One of the oldest methods of marketing goods and services is through direct selling. With the advent of mass media communications, merchandising and super-stores, it began to take a somewhat background role, at least as far as consumer goods selling was concerned. In recent years, however, it has experienced some-thing of a comeback, and is now a developing area of marketing.

Many people dislike crowded shops and shopping precincts, preferring to shop at leisure from their own homes. In addition, despite the fact that large retail supermarkets and hypermarkets, not to speak of sophisticated shopping conglom-erations, abound in urban areas, many people live in rural areas and do not have easy access to such facilities.

Direct selling provides service at the point of sale. It can be argued that it is the change in retail patterns away from local retailers that has led to customer choice being stifled and less innovative products being sold. Direct selling promises to redress this shortcoming through the provision of personal service and innov-ative products which can be offered through catalogues.

Direct selling is remarkably resistant to changing economic cycles, and is a proactive approach to retailing. It is particularly attractive to customers who may be old or infirm, or who live in rural districts. Essentially it amounts to relation-ship marketing. Anything that is bought from a department store can be bought from a direct selling company: cosmetics, fashionwear, jewellery, accessories, toys, household products, kitchenware, books – all are products that benefit from being demonstrated in the home or place of work.

Direct selling needs efficient distribution and management because of the costs involved. It can involve selling one to one, or to a group (party selling). The choice of strategy is dictated by the nature of the product.

SUMMARY

Selling plays an important role within the marketing communications mix. It influ-ences attitudes towards a product or service, moves people towards a desire to purchase a product or service, and tries to convince people that it is the right decision to make. Selling is concerned with actually getting people to take the purchasing step, and reassuring the person that he or she has made the right decision.

A salesperson carries out a number of different roles. The nature of the role varies according to the type of products being sold and the kind of selling situation. Some products and situations, such as are found in selling industrial products, require a good deal of technical product knowledge as well as persuasive skills. In some cases when dealing with retail buyers, knowledge of the buyers' business activities and problems is essential.

While there are no clear-cut ways concerning how best to hold a sales interview, there are guidelines which can help in developing different kinds of selling skills and strategies.

Selling involves getting marketing communications across to an audience with the aid of people. People have to be motivated to do well. Sales managers have to be aware of the ways in which staff can become motivated and need to provide the basis for this to happen.

Sales managers have certain other functions to carry out. These include determining the best size of sales force, and organizing it in the most effective manner, particularly with respect to assigning people to territories.

Telemarketing is an area which, despite apparent limitations, is increasing in importance as an element within the communications mix.

Direct selling has undergone a resurgence in recent years and involves one-to-one selling, or selling to a group of people in the home or in the workplace. While costs have to be carefully controlled to make it an efficient and effective method, it is considered particularly useful for introducing new products.

DISCUSSION QUESTIONS

1. Discuss how selling fits in as part of the marketing communications mix. What particular marketing communications tasks is selling most suited to perform?

2. 'A salesperson has many different roles to perform.' Discuss this statement.

3. There are different kinds of selling situations. What are the factors that produce these different situations and what implications do the situations have for the salesperson?

4. What are selling skills and strategies? Give examples.

5. Not everyone is motivated to work hard for the same reasons. How can a sales manager take account of this when trying to provide a basis for sales staff to be motivated?

6. How can sales managers determine the best size of sales force to employ?

7. What factors should be taken into account when organizing a sales force in the most effective manner, particularly with respect to assigning people to territories?

8. What are the advantages of telemarketing?

9. Why should there have been a recent resurgence of interest in direct selling and what special advantages does it have to offer?

REFERENCES

Cron, W.L., Dubinsky, A.J. and Michaels, R.E. (1988) The influence of career stages on components of salesperson motivation, *Journal of Marketing*, January, 78–92.

Denny, R. (1988) *Selling to Win*, Kogan Page, London.

Enis, B.M. (1979) *Personal Selling: Foundations, Process and Management*, Goodyear, Santa Monica, Calif.

O'Hara, B.S., Boles, J.S. and Johnson, M.W. (1991) The influence of personal variables on salesperson selling orientation, *Journal of Personal Selling and Sales Management*, Winter, 61–8.

Pradeep, K.T. and Block, C.E. (1983) Monetary incentive and salesmen performance, *Industrial Marketing Management*, October, 263–70.

Thompson, J.W. and Evans, W.W. (1969) Behavioural approach to industrial selling, *Harvard Business Review*, **47**, March–April, 69–83.

FURTHER READING

Abratt, R. and Smythe, M.R. (1989) A survey of sales incentive programs, *Industrial Marketing Management*, August, 209–14.

Mercer, D. (1988) *The Sales Professional*, Kogan Page, London.

Pederson, C.A., Wright, M.D. and Weitz, B.A. (1986) *Selling: Principles and Methods*, Irwin, Homewood, Ill.

Wotruba, T.R. (1978) *Sales Management: Planning Accomplishment and Evaluation*, Holt, Rinehart and Winston, New York.

CASE PROBLEM 15.1

LEMON COMPUTERS: NEW TRAINING IN COMPUTER SELLING

Lemon Computers is planning to introduce a new sales training programme. It will consist of four weeks of classroom training. The aim of the course is to make salespeople more knowledgeable about all products and to improve their selling skills. Training includes learning the steps of gaining a sale:

● gathering information on customers

● evaluating potential customers

● getting an interview

- presenting concepts

- demonstration of hardware/software

- advising on the required system configuration

- closing the sale

- installing the equipment and training the customer.

It is thought that if 90 % of attenders experience increased sales after training, the programme will have been successful.

QUESTION

1. Comment on the sales training strategy.

CASE PROBLEM 15.2

MELON GROUP: DIRECT SELLING FOR TELEPHONES

Vacuum cleaners were seen as modern wonders of the world when they first arrived on the scene. They helped to take the drudgery out of life and free up considerable time for the housewife. It was common to find them being sold door to door in the 1950s and early 1960s. The usual pitch employed by a door-to-door salesman was:

'Excuse me, Madam, but how would you like to have a lot more time to do the things that you enjoy doing most?'

To which the usual reply was:

'Very much indeed.'

Allowing the salesman to answer:

'If you can spare me ten minutes of your time I can show you just how this can be achieved.'

Not surprisingly, many housewives were suitably impressed by this message and invited the salesman into their homes. Anyone who has had to remove dirt, dust and other materials from carpets with the aid of a brush and shovel will appreciate the miracle of the vacuum cleaner. Direct selling is a good way of getting new products into the homes of consumers. This is particularly the case where the benefits of a product can be demonstrated.

Of course there are many products which could in theory be sold direct to people in their own homes. One idea currently being considered by the

Melon Group is to sell telephone and related equipment in this way. James Price the managing director feels that the firm should recruit and train a sales force to sell direct to members of the public in their own homes. The firm is considering the possibility of marketing a range of telephones, from handheld portables to fax machines and answering machines.

James Price argues that the consumer is more likely to move through the stages of attention, interest, desire and action if he or she has the opportunity to discuss and study the product at leisure and in a relaxed manner in their own homes or even in their place of work. The idea he puts forward involves selling with the aid of a special catalogue.

'What we have to do,' he says 'is to identify opinion leaders in the community who can spread good word of mouth communication about the products we want to sell. Good starting points will be places of work.

'Clearly the different products will be of interest to a wide variety of people, so we have to find a method which will be effective in reaching the whole of the target market. So who is the target? Well this depends largely on the product. In the case of handhelds this is executives, in the main, but for answering machines then almost anyone is a potential user.

'Now identifying the opinion leaders is a more difficult problem and getting executives to run a club seems impossible. However there must be an innovative way of approaching the problem.'

QUESTIONS

1. Do you agree with the definition offered of the target market?

2. Do you think telephone equipment can be sold by direct selling methods as outlined above?

3. What action do you think the firm should take?

16 SALES PROMOTION AND OTHER METHODS

This chapter considers the nature, purpose and role of sales promotion within the marketing communications mix. How organizations make use of public relations in marketing communications is then discussed, together with the nature and importance of direct marketing, direct mail, directories and exhibitions. Finally, the growth in sponsorship and how it helps both the sponsor and the organization being sponsored is examined.

OBJECTIVES

After studying this chapter you should be able to:

- understand the nature, purpose and role of sales promotion within the marketing communications mix, and describe the various mechanisms used in sales promotion

- understand the nature and role of public relations and in particular how organizations can make use of public relations in marketing communications

- appreciate the nature and importance of direct marketing, direct mail, directories and exhibitions and the growth in sponsorship.

INTRODUCTION

This chapter provides an introduction to a number of different promotional methods other than selling and advertising.

Sales promotion – its nature, purpose and role within the marketing communications mix – is considered. In comparison with other marketing mix variables, sales promotion has become an increasingly more popular promotional tool. The reasons for this are explored here. Sales promotion makes use of a variety of promotional mechanisms, which are described in some detail. It takes on two forms in the case of firms marketing goods: it may be directed at consumers, or it may be directed at salespeople and resellers in the trade.

Public relations is an important weapon which can be effectively employed in marketing communications. As is the case with sales promotion, it comprises a variety of tools – for example, publicity, institutional advertising, lobbying, and the use of company journals and magazines.

Another rapidly developing marketing communications method is direct marketing, and this also is explored in this chapter, together with the use of direct mail and the role played by directories in the marketing communications mix.

The use of exhibitions is next explored, before finally attention is given to the growth in sponsorship and how it helps both the sponsor and the organization being sponsored

Sales promotion

At one time sales promotion was considered to be all that is left over after taking account of advertising, personal selling and public relations. Nowadays, however, the American Marketing Association (1988, p.16) defines it as:

> media and nonmedia marketing pressure applied for a predetermined, limited period of time in order to stimulate trial, increase consumer demand, or improve product quality.

Sales promotion has grown rapidly in terms of importance in recent years, the stimulation for growth coming from both consumers and business. Sales promotion offers consumers the chance to get more than they expected and at the same time reduces the risk associated with buying. For example, product sampling affords consumers the opportunity to try a product without actually buying it. Moreover, in terms of providing motivation to purchase, an extra discount or rebate means that the consumer is more likely to buy a product.

The evolution of sales promotion has been stimulated by business. Many product managers find it difficult to differentiate their product in a real way from that of their competitors; sales promotion methods enable product managers to achieve this end. Every time we need to visit the petrol station to fill up our car's tank of petrol we are enticed to visit one or other station because of special promotions that are being offered – free air travel mileage, redeemable tokens which we can eventually exchange for goods, or even drinking glasses. We may in fact not perceive or be conscious of any differences between the brands of petrol at the different filling stations, but we can differentiate in terms of the kinds of promotions that are being offered. One promotion may have more appeal than another, and we may purchase the product from that source because of the promotion.

From management's point of view, sales promotions often provide exactly what is most required: an immediate boost in sales. New life, albeit temporary, can be pumped into ailing brands by dropping coupons in the mail.

At a more general level, the use of sales promotion has been stimulated by factors that have adversely affected advertising – such as the high costs of mass media advertising. In addition, retailers, working on small profit margins and needing the increased sales volume generated through sales promotion, have encouraged the growth of sales promotion.

The severest criticism of sales promotion is that it diminishes the value of the brand. The move from brand-building advertising to trade promotions and couponing, critics argue, can lead to consumers who view all products as commodities. Other critics say that the management of sales promotion over a long period of time is fraught with difficulties. Many sales promotion tools are short run, tactical devices. Coupons, premiums and contests, for example, set out to produce immediate responses.

Whereas advertising provides reasons why a customer should buy a product or service, sales promotion provides the incentive to buy. It can take many forms (see Figure 16.1).

Some of these apply to sales promotion to consumers, and others to sales promotion to the trade. First we will look at sales promotion to consumers.

Figure 16.1 Types of sales promotions.

SALES PROMOTION TO CONSUMERS

It has been found that decisions to purchase brands of many consumer goods are actually made in the shop where goods are displayed. Point of sale selling aids are therefore key elements in the sales promotion process. The job of sales promotion in retail consumer markets is a significant one, and sales promotions are often carried out by teams of sales merchandisers in stores.

We will now look at some of these in more detail.

Consumer sampling

Getting the customer to try out the product is one of the keys to making it successful. This can be achieved through consumer sampling, whereby the product is given to the consumer free or for a small fee.

Sampling should really only be used as a technique when the product sells itself. The product must possess benefits or features that are easily discerned by the consumer. In addition the consumer should be given enough of the product to enable him or her to accurately judge the quality of the product. Products that are sampled tend to be low in price and to have a high turnover, but, of course, it is possible to sample more expensive products.

Samples are often distributed door to door by organizations that specialize in providing this kind of service. Products can also be sampled directly through the retailer, who sets up a display unit near the product or hires a person to give it out to consumers as they pass by.

Sampling appears to help marketers get to grips with the problem of getting consumers to notice their product, particularly a new one, when speed of trial is often the most important ingredient in the brand's success. On the other hand, sampling costs may be excessive, and measuring its effectiveness is not easy. Another major difficulty concerns a product's suitability for sampling. A sample will only convince a customer to buy the product if the product is unique or of an exceptionally high quality.

Price deals

There are four different types of price deal: price discounts, price pack deals, refunds and coupons.

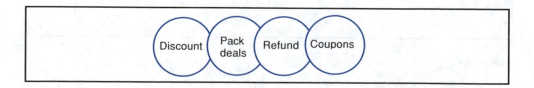

Figure 16.2   Price deals.

- **Price discounts**   Customers are informed of price discounts either through advertising or at the point of sale. Advertising mechanisms include flyers, newspaper and TV ads. At the point of sale, the price reduction may be indicated on the package or on signs near the product or in shop windows. Price discounts are found typically in the food industry, where 15% to 20% off the regular price is the normal practice. Price discounts by themselves do not encourage people to buy for the first time, but may cause existing customers to buy in larger quantities. Since up to half of purchase decisions are unplanned, a price discount may prompt people to buy when they did not expect to do so.

- **Price pack deals**   These take one of two forms: a bonus pack or a banded pack. Where a bonus pack is offered an additional quantity of the product is given away free when the standard product is purchased at the regular price. It is a method which is often used in promoting sales of cleaning products, foods, and health and beauty aids. When two or more units of a product are sold at a reduced price compared to the regular single-unit price, a banded pack offer is made. Usually, the products are offered in multiple format, or a smaller size of the product may be attached to the regular size.

- **Refunds**   A refund is an offer to give back money when the product is purchased alone or along with other products. It is used to increase the quantity or frequency of purchase and to stimulate the purchase of postponable goods (e.g. major appliances). Unlike price discounts, it is suggested that refunds are considered by customers to be rewards for purchases and this tends to build brand loyalty (Haugh, 1980).

  Refunds should be as uncomplicated and as unrestricting as possible. Good ideas include a cash rebate plus a low value coupon for the same product or another company product, or a high value coupon alone.

- **Coupons**   Coupons are legal certificates offered by manufacturers and retailers that grant specified savings on selected products when presented for redemption at the point of purchase. Coupons appeal to customers who are price-sensitive. Research indicates that the tendency to use coupons increases when consumers tighten their budgets, when they like to experiment with new products, and when applied to products that are purchased at regular intervals throughout the year. Coupons have the ability to attract new triers and brand switchers, and to maintain or enhance repeat purchase rates (Blattberg and Neslin, 1990). Moreover, when coupons are used there is an opportunity for the marketer to achieve optimum co-ordination with other promotional activities.

Competitions, contests and sweepstakes

Contests and sweepstakes generate a great deal of interest and excitement. A good contest can gain a good deal of customer involvement, revitalize a poor sales record, help displays and merchandising at the retail level, add to advertising themes and create enthusiasm and interest in a low interest product.

CASE EXAMPLE

GAYMER: USING COUPONS IN SALES PROMOTION

Finding a way of appealing to a younger audience when a firm is traditionally associated with an older audience is a challenge. Gaymer's Olde English cider possessed an image of appeal to older gentlemen, but Gaymer wished to appeal to younger men aged 25–44.

The first step was to choose a medium through which to address the target group. Commercial radio was thought to be appropriate, and Capital Gold was chosen, its core listeners being in the over-25 age bracket. In addition to using radio, in the summer of 1992 Gaymer employed a targeted mail drop which both supported the radio communication and provided trial use. It also provided a means of evaluating the campaign's success.

It was Gaymer's intention not just to boost awareness but to get the new group of customers to try its product. Some 300 000 households within the station's listening area were involved in the mail drop. The promotion comprised a leaflet containing a money-off coupon that also explained how to enter a competition on Capital Gold.

As a first step, households with men aged 25–44 within the designated area were identified. Next, the TGI (Target Group Index) was used to discover which of these households were regular or heavy drinkers of competitive cider products. Lastly, Checkout, a database which provides information about where consumers shop, was employed to reduce the number to those within a certain distance of grocers which sold Olde English.

The promotion proved remarkably successful and redemptions of the coupon were nearly four times the industry average. At the same time, Olde English's market share went from 1.5% to 4%.

(*Source:* Marketing, *27 January 1994, p.24)*

QUESTION

1. What other kinds of products could be promoted in a similar fashion?

CASE EXAMPLE

MCVITIE'S FOOD SERVICE: SALES PROMOTION

Using snooker as a theme, cash and carry and delivery wholesalers are taking part in a 16-week sales promotion for McVitie's Food Service, starting in April. The promotion involves having customers match a playing card with a playing grid. The cards appear in special promotional packs of Crawford's Minipacks, Sweet Assortment, Biscuits for Cheese and Rover, as well as in McVitie's All Butter Shortbread, Digestives and Mini Cheddars. Should a card reveal a winning combination of snooker balls, the customer can obtain one of a wide range of sports prizes.

(Source: The Grocer, *12 February 1994, p.25)*

QUESTION

1. What do you see as the advantages and disadvantages of this particular promotion?

Contests require participants to compete for a prize or prizes on the basis of some sort of skill or ability. This contrasts with sweepstakes where one only has to supply a name and address.

Some people, however, maintain that contests and sweepstakes can generate more ill will than goodwill, suggesting that losers may become opinion leaders against the company.

Premium offers

Getting an extra amount of a product is a premium, as is receiving free glasses with petrol. Companies usually choose premiums that tie in with their product or that appeal to their most obvious customers.

Premiums may be used to attract people to a particular shop, or to stimulate purchase of large amounts of a product. Marketers look at premiums as a way of rewarding customers without actually cutting prices. Premiums are regarded as a true value added item and are tending to replace refunds and couponing.

Continuity programmes

Rather than one-off premiums, firms may prefer to run continuity programmes. The idea here is to hang on to a brand user for a long time by offering ongoing incentives. This requires customers to keep saving something before they actually obtain the premium. In the past, trading stamps were good examples of this.

Petrol gift tokens fulfil a similar role. Continuity programmes provide differentiation and are effective in combating a new and threatening competitor by offering established customers a reward for their loyalty.

To be successful, a continuity programme must offer something which reflects a thorough understanding of customers and their motivation. There is also the need to evaluate the benefits of maintaining loyalty versus the costs.

Leafleting

Door-to-door leafleting and providing free samples can be a cheap and effective way of communicating with prospects. Leaflets can be distributed by the post office or inserted in free newspapers. Alternatively, people can be hired to deliver leaflets on foot.

Research seems to indicate that leaflets are in fact read by recipients and are often considered to be interesting. Free samples delivered through the letter box are also well received.

Having looked at sales promotion methods to consumers, we will now go on to look at sales promotion methods to the trade.

SALES PROMOTION TO SALESPEOPLE AND RESELLERS

Sales promotion can be a very important communications mix tool which facilitates getting new products into stores, gaining shelf space, and motivating intermediaries and sales personnel.

Sales force sales promotions

Promotion activities directed at the sales force are intended to motivate sales-people to increase overall sales. The short-term goals may include signing up new dealers, promoting sales of new or seasonal items, communicating special deals to retailers, increasing order size, and reducing sales expense. Often such activities are aimed as much at raising the morale of the sales force as at creating sales.

Sales promotions directed at the sales force are classified into two categories. The first comprises programmes that prepare sales people to do their jobs. These programmes include sales manuals, training programmes and sales presentations, as well as films, slides and other visual aids. The second set comprise promotional efforts that motivate people to work harder. In the latter case, prizes or awards form the core of the incentive programmes.

Trade promotions

Objectives of promotions aimed at the trade try to accomplish four overall goals:

1. To develop in-store merchandising support or other trade support. Retail support can take the form of featuring a special price on advertisements or signs, point-of-sale materials, or superior store locations for the product – usually shelf space.

2. To increase or deplete inventory levels and to eliminate peaks and troughs which characterize seasonal sales. Increases are of course desirable when a product is introduced, or at the start of a special promotion. Depletion is desirable at the end of a promotion or the end of a season, or when a product is being deleted.

3. To open up new areas or classes, or to gain distribution for new sizes of the product. Keeping and gaining shelf space is the critical objective.

4. To generate excitement about the product among those responsible for selling it.

There is a wide range of promotional devices that can be used to motivate channel members to support a product. These include point of purchase displays, contests, trade shows, sales meetings, trade coupons and trade deals.

PUBLIC RELATIONS

Public relations presents stories about an organization to its various publics. It involves the use of information and communication of that information through a variety of media to influence public opinion. Public relations is not a modern innovation – its practice can be traced back to antiquity. Counsellors, heralds,

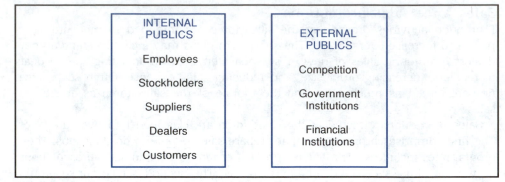

INTERNAL
PUBLICS

Employees

Stockholders

Suppliers

Dealers

Customers

EXTERNAL
PUBLICS

Competition

Government
Institutions

Financial
Institutions

Figure 16.3 Some examples of an organization's internal and external publics.

bards and even court artists sometimes assumed the functions later ascribed to public relations (Burnett, 1993, p.413). Indeed the first serious outflow of public relations was in the field of religion and concerned literate people in the 15th and 16th centuries.

In any organization, a public relations unit is responsible for creating and maintaining a positive and beneficial corporate image with both the company's internal and external environments. Public relations must be sensitive to two types of public: internal and external.

The internal public of an organization is the people with whom it normally communicates in the ordinary routine of work. The usual internal publics in industry are employees, stockholders, suppliers, dealers and customers.

The external public is the people with whom an organization communicates, without having close associations. Forces in the external environment are able to influence a company's operations. The source of the influence may be competitors, government institutions, financial institutions, economic forces, political pressure, ethical considerations, and sociocultural or technological change. All of these represent 'publics' to an organization.

An organization has to deal with its various publics in such a way as to give the impression that it is acting in the best interests of them all. The public relations function in a firm strives to help the organization develop and maintain a climate or environment which is favourably disposed towards its operations.

Public relations activities include:

● identifying specific interest groups and how they are likely to influence the activities of the organization

● providing advice to management about what is happening with respect to its various publics

● product publicity

● media relations, whereby efforts are made to put forward newsworthy information about the firm in the public eyes. This can be used to attract public attention to a particular product, service, activity or enterprise

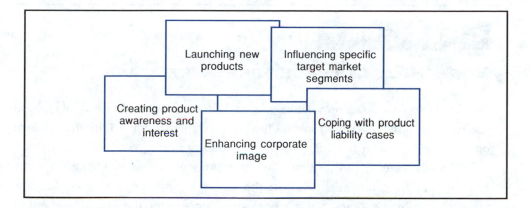

Figure 16.4 Tools for marketing public relations.

- corporate communications which concentrate on creating awareness, understanding and positive attitudes towards the organization itself

- lobbying legislators, influential government officials or professional bodies over matters that have direct consequences for the organization.

Some firms have used public relations as an effective marketing tool and as a cheaper and more effective option to advertising. In this respect PR can be very effective in terms of:

- creating product awareness and interest

- launching new products

- influencing specific target market segments

- coping with cases which involve product liability

- enhancing corporate image.

Next we will look at some of the tools of public relations in more detail.

PUBLICITY

Most publicity is delivered in the form of a news release or press release. A news release is produced in a style which is acceptable to the media for which it is intended. Press conferences are another way of achieving publicity. Press conferences can be very searching, so the organization has to be prepared to answer all the questions that might be asked at such a meeting.

CASE EXAMPLE

EDGE HILL COLLEGE: PRESS RELEASE

Donald McIntyre, Reader in Education at Oxford University, is to meet local teachers and other experts from the field of teacher training at Edge Hill College on 25 June to launch the College's professional mentoring centre.

Dr Anne Proctor, Head of Junior Teaching programmes at Edge Hill, says the scheme has great potential and that the mentoring system is one of the best ways of combining practical classroom experience with the sound theoretical knowledge students gain at college.

Mentoring entails trainee teachers receiving individual tuition in developing their classroom skills during the course of teaching practice. An experimental scheme has been in operation between Edge Hill and local secondary schools since last September and the college is now hoping to extend it to all the teacher training courses. Students receive personal guidance from teachers who have been specially trained as mentors by the college. The new scheme is intended to give student teachers the chance to learn directly from the experience of qualified school teachers.

(*Source:* Ormskirk Advertiser, *23 June 1994*).

QUESTIONS

1. Rewrite the above as a press release.

2. What do you think is its prime purpose?

INSTITUTIONAL ADVERTISING

Sometimes called corporate advertising, or public relations advertising, unlike publicity, institutional advertising is paid for by the sponsor, which enables the sponsor to tell the story when the sponsor chooses and to the audience it selects. In this case the appearance of the advertising is exactly the way the advertiser wants it to appear. Unfortunately, this form of advertising is often interpreted by an audience in an unfavourable way and audience resistance may be raised. Audiences are apt to see it as paid pleading. Many critics believe that institutional advertising is in fact ineffective – however, this yet remains to be shown empirically.

There are several reasons why a firm may indulge in this form of promotion. A company may want the advertising to create confidence in the company that will help to sell its products.

Alternatively, a company may want to explain the management's stand on a key issue, for instance a disastrous product. Another objective might be to put forward the company's philosophy about government, politics or other aspects of society.

COMPANY JOURNALS AND MAGAZINES

Many companies produce in-house journals or magazines. They often enjoy a wide circulation, and in addition to people within the firm they may also reach customers or potential customers. Their objectives include selling company products, informing readers of product uses, and creating general prestige, good-will and understanding. Since these publications enjoy such a wide readership they should be friendly, reliable, and frank.

LOBBYING

Lobbying is an area of some sensitivity, and it requires a low pressure strategy, personal contact, and thorough knowledge of the industry. Some public relations practitioners become professional lobbyists, generally representing a particular industry or special interest group.

An example of successful lobbying was that reported in *The Grocer*, 14 May, 1994. The report indicated that MPs had voted to allow off-licensing between 12.30 pm and 10 pm on Sundays in supermarkets, grocers and off-licences in Scotland. This followed a two-year campaign by independents, multiples, co-ops and suppliers.

OTHER PROMOTIONAL METHODS

DIRECT MARKETING

Direct marketing involves cutting out the wholesaler and the retailer from the sales distribution chain. Mail order, direct mail and party plan selling are all examples of direct marketing. Use is made of the post, the telephone and direct response advertising to establish contact with potential customers. It presents a method of marketing goods to both private individuals and businesses alike.

Direct marketing has become the major area of growth in the world of personal computers, where more and more companies have come on the scene, offering better support, more technical knowledge, and better and cheaper products than the established dealers and channels have been able to offer.

Mail order

We look at mail order again in chapter 17. Here, we will simply remind ourselves of the familiar large mail order catalogues which have become a feature of everyday life. In more recent years there has been a rise in the number of small specialist catalogues which focus upon a particular area – fashion, gifts, etc. Mail order is carried out in the comfort of people's own homes, and payment for goods can be made on credit.

Direct mail

Direct mail comprises personalized sales letters sent out to individual prospects. People using direct mail can buy lists of mailing prospects from companies who compile them, or alternatively they can put together their own mailing lists. Mailing lists are kept in large databases and must be regularly updated. The usefulness of such a database is clearly defined by how up to date it is.

Because of the time and effort necessary to maintain a good quality mailing list it is becoming more common to rent a mailing list. Indeed, some mail order firms may never even see their mailing list – everything is sent to an independent mailing house which attaches labels to envolopes which the firm supplies. This approach reduces the risk of the mailing list being copied, and it is much cheaper than actually purchasing a list. BRAD, for example, have a directory containing more than 3000 business and consumer mailing lists which are available for rental.

Party plan selling

In the previous chapter, we looked at direct selling. Party plan, which is also called 'shopping at home', is another name for direct selling.

DIRECTORIES

Directories can be of enormous help to marketers. It is often the case that they contain unique information about an industry, sector or market, or alternatively information which would be very difficult to come by elsewhere.

In the case of the computing industry a reader would need to study dozens of different magazines to collect all the information contained in a single directory. In a year, a single magazine might deal with perhaps 500 products, whereas a directory can list 16 000 plus suppliers. When purchasing a directory the payment is not so much for the book, or CD-ROM, as the case may be, but for up-to-date research.

Directories provide companies with the opportunity to present themselves to highly targeted and specialized audiences, often for free. The importance of directories as an advertising medium, particularly for small businesses, should not be underestimated. TV, national press and radio are important for some firms, but the bulk of companies use directories, direct mail and local press. Users normally regard directories as serious and trustworthy works of reference. While

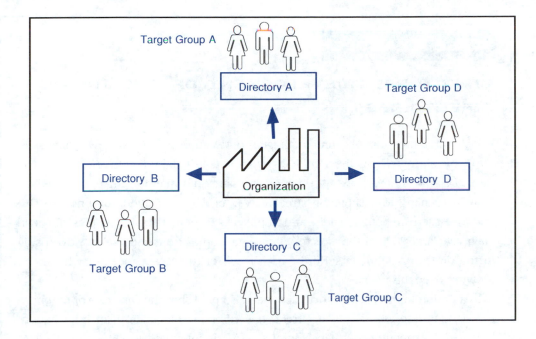

Figure 16.5 Directories facilitate addressing specific segments of target markets.

directories in book format allow little scope for creativity in artwork, CD-ROM facilitates moving pictures and even interactive advertisements. For example, when advertising computer software on CD-ROM, demonstrations are possible.

EXHIBITIONS

An exhibition is the public showing of facts and features relating to a product or service. Exhibitions can be manned or unmanned, and have the advantage of bringing trained and experienced sales personnel into contact with potential buyers, as well as making technical experts available to the customer. Exhibitions are widely used by producers of industrial products and also by suppliers of a wide range of consumer durable goods.

Travelling exhibitions or roadshows have been used by a number of different marketers. They have the benefits of static exhibitions but can be brought to a variety of locations. For example, in 1994 the Health Education Authority arranged a travelling roadshow which visited cities around the country providing computerized dietary analyses, cookery demonstrations, tastings and information (*Marketing*, 3 February 1994, p.10).

DIRECTORIES: DEVELOPMENT OF ELECTRONIC DIRECTORIES

A fashion clothes manufacturer managed to pull in over £1m of new business in 1993 by simply using the *Retail Directory*, published by Newman Books. The *Retail Directory*, now in its 49th edition, contains information ranging from who's who in retailing to a shopping street survey of prime locations around the UK, and is aimed at both retailers and suppliers. Several thousand copies are sold each year and 90% of the directory's revenue comes from copy sales. Advertising in the directory, although suffering as a result of the recent recession, has been growing over the years.

In addition to the UK directory, Newman also publishes the *Directory of European Retailers,* in line with a growing trend towards publishing European information. Moreover, competitor Maclean Hunter's BRAD is intending to launch a CD-ROM in March incorporating both European and UK data. There is constant demand for additional information. People want more than just raw data, they want the directory to do more work for them. In 1994 BRAD relaunched its main directory incorporating a new emphasis on its monthly frequency, in the hope of encouraging subscribers to update each month. One of the few directories with a high frequency, it was recently launched on-line, with automatic updates on a daily basis.

(Source: Marketing, *1994a)*

QUESTION

1. Consider the potential of electronic directories. How do you see them developing in the future?

SPONSORSHIP

This is the supporting or subsidizing of some activity with hard cash in return for publicity and/or free exposure in the media. Sporting events and sporting personalities predominate in the kind of activities that receive sponsorship. In 1994, for example, two food industry firms agreed to back the 1994 Vauxhall Cup Tennis Tournament – Onken Dairy and NutraSweet. In addition, a number of UK meat companies sponsored a 350-mile bicycle endurance test in 1994.

IPC AT HOME: USE OF EXHIBITIONS

IPC is matching Associated Newspapers' Ideal Home Exhibition with its own exhibition. The two exhibitions will be six months apart, but At Home will be on a much smaller scale. The Ideal Home Exhibition attracted 560 000 people in 1993 over 26 days. At Home is hoping to attract 65 000 people over six days.

Some £1m. will be spent on promotional activity around the event, including a sales brochure, advertising and PR. In addition, the At Home event is be promoted in relevant IPC magazines; titles such as *Ideal Home, Homes and Ideas, Homes & Gardens* and *Country Homes & Interiors* will be brought to life through the exhibition. IPC has linked up with the Independent Event Company to launch At Home, which will encompass all facets of furnishing, cookery and gardening. The purpose behind the exhibition is to build on IPC's magazine brands by enhancing relationships with advertisers and readers.

(Source: Marketing, *1994b)*

QUESTION

1. Evaluate IPC's strategy in this instance.

From the point of view of the sponsor there is a general benefit in being able to keep the company's name in the eye of the public who follow the event or personality receiving sponsorship. From the point of view of efficient target marketing, however, its effectiveness as a medium is less obvious. In addition to sponsoring sports events and personalities the arts also receive sponsorship.

SUMMARY

Sales promotion has grown rapidly in terms of importance in recent years. It offers consumers the chance to get more than they expected and at the same time reduces the risk associated with buying. The evolution of sales promotion has been stimulated by business. Many product managers find it difficult to differentiate their product in a real way from that of their competitors, and sales promotion methods enable product managers to achieve this end. It provides exactly what is most required: an immediate boost in sales. New life, albeit temporary, can be pumped into ailing brands. The use of sales promotion has been stimulated by factors such as the high cost of mass media advertising. In addition, retailers working on small profit margins and needing the increased sales volume have encouraged the growth of sales promotion. Sales promotion can take many forms including free samples, price deals, coupons, free gifts, and competitions.

Public relations is the use of information and communication of that information through a variety of media to influence public opinion. It has to be sensitive to two types of public: internal and external. The internal public is the people with whom the organization normally communicates in the ordinary routine of work. The external public is the people with whom an organization communicates but does not have close associations.

Some firms have used public relations as an effective marketing tool and as a cheaper and more effective option to advertising. In this respect PR can be very effective in terms of creating product awareness and interest, launching new products, influencing specific target market segments, coping with cases which involve product liability and enhancing corporate image.

Direct mail comprises personalized sales letters sent out to individual prospects. People using direct mail can buy lists of mailing prospects from companies who compile them; alternatively they can put together their own mailing lists. Mailing lists are kept in large databases and are regularly updated.

Directories often contain unique information about an industry, sector or market, or alternatively information which would be very difficult to come by elsewhere. Directories also provide companies with the opportunity to present themselves to highly targeted and specialized audiences, often for free. The importance of directories as an advertising medium, particularly for small businesses, should not be underestimated. TV, national press and radio are important for some firms, but the bulk of companies use directories, direct mail and local press. Users regard them as serious and trustworthy works of reference.

While directories in book format allow little scope for creativity in artwork, CD-ROM can incorporate moving pictures or even interactive advertisements. For example, when advertising computer software on CD-ROM, demonstrations are possible.

An exhibition is the showing of facts and features relating to a product or service in public. Exhibitions can be manned or unmanned, and have the advantage of being able to bring trained and experience sales personnel into contact with potential buyers, as well as providing a means of making technical experts available to the customer. Exhibitions are widely used by producers of industrial products and also by suppliers of a wide range of consumer durable goods.

Sponsorship amounts to supporting or subsidizing an activity with hard cash in return for publicity and/or free exposure in the media. Sporting events and sporting personalities predominate in the kind of activities that receive sponsorship.

From the point of view of the sponsor there is a general benefit in being able to keep the company's name in the eye of the public who follow the event or personality being sponsored. From the point of view of efficient target marketing, however, its effectiveness as a medium is less obvious. In addition to sponsoring sports events and personalities, the arts also receive sponsorship.

DISCUSSION QUESTIONS

1. Define sales promotion and discuss the role it plays in the marketing communications mix.

2. What factors do you think account for the growth in terms of importance of sales promotion in recent years?

3. What do you consider to be the benefits of sales promotion as far as the customer is concerned?

4. What benefits do you think the marketer gains from using sales promotion?

5. Discuss some of the forms that sales promotion can take.

6. How would you define public relations?

7. What are the two main kinds of public that public relations has to address?

8. It can be argued that some firms have used public relations as an effective marketing tool and as a cheaper and more effective option to advertising. Discuss.

9. Discuss the role of direct mail in the marketing communications mix.

10. Evaluate the usefulness of directories to companies.

11. What do you consider to be the purpose of exhibitions?

12. A relatively new promotional tool is sponsorship. Discuss the benefits that might accrue to both sponsors and organizations receiving sponsorship.

REFERENCES

American Marketing Association (1988) *Marketing definitions: A glossary of marketing terms*, AMA, Chicago, Ill.

Berry, S. (1994) Scottish ensemble keeps the BT, *Insider*, **11**(6), 12–14.

Blattberg, R.C. and Neslin, S.A. (1990) *Sales Promotion: Concepts, Methods and Strategies*, Prentice Hall, Englewood Cliffs, N.J.

Burnett, J.J. (1993) *Promotion Management*, Houghton Miflin, Boston, Mass.

Haugh, L.J. (1980) Cash refunds multiply, *Advertising Age*, 5 May, 48.

Marketing (1994a) Directories and their role in the business world, 27 January, 30.

Marketing (1994b) IPC challenges the Ideal Home, 3 February, 9.

FURTHER READING

Cutlip, S.M., Center, A.H. and Broom, G.L. (1985) *Effective Public Relations*, Prentice Hall, Englewood Cliffs, N.J.

Rapp, S. and Collins, T. (1990) *The Great Marketing Turnaround*, Prentice-Hall, Englewood Cliffs, N.J.

CASE PROBLEM 16.1

BT SCOTTISH ENSEMBLE: SPONSORSHIP

The Scottish Ensemble is now the BT Scottish Ensemble and in return for funding of £70 000 a year this is a title it must keep for another two years. Some people saw the agreement as over-restrictive and a move towards the 'piper playing the tune', but in fact under the agreement the ensemble has to do around 10% extra programming and can set up other sponsorship deals. It could be that these kinds of arrangement will set a new pattern for future arts sponsorship, particularly as public sector support (both through the Arts Council and the regional councils) continues to decline.

The ensemble has benefited from the agreement in that its image has been raised as a result of expensive new promotional literature provided at a below-the-line cost. In addition, the ensemble can also call on BT Scotland's PR and Marketing department.

BT received the first big payback for its investment during Easter week, when the Ensemble performed James MacMillan's *Seven Last Words from the Cross* nightly on BBC2. Arts sponsors dream of this variety of media coverage, but don't receive it very often since reviewers and arts promoters are still reticent about mentioning sponsorship support.

At the present time BT business subscribers in Scotland can listen to the BTSE playing when they are put on hold by a BT operator. Among the current proposals are a promotional phonecard featuring the Ensemble and a proposal to present invited audience members with autographed scores of new works.

(Source: Berry, 1994)

QUESTIONS

1. How might BT evaluate the return it has obtained from supporting the Ensemble?

2. How might the Ensemble evaluate the value of the sponsorship it has received?

3. Do you think that sponsorship could be applied to museums, art galleries, historic monuments, and the like? Why, or why not?

CASE PROBLEM 16.2

CONSUMER BANK: DATABASES IN MARKETING

Consumer Bank will contain information on more than 40 million people. The new database will use electoral roll data as well as information from CMT's National Shopper Survey (NSS) and from sister company NDL's Lifestyle Selector. CMT is to extend its National Shopper Survey programme, with additional surveys conducted throughout the year. The NSS is distributed annually to millions of households and gathers consumer data on 4 million households. Information obtained includes details of which brands they use, how often they purchase and use them, plus demographics, lifestyles and attitudes.

(Source: Marketing Week, *28 January 1994, p.31)*

QUESTION

Suggest ways in which such data can be used by the survey's sponsors to decide how they should be approaching existing and potential customers.

17 DISTRIBUTION

This chapter considers the various channels of distribution and their characteristics, along with strategic decisions relating to distribution. How producers can assist or motivate intermediaries to promote goods is discussed, along with the various elements that go into making up a physical distribution system. Finally, the nature of the logistics concept is explored, together with how this can lead to maximising overall efficiency and effectiveness.

OBJECTIVES

After studying this chapter you should be able to:

- distinguish the various channels of distribution and their characteristics
- appreciate the nature of distribution decisions that have to be taken
- understand the various ways in which producers can assist or motivate intermediaries to promote goods
- outline the various elements that go into making up a physical distribution system
- understand the nature of the logistics concept and how this can lead to maximizing overall efficiency and effectiveness.

INTRODUCTION

Distribution is customarily referred to as the element of 'place' in the 'four Ps' of the Marketing Mix. It involves activities and decisions concerned with the transfer of goods from the producer to the customer. The physical aspects of this are referred to as 'physical distribution', and the strategic dimensions are known as channel management. Physical distribution includes warehousing, transportation and inventory management. Channel management, on the other hand, concerns choice of suitable middlemen to act as intermediaries in the distribution process.

The chapter outlines the various channels of distribution by which firms can reach the market – direct, through wholesalers and retailers, through agents and distributors, etc. and indicates the nature of different kinds of wholesale and retail establishments and the functions they perform. Attention is then given to the nature and advantages of franchising as a specific distribution strategy.

The chapter goes on to consider the various channel decisions that have to be taken, and looks at the various ways in which producers can assist or motivate intermediaries to promote goods and services on their behalf. Following this, attention is given to the evolving nature of distribution channels.

Attention is then focused upon the physical distribution system and the various elements that it comprises. The impact that good inventory management can have on profitability, and the importance of understanding the relationship between inventory management and customer service, are emphasised. Transportation has a strong impact on distribution strategy, and attention is given to evaluation of different transportation methods.

The chapter concludes by examining the nature of the logistics concept and how this can lead to maximizing overall efficiency and effectiveness.

CHANNELS OF DISTRIBUTION AND CHANNEL DECISIONS

In the case of marketing services, providers either use agents/brokers or deal directly with customers. Producers of goods, on the other hand, have different methods at their disposal. These are outlined below:

PRODUCER–CUSTOMER

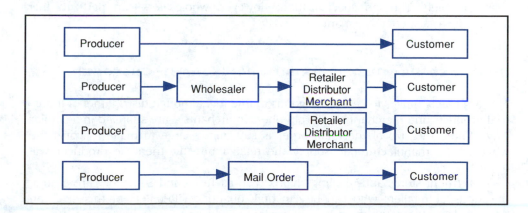

Figure 17.1 Different channels of distribution.

All goods, in theory, may be distributed direct to customers. It is commonplace to find many industrial goods distributed in this manner, but it is less frequently encountered in the case of consumer goods. Where industrial goods are involved, the financial value of the order can make it economical for the producer to deliver direct to the customer. Mainframe computer manufacturers, for example distribute direct to customers. This does not necessarily mean that the producer will have its own fleet of transportation vehicles – specialist delivery firms may provide this service. Indeed, as far as distribution is concerned, firms only take on those activities which they consider to be an economic proposition.

As we saw earlier in the book, there has been a growth in direct marketing. Many different types of consumer goods can be supplied direct to customers – encyclopedias, cosmetics and vacuum cleaners are well-known examples of products that are distributed in this fashion. In these instances the producer has chosen to carry out all, or most of the various aspects of physical distribution. Through specialization and experience, the producer is able to perform the function as well as an intermediary would.

Mail order is a way of both selling and distributing direct to customers. A wide variety of consumer goods are distributed in this way and a producer which specializes in this method can become very efficient and effective.

PRODUCER–WHOLESALER–RETAILER–CUSTOMER

This is a popular method of achieving distribution for goods and is characteristic of much of consumer product marketing. The producer supplies to a wholesaler, who in turn supplies a retailer. The retailer then makes the goods available to the customer.

Consumer goods producers use this method when seeking to make goods available through a large number of small retail outlets which may be dispersed geographically. In such a case, probably it would not be cost effective to supply directly to such a large number of retailers. Orders would tend to be small and would also tend to be placed relatively frequently. The costs would therefore be relatively high. Through specialization, however, wholesalers can perform this activity in a cost-effective manner.

PRODUCER–RETAILER/DISTRIBUTOR/MERCHANT–CUSTOMER

This approach applies to consumer goods marketing, although distributors of industrial products and merchants – e.g. plumbers' merchants – are supplied in a similar way. Where the size of the retail order is sufficiently large to make it worth the while of the manufacturer to supply the retailer directly, then the producer will do so.

Department stores and retailing chains such as Tesco and Sainsbury are among the kinds of retailers who can buy in bulk quantities. Retailers of this size can buy goods at the same price as wholesalers would pay. The wholesaler's margin

CASE EXAMPLE

CATALOGUES: GROWTH OF UPMARKET CATALOGUES

Not only the specialist clothing market is turning to mail order, but also producers of a wide range of other goods. Expensive collectable goods (such as designer plates and miniature models), DIY, crafts, business-to-business goods, computers, specialist goods and even food are now being marketed through catalogues.

UK mail-order catalogue business was at one time associated in people's minds with cheap goods and uncertain quality. Indeed, premium merchandisers would not consider distributing goods to consumers through this medium, in case they were associated with a low-quality image. However, in 1987 high street retailer Next became involved in catalogue selling, adding credibility to the mail order business and capitalizing on its own already successful operations. There was already consumer familiarity with the quality of Next's products and styles, and people were easily persuaded to believe the same quality could be distributed through mail order.

Prior to the entry of Next, the market had been dominated by Great Universal Stores, Littlewoods, Freemans, Grattan and Empire. These five companies still control 85% of the UK mail order business, but because they appeal to the down-market buyer, they are not well considered by the premium purchaser. Two quality household catalogues were in the market before Next – Scotcade and Innovations – but no one built on their success. Those that followed Next included Racing Green and Land's End. The latter is a US mail order business that has done well in the UK market, having had the benefit of a substantial promotional budget to help it with its task.

(Source: Marketing, 1994)

QUESTION

1. Why do you think mail order shopping as a mode of distribution has only recently started to appeal to up-market producers?

can then be partially passed on to customers, in the form of lower prices. Large retailers, however, incur higher costs as a result of carrying out the wholesaler's function – e.g. carrying higher stocks which requires additional storage and display space. Higher stocks also tie up a retailer's cash and prevent it from being put to more profitable use.

Large retailers operate on high volume sales and this enables them to achieve satisfactory profits with lower profit margins. The net effect of all these factors is often lower prices to the customer than would have been the case if wholesalers and small retailers had been involved in the distribution chain.

Producers can, of course, use any or a combination of the three methods outlined to distribute their product.

TYPES OF DISTRIBUTOR

Having looked at the different ways in which distribution to the market can be achieved, we will look in more detail at the characteristics of the channel members.

Wholesalers

Wholesalers buy in bulk from producers and sell in small quantities to retailers. They specialize in a class of goods, for instance fish, vegetables, newspapers, etc. Some operate from central markets while others maintain warehouses and employ representatives.

Brokers

Brokers perform a similar function to wholesalers except that they do not hold stock. Brokers operate in commodity markets such as metals and tea. They are also to be found selling insurance and financial services, and deal with share transactions on the stock exchange. There are also food brokers.

No two brokers offer exactly the same service. While they all sell on behalf of clients, what makes them different from agents or importers is the facilities that they offer. Brokers can perform selling and marketing functions at a lower cost than a manufacturer can usually do in-house. They have contacts with retail buyers, can be flexible, are able to tailor their services to the needs of clients, and have expertise and contacts in many areas.

Retailers

Consumer goods distribution was traditionally carried out by middlemen or wholesalers who broke up supplies into smaller lots and shipped them off to hundreds of small retailers. The wholesaler provided an important function of breaking bulk and holding stock. Wholesalers maintained their own sales forces, and because they specialized as distributors were able to perform the task much more cheaply than a producer.

Over the last 30 years or so, however, there have been massive changes in

Estimated UK shop numbers and turnover shares by type of organisation

	Number of shops		% share of all commodity turnover	
	1971	1990	197	1990
Co-operatives	7,745	2,545	13.2	10.3
Multiples	10,973	4,439	44.3	75.7
Independents	86,565	41,223	42.5	13.9

Source: Marketing Pocket Book, *1993 p. 52*

Figure 17.2 Different types of retailers.

retailing patterns. The development of self-service methods giving rise to super-markets and hypermarkets led to massive sales volume being conducted through such outlets. Moreover, supermarkets and hypermarkets developed as chains, with centralized buying departments. The emergence of these types of retailer made it more attractive for the producer to supply direct to the retailer.

Supermarket retailers

Many supermarkets are part of a chain of several hundred stores, but sometimes they are managed as single units. A wide variety of fast moving consumer goods such as food, drink and other household items is offered in such stores. An important feature is self service with a number of check-out points. Hypermarkets are a development from supermarkets, and are in reality very large supermarkets usually located out of town and carrying a much wider range of goods than a normal supermarket. Hypermarkets may offer clothing, gardening goods and so on, in addition to food and other household goods.

Superstore retailers

Superstores are a fairly recent development and include mass merchandisers supplying more specialized goods such as DIY items and car accessories – examples include Halfords, B&Q, Texas, etc. Smaller stores may be found in town centres, and much larger ones are often found in retail parks on the edge of towns and cities.

Cash and carry retailers

The cash and carry warehouse is effectively a wholesaler who provides for small retailers. Bulk supplies may be bought at the wholesale price, but no credit or transport facilities are provided. Individual consumers can also buy from these stores.

Symbol group retailers

Symbol groups are made up of a wholesaler and a number of retailers who have entered into a specific kind of business agreement. Originally, symbol groups developed to help smaller retailers compete more effectively with supermarkets. Wholesalers were keen to support the idea, since they too were losing business. SPAR is an example of a symbol group.

It is usual in such groups to find that in exchange for buying almost everything from a single wholesaler, special trade terms are offered by the wholesaler to the retailer. Each shop displays the wholesaler's symbol, and the wholesaler provides advertising support.

Discount store retailers

Discount stores buy in bulk and are able to sell expensive consumer durables such as washing machines at cut-prices. Often such stores do not provide servicing, although larger firms such as Comet make provision for servicing.

Department store retailers

Department stores are large stores with numerous departments, usually including furnishing, soft-furnishing, clothing and household goods. Many have amalgamated into large national chains, such as Debenhams. Like superstores they usually buy direct from producers, since they can negotiate advantageous terms by buying in bulk.

Co-operative retailers

Co-operative stores were originally based on customer ownership and profit-sharing by means of dividends proportional to purchase. Dividends have in some cases been replaced by trading stamps, and some local societies have now amalgamated under national ownership. The co-operatives have their own wholesaling organization and own some factories.

The last two sections have looked at ways of getting goods to the market through distribution channels and have also examined the nature of channel members. In the next section we will look at the various strategic options open to producers in distributing their goods.

DISTRIBUTION STRATEGY

There are many different kinds of outlet; some products may be sold through every possible outlet, while those products of a more specialized or high image nature may be sold only through selected or appointed dealers. In the latter case it usually means that the dealer does not sell competing products and thus gives an exclusive sales outlet to the producer. The dealer of course can sell complementary products.

Name	Operation
Hertz	Vehicle rental
Body Shop International	Cosmetics and beauty products
ANC Holdings	Parcel and courier service
Mr Softee	Mobile Ice Cream sales
Spud U Like Ltd	Baked potatoes, fast food
Safeclean	Carpet cleaning
Tie Rack PLC	Ties, scarves, accessories

Figure 17.3 Some franchising operations.

FRANCHISING

Franchising refers to the situation where a distributor is independent and controls the business to his or her own liking, but has a special agreement with a producer with respect to distributing the producer's product. The arrangement usually requires an investment and a commitment to buy the franchiser's product, in return for which the retailer receives advice or assistance in managing or promoting the business. Some franchises operate under a common name with a standard corporate identity, such as Wimpy bars. Others such as launderettes may make use of a certain make of machine. Franchising is particularly popular with service firms (see, for example, Fortune, 1991).

CHANNEL DECISIONS

There are six basic channel decisions to make.

1. Whether to distribute direct to the customer, or indirectly through middlemen

The advantages of going direct are that it enables firms to exercise more control over marketing activities and it reduces the amount of time spent in the channel. The disadvantages are that it is difficult to obtain widespread distribution, and more resources are required to maintain distribution.

Going direct is the method widely used by industrial goods producers. In the case of consumer goods, examples of going direct to the customer include cosmetics and encyclopedias.

Using intermediaries instead of going direct to the customer can increase the number of marketing activities and has a wider distribution potential. On the other hand it does mean that firms have less control over marketing activities, are more 'distanced' from the customer, and the product spends more time in the channel.

Control over marketing activities is desirable, but firms have to balance the costs and benefits of exercising control. Moreover, where goods are perishable there is clearly a need to get them through distribution channels as quickly as possible. This favours shorter distribution channels.

2. Whether to adopt single or multiple channels of distribution

The advantages of using a single channel are that it guarantees a minimum level of sales, and the exclusivity of using a single channel guarantees attention to the product. In the first case intermediaries can be asked to accept a minimum non-returnable order quantity. In the second case the fact that a product is only available from very specific outlets suggests that it is difficult to obtain because it is exclusive. The harder it is to get, the more people will want to know about it – or so the argument goes. On the other hand, the disadvantage of exclusivity is that it does limit sales.

In contrast, the use of multiple channels should lead to increased sales and a potential for wider distribution. It must be argued that the more establishments put the product on view, the more likely it is that sales will be substantial. Restricting the number of channels through which the product is sold restricts the number of people who can come into contact with it.

There are disadvantages with using multiple channels, however. First, greater investment, more salespeople in the field, more marketing effort in general and more administration are required. Secondly, it can lead to damaging competitive rivalry among channel members – channel members who find themselves competing with one another to sell the same product may not behave in the best interests of the producer.

3. How long the channel of distribution should be

In determining the best channel length to adopt, the following factors have to be taken into account:

- The financial strength of the producer – those in a strong position can carry out the functions provided by intermediaries.

- Size and completeness of the product line – the costs of carrying out the distribution function can be spread across the various items in the product line. The more items, the more economical it might be to consider a shorter distribution channel.

- The average order size – large orders may be distributed direct to customers.

- The geographical concentration of customers – geographically dispersed customers merit a longer distribution channel, since servicing them requires substantial investment of resources.

- The distance of the distributor from the market – geographical distance makes it less attractive for the producer to supply direct.

The above are guidelines, and of course exceptions may be encountered in practice.

4. The types of intermediaries to use

This effectively means choosing between different types of retailer, in the case of consumer goods – e.g. supermarkets as opposed to cash and carry – and different types of distributor, in the case of industrial goods – e.g. whether to use franchised dealerships or not.

5. The number of distributors to use at each level

In principle, more distributors are required if:

- the unit value of the product is low and/or the physical quantity of stock held is likely to be high

- the product is purchased frequently

- there is a high degree of technological complexity in the product

- the service requirement is high

- the inventory investment is high

- geographic concentration is low

- total market potential is high

- the market share of the producer is high

- competition is intense.

6. Which intermediaries to use

This is a qualitative decision and reflects whether the image of the particular outlet, the way in which it performs and the deals which can be struck with the distributor, are satisfactory. It may mean choosing C&A rather than Marks and Spencer, or Tesco rather than Finefare.

Even when strategies have been selected they have to be implemented, and this involves producers and intermediaries working together in the most effective manner possible. We will explore this topic in detail in the next section.

GETTING PRODUCERS AND INTERMEDIARIES TO WORK TOGETHER

Channel management is a co-operative effort in which both distributor and producer are working together for mutual benefit. It amounts to both parties collaborating in whatever way they can so that benefits accrue to both.

There are some general ground rules that need to be followed and closely adhered to. From the point of view of the producer help can be given to intermediaries by:

- providing a good, desirable assortment of products – well designed, properly priced, attractively packaged, delivered on time and in adequate quantities
- building up consumer demand for these products by advertising them
- furnishing promotional assistance
- providing managerial assistance
- honouring product warranties and providing repair and installation services.

Intermediaries can respond by increasing product sales through:

- carrying adequate stocks
- providing effective promotional displays and undertaking some advertising
- providing services to customer – credit, delivery, installation, etc.
- honouring the product warranty conditions.

MOTIVATING CHANNEL MEMBERS TO ACT IN THE PRODUCER'S INTEREST

While getting the best out of relationships between producers and intermediaries requires contributions from both sides, producers can instigate the process. Producers need to get intermediaries to act in the best interests of the producer and are in a position to take the leading role. Three approaches may be tried.

Co-operation
Here the producer uses the 'carrot and stick' method. Positive incentives are given in the form of higher margins, special deals, co-operative advertising allowances, display allowances and sales contests. Negative sanctions in the form of reducing margins, slowing down on deliveries, etc. may also be applied.

The weakness of this approach lies in the fact that the producer may not really study the needs, problems, strengths and weaknesses of the distributor. If distributors are unable to do all that the producer requires of them then there is very little that can be done about it, no matter what incentives or sanctions are applied.

Partnership
The idea of partnership provides a definite step in the right direction. Here, both producer and distributor agree on what the distributor should accomplish in terms of:

- market coverage
- product availability

CASE EXAMPLE

FOOD INDUSTRY: FORMATION OF ALLIANCES

Product life cycles in the food industry are becoming shorter, and the days of seasonal produce are gone. Customers expect fresh produce to be available throughout the year.

In the food industry, partnerships between producers and multiples will grow rapidly right across Europe. EC food safety legislation, backed by consumer concerns about how, where and by whom their food is produced, is one of the main causes.

Retailers and suppliers are under pressure to form partnerships, having much to lose from poor supply chain management. The pressure will increase to form partnerships – key distributors, fresh produce consolidators, food processors and manufacturers will become bound to long-term relationships with major clients. Suppliers, too, will seek to enter into supply agreements with their raw material suppliers, farmers and growers.

A concentrated retail sector, in which major firms will use own-label produce strategies to differentiate themselves from competitors, will become the norm throughout the EC. The result of this will be that the big firms will get bigger, and will concentrate on building stronger, core brands. The best small firms will survive by providing high-quality 'boutique' food products and high levels of service.

(*Source*: The Grocer, *11 June 1994, p. 49*).

QUESTION

1. What factors do you think lie behind successful food industry partnerships?

- market development
- account solicitation
- technical advice
- market information.

Rewards for attaining targets are financial, it being assumed that money is the prime motivator. Indeed, it is common practice for the producer to pay sales commission as follows:

- for carrying the proper inventory level
- for meeting the sales quota
- for servicing customers correctly and effectively
- for the proper reporting of customer purchase levels
- for the prompt payment of accounts due.

Distribution programming

In both of the previous cases one important point is not considered: the needs of the distributors. These are needs that cannot be addressed by financial help alone but require a different form of approach. Distribution programming identifies distributor needs and builds up merchandising programmes to help distributors operate optimally. Producer and distributor undertake joint planning of merchandising plans, inventory levels, space and visual merchandising plans, sales training and other promotions.

SELECTING THE RIGHT INTERMEDIARIES

This is a critical decision on which the success or failure of the marketing of the company's products may depend. Factors which should be taken into account include:

- familiarity with the market
- coverage of the market
- interest or enthusiasm in the firm's product
- strength of the marketing personnel
- product familiarity
- amount of contact with own customers
- previous track record
- cost of operation
- experience in dealing with competitors
- ability to provide customer service
- quality of service stock
- stock holding facilities
- credit worthiness
- image in the market place
- geographical location

- compatibility of distibutor's marketing policies with suppliers

- sufficiency of promotional activities and budgets

- whether the distributor is someone with whom the supplier can work.

Some of these points, such as the last one, of course, are more critical than others.

EVOLVING CHANNELS

Over time, the nature of channels changes. Change is brought about by changes in the marketing environment such as evolving customer needs, and technical progress and innovation which bring about new and better ways of delivering value to customers.

The development of low-cost channels and the growth of vertical, horizontal and multi-channel systems are now apparent.

Growth of low-cost channels

The growth of low-cost channels results from market evolution and the decline in the value added by a channel. At the early stages in market development, intermediaries provide high-level support in helping manufacturers to find customers and in offering help and service to customers. Later on, customers become more familiar with the product, prices decline and product reliability improves. A shift then takes place from specialist to higher volume, low added value channels. Eventually mass merchandising channels may be used and even mail order and discount shops may distribute the product.

This has been characteristic of the changing pattern in distributing personal computers over the past decade. Initially they were only available from specialist dealers who helped to educate the customer how to use the machines. While post-purchase technical service is still required by most users today, the market has evolved to a stage where customers are quite knowledgeable about the products available. This is helped to some extent by the availability of computer magazines which provide information on different models, their capabilities, etc. Consumers today are much more informed about PCs and their operation and capabilities than they were ten years ago and many now buy through mail order.

The technical complexity of the product obviously plays an important role in determining the speed at which low-cost channels can develop. Given an educated consumer who has access to informative magazines, and given also a not too complex product, the speed of development of low-cost channels can be quite rapid, as is evidenced by the camcorder and mobile telephone markets where low-cost channels feature fairly early in the life cycle.

Development of vertical marketing systems

The trend is towards vertical marketing systems in which channel activities are integrated and managed by one member of the channel – either a manufacturer, intermediary or a retailer (Doyle, 1994, p. 325). Such systems reduce cost, minimize conflict among channel members, and build on the experience and expertise of channel members.

Corporate vertical marketing systems occur in vertically integrated companies which have their own manufacturing, wholesaling and retailing operations. The current trend, however, is to build administered vertical marketing systems and contractual vertical marketing systems. In the former case channel members maintain their financial independence and legal autonomy, but are led by the most powerful member of the channel. In the latter case, channel members' rights and obligations are defined by legal agreement in the form of collaborative or franchise agreements.

CASE EXAMPLE

WAREHOUSE: IMPROVING EFFICIENCY

Gareth Jones is the warehouse manager for a large DIY chain which operates throughout the UK. Its Midlands-based main warehouse occupies some 300 000 square footage containing 30 000 storage locations for over 3,000 products, which range from doors to mirrors, to bathroom suites and fittings, to kitchen furniture, to lounge suites.

Gareth is keen to improve the efficiency of the warehouse. At present pallets of goods are received by the lorry-load from a variety of suppliers. After being checked against the order placed they are entered into the computer for inventory recording purposes. They are then assigned a suitable storage location number, bearing in mind the location space and the physical dimensions/characteristics of the items concerned. This is then tagged to the delivered items. Items are temporarily stored in a specific area of the warehouse, on the floor. Warehousemen driving forklift trucks put the items away into the designated storage locations continuously throughout the day.

The racking used for storing items is flexible in the sense that the size of space in a location can be changed. Racking is currently back to back in parallel blocks throughout the warehouse, and is five or six storeys high, depending on the roof height. In one block of back-to-back racking there can be as many as 600 locations.

The DIY company has a large number of stores all over the country, and all items are supplied from this central warehouse. Orders from the stores for items are placed on a regular basis and a single order usually is for a variety of items

CASE EXAMPLE *CONTINUED*

which have to be picked from the individual storage locations to make up the order. Typically, a driver will have to pick the required amounts of items from various locations throughout the warehouse – the order having previously been processed through the computer to identify storage locations and to assess and adjust stock levels. A list of items to pick and their locations is given to a warehouseman to assist him make up an order.

This process, naturally, leaves many part-filled locations which then have to be replenished when they become empty. When an order is picked it is then taken to a specially reserved area of the warehouse to await collection by one of the firm's delivery vans.

Apart from wanting to improve the overall system, Gareth has noticed a number of bottlenecks and problems with the current system. When picking orders all the heavy items, such as doors, must be picked first. Congestion can occur in the aisles between the racking, as one forklift truck driver blocks another's progress while he is picking items from a location. Determining a proper picking order seems to present a particular difficulty.

Gareth has past records of demand from the stores, delivery patterns from the suppliers, and details of the times it takes warehousemen to pick orders.

QUESTION

1. How should Gareth approach this problem?

Development of horizontal marketing systems

Strategic alliances and networks facilitate the development of horizontal marketing systems. They reflect the readiness of two or more autonomous units, which may even be competitors, at the same level in a channel to co-operate. Co-operation reduces the risks for an individual firm, facilitates access to other channels of distribution thereby accelerating market penetration, and provides access to new technologies and know-how.

Development of multi-channel marketing systems

As a result of markets becoming highly fragmented with customers having different product and service needs as well as price sensitivities, different channels have emerged to meet customers' expectations. While a multi-channel marketing system provides the opportunity for a firm to serve a range of segments, it is a potential source of channel conflict. A producer has to guard against the problems that this can create by being seen to be as fair as possible in dealing with channel members.

Having looked at channel selection and other strategic issues to do with channel management, in the next section we will look at the physical aspects of distribution.

Physical distribution

As the name suggests, physical distribution is concerned with the physical movement of goods from the producer to the consumer. An unco-ordinated physical distribution system may produce undesirably high costs. This is especially so in consumer products' markets such as food items, where delay can result in goods being unfit for consumption.

The physical distribution system forms part of the firm's competitive advantage. Efficient management of the physical distribution system can lead to lower costs, which in turn produce lower prices. Cost savings can be effected through better co-ordination, lower average delivery times and better service and quality.

Warehousing, stock control and transportation

JIT (just in time) management is now an accepted way of operating. What this means is that producers try to minimize their holding of finished stock. They produce to order, and produce just enough to meet what they anticipate will be required.

Stocks are held by wholesalers, retailers and, to some extent, by producers. Holding stock effectively ties up cash, so all members of the distribution chain are keen to keep this to a minimum. There are opportunity costs associated with the cash tied up in stock – the same cash, if it were left in an interest-bearing bank account, would earn money. It is also likely that organizations have bank loans or overdrafts which incur interest changes. Stock also takes up physical space, and the more stock that is held the greater is the amount of space required to house it. Buildings cost money to put up and maintain, and land has considerable value.

There is every incentive for all businesses to minimize their stocks to such an extent that they just match with demand. This is a difficult task – if too little stock is held, customers' demands cannot be met and not only is a sale lost but a frustrated customer is an unsatisfied one who may then switch to a competitor's product. The previous case example highlights the problems of warehouse management and of balancing supply with demand.

INVENTORY MANAGEMENT AND LEVEL OF SERVICE

A factor which affects the efficiency of the marketing operation is the level of customer service provided. Level of service refers to delivery frequency and reliability, stock levels and order cycle time as they impact upon product availability.

Product availability is usually measured in terms of the percentage of demand that can be met from stock. In principle, the larger the stocks that are held, the greater will be the product availability. The cost of holding stock and making the product available rises exponentially (i.e. disproportionately) as the percentage of demand that can be met from stock rises. This is largely because additional safety stocks have to be carried to lessen the risk of a stock-out.

The decision to be made relates to the trade-off between the cost of holding stock and the cost of a stock-out. One therefore has to balance the cost of a stock-out against the cost of holding stock.

Unfortunately there is no precise way to measure the cost of a stock-out on profitability. The possible consequences of a stock-out could be any of the following:

- loss of sale to competitor
- loss of customer to competitor
- loss of sale on related items
- loss of other customers, who may learn of poor product availability
- additional cost of shipping goods from other depots
- having to expedite a rush order with heavy on-costs
- having to progress a customer's re-order.

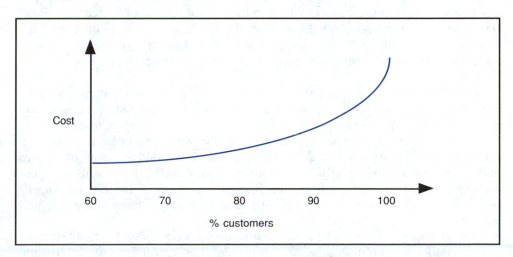

Figure 17.4 Level of service given versus cost of providing that level of service.

To tackle the problem, the probability of each one of these eventualities happening has to be worked out in some way or other, together with the ensuing financial impact on profitability. Market experiments to assess the precise impact of non-availability on market share indicate that over a certain range, improvement in level of service does have an impact on sales. There also appears to be a saturation point beyond which the customer does not seem to distinguish between improvements in stock availability.

Finding the point where trade-offs balance is a key problem for marketing management.

TRANSPORTATION

Choice of transportation method is relevant to all members of the distribution chain. Strategic decisions include:

● whether to use road, rail, sea or air transport

● whether a producer should have its own transport system.

In the case of transportation within the UK and Europe, road transportation takes the largest share. There has been a gradual shift over time away from rail transportation in the UK. Even if the railways were to double the amount of freight they carry, it would only reduce by 10% the amount of freight carried by road.

Road transport provides considerable flexibility, offering a door-to-door service. With respect to rail transport, very few industrial companies have their own railway sidings so that goods have to leave the factory by and large by road before they can be put onto rail with all the extra handling that this involves.. The incentive, therefore, is to use road transport since goods can be loaded at the factory and delivered straight to the customer. Even remote rural areas can be reached. Road transport is economical since the road haulage industry is competitive and the continuing development of motorways in the UK and on the continent of Europe has linked up the main centres of population making transportation between them speedy.

Containerization has had an enormous impact on transportation methods. Freight is packed into large containers at the point where they are produced, and the containers are sealed. Containers can be packed before lorries arrive. Furthermore they are standardized and are usable with any operator's vehicles. When goods are sent overseas they can be easily loaded on and off lorries and ships. Firms using containers often incur a heavy initial investment to acquire the containers. However, goods are much safer in containers and the system has been developed to cater for all kinds of goods, including refrigerated goods and liquids.

Road transport is not suitable for transporting goods of great bulk such as iron ore. Moreover, rail transport can be speedier than road transport under some circumstances, and the railways have developed a freightliner system which makes use of containerization to good purpose. The railway maintains its own fleet of lorries which picks up containers from customers, loads them onto trains, transports them to an intermediate destination and finally offloads them onto British Rail lorries for delivery to the customer. Containerization and the freight-liner system are likely to play an important role in distributing goods to Europe from the British Isles.

INTERNATIONAL TRANSPORTATION

In the case of international trade, 95% of the volume (and 75% of the value) takes place by sea transport. Transport by sea offers flexibility and exporters can get shipping space easily. Containerization has assisted the smooth running of sea transport operations and has been accompanied by the building of special container vessels. Nevertheless, in recent years there has been a steady increase in air freight. In keeping with this trend, new and larger aircraft have been developed which are capable of carrying larger loads.

Air transport is frequently used where speedy delivery is required. Mail, medical supplies and newspapers come into this category, as do spare parts for industrial machinery, and components for cars and computers. The cost per tonne carried is higher by air than by sea, but the cost of transport needs to be looked at in the light of the value of the goods being carried. The price of low-value items might have to be increased considerably if they were to be sent by air, whereas the price of high-value items increases much less appreciably if they are airfreighted.

LOGISTICS

In this final section we look at logistics, a concept which views the process of goods as they move through the manufacturing process and pass eventually to the customer as a total system. In this concept other elements of marketing, production and purchasing should also be viewed as part of a total system. In order to optimize the output of this total system it may be necessary for some or even all of its components to operate sub-optimally – marketing may have to offer a lower level of customer service than the optimum; production might have to schedule shorter production runs, etc.

The logistics mix is made up of the following:

● **Facilities**   Companies have to provide and invest in facilities for holding stock and enabling it to be distributed to further distribution points. Factory ware-house facilities and strategically sited depots near to large concentrations of customers are what is required. There may even be several production plants, depending upon the level and concentration of demand.

There is no doubt that good relations with intermediaries can help towards overcoming stockholding problems, but even the most willing intermediaries will not want to tie up excessive amounts of working capital in stocks. Striking a balance between centrally sited production and warehousing facilities and strategically sited depots or other production plants to maintain an acceptable level of customer service is thus a key issue in logistics management.

- **Inventories or stock levels** We have already looked at the key role of inventory management and its relationship to providing customer service above. It plays an important part in logistics management, and striking the balance with maintaining a given level of customer service is again the key issue.

- **Communication decisions** Accompanying goods as they flow through the distribution system is information. This information is part and parcel of the demand forecasting, order processing and invoicing systems. This is necessary to provide a satisfactory customer service at an acceptable cost.

  The more efficient and even user-friendly such communications are, the more they contribute to overall customer service. Where such communications are poor they can result in mistakes and delay, which can be costly and do nothing to improve customer relations.

- **Utilization decisions** These relate to the packaging of goods and their subsequent assembly into larger batches, having major implications for logistics economics. The producer has to provide the product in such a way as to minimize subsequent handling and storage costs. However, not only must the producer think about minimizing his or her own costs, but attention has also to be given to the handling costs of distributors and even of end-users, particularly in the case of industrial goods. If goods are not packaged in a way which satisfies distributors and end-users, they may switch to buying from an alternative source. For example, it might well suit the producer to package a product in drums, but the final user may have a preference for buying the product in bulk for direct delivery into his or her own containers.

- **Transport decisions** These involve the choice of the best medium of transport, so that goods arrive at the next stage of the channel on time and in the best possible condition. Once again it is a question of establishing a balance between costs and meeting the customer's requirements. There are a wide range of options by land, sea and air, and some carriers offer specialized services.

Together, these five areas account for the total costs of distribution. In addition, decisions taken in one area can have implications for one of the other areas. For example transport costs are obviously affected by the siting of distribution depots, as also will be stock levels.

CUSTOMER SERVICE

The five areas of logistics management highlighted are related to providing customer service, and all aspects of logistics are traded off against some notional service level. Customer service involves:

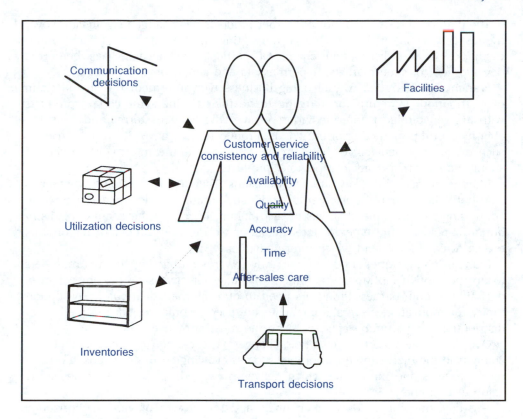

Figure 17.5 Logistics components and customer service.

- consistency and reliability of delivery
- availability (the time by which the customer requires the product or service)
- quality of the goods/service
- accuracy of transactions
- time taken to process an order
- quality of after-sales care.

SUMMARY

One of the keys to effective marketing is gaining distribution for a product. There are different distribution routes from which the producer can make a selection. However, not all methods are suitable for all products, and in many cases there are strategic advantages to be obtained from selecting one method over another. Producers can reach the market direct, through wholesalers and retailers, through agents and distributors, etc.

The pattern of distribution for consumer products has changed significantly over the last 30 years. This has resulted in the setting up of all kinds of different intermediaries in the distribution chain. Of particular significance has been the development of supermarkets, hypermarkets and superstores.

Franchising is a good way of doing business with intermediaries in the chain of distribution. In return for agreeing to tie their business for certain products with a given producer, intermediaries receive advantageous terms and considerable help in the marketing of the goods. Producers, too, have much to gain from such an arrangement since they can be assured that the intermediary will not supply its customers with competitors' products.

Channel decisions are key strategic decisions. They involve deciding whether to distribute direct to the customer or indirectly through middlemen, whether to adopt single or multiple channels of distribution, how long the channel of distribution should be, the types of intermediaries to use, the number of distributors to use at each level, and which intermediaries to use.

Franchising agreements go only part-way towards motivating channel members to do their jobs well. Moreover, franchising may not always be possible or even desirable to both parties. Producers need to offer all their distributors the opportunity for motivation. Several approaches are used in practice, but the method of distribution programming appears to be the most attractive.

Over time the nature of channels changes. The change is brought about by changes in the marketing environment such as evolving customer needs and technical progress and innovation which delivers new and better ways of delivering value to customers.

The development of low-cost channels and the growth of vertical, horizontal and multi-channel systems are apparent at the present time.

Good inventory management and providing an adequate level of customer service are important contributors to the profitability of any firm. Achieving the right balance between the two, however, is quite hard to achieve.

Transportation is a key element in achieving efficient distribution. Moreover, different methods of transportation have different associated costs, different levels of effectiveness and in some cases may not even be available. Containerization has done much to revolutionize the way in which many goods may be transported.

Appreciating the nature of the logistics concept can lead to maximizing overall efficiency and effectiveness, even if some of the elements of the distribution mix are not implemented in an optimum fashion. The distribution mix comprises facilities such as warehouses and production plants, inventories, communications accompanying goods as they flow through the distribution system, the packaging of goods and their subsequent assembly into larger batches, and transport.

DISCUSSION QUESTIONS

1. Why is distribution one of the keys to effective marketing?

2. Outline the different distribution routes from which the producer can select the most appropriate.

3. What factors have to be taken into account when selecting an appropriate channel of distribution?

4. Describe how the pattern of distribution for consumer products has changed significantly in the last 30 years.

5. Why is franchising a good way of doing business for producers with intermediaries in the chain of distribution?

6. Indicate the nature of the key strategic channel decisions that have to be taken.

7. Several approaches to motivating intermediaries are used in practice, but the method of distribution programming appears to be the most attractive. Explain why this is the case.

8. What factors give rise to the development of low-cost channels and the growth of vertical, horizontal and multi-channel systems?

9. Why is it difficult to achieve the right balance between the level of service and good inventory management? Why is it important to try to do so?

10. Show how containerization has done much to revolutionize the way in which many goods may be transported. What are the implications for marketing of this?

11. How can the logistics concept lead to maximizing overall efficiency and effectiveness even if some of the elements of the distribution mix are not implemented in an optimum fashion?

REFERENCES

Doyle, P. (1994) *Marketing Management and Strategy*, Prentice Hall, Englewood Cliffs, N.J.
Fortune (1991) Look, who likes franchising now, 23 September, 125–30.
Marketing (1994) Business by the book, 3 February, 28.

FURTHER READING

Christopher, M. (1986) *The Strategy of Distribution Management*, William Heinemann, London.
Cooper, J., Browne, M. and Peter, M. (1991) *European Logistics*, Blackwell, Oxford.
Fernie, J. (ed.) (1990) *Retail Distribution Management: Strategic Guide to Developments and Trends*, Kogan Page, London.

CASE PROBLEM 17.1

PLIMSOLL PORTFOLIO ANALYSIS: SURVEY OF RETAIL DISTRIBUTION EFFICIENCY

A survey undertaken by Plimsoll Portfolio Analysis concluded that almost half the firms bringing fresh fruit and vegetables to market in the UK are financially weak, and some are in danger of failure. Examining the period from July 1992 to July 1993 the firm looked at the balance sheets of 1615 companies, 90% of the sector, concerned with growing, processing and distributing, importing and wholesaling fresh produce. Across the whole sample average sales growth in the year to July 1993 was zero, even the top quartile showing only an average 5% increase. Average pre-tax profit margins were 2%, while the best was only 3%.

(Source: The Grocer, *11 June 1994, p.55)*

QUESTIONS

1. What factors do you think contribute to the financial problems facing distributors of fresh fruit and vegetables?

2. What other distributive businesses do you think are likely to suffer from the same kind of problems?

3. What action do you think can be taken to improve the situation?

CASE PROBLEM 17.2

OUT OF TOWN RETAILING: CITY CENTRE SHOPPING RESPONSE

There is a conflict between those who envisage the future of retailing in town centres, and those who favour the retail park or out-of-town shopping mall. Certainly in the 1980s very little seemed to be done to prevent large retail developments, targeted almost exclusively at the car-owner. The 40% increase in the number of cars on the roads over the past decade has tended to lend support to the argument for this form of retailing.

Opponents of out-of-town shopping argue that these developments have been detrimental to the traditional high street shops. Local councils, supported by retailers including Marks & Spencer and Boots, lend support to this point of view. As a result, town centre managers, whose role is to promote such shopping areas to potential investors and customers, have come into being.

Marks & Spencer has seconded two staff as town centre managers in Oxford and Liverpool and has provided funding towards a further 18. Boots is sponsoring some 48 officers. Town centre managers' budgets range from Liverpool's City Centre Partnership, with annual finance of £240 000, excluding the salary of the town centre manager, to those with no specific funding at all.

Michael Stansbury is the manager for Ilford town centre, which has to compete not only with Romford, but also with the extensive Thurrock Lakeside development and the West End of London, less than 30 minutes away by Underground. Stansbury admits that his budget cannot compete with the malls. The town has been boosted by the Exchange, a £100m. shopping centre developed by Norwich Union. Winning such investments meant using exhibitions, brochures, seminars and conferences. However, more difficult still is winning back shoppers. Stansbury's funds run from around £10 000 a year for entertainers to £60 000 for Christmas lighting, supplemented by campaigns run by the Exchange.

Thurrock Lakeside does not see itself as a threat to the town centre, but believes that the two types of shopping can coexist. It feels it is a complement to the town centre, arguing that apart from very local people, shoppers take selective trips to Lakeside and it is certainly not an every-week shopping experience. Its own research shows that the majority of people visit Lakeside only three or four times a year.

(Source: Marketing, 27 January 1994, p.21)

QUESTION

1. Are town centre managers a waste of time? Who is right – the out-of-town shopping supporters, or their opponents?

18 MARKETING CONTROL AND ORGANIZATION

The nature of control and the need for it in marketing are the focus for this chapter. The nature of the different forms of marketing organizational structure that are possible are examined, along with different managerial styles. How situations involving change need to be managed, together with the importance of creativity in marketing and management, are also explored.

OBJECTIVES

After studying this chapter you should be able to:

- appreciate the nature of control and the need for it in marketing
- appreciate the nature of the different forms of marketing organizational structure that are possible
- understand the less effective and the more effective managerial styles
- understand how situations involving change need to be managed
- appreciate the importance of creativity in marketing and management.

INTRODUCTION

The previous chapters emphasized planning and decision making with respect to the various elements of the marketing mix. In this chapter we look at the function of control in the marketing management process and how it is related to objective setting and decision making with respect to the marketing mix elements.

Planning, decision making, implementing decisions and control all depend upon people being organized and managed in an effective manner to carry out these various activities.

In this chapter we also look at the human side of enterprise, exploring different managerial styles and the impact they are likely to have on actually getting people to do things in an organization. The chapter concludes by examining the need for creativity in organizations, the factors which can stifle it and how creativity may be positively encouraged.

CONTROL

Once objectives have been operationalized, it is not only useful but actually imperative to monitor progress towards achieving those objectives and to have guidelines with respect to corrective action, should deviations from plan occur. Unless this is done then planning is futile.

Control is the process of ensuring that activities are carried out as intended and it involves monitoring aspects of performance and taking corrective action where necessary. Control of expenditure, for example, involves regular monitoring of expenditure figures, comparison of these with budget targets, and taking decisions to cut or increase expenditure, where any variance is believed to be harmful.

TYPES OF CONTROL

Several types of control can be found in an organization:

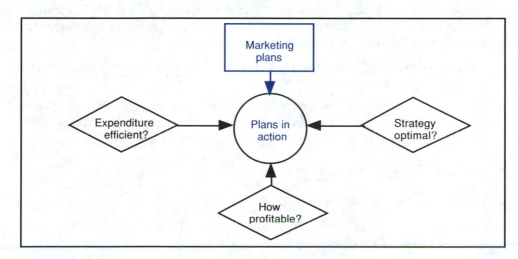

Figure 18.1 Nature of control.

- **strategic control** – this concerns whether the company is pursuing its best opportunities with respect to markets, products and channels

- **efficiency control** – this involves evaluation of spending efficiency, together with attempts to improve the spending efficiency and impact of marketing expenditures. It is applied to the sales force, advertising, sales promotion and distribution

- **profitability control** – this involves examination of where the company is making or losing money. Profitability by product, territory, customer group, trade channel and order size are studied.

STRATEGIC CONTROL

The interface between marketing and corporate strategy and planning is close as the two are intertwined and interrelated. At the strategic level the company survives by outwitting its rivals and anticipating the changing conditions which may occur as a result of new entrants, substitute products and the changing power of buyers (see Porter's competitive forces model in Chapter 4). All of these forces have to be monitored continuously and closely. The source from which threats arise varies from one type of business to another, but experience seems to indicate that new technologies and new entrants to an industry or market go together. It is vitally important to keep watch on the emergence of new technologies, monitor how they are developed by competitors or potential competitors, and assess the implications of these developments.

In the shorter term, one way to develop and maintain a strategy which helps to separate a firm from its present-day rivals is the **benchmarking method**. This is a technique which provides management with valuable control insights into the firm's standing on a number of criteria.

- Critical success criteria are identified for a given market or industry. Examples of such measures usually include return on capital, productivity, capacity versus output, and sales volume per sales person.

- The performance of the most successful firms in the industry are then analysed and rated against the criteria identified.

- The firm conducting the analysis then compares its own performance against each of the criteria identified. This helps to highlight strengths and weaknesses and to identify future corrective measures that may be introduced.

At this level of control attention must be paid to:

- the effectiveness of the customer philosophy

- the attainment of the firm's marketing strategy, in whatever terms it was expressed in the first place

- the attainment of the marketing objectives

- the appropriateness of the marketing organization
- the quality of marketing intelligence
- general operational efficiency.

EFFICIENCY CONTROL

Control procedures are necessary for measuring both the efficiency and the effectiveness of the various elements of the marketing mix. Particular attention has to be given to those areas which impact upon results. In this connection the most significant areas are sales, distribution and promotion.

Having looked at control in marketing in general terms we now look at specific aspects of marketing where control can be effected.

Sales control

The sales pyramid is a valuable system for monitoring levels of performance. It is based upon the idea that an erosion rate exists between actual sales and the various stages of the selling effort (Majaro, 1993). The model relates specifically to the selling of industrial products, but can be transferred to most selling situations. At the first level of the pyramid (the base), initial contacts are made, at the second level a number of visits are made, at the third level a number of proposals are made and at the apex a number of sales are achieved.

According to the principles behind the sales pyramid, sales attained are related to the number of proposals submitted to customers. This in turn is a function of the number of visits, which in turn arise from the number of initial contacts. The pyramid effect (reducing numbers) comes as a result of not all the initial contacts leading to visits, and not all visits leading to a proposal being requested and submitted. Similarly, at the apex of the pyramid, only a portion of the proposals result in orders being placed.

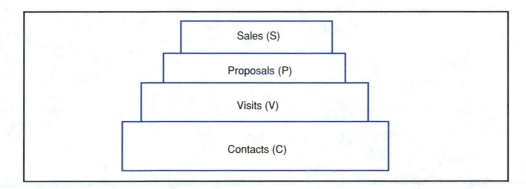

Figure 18.2 The sales pyramid.

For example:

Suppose   500 initial contacts (C) lead to 400 visits (V);
          400 visits (V) lead to 350 proposals (P);
and   350 proposals (P) lead to 245 sales (S).

then $S = 0.7P$; $P = 0.875V$; and $V = 0.8C$.

To increase S, one must increase the ratio of V/C, P/V or S/P or the size of C.

Data collected from salespeople reflecting the number of prospects taken to each stage of the selling process (or sales pyramid) are essential for management control helping to pinpoint where problems arise. In addition, the information provides guidance with respect to the kind of corrective action that is required.

Advertising control

Advertising effectiveness is difficult to measure, and this means that control in this area is more difficult. If any control is to be effected, then it is of paramount importance that the objectives for the advertising are clearly understood and specified precisely. Only with this in mind can any attempt be made to address the subject of its effectiveness.

A close check needs to be kept on advertising expenditure and what it is achieving. Measures which can be used to control advertising efficiency include the following:

● cost per thousand reached

● media effectiveness comparisons

● impact on customers

● retention rate of message

● attitude change to product or service

● enquiries resulting from advertising.

Most of this information cannot be obtained from internal sources, so market research is needed to provide the necessary feedback.

Distribution control

The most important efficiency controls are as follows:

● inventory levels/stock turnover

● stock-out situations

● customer complaints

● warehouse efficiency ratings

● physical distribution costs.

```
1. Company profit and loss statement (£)

Sales                                        260000
Cost of goods                                130000
Gross profit                                 130000

Expenses (cost of sales)

Sales                        66800
Overheads                    26600
Materials                    14000

Total                                        107400

Net profit                                    22600
```

Figure 18.3 Company profit and loss account.

This kind of information should be available from internal records. Stock turnover, for example, is the ratio of sales to stock. The more sales that can be obtained from existing stocks, the more chance there is of increasing return on investment in inventory. One should be looking to maintain or increase this ratio.

PROFITABILITY CONTROL

From a corporate standpoint, one should attempt to measure the profitability of a product line of the business in terms of return on capital employed. It can be difficult, however, to allocate overheads against profits, and an alternative method may be to look at the contribution that every product and product line is making to overheads and profits. Sales and profit interaction effects with other products and lines are more difficult to measure, or even to detect.

Figure 18.3 shows a simple profit and loss account for a trading company (stage 1).

Figure 18.4 shows the follow-through in which the profitability of the firm's three products, alpha, beta and gamma, is assessed (stages 2–4).

Stage 2 shows how the various overheads of the firm are apportioned to the various functional areas of the business – selling, advertising, delivery and administration. Stage 3 shows then how these functional costs are then allocated to individual products. In this case, the average selling cost per call, cost per advert, cost per delivery and administrative cost per order are calculated. Some 310 calls were made with respect to selling product alpha, 140 for beta and 75 for gamma, a total of 525. Since the total functional cost of selling was £53 700, this means that the average cost per call was £102.2857. Average costs per unit of measure for the other functions (advertising, delivery and administrative) are derived in a similar way. In stage 4 a profit and loss statement is presented showing costs allocated against each product. The expenses shown against each product are obtained by multiplying the average per unit cost for each function derived in stage 3 by

2. Apportionment of expenses to functional areas

	Total	Selling	Advertising	Delivery	Admin.
Salaries	66800	33400	6680	10020	16700
Overheads	26600	13300	2660	3990	6650
Material	1400	7000	1400	2100	3500
Total	107400	53700	10740	16110	26850

3. Allocation of functional costs to individual products

Product	No. calls Selling	No. ads Advertising	No. deliver. Delivery	No. orders Admin.
alpha	310	60	90	80
beta	140	40	40	40
gamma	75	20	20	30
Total	525	120	150	150
Functional expenses	53700	10740	16110	26850
Average cost/unit	102.2857	89.5	107.4	179

4. Profit loss per product

	alpha	beta	gamma	total
Sales	110000	70000	80000	260000
Cost of goods	55000	35000	40000	130000
Gross profit	55000	35000	40000	130000

Expenses (cost of sales)

	alpha	beta	gamma	total
Selling	31708.57	14320	7671.429	53700
Advertising	5370	3580	1790	10740
Distribution	9666	4296	2148	16110
Admin	14320	7160	5370	26850
Total	61064.57	29356	16979.43	107400
	−6064.57	5644	23020.57	22600

Figure 18.4 Profit and loss by product.

the frequency of occurrence, also shown in stage 3. Thus the selling expenses for product alpha of £31 708.57 are a product of the average cost per call of £102.2857 and 310, the number of sales calls made for product alpha in the period.

Inspection of the data at stage 4 reveals that product alpha is making a negative contribution to profits i.e. it is losing money. Unless profitable sales interaction effects with the other products can be detected and assessed, consideration might well be given to dropping the product from the mix and replacing it with a more profitable item. The data shown in Figures 18.3 and 18.4 above can very easily be entered into a spreadsheet and a sensitivity analysis carried out. Sensitivity analysis can disclose how variations in numbers which are input into the model affect overall outcomes. For example, if it were possible to substantially reduce sales calls, deliveries and administrative costs associated with product alpha (the actual amount would have to be assumed or estimated from known data), the product would then be more profitable.

In addition to allocating costs to products, some form of sensitivity analysis is called for in exercising control. The rules for allocation of costs shown above were considered reasonable in this case, but in different circumstances a different way of allocating costs might be seen as more reasonable.

EVALUATING THE MARKETING EFFORT

The principal marketing plan is the annual plan, and in relation to this plan the purpose of control is to monitor whether planned results are being achieved. Towards this end sales analyses, market share analyses, sales to expense ratios, financial analysis and monitoring of the attitudes of users all form part of the control process.

Financial statistics are suitable for measuring financial performance, but the performance measures that help a company focus on improving customer satisfaction include:

- how customers perceive speed, accuracy and reliability of the firm's operations

- how customers rate the value of products in use, through channels such as formal rating, hotlines, market research, focus groups

- other firms' performances, against which the self-evaluating firm can benchmark itself

- critical incidents such as late delivery, unfulfilled orders, volume and frequency of complaints, time taken to resolve complaints

- strength of relationship with customers, indicated by market share, brand loyalty, repeat orders.

Having looked at the mechanisms of control, let us now look at how control is implemented.

THE PROCESS OF CONTROL AND EVALUATION

The control process consists of a comparison of actual performance with objectives and goals that have previously been set. Objectives and goals are established within budgets (a quantitative and financial plan of activities to be pursued during the financial year to achieve the year's objectives) which relate the responsibilities of departments and employees to the requirements of plans and policies. This is accompanied by a continuous comparison of actual results with the targets set in the budget, so that the latter may be achieved, or alternatively adjustments made to the objectives upon which they were founded.

Control exercised in this way is usually referred to as budgetary control. The basic notion behind this is that of Responsibility Accounting, whereby areas of employee responsibility such as sales or distribution become control centres within an organization.

There are two kinds of control centre:

- cost centres which are responsible for costs
- profit centres which are responsible for costs and revenues (profits).

Marketing is usually regarded as a profit centre, while departments which specialize in advertising or distribution are considered cost centres.

When exercising control, variances from expected performance are of interest. In the following sections we will look at how variances are analysed.

ANALYSING VARIANCES

An important aspect of control involves measuring the variations of costs, revenues, etc. from the budget and analysing why variations have occurred. As a result of these analyses corrective action can then be taken. In a company which is offering many products or services, the task of analysing variances and suggesting appropriate courses of action is an extensive one.

CUSTOMER PROFITABILITY ANALYSIS

Discounts of many varieties may be offered to intermediaries and retailers in an attempt to attain the sales volume laid down in the budget. Although it is difficult for a company to estimate the effect that such discounts will have on margins, customer profitability analysis will provide a means of coming to grips with this problem.

An analysis of the revenues and costs attributable to any one customer or distributor needs to be carried out. This enables a firm to identify those accounts that are making the greatest contributions to profit, and those which are making the least contributions. It also enables the firm to establish why this is the case. Appropriate action can then be considered with respect to either trying to raise the profitability of the accounts concerned, or alternatively consideration can be given to no longer servicing those accounts, if it is thought wasteful of resources to continue doing so.

This kind of approach enables firms to look closely at large customer accounts where margins may be low and sales turnover high. It can then be established whether the margins are adequate in terms of their ability to generate contributions to profits and overheads. It can also be established whether there is sufficient leeway to offer better terms at the next round of negotiation of contracts.

Planning, execution and control all require an organizational structure which enables them to be implemented. In the following section we will look at different types of marketing organization.

MARKETING ORGANIZATION

Organizations can be thought of as social groupings arranged to achieve goals. Business organizations pursue multiple goals and hence the structure which they adopt has to reflect the nature of the principal goals they pursue. Hence an organization whose prime goal is to serve international markets will adopt a structure which reflects such an orientation.

A suitable organization structure has to be in place to enable goals to be pursued and marketing plans and control to be put into operation. Within the overall organization the key functional areas have their own individual organizational arrangements or structures. Marketing is a key functional area in business and at the same time is one of the main tasks of a business. Perhaps it is surprising therefore that marketing does not always have a formal organizational structure within the overall structure of the firm. This is because although its functions may be recognized as being important, the marketing functions are carried out by a variety of people in the organization who do not necessarily belong to a formal marketing department.

The absence of marketing within the formal structure of an organization is perhaps most noticeable in very small firms and public sector organizations, such as the health service. In the case of very small firms, the chief executive may well carry out all the marketing functions. In this case, the size of the organization is too small to give rise to a separate marketing function within the organization. In the case of public sector organizations the decision making for pricing, promotion, distribution and product development is highly dispersed and no co-ordinating role exists.

Where marketing – or aspects of it, such as sales – have become recognized as important activities that require specialized knowledge and expertise in their own right, organizational structures may have evolved to support these activities. For example, it is common in many firms for selling to be recognized as an important activity in its own right. A specialized department under the direction of a sales manager often develops as a result. Marketing departments, however, emerge less frequently, since decision making, planning and control relating to the

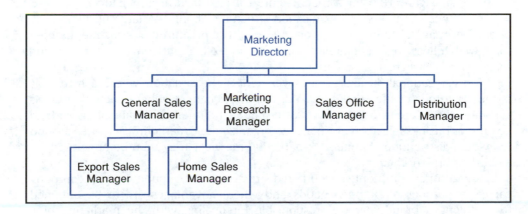

Figure 18.5 Functional marketing organization.

marketing mix variables tend to be dispersed in many organizations. Largely as a result of education and the development of a professional approach to marketing, however, more and more firms have come to recognize the benefits of having a marketing department or sub-organizational structure within the overall structure of the firm.

Where marketing organizational sub-structures occur within firms, it is common to find them adopting a task-based or functional type of organization structure. A typical functional marketing structure is shown in Figure 18.5.

Under this kind of organizational structure, the marketing director co-ordinates, controls and appraises the activities of all the people below his or her level in the organization. In the illustration, each of the four people who report directly to the marketing director have functional responsibility and accountability for particular aspects of marketing. To each one of them in turn there are other people who have responsibility and accountability. All organizations have to carry out the same kinds of marketing activities, and so all firms adopting a functional marketing organization structure will adopt some variant on the above approach.

How tasks are allocated in an organization will reflect custom and practice and the importance the company attaches to that task. In the above example, pricing policies may be laid down by the marketing director in conjunction with the chief executive and the director of finance. The day-to-day running of the sales force, however, will be left to the sales manager who is accountable to the marketing director. The sales office manager deals with all the paperwork associated with sales. This includes progressing orders and invoicing for payment. The sales office manager is **not** accountable to the sales manager for what he or she does, but is accountable to the marketing director. If an account is not settled by a customer, then responsibility for dealing with the matter may be shared between the company's finance department, its legal department (or else the company secretary) and the sales office.

A functional organizational approach to marketing is often found in manufacturing companies. However, some manufacturing companies adopt a production-based structure in which a product manager takes responsibility for the marketing of a group of products sharing common characteristics. An example organization is shown in Figure 18.6 for a manufacturer of lead acid accumulators.

Other types of marketing organization structures abound. A large business may operate in many different regions or countries. The organization structure adopted may well reflect this geographical division. Indeed, there may be a marketing manager for each region or nation.

The organizational structure may even reflect the situation where a firm sells its goods through different kinds of distribution channel, where each channel is substantially different to the other. Given that each one of the channels has a high volume of business, firms may choose to organize their marketing activities around individual distribution channels. A marketing manager may then be appointed for each distribution channel.

Lastly, another commonly encountered structure is to be found where a company carries a number of branded goods and where advantages are to be obtained from having a brand manager responsible for dealing with the marketing of a particular brand.

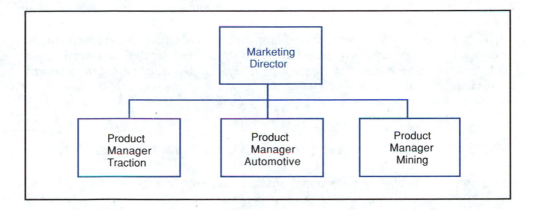

Figure 18.6 Marketing organization – production-based structure.

CASE EXAMPLE

PROCTER & GAMBLE: REORGANIZATION

Procter & Gamble changed its marketing organization in 1993. The advertising/marketing hierarchy changed to run from assistant brand manager to marketing director to category general manager. The associate ad manager and ad manager titles were eliminated and replaced by the single title of marketing director. The brand assistant title also disappeared.

The restructuring included a reassessment of how pan-European and national marketers work together. The company was aiming for a flatter organization with a broader spread of responsibilities, to speed up decision making. Responsibility for pan-European brands was identified as an important item for organizational review. There was a need to optimize the joint contribution of the European level brand group and the national level. Moreover, it was decided that a lot of things could be done at the regional level, such as dealing with local competition, customers and pricing.

(*Source*: Marketing, *3 February, 1994, p.17*).

QUESTION

1. Suggest how a firm such as P&G might structure its pan-European marketing organization.

Organizational efficiency can be improved through reorganization, as the case example indicates.

For effective planning, control and implementation, organizations have to be managed and that means people have to be managed. In the next section we will look at ideas relating to management style and getting people to perform satisfactorily in their jobs.

PEOPLE MANAGEMENT – ALTERNATIVE STYLES

Setting up a suitable organizational structure is only part of the management task. There is also the task of getting people to do things, and this is not a simple matter of telling them what has to be done. A manager has to know how to deal with situations and individuals to get the best out them. Much has been written about management, and about leadership in particular, but the only real conclusion that can be drawn is that there is no single best method to get a job done.

Managers spend most of their time dealing with contingencies, and people problems are no exception to this. Indeed managers may spend as much time trying to sort out people as they do getting on with the functional aspects of their job. When dealing with people a manager has to adapt his or her style of management to deal with the needs of individuals. The objective is to find out how subordinates are motivated to perform well in their jobs, and then to find ways of making it possible for them to achieve targets that are set for them along with satisfaction in performing their work.

Managers adopt a variety of management styles and indeed tend to exhibit a preferred style of managing. At one extreme a manager may adopt an autocratic stance, while at the other extreme another manager may be much more democratic and encourage subordinates to share in the decision making.

In certain circumstances a particular style of management may appear to work for a particular group of individuals. However, if the make-up of the group changes substantially and entirely different personalities join the group, then the same style may not work at all.

A manager's task is a difficult one, since he or she will be unable to please everyone and personality clashes with the staff are almost inevitable. A manager who adopts a democratic style of management may be seen as too easy-going by some members of the group, while by others the style may be viewed as appropriate for the situation.

Different managers may have a preferred style of interacting with people, and it may be a pervasive characteristic of the way they behave. Several writers on organizations have come up with ideas or suggestions which relate to effective and ineffective management styles. Reddin (1987), for example, differentiates between less effective and more effective managers. A summary of the types he identifies is given below.

LESS EFFECTIVE MANAGERIAL STYLES

- The 'missionary', who is zealous about new ideas, tries to sell them to other people, but loses interest in the job and moves on to other things.

- The 'deserter', who has become disappointed with the organization and does the minimum required.

- The 'autocrat', who shows most concern for getting the job done and relies on power. Such a person tends to keep information to himself or herself and communicates downwards. Fear and threats are used constantly to coax people into doing things.

- The 'compromiser', who prefers things to run smoothly and tries to avoid conflict.

MORE EFFICIENT MANAGERIAL STYLES

- The 'developer', who likes to teach, train and help others to put ideas into practice.

- The 'bureaucrat', who sticks to the rules, remains impartial and stays remote from the action.

- The 'benevolent autocrat', who delegates a little but keeps close policy control, giving rewards rather than punishments to motivate people. Loyalty to the organization is perceived by such managers as being an important quality in staff.

- The 'executive', who exercises authority when occasion demands, but who also consults and involves people in decision making.

In practice we may find managers showing a mixture of the various styles suggested by Reddin.

Managers are accountable to others for their work and for their responsibilities. While they delegate their work to others, they are still accountable for how well the work is performed. No manager can afford to overlook this point. An employee who fails to perform satisfactorily in accordance with the work that has been delegated to him or her can expect little sympathy in the long term from a good manager.

MANAGEMENT OF CHANGE

Planning to some extent will always involve introducing change of one kind or another into an organization. This being the case, it is important to remember that when introducing change into the organization the following points should be taken into account.

- People should be given ample warning and indications of the kind of change that is likely to occur.

- An explanation should be offered as to why the change has taken place.

- People should be involved at all stages in the discussions relating to the change.

- People should understand what the benefits and rewards are that result from the change.

- Training should be provided in relationship to changes in practice.

The launching of new products or services, and changes in marketing methods, are examples of where changes take place. Members of the organization itself and its distributors should be involved.

Change can occur with unexpected rapidity, so it is important to have control mechanisms which facilitate quick reactions to change. Not only are contingency plans required, but it also necessary to think in a creative and innovative way. Given the constantly changing nature of the marketing environment it is important that marketing executives accept that dealing with a continually changing situation is a normal part of their jobs. At all cost, executives should not bury their heads in the sand when new or different problems arise.

Marketing executives need to keep themselves well informed about developments in their industry or profession. They should also monitor the environment for signals, trends and developments in the attitudes and behaviour of competitors, customers and the market. One way to stimulate a positive attitude to change is by encouraging colleagues to discuss new ideas and issues on a regular basis, and encouraging staff to raise issues concerning their work. Future plans and issues should also be discussed with staff, both individually and as a group, on a regular basis. There should also be a willingness to be experimental and flexible with people's ideas, trying out new techniques and ideas whenever appropriate.

Organizations are constantly changing as people come and go. Changes should be communicated to staff unless there is good reason not to do so. A working atmosphere needs to be created in which ideas and issues do not fall between bureaucratic cracks.

MARKETING, CREATIVITY AND ORGANIZATION

Attempting to do things in the same way as they have always been done in the past can lead to difficulties in a business environment which is experiencing rapid cultural, economic or technological change. Change is an ever-present phenomenon to which businesses of all kinds are forced to respond, if they want to stand the best chance of survival and prosperity.

The rapid growth of competition in business and industry is often quoted as a reason for wanting to understand more about the creative process. Many firms are under continuous pressure to enhance old systems and products. Growth and survival can be related directly to an organization's ability to produce (or adopt) and implement new products or services and processes.

Managers also need to discover new and better ways to solve problems. In particular, for an increasing number of problems there are few or no precedents, hence there are fewer tried and tested ways of approaching them with the prospect of reaching a successful outcome.

Creativity is a valuable and even vital asset for any person who is involved in leadership. Creative leaders actively hunt for new problems and are especially successful in handling new challenges which demand solutions outside the routine of orthodox strategies. Such people often possess significant vision and are able to inspire others by their creative talents.

Creativity is an important human resource which exists in all organizations. Creative thinking benefits all areas and activities of management, and organizations have to try to make use of this resource by devising settings which permit creative talents to thrive. Creativity is required to dream up better ways of marketing goods, to devise new production methods, to find new ways to motivate people, and so on. Creativity turns up in every business situation where there is a chance that things can be done in a more business-like, more profitable or in a more satisfying way.

Typical problems requiring creative thinking are:

- how to improve a product's appeal to customers

- how to appeal to customers' wants and needs

- how to identify new and profitable product market opportunities

- how to get skilled and experience staff to stay with the company without paying them excessively high salaries.

Problems which require creative thinking are 'open-ended' – there is more than just one solution.

The case example on the following page provides some evidence of creativity in a work setting.

BLOCKS TO INDIVIDUAL CREATIVE THINKING

Significant blocks to discovering new problem perspectives arise from personal bias. Jones (1987) has identified four typologies of blocks.

- Strategic blocks: 'one right answer' approaches, inflexibility in thinking.

- Value blocks: over-generalized rigidity influenced by personal values.

- Perceptual blocks: over-narrow focus of attention and interest.

- Self-image blocks: poor effectiveness through fear of failure, timidity in expressing ideas, etc.

CASE EXAMPLE

KWIK-FIT: CREATIVE THINKING

Customer satisfaction is not sufficient for Kwik-Fit. Its target is '100% customer delight'.

Many companies take a new look at the way they work in order to find a way of improving customer satisfaction. Kwik-Fit has analysed customers' expectations, from the moment they enter a service centre and beyond. Its operations are now organized to meet customer expectations at each point of the process of interaction with the customer. Training staff to give helpful and friendly service receives priority, and for the comfort of customers pleasant waiting rooms are provided. Terminals at all centres are linked into the company's mainframe and this enables fitters to source parts quickly. When it comes to payment, fitters use the terminals to raise the invoice on the spot.

(Source: Insider, *March 1994, p. 3)*

QUESTION

1. Which of the above ideas do you think show creative thinking?

Strategic blocks can be challenged through creative problem-solving training. Values, however, are a more difficult problem, but creating an awareness of personal values in the individual offers some respite. Perceptual blocks can be freed through observation, and self-image blocks can be dealt with by assertiveness training.

FACTORS STIFLING ORGANIZATIONAL CREATIVITY

Although there is an obvious need for creative thinking in organizations, there are a variety of factors that can stifle it. One important factor is an over-emphasis on managerial control. Where long-term innovation is concerned, traditional financial controls are not appropriate. Organizations have a propensity towards short-range thinking, looking specifically for quick returns with financially measurable results. Too much time may be spent analysing ideas, and any competitive advantage lost in doing so. In addition, organizations are apt to search for one big potential winner, rather than a number of smaller ones. As a consequence, good small opportunities can often be overlooked.

Another set of factors working against creativity emanate from rigid hierarchical organizational structures. Such structures are also not suitable in an unpredictable environment which requires a responsive organizational structure.

Organizations are under pressure to get more done with fewer resources. This also introduces an additional problem, since departments are often punished for cutting costs, instead of being rewarded. The more a department saves one year, the less it has to play with the next. Strange as it may seem, this means that the more organizations have to cut back, the more creative they must become. In addition, so-called marketing oriented organizations may place an over-emphasis on market research at the expense of good ideas which come out of R. & D.

ENCOURAGING CREATIVITY AND INNOVATION IN AN ORGANIZATION

Control enables planned courses of action to be monitored, but it can lead to the stifling of creativity. Being aware that this can happen is of itself important. Simply devising appropriate organization structures which facilitate planning and control will not get around the problem, and, as we have seen, too rigid organizational structures can themselves be detrimental to creative management creativity.

In view of the importance of creative thinking in an organization, the organizational climate should encourage circumspect risk-taking. Generating creative ideas requires freedom of thought and some degree of autonomy. Managers should link rewards with specific performance, and must not only tolerate but encourage different viewpoints. Creating and maintaining an innovative climate begins at the top, and organizations require a continual flow of ideas, which should be encouraged.

In creative thinking one has often to put to one side long-held beliefs, and sometimes entertain the impossible. Through a series of steps one may proceed to change the impossible to the possible. Creative thinking and creative problem-solving can be extremely difficult mental exercises, but fortunately there are techniques which help with the process. A variety of techniques have been evolved, perhaps the best known of which are brainstorming, synectics, lateral thinking and morphological analysis (see De Bono, 1971; Hicks, 1991; LeBoeuf, 1994; Majaro, 1992).

The use of creative problem-solving techniques may help to lessen many of the barriers to creativity in individuals and teams. Their use encourages a better atmosphere and unusual patterns of thought. Some techniques are more appropriate for certain types of problems than others, so it is difficult to assess the comparative effectiveness of the techniques.

SUMMARY

In themselves, plans are not sufficient to ensure that an organization achieves its desired objectives. Marketing budgets have to be established to provide specific targets to achieve and resources to allocate. Control has to be effected to ensure that the organization keeps to the specified plans.

Marketing effort is evaluated through the use of sales analyses, market share analyses, sales to expense ratios, financial analysis and monitoring of customer attitudes.

Planning and control is implemented through the management of people, and it is important to appreciate the alternative management styles that can be used.

An awareness of the importance of creativity in organizations is fundamental; the factors which impede its development must be understood, together with the conditions which encourage creativity.

DISCUSSION QUESTIONS

1. Explain the nature of control and the need for it in marketing.

2. Discuss the three major types of control that need to be exercised in an organization.

3. Explain the nature of strategic control and how it is operationalized.

4. What is implied by efficiency control and how is it put into effect in the case of each of the marketing mix variables?

5. Suggest how one might identify the profitability of individual items of the product mix.

6. Why is there a need to evaluate the marketing effort and construct sales analyses, market share analyses, sales to expense ratios, financial analyses and the monitor of the attitudes of users?

7. Describe the nature of the process of control and evaluation.

8. Why is there a need for customer profitability analysis, and what is involved in undertaking this form of analysis?

9. Indicate the nature of the different forms of organizational structure that are possible.

10. Contrast the less effective and more effective managerial styles.

11. How do situations involving change need to be managed?

12. Account for the importance of creativity in marketing and management.

13. What are the various factors which stifle creativity in organizations?

14. How might creativity be encouraged in organizations?

REFERENCES

De Bono, E. (1971) *Lateral Thinking for Managers*, Pelican, London.
Hicks, M.J. (1991) *Problem Solving in Business and Management*, Chapman & Hall, London.

Jones, L. (1987) The development and testing of a psychological instrument to measure barriers to effective problem solving, unpublished MBSc dissertation, Manchester Business School.
LeBoeuf, M. (1994) *Creative Thinking*, London: Piatkus.
Majaro, S. (1992) *Managing Ideas for Profit*, McGraw-Hill, Maidenhead.
Majaro, S. (1993) *The Essence of Marketing*, Prentice Hall, Englewood Cliffs, N.J.
Reddin, W.J. (1987) *How to Make your Management Style More Attractive*, McGraw-Hill, Maidenhead.

FURTHER READING

De Bono, E. (1971) *Lateral Thinking for Managers*, Pelican.
Hicks, M.J. (1991) *Problem Solving in Business and Management*, Chapman & Hall.
LeBoeuf, M. (1994) *Creative Thinking*, London: Piatkus.
Majaro, S. (1992) *Managing Ideas for Profit*, McGraw-Hill.
Proctor, T. (1995) *The Essence of Management Creativity*, Prentice Hall, Hemel Hempstead.
Reddin, W.J. (1987) *How to Make your Management Style More Attractive*, McGraw-Hill.

CASE PROBLEM 18.1

SENSITIVITY ANALYSIS: AN EXAMPLE

Refer to the information given in Figures 18.3 and 18.4. Enter the data into a spreadsheet in such a way that it allows you to undertake a sensitivity analysis.

Assess what impact each of the following would have on (a) overall net profits, as given in Figure 18.3, and (b) on the net profitability of individual products given in Figure 18.4:

- increasing selling salaries by 10% and distribution salaries by 5%
- increasing advertising expenditure across all products by 5%
- increasing the number of sales calls per period for alpha by 10%
- decreasing the advertising expenditure on beta by 10%, alpha by 20% and gamma by 10%
- reducing the cost of all goods sold by 10%
- increasing sales of alpha by 10%
- increasing all administrative expenses by 10%.

CASE PROBLEM 18.2

LEVER BROS: MARKETING REORGANIZATION

As part of a wholesale restructuring of its marketing organization, Lever Brothers has abolished its marketing director post and replaced traditional marketing and sales departments with consumer and customer management teams. The marketing reorganization is directed at getting closer to customer requirements.

New 'category marketing' teams, whose task is to ensure that brand plans win the approval of retailers, have also been established. Two new business group managers, one for fabrics and one for home care, have taken over a restructured role. They each have their own consumer and category marketing teams reporting to them, and they in turn report direct to the managing director. The customer management teams report to the sales director.

(Source: Marketing, *3 February 1994, p.1)*

QUESTION

1. Evaluate the new approach to marketing organization adopted by Lever.

19 INTERNATIONAL MARKETING

Incentives for international trade and how firms can become involved in international marketing activities are examined in this chapter. International marketing research, together with the factors that firms should take into account when screening potential international marketing opportunities, are discussed, and consideration is given to the factors that should be considered when pricing, distributing and promoting goods in international markets.

OBJECTIVES

After studying this chapter, you should be able to:

- understand why firms should become involved in international marketing
- describe the various ways in which firms can become involved in international marketing activities
- describe the various factors that firms should take into account when screening potential international marketing opportunities
- know what factors firms have to take into account when pricing, distributing and promoting their goods in international markets.

INTRODUCTION

Not all firms engage in international marketing activities. There are various reasons for this, which we will explore below. The chapter starts by looking at the benefits of international trade. Despite the fact that there are advantages to international trade, there are also both natural and artificial barriers which prevent or dis-courage it from taking place. Next we examine why firms should become involved in international marketing and describe the various ways in which firms can become involved in international marketing activities. These range from simply supplying goods to intermediaries who then look after the shipping of the goods to various overseas markets, to actually setting up in business in the countries concerned.

Prior to undertaking international marketing, firms should undertake analysis of marketing opportunities. In this context, consideration is given to how international marketing research is conducted. Subsequent to research having been conducted, various factors have to be taken into account when screening potential international marketing opportunities from the point of view of deciding whether or not to exploit these opportunities. The chapter examines the factors which need to be considered.

Consideration is given in the chapter to how firms might identify international marketing opportunities and to those factors firms have to take into account when pricing, distributing and promoting their goods in international markets.

Finally, attention is given to the difference between global and international marketing.

INTERNATIONAL TRADE: PROBLEMS AND MOTIVATIONS

Before countries can become involved in international marketing, they must have reached a certain stage of economic development. Joanna Kinsey (1988) indicates four levels of economic development, the corresponding extent to which there is an emphasis on marketing, and the extent of the market.

1. **Self-sufficient barter economy** – emphasis is on the exchange of basic necessities; extent of the market is local.

2. **Emerging, expanding economy** – emphasis is on distribution, development of trade, specialist and intermediaries, and product orientation; extent of the market is expanding.

3. **Industrializing** – emphasis is on the use of the marketing mix and consumer orientation with product differentiation and market segmentation; emphasis is on national and international markets.

4. **Industrial/post-industrial** – as in 3, but with emphasis on consumer values and social orientation; emphasis is on global markets.

What this kind of analysis suggests is that, because not all countries in the world are at the same stage in economic development, the status of marketing and the scope for marketing, both nationally and internationally, is likely to vary considerably.

Economic theory argues a good case for countries to get involved in international trade. The argument is that some countries can produce certain goods, extract certain raw materials or provide certain services more economically than others. In the case of producing goods, this may be because they have access to cheap labour or have automated manufacturing processes. With respect to raw materials, these may be more readily accessible and cheaper to obtain. Over time, some countries will have developed efficient service industries such as banking and insurance. By specializing in producing those goods, materials and services which countries can produce most economically, and then engaging in trade, all countries will benefit as a result.

One does not need to be an expert on international economics to recognize obvious truths in this. For example, countries which are rich in natural resources such as oil and metals, but which have no means of producing consumer products, can supply other countries which do not have these natural resources. The latter countries in their turn may be better endowed with manufacturing facilities and can then supply consumer goods to the former countries. In theory, all the countries involved should benefit from the exchange.

BARRIERS TO INTERNATIONAL TRADE

Despite the benefits of international trade, there are a number of problems which do tend to discourage it.

1. Financial barriers

- Shipping costs – adding to the cost of imported goods.

- Tariffs – taxes imposed by governments to tax or even to discourage the import of certain kinds of goods.

- Credit risks – creditworthiness is not too difficult to ascertain in most Western, developed countries. In underdeveloped or developing nations, however, this may be much harder.

- Currency risks – high rates of inflation exist in some countries. This has the effect of making it more difficult to obtain the agreed price for goods supplied.

Where inflation is running at 400% per annum, then this is more than 1% each day. If goods to the value of £100 000 are supplied, then every day's delay in the payment for such goods reduces the amount actually received by more than £1000. Clearly where very large order are concerned the effect can be substantial.

Legal barriers

- Protectionism – on top of tariffs, quotas on goods which can be imported may be imposed. This may be to protect domestic industries and/or to save scarce foreign currency.

- Foreign legal restraints – laws may also exist which govern and restrict what foreign companies can do.

- Foreign government interference.

- Requirements for participation of local concerns. Some countries encourage foreign companies to invest, but on the basis of a joint venture operation.

Cultural barriers

- Nationalism – there is a strong preference for home-produced products in many countries. This makes it difficult for would-be exporters to enter those markets.

- Cultural differences – this creates particular problems for all aspects of marketing.

- Different business relationships and practices

Psychological barriers

- Racial or ethnic prejudice against imported goods from certain countries. Prejudices arise for many different reasons.

- Risk – this applies especially to machines and other mechanical and electrical contraptions. Such goods produced at home can be supplied with spare parts and readily be repaired. This does not always apply to imported goods.

Other barriers

- Limited mass communication systems – these make it difficult for firms wanting to advertise their wares.

- Limited transportation systems – these make it difficult to implement physical distribution.

- Cost of adapting goods to the needs of individual countries – even where goods are standardized they may need some minor modification, e.g. consumer electrical goods in some countries.

The following case example highlights changing government views on international trade in Japan.

CASE EXAMPLE

MARKETING IN JAPAN: IMPORT REFORMS

Japan has faced exceptional difficulty with the longest and most serious recession since the Second World War. Steps are now being taken to promote imports in Japan, along with a further opening up of the domestic markets. There is no doubt that reform of the Japanese economic system and gearing it more towards domestic demand and greater freedom of choice for consumers, will increase foreign access to Japanese markets, including both imports and investments. Japanese markets could represent a significant opportunity for companies in the United Kingdom.

Continuing (controlled) deregulation in Japan has led to the slackening of restrictions on big retailers. These restrictions were put in place to protect small family shops, but one recent example of deregulation was that an American-affiliated toy distributor was able to set up operations in many parts of Japan. In another instance the government reduced the minimum quantity of beer to be produced by a single brewer from 2000 kilolitres to only 60 kilolitres. As a result, more small businesses are now preparing to enter the brewing industry, which has in turn created possibilities for foreign brewery equipment.

In March 1994 an External Economic Reform Plan was adopted, which included measures to increase foreign access to Japanese markets, including both imports and investment. However, there is increasing concern in Europe that Japan may only accommodate pressures from the United States for greater access to import markets, in order to reduce the trade surplus of Japan with the US. Only time will provide an answer for these concerns. There is an alternative view which argues that Japan regards trade relations with the European Union as being of equal importance to their US trade relations, since it is important for Japan to maintain balanced trade.

(Source: Sinclair, 1994)

QUESTION

1. Assuming there are opportunities in Japan for European goods what kinds of goods would be in most demand?

WHY FIRMS SHOULD ENGAGE IN INTERNATIONAL MARKETING

While the argument in favour of countries engaging in international trade seems clear, it does not explain why individual firms should engage in international trade. Indeed, it would seem simpler for firms to concentrate their efforts in the domestic market, rather than becoming entangled in having to deal in international markets. However, there are a number of reasons why firms become involved in international marketing:

- **To sustain growth** Reliance on a single market can be risky. If agricultural tractor manufacturers, for example, were to rely solely on their domestic markets they would experience substantial variation in demand from year to year, and no overall growth in the market. Moreover, all the producers of agricultural tractors would have much smaller sales volumes if they did not engage in selling to overseas markets. Where the domestic market is static or shows only a slow rate of growth, or is highly competitive, then international marketing may be used to gain expansion. The only thing a firm must ask itself is whether it could achieve growth in a less risky and/or more profitable way.

- **To achieve economies of scale** It is possible to achieve a competitive advantage from economies of scale resulting from the increased volume of output and lower unit costs. The additional sales generated from export opportunities can enable firms to obtain this advantage.

- **Competition** Competitive pressures may make it necessary to supply to international markets. Given that all or most other firms in an industry operate internationally, then those that do not follow suit risk loss of status in the eyes of the customer/industry and then loss of market share in the domestic market.

It would seem that it is becoming easier for firms to consider entering international markets. Many countries now have large retail chains, TV advertising and credit cards, and tariff barriers are falling. Advances in technology have reshaped industries and shifted product leadership to new countries, thereby stimulating the need for international trade. Improvements in communications have overcome geographically imposed barriers to trade and have made buyers increasingly aware of global markets.

INTERNATIONAL MARKETING VERSUS MARKETING NATIONALLY

International marketing, by and large, is an extension of national marketing. The same kinds of topics are invloved as in domestic marketing. The key difference is in terms of individual outlook and personal attitudes, plus the fact that there may be certain additional issues which can create problems if they are not attended to properly.

There is a need to understand the subtlety of business practices and customs in foreign countries. For example, in Japan, negotiations should be conducted by making the point without obviously winning the argument: thus the adversary need not lose face.

One has also to be aware of the differences that exist in terms of business ownership. It is common to find family-owned firms abroad, particularly in developing countries. Attitudes of executives in similar sized firms may also vary a good deal from country to country. Executives of a particular rank may carry different levels of authority and responsibility in different countries. Moreover, attitudes of consumers, trade unions and government may also vary considerably.

INTERNATIONAL MARKETING MANAGEMENT

As marketing has become more internationalized, the function of the home-based organization has changed somewhat. There has been a shift towards being more knowledgeable about what is going on at a local level while at the same time, as international business has become more globalized there has also been a shift towards integration. The role of headquarters staff is to preserve a long-term global view and decide which products should be sold in which markets, and what should be the broad marketing mix in each case.

Another important aspect of international marketing management concerns the management of technology and technological progress.

The linkage between R.& D. and marketing is crucial in this context. Technology and the ability to move easily across national borders are major sources of competitive advantage.

Having looked at why firms should become involved in international marketing, we will now move on to look at the various way in which they can do so.

APPROACHES TO INTERNATIONAL MARKETING

Firms can get involved in marketing their goods and services in international markets in a number of ways. Choice of strategy depends upon the amount of resources firms have at their disposal and the amount of control they wish to exert over the international marketing of their goods and services.

EXPORTING THROUGH INTERMEDIARIES IN THE HOME COUNTRY

Export houses in the home country may be used to gain access to international markets. These export houses are rather like wholesalers, but they specialize in supplying goods to foreign markets. Using export houses can sometimes be a first step taken by firms wanting to increase sales by selling to international markets. In adopting this approach, of course, firms usually have no control over what happens to the goods after they have been supplied to the export house. As a consequence, firms are not in a position to make sure that the product matches to the needs of the market. Such an approach to international marketing is in effect an extension of the domestic market, but without being able to know much about how the product is received.

CONFIRMING HOUSES

Confirming Houses are organizations which place orders with manufacturers on behalf of an overseas buyer. The confirming house sees to the shipping arrangements and pays cash for the goods supplied. Confirming houses also act as export houses and obtain orders for manufacturers, but without carrying the overseas risk. A set fee or a percentage of each invoice is payable as commission.

DISTRIBUTORS IN THE DOMESTIC MARKET

Where a firm's existing distributors in the home market operate on an international basis, it may be possible for a producer to make use of its existing intermediaries to effect entry to international markets.

OTHER SUPPLIERS/MANUFACTURERS IN THE DOMESTIC MARKET

Other suppliers/manufacturers with which the firm is on good terms and not in direct competition may be used. They may be keen to carry products which complement their own product lines.

IMPORT HOUSES

Just as there are export houses in the country of origin, so there are specialist importing houses in countries of destination. Goods can be supplied direct to import houses, but of course the producers or suppliers lose control of the marketing of the goods. On the other hand, they have knowledge of the goods' country of destination and can research the foreign markets for themselves to get some idea of customers' wants and needs.

DIRECT EXPORT

Here the exporting company has its own sales staff who solicit orders in overseas markets. Products are then shipped directly to the customer. Sometimes there is a local office in the country of destination to handle paperwork and other matters.

There are many advantages of this method, from the point of view of the supplying firm. In particular it can exercise complete control over the marketing of its goods and services.

CASE EXAMPLE

NIPPON EDWARDS: A NEW PLANT IN JAPAN

A new Japanese factory, at Ina City in Nagano Prefecture, about 200 km north-west of Tokyo, started operation at the end of September 1994. It is owned by Edwards High Vacuum International, a world leader in the supply of high vacuum equipment for a wide range of R.&D. and industrial applications. Edwards, a member of the BOC Group, has been well established in the Japanese market for over 20 years under the name Nissan Edwards Shinku (NES). The new factory is next door to OSK, a BOC Group company manufacturing high purity gases for the semiconductor industry.

In February the Japanese company was also recapitalized and renamed Nippon Edwards KK (Edwards Japan Ltd).

(Source: Japan Contact, *June 1994, p.5)*

QUESTION

1. This case example seems to illustrate the fact that only high-tech companies are likely to be able to set up manufacturing bases in a country such as Japan. Would you agree?

Supplying through local agents

This is similar to direct export, except that there is no expense involved in setting up a local office. Local agents who have a good knowledge of the market are employed. The effectiveness of this method depends on the quality of the local agents.

LOCAL ASSEMBLY

The competitiveness of products in international markets can be curtailed by tariff and quota restrictions on finished products. Where it can be shown that there is a specific 'local manufactured content' in goods supplied by foreign firms, then lower tariff rates may apply.

A good way to achieve this is to assemble products in the country of destination. This develops naturally from marketing direct and having a sales office in the country concerned. Although a higher level of investment on the company's behalf is demanded, it can lead to a more effective means of marketing goods. Nevertheless, availability of suitable premises and personnel are important factors to take into consideration.

LOCAL MANUFACTURE

The establishment of a full-scale manufacturing plant, rather than just an assembly operation, can be an attractive proposition. This is particularly the case when the country concerned enjoys political stability and offers good tax and other incentives to foreign firms to make such an investment. Japanese firms have been encouraged to do just this in the UK. The countries where such manufacturing plants are set up also benefit since it provides employment.

LICENSING

Licensing arrangements can be used in several ways. They can entail arranging for a product to be assembled, manufactured or even marketed by local companies based in a foreign market. The supplying company can receive periodic, or once and for all time payments, called royalties. It is usually the case that such agreements restrict the licensees to supplying goods to the domestic markets in the countries in which they are based. Where there is hyper-inflation, political instability or other hostile business conditions, licensing arrangements may be the only realistic way of marketing.

FRANCHISING

In the case of franchising, a distributor can operate a business independently, to his or her own liking. The franchisee is usually required to make an investment and a commitment to buy the franchiser's product. In return the franchisee receives advice or assistance in managing or promoting the business.

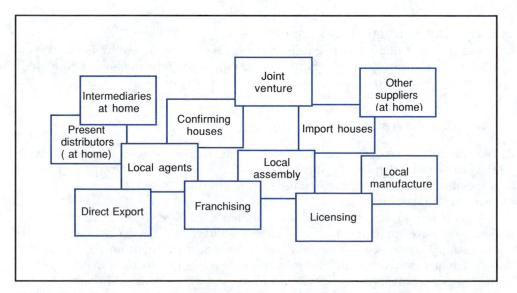

Figure 19.1 Twelve ways of getting involved in international marketing.

Joint ventures

Joint venture arrangements require manufacturing and/or distribution to be undertaken by a company established and jointly owned by the exporting company and local shareholders or the government of the country of destination. This method of entry may be imposed on the exporter by the government of the country concerned as the only acceptable way of gaining access to the market.

Having looked at the various ways in which products can be sold internationally, we will now turn to look at how one analyses international marketing opportunities to decide which ones to pursue.

Analysing international marketing opportunities

Most firms involved in international marketing activities at least know the destination of their goods. Clearly, this means that such firms really need to understand the foreign market place as well as they understand their domestic market place.

Any company engaged in international marketing should be aware of foreign government policies about importing the range and type of products it produces. This includes the imposition of tariffs and quotas. In addition, because of the complexity of international marketing, there will be legal and financial regulations to understand. The marketing and commercial infrastructures of countries differ considerably, and it is important to understand how these vary from country to country.

As far as consumer behaviour is concerned, what is true of the home market is not necessarily true of different foreign markets. Life cycle patterns, bases of motivation, cultural values and lifestyles may be very different from what we are used to, and may require entirely different marketing approaches. Many blunders have been made by firms that have failed to study local customs carefully. For instance, in some countries it is considered unacceptable – even offensive – to portray physical contact between the sexes in promotional material. In Thailand, a firm that was trying to introduce a mouthwash showed, in its advertisements, a young couple holding hands. This caused offence, but by changing the advertisement so that two women were holding hands, the commercials became acceptable (Ricks, 1993, p.58). Another interesting case is presented in the following case example.

Marketing communication channels must be studied in order to identify how information relating to products and services can be brought effectively to the attention of the consumer. Common barriers include those posed by literacy and language, and these have to be overcome.

A key factor is the capacity of the market to pay for the goods and services supplied. This is influenced by such things as personal disposable income, and government restrictions on the expenditure of foreign currency reserves. In the

CASE EXAMPLE

ICELAND: FREEZER CHAIN IN EUROPE

Iceland is performing well in the UK, but its French freezer chain Au Gel closed down after around a year's difficult trading. Iceland will have learned some valuable lessons which will be useful in the context of future European expansion plans. Six of Au Gel's 14 stores were shut down in March 1994. The remaining eight, of which four traded as Iceland, and its distribution centre closed in June 1994. According to Iceland, the Au Gel assets were written off in its 1993 accounts, and combined trading losses amount to £1.5m.

Iceland moved into mainland Europe in December 1991, after having acquired a 50% holding in the French freezer chain.

Iceland planned that Au Gel would be a low-cost experiment in continental retailing, rather than a strategic move. The company is not ruling out other European expansion projects and is increasingly exporting own label products to both western and eastern European markets.

(*Source:* The Grocer, *2 July, 1994*).

QUESTIONS

1. What do you think happened as far as the venture into France was concerned? Discuss.

2. Should Iceland consider entering the European market on such a scale again? If so, where and how? If not, why not?

case of larger items and industrial projects, loan terms, interest and capital requirements are also important factors.

INTERNATIONAL MARKETING RESEARCH

The majority of marketing research work is carried out by local researchers, but the whole process tends to be directed and co-ordinated by headquarters staff. Headquarters staff also have to put considerable effort into 'country market screening' – looking at the relative size of each potential market, the size of its purchasing power and its concentration, and the likely rate of future growth. In addition, an assessment of the competitive forces at work in each potential market has to be made.

INTERNATIONAL SEGMENTATION

Market segmentation amounts to dividing markets into groups of consumers with similar buying needs and who are likely to respond similarly to specific marketing mixes.

Segmentation helps firms to market their products in the most effective way. It is important to note that all segments should be measurable, accessible and of reasonable size. The international marketing strategist seeks to consolidate numerous small segments across a number of countries into a slice of the global market that is worth serving.

Target market selection

The process involves narrowing down potential country markets to a feasible number of countries and market segments within countries. It is argued that instead of trying to appeal to everyone, firms make best use of their resources by identifying potential markets for entry and expanding selectively over time to those that are considered attractive.

The four stages of screening are:

1. preliminary screening

2. estimation of market potential

3. estimation of sales potential

4. identification of segments.

Preliminary screening relies on secondary data; in particular, indicators of overall buying power in country markets are useful.

Estimation of market potential is often undertaken with the aid of secondary data-based analytical techniques which focus on or utilize demand patterns, income elasticity measures, etc.

Estimating sales potential involves assessing the market share that is likely to be achieved. Information on competition, degree of relative product advantage and access to retail outlets must figure pre-dominently in these assessments.

Selecting markets

It is often the case that opportunities in foreign markets present themselves to would-be exporters or international marketing firms from time to time. Such cases have to be evaluated on their individual merits. It may also be, however, that a firm is actively searching for such opportunities; in either case it should bear in mind the following points.

1 There has to be enough potential in the market to justify a firm's marketing efforts in approaching the market.

- The firm's products should stand out well against competitors' offerings when it comes to quality, performance and price.

- Where pricing is very keen, care should be taken. One should look for opportunities where price is not all-important and where profit margins will not easily be eroded.

- There should be some indication of growth in the sector or sectors of interest (5 to 10% growth per annum at least).

- It is better to avoid countries where there are likely to be problems in obtaining money for goods supplied and/or transfer currency back to the country supplying the goods.

The kind of information which needs to be obtained should answer questions about:

- the approximate size of the market production/imports/exports/consumption

- the products which are currently available (how well they satisfy tastes, habits etc.)

- the leading competitors, their market shares, promotion methods, services and facilities offered

- the channels and costs of distribution

- the legal requirements, standards etc.

- tariffs, quotas, import licences

- ease of transportation (speed/frequency/costs)

- the political/economic stability of the market

- the growth trends in the market.

CONCENTRATION VERSUS DIVERSIFICATION AS A STRATEGY

A firm's major alternatives are to concentrate on a small number of markets or to achieve growth by diversification in a large number of markets, in the early stages of international market expansion. The choice of expansion strategy is influenced by market-related, mix-related factors.

MOVEMENTS TOWARDS A FREE MARKET: A BOON FOR THE INTERNATIONAL MARKETING STRATEGIST

The international marketer works in a complex business world. This complexity could be greatly simplified by the existence of markets in which trade barriers did not exist and where there was a common currency and economic equality in terms of development between countries. Such a Utopia would make business negotiations and transactions much easier.

In many areas of the world steps are being taken to bring about such a situation. These steps involve the creation of customs unions or common markets, markets shared by different countries with a long-term view of working toward the reduction of trade barriers, and even economic union. The European Community is an example of this kind of co-operation.

Goods, services, capital and people may now move freely between the member countries of the EC, where the elimination of physical, technical and fiscal barriers is intended to make international trade much easier and cheaper. At the same time, the market has become more competitive, in the sense that what were formerly national markets enjoying varying degrees of protection are now open to greatly increased competition. The competition comes not just from within fellow European countries, but also from other countries such as those in the Far East.

Having looked at ways of analysing international markets and current trends in Europe, we will move on to look at how the task of marketing management has to be adjusted to fit the needs of international markets.

MARKETING MANAGEMENT

A key issue concerns the extent to which the marketing mix variables can be standardized. Standardization normally means cross-national strategies, rather than a policy of viewing foreign markets as secondary and not important enough to have products adapted for them. The international marketer should think globally and act locally, focusing neither on full standardization nor full localization. In some instances it will be possible and desirable to standardize, whereas in others it may not be.

Globalization is a business initiative that stems from the belief that the world is becoming more homogeneous, and that differences between national boundaries are vanishing. Companies sharing this conviction are trying to globalize their international strategy by formulating it across country markets to take advantage of the underlying market, cost, environmental and competitive factors. Coca-Cola and Levi Strauss have adopted this approach successfully. The global approach looks for similarities between markets and for homogeneities in products, image, marketing and advertising message.

INTERNATIONAL PRODUCT STRATEGY

A firm must aim to satisfy customers' own defined needs. Where a product is standardized, a decision has to be taken regarding what product adaptations are needed by a particular foreign market and whether they justify either the cost or departure from the notional standard. Several factors should be taken into account when evaluating the need for a product modification, for example technical factors relating to the product in use; local safety standards relating to product specifications; and local income and the ability of local residents to pay for the modified product.

In determining how to adapt to foreign market conditions account needs to be taken of regional, country or local characteristics, as well as the product characteristics and company considerations.

- **Regional or local characteristics** Government regulations have to be taken into account. Often no concrete product changes are required, only changes in the positioning of the products. The availability of power to drive a product is also important, along with the availability of service and repairs.

- **Product characteristics** Products should never contain ingredients which violate legal, religious or social customs. Packaging is one area where modifications may well have to be made. Greater time spent in distribution channels means that firms need to use more expensive packaging materials. Labelling is a key issue, and the specific requirements of individual countries must be met. Establishing world-wide brand names may be difficult. In some cases brand name changes are demanded by local requirements.

Whether or not it is worth adapting a product to meet the needs of the market depends upon the costs involved and the impact this has on profitability.

Some firms only provide for a particular market segment at first, expanding gradually to cover an entire market. For example, after establishing themselves in the small car market, Japanese manufacturers moved into the luxury car market. Inevitably, because of specific local tastes and cultural values, brands or labels may be developed locally but may never develop into international brands or labels.

A major problem area is that of trademark counterfeiting. This costs firms considerable amount of lost revenue. Counterfeiting even extends to raw materials and components. Various measures have been introduced to counteract the problem. For example, new authentication materials in labelling, which are almost impossible to duplicate, are now being used. As a result of counterfeiting, firms can lose not only sales but also goodwill in the long term, because customers may believe they are getting the genuine product when in fact they are not.

INTERNATIONAL PRICING STRATEGY

The strategy to be avoided is that of underpricing products in foreign markets, and this applies especially to new entrants. Competitors will take a harsh view of firms entering their market with a low price and they will respond accordingly. Something else that should be borne in mind is that it is much more difficult to raise prices from an unduly low level than it is to reduce prices from a comfortable margin, when competition is in evidence. The general rule is that prices should always be related to what the market will bear.

It is expected that during the 1990s, businesses in the European Community will experience:

- a general drop in costs
- the opening up of public purchasing contracts to broader competition
- extra foreign investment in the European Community, leading to an increase in production capacity
- more rigorous enforcement of competition policy
- generally increased competition.

The overall result should be a downward pressure on prices. Possible changes in specific industries include:

- increased price rivalry on airway routes after deregulation
- the opening up of markets for financial services internationally, with a consequent drop in the average price for banking, insurance and securities
- increases in freight capacity as a consequence of more efficient border crossings leading to enhanced price competition among carriers.

Price cutting will be used as a short-term strategy to gain market share, but it is not clear whether pricing will play a more prominent role in competition than the non-price elements of the marketing mix.

In 1990 there were wide differences in prices for similar products throughout EC countries. It was common for these differences to reflect calculated manufacturer strategies to vary product positioning according to the stage of economic development in each country. Different taxation policies and distributor margins in the particular countries also played their part. With the beginning of the 1992 harmonization process to improve market integration it was expected that this might lead to smaller price variations between individual countries for similar products. This issue concerns the price elasticity of consumer demand for individual products in individual countries in the EC, and product substitution effects at different price points.

The price set in any particular set of circumstances will vary from as low as the firm's cost of production at one extreme, to whatever the market will bear at the other extreme. Those firms that are most active in global markets will harvest the benefits of internationalization most rapidly – the direct result of the effects of the experience curve. In addition to these effects, there are three other factors which influence pricing. First taxes and tariffs; secondly, exchange rate fluctuations; and thirdly, inflation.

THE PROBLEM OF TRANSFER PRICING

International firms need to pay close attention to transfer pricing – the pricing that takes place for transactions between subsidiaries of the same company.

Governments are often suspicious of such arrangements being manipulated to gain tax advantages – exporting country regulatory bodies may think that a transfer price is too low, whereas the authorities in the importing country may consider them to be too high.

THE PROBLEM OF DUMPING

Dumping is another problem which leads to accusations of unfair practice. Dumping amounts to selling at a price less than the cost of manufacture – often simply to acquire foreign currency or to increase market share. Inexpensive imports often trigger accusations of dumping, which may be intentional or accidental.

PRICE SETTING METHODS

There are three general price setting methods:

- Standard world-wide pricing which is based on average unit costs of fixed, variable and export related costs.

- Dual pricing, often based on marginal cost pricing, resulting in a lower export price than the domestic price. Fixed costs have to be recovered by sales in the domestic market, but export sales need only recover the variable and export costs.

Cost oriented pricing suffers from being based on arbitrary allocations of costs and takes no account of different market conditions (is not demand oriented).

- The third method, market-differentiated pricing, is a demand-oriented strategy and is more in keeping with the marketing concept. It also takes into account competitors' actions.

Lack of information about the market often forces firms to adopt a marginal pricing approach.

INTERNATIONAL PROMOTIONAL STRATEGY

Promotion includes the whole communication package about the product which is presented to potential customers. The strength and recognizability of the brand name is a powerful determinant of promotional strategy. While personal selling, sales promotion and public relations activities are helpful, for most consumer goods in most market economies the best tool is advertising.

Care has to be taken with translations and cultural values which are communicated. Local advertising agencies or a global agency should be used, where the firm has a globally known brand or label.

Advertising

Key decision areas relate to media strategy, promotional message and organization of the promotional programme.

Choice of media strategy may be limited. Television advertising is severely restricted in some countries – for example it is prohibited altogether in Sweden.

Some media vehicles have been developed that have target audiences on several continents. For example, there are 133 editions of *The Times*, enabling advertising to reach a particular country, continent or the world. In broadcast media, pan-regional radio stations have been joined in Europe by satellite television broadcasting.

In all cases it should be borne in mid that the promotional message that is being imparted must match with what the customer is really buying – the product benefits. This will reflect the customer's motivations.

Personal selling

In most cases this takes place at a local level. The idea is to establish a solid base of dealerships staffed by local people.

Sales promotion

For sales promotion to work, campaigns planned by manufacturers or their agencies have to gain the support of the local retailer population. Attendance at an appropriate trade show is one of the best ways to make contact with government officials and decision makers.

Public relations

Public relations activity includes anticipating and countering criticism. The criticisms range from general ones against all multinational corporations, to specific complaints.

INTERNATIONAL DISTRIBUTION STRATEGY

From the viewpoint of channel management, the multinational company has to find the best combination of local sales subsidiaries, wholesalers and retailers to help it achieve its distribution targets.

The nature and complexity of distribution channels varies considerably from country to country. They can be relatively simple (as in the case of the UK) or highly complex (as in the case of Japan). Complexity can involve delay, inefficiency and additional cost. Firms can, of course, set up their own distribution systems, in which case key decisions then have to be made concerning whether to hire local or expatriate personnel.

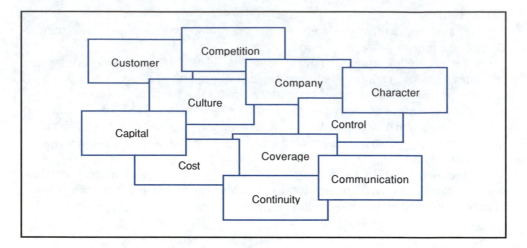

Figure 19.2 The '11 Cs' of channel design.

Distribution policy

Channel design refers to the length and width of the channel employed and is determined by factors that can be described as the '11 Cs': customer, culture, competition, company, character, capital, cost, coverage, control, continuity and communication.

- **Customer**: demographic and psychographic characteristics of consumers may require a product to be distributed through specific distribution channels.

- **Culture of the distribution system**: different countries operate entirely different systems of distribution. Unless the culture of the system is clearly understood, penetration of the market will not be possible.

- **Competition**: channels used by competitors form another basis for planning. One can either use the same channels (safe strategy), or try to gain a competitive edge by innovating.

- **Company objectives**: account has to be taken of company market share and profitability objectives.

- **Character of the product**: the more specialized, expensive, bulky, or perishable the product, and the more after-sales service it may require, the more likely it is that there is a need for the channel to be relatively short.

- **Capital**: this refers to the financial requirements required for setting up the system. The financial strength of the exporting company will determine the type of channel and the basis on which channel relationships will be built. The stronger the financial resources, the greater the possibility that the firm will be able to control or own its intermediaries.

- **Cost**: this is the expenditure incurred in maintaining a channel once it is established.

- **Coverage**: this reflects both the number of areas in which the marketer's products are represented and the quality of that representation.

- **Control**: the looser the relationship between the marketer and the intermediaries, the less control can be exerted. For example, the longer the channel of distribution, the less control the marketer has on pricing.

- **Continuity**: marketers are trying to make decisions which have long-term standing. They will be looking for good distributors who are likely to establish this kind of relationship.

- **Communication**: proper communication will perform important roles for the international marketer. It will help convey the marketer's goals to the distributor, help solve conflict situations, and aid in the overall marketing of the product.

Selecting and screening intermediaries

The appointment of a foreign distributor should be made with the same degree of care and attention as that given to permanent management posts within the company. A bad appointment can be very detrimental to a firm. Not only will under-performance occur and goodwill with customers be lost but, in addition, contracts made with distributors can be difficult to terminate. When evaluating potential distributors, attention should be paid to such factors as the potential distributor's financial standing, sales record and degree of professionalism.

GLOBAL VERSUS INTERNATIONAL MARKETING

Some people hold the view that there is a difference between international marketing and global marketing. It can be argued that international marketing involves the marketer in adapting products, services, and methods of marketing to meet the needs of individual countries. With global marketing, standardized products, services and methods of marketing are designed to be suitable for every country.

Proponents of international as opposed to global marketing believe that the marketing concept is only really satisfied by interpreting the different wants and needs of different countries individually. Those who favour global marketing think of having standardized products and methods of marketing. They maintain that as a result of rising standards of living, differences between countries at similar stages in economic development are disappearing because their wants and needs are similar. Using this argument it is therefore possible to market the same product and use the same methods of marketing communication in different countries. McDonald's is an example of an organization which uses global marketing, though it has sold beer in Germany, wine in France, mutton pot pies in Australia, and MacSpaghetti in the Philippines (Ricks, 1993, p.25).

Baker (1991, p.541) argues that globalization is production-oriented in the sense that it seeks to 'drive' the wants and wishes of potential users toward commonality, rather than modifying the supply to match a varying demand.

SUMMARY

Firms get involved in international marketing for a number of reasons. These are to sustain growth, match competition and to achieve economies of scale.

There are many ways in which firms can get involved in international marketing activities. Supplying to confirming houses in the home market is perhaps the easiest way to start, but eventually firms may set up their own manufacturing facilities and retail outlets in foreign countries.

When firms get involved in international marketing they need to establish a variety of facts. These include the stated government policies about the range and type of imports that will be accepted into the country and the extent to which the government imposes tariffs and quotas to protect industry at home.

The marketing and commercial infrastructures of countries differ considerably and it is important to understand this fact. Firms also need to understand consumer behaviour – what we assume to be true of the home market is not necessarily true of different foreign markets.

Life cycle patterns, bases of motivation, cultural values and lifestyles may differ markedly from country to country, and may require an entirely different marketing approach. Marketing communication channels need to be explored to identify how effectively information regarding products and services can be brought to the attention of the consumer. Most important of all, as far as the firm is concerned, is the capacity of the market to pay for the goods and services supplied.

Pricing goods in international markets has to be handled with care. Firms have to study the various factors that influence prices and ensure that they do not underprice their goods. While personal selling, sales promotion and public relations activities are helpful, for most consumer goods in most market economies the best tool is advertising.

Care has to be taken over translations and cultural values which are communicated. Use should be made of local advertising agencies, or a global agency where the firm has a globally known brand or label.

The nature and complexity of distribution channels varies considerably from country to country. They can be relatively simple or complex; complexity can signal delay, inefficiency and additional cost. Firms can, of course, set up their own distribution systems, in which case key decisions then have to be taken concerning whether to hire local or expatriate personnel.

A distinction is made between global and international marketing. Global marketing is an attempt to achieve some degree of standardization in terms of the products and services which are offered in different countries. International marketing, on the other hand, stresses that the needs and wants of consumers in different countries will always be different, and that as a consequence it is necessary to meet their specific requirements.

DISCUSSION QUESTIONS

1. Discuss the benefits of international trade.

2. Distinguish between natural and artificial barriers to international trade. Why should artificial barriers to international trade be created?

3. What motivates firms to become involved in international marketing?

4. Explain the various ways in which firms can become involved in international marketing activities.

5. Suggest how firms should analyse international marketing opportunities.

6. Examine what is involved in conducting international marketing research.

7. What factors should firms pay particular attention to when screening potential international marketing opportunities?

8. Describe various ways in which firms can identify international marketing opportunities.

9. What factors do firms have to take into account when pricing goods in international markets?

10. What factors do firms have to take into account when promoting goods in international markets?

11. What are the '11 Cs' of international distribution?

12. Differentiate between global and international marketing.

REFERENCES

Baker, M.J. (1991) *Marketing : An Introductory Text*, 5th edn, Macmillan, London.

Kinsey, J. (1988) *Marketing in Developing Countries*, Macmillan, London.

Ricks, D.A. (1993) *Blunders in International Business*, Blackwell, Oxford.

Sinclair, A.J. (1994) All to gain from import reforms in Japan, *Japan Contact*, **28**, June, pp. 1–2.

FURTHER READING

Cateora, P.R. (1990) *International Marketing*, Irwin, Homewood, Ill.

Dahringer, L.D. and Muhlbacher, H. (1991) *Marketing: A Global Perspective*, Addison Wesley, Reading, Mass.

Majaro, S. (1991) International marketing – the main issues, in *The Marketing Book* (ed. M.J. Baker)

CASE PROBLEM 19.1

SINGLE MARKETING: GLOBAL MARKETING APPROACH

In France, Germany and Benelux, grocery retailing is both concentrated and very competitive. Net profit margins elsewhere in Europe are also beginning to converge, as the UK conforms with other countries.

Jeff Bayley set up Single Marketing in 1991 in the belief that there is no reason why packaged foods cannot be sold at the same price levels all across Western Europe. Indeed his company believes this is what marketing in the single market is all about – hence the company name. Jeff holds the view that the UK consumer should have access to leading brands and products at the same price level as they are available in other EC countries. Separating out differential taxes such as VAT and excise duties, total distribution costs should not be that different from country to country, particularly as trade structures converge further in the major European countries.

(Source: The Grocer, *11 June 1994, p. 30)*

QUESTION

1. Do you agree with Jeff Bayley's beliefs about pricing? Why, or why not?

CASE PROBLEM 19.2

MALAYSIA AND THAILAND: COMPARATIVE MARKETING OPPORTUNITIES

Following a recession in 1985–6, the retailing industry in Malaysia bounced back and enjoyed a phenomenal success. In Kuala Lumpur shopping malls, every inch of space is occupied by retailers selling a vast range of goods seven days a week. These malls are open until late in the evening and are thronged with people. Managers of the City Square, Petaling Garden's Pudu Plaza, the Atria, Lot 10 and Bangsar Complex are confident about continued prosperity.

CASE PROBLEM 19.2 *CONTINUED*

More recently, the most noticeable change has been the arrival of several public-listed companies into the retail sector, for example Parkson's and 7-Eleven. Economic recovery attracted a growing presence of foreign retailers, undaunted by the failure of Kimisawa, Chushinya and Printemps in the mid-1980s recession. Foreign retailers such as Japan's Isetan, Yaohan, Jaya Jusco and the US-based Toys 'R' Us have opened up stores. Parkson Grand in Subang Jaya stocks designer labels for the upmarket consumer, while 7-Eleven stores, strategically located in the urban areas, are popular with younger shoppers.

Over the past 20 years Malaysia has prospered economically, although in the recent past it was almost totally dependent on world commodity prices (rubber, palm oil, tin and timber). These days it is diversifying its economic base and is one of the fastest growing economies in Asia. In recent years Malaysia'a GNP has been growing at around 8% and its light industrial base has been expanding rapidly to provide real export income. Oil, too, has helped to make the economy buoyant. Malaysia is seen as one of the next generation of 'tigers' (the booming economies of Korea, Taiwan, Hong Kong and Singapore), and this healthy economic base reinforces Malaysia's position as one of the best-off countries in Asia. Education has pride of place in the country. Many thousands of students come to Britain and the USA for higher education, and British universities offer distance learning MBA programmes to Malaysia's aspiring business executives. Much of the content of daily newspapers is given over to discussing educational matters.

To the north, next-door neighbour Thailand is another up-and-coming regional economic powerhouse and over the six years to 1993 its economy grew by almost 10% each year. However, the rapid pace of change in the country has been accompanied by social, economic and environmental problems. Bangkok's transport system is on the verge of collapse. In the poor North East, incomes have stagnated, exacerbating social tensions, and in the Central Plains, scarcity of land is forcing landless farmers to migrate to squatter communities in Bangkok in search of work. Tourism has also created problems, and Thais blame tourists for the explosion of the sex industry and the proliferation of AIDS. However, despite such anxieties, politicians, workers and academics alike are generally optimistic about Thailand's future.

Some people argue that Thailand will join the exclusive club of 'newly industrialising countries'. Several years of high economic growth, a massive inflow of foreign investment from the late 1980s, perceived political stability, and a fiscally conservative government have made Thailand 'look the part'. However, this view of Thailand overlooks a number of worrying facts. First, and most important, economic activity is highly concentrated, mainly in and around Bangkok, where the city radiates wealth and refinement. Poverty and malnutrition are widespread in the countryside – one in six households remains in poverty. Growth in Thailand has been founded

CASE PROBLEM 19.2 *CONTINUED*

upon foreign technology and capital –Thailand is not a Taiwan or South Korea with its own creative, innovative class of industrialists. Lack of education is highlighted by most economists as one of the major constraints facing the country as it endeavours to develop. Only 20% of workers have anything more than a primary education, and without the skills that come with education it is unlikely to continue enticing foreign companies to invest.

Today agriculture contributes just over 15% of Thailand's GDP while manufacturing alone contributes over a quarter. The main exports are rice, textiles, electronics and tourism. However, although the economy has diversified, most Thais are still farmers. Growth in the agricultural sector has been slow in comparison with industry, and this has meant that the gulf between town and country has widened. This has caused many rural Thais to experience feelings of frustration: they are well aware of the consumer goods that can be bought, but they are unable to afford them.

QUESTION

1. How would you evaluate Malaysia and Thailand from a marketing perspective? What conclusions would you reach?

INDEX

LECTURERS' RESOURCE MANUAL

This book comes complete with a comprehensive lecturers' resource manual which is free to lecturers and teachers recommending the text book as an essential purchase for their students.

For more information call Mark Wellings (Senior Commissioning Editor) on 0171 865 0066 or order direct from the address below:

Anita Barnecut
Inspection Copy Requests
Chapman & Hall Ltd
Cheriton House
North Way
Andover
Hants SP10 5BE

Tel: 01264 342932
Fax: 01264 342765
email: rchinspection@itps.co.uk